ECHOES OF SCHOOL BELLS

History of Jasper County
Rural Schools
Jasper County, Missouri

COMPILED BY
Helen K. Hunter
Copyright 2013

ALL RIGHTS RESERVED.

This book contains material protected under International and Federal Copyright Laws and Treaties. Any unauthorized reprints or use of this material is prohibited. No part of this book may be reproduced or transmitted in any form or by any means, electronic or mechanical, including photocopying, recording, or by any information storage and retrieved system without express written permission from the author / publisher. Please do not participate in or encourage piracy of copyrighted materials in violation of the author / publisher rights. Purchase only authorized editions.

For information, address:
Drop Cap Publishing
2139 S. Maple
Carthage, MO 64836
www.dropcappublishing.com

ISBN-13: 978-0615932965
ISBN-10: 0615932967

PRINTED IN THE UNITED STATES OF AMERICA

Table of Contents

Map........................Jasper County School Map West - Page VII

Chapter 1..........................1830's - Out of the Wilderness - Page 1

Chapter 2..........................1840's - A New County is Born - Page 5

Chapter 3..........................1850's - Progress and Unrest - Page 15

Chapter 4..........................1860's - Years of Pain - Page 21

Chapter 5..........................1870's - A Time of Rebuilding - Page 27

Chapter 6..........................1880's - Time of Growth - Page 33

Chapter 7..........................1890's - A Time of Refinement - Page 37

Chapter 8..........................1900's - A New Decade - Page 41

Chapter 9..........................The Rural Schools - Page 55

Chapter 10........................Looking Back in Time - Page 57

Map........................Jasper County School Map East - Page 334

Acknowledgements

We wish to thank each and all who participated in the making of this book. Without their input, this project would not have been possible. Heartfelt appreciation goes to: Joel T. Livingston, author of A *History of Jasper County Missouri*, and Marvin VanGilder, author of *Jasper County – The First Two Hundred Years*, whose research and information has been invaluable. Thanks to Steve Weldon, Director of the Jasper County Records Center, whose determination to see this book to completion kept me focused; Marjorie Bull, Doris Carter Wardlow, Jeanie Hill, Jo Stocker, Barbara Little, Ellen Yoes, Shirley Kennedy, Reba Keeper and Carolyn Hamilton who generously give their time as volunteers at the Records Center and whose input has made this book richer, and to Kathy Sidenstricker who was so generous with her information. Last but not least, to Chrystina Hanna for her artistic work that has helped bring this book to life. To those individuals who took the time to share their stories with us so that we may take a trip back through history and to those whose passionate determination may yet save the remaining schools.

We tried to be complete in this condensed history of our rural schools and believe the information contained herein is authentic; we have made every effort to make it so.

The printing of this book is made possible by the contribution of the Jasper County Record Center, the office of Jasper County Clerk, Bonnie Earl, the Jasper County Commissioners: Presiding Commissioner John Bartosh, Eastern Jasper County Commissioner Jim Honey, Western Jasper County Commissioner Darieus Adams.

The photos in this book are courtesy of the Jasper County Record Center unless otherwise stated.

Forevvard

This book is meant to be a memorial to all teachers and children that have stepped foot in a country school, even for a short time.

It is a tribute to the early pioneers that saw the necessity of educating their children.

It is meant to honor the schools themselves, those long lost to history and the ones still standing, like sentinels, guarding the past. They have heard children's laughter during a game of Red Rover or Kick the Can, saw tears over a scraped knee and the sound of a teacher's school bell announcing "schools in." They were our second homes, churches, funeral parlors, a courthouse and military headquarters. "The one-room school is the foundation of today's education," Virginia Snyder said, author of *Books, Pies and Spelling Bees - The One-Room Country School Revisited*.

We have attempted to relay historical facts, as well as personal accounts from former teachers who taught there, students fortunate enough to have attended their classes and others who have stories to tell about them.

We hope this book takes you on a journey back in their rich history through pictures, school days as seen through a student's eyes, a teacher's perspective, rules for student conduct and expectations of the school superintendent.

The rural schoolhouse history is full of interesting anecdotes and is important because it tells a story of our progress and memorializes the names and actions of those who help mold lives. By knowing our past, we make ourselves and future generations richer.

THE COUNTRY SCHOOL HOUSE SPEAKS

I am a country school house. I am legion for I am found throughout this United States of America from east to west and from north to south. I stand on steep mountains sides, in canyons, in rich valleys, and on wind swept plains. I stand by the broad paved highways that band our land from state to state, by the seldom traveled by-road, by the cow path that crosses the vast stretches of prairie; and by the mountain trail that winds its tortuous way up the steep slopes.

Over the threshold countless thousands of boys and girls have passed. I have been a power of force for the training of leaders in the great land of America.

In the past, my doors opened to an opportunity for educational training that was equal to the best, but not so today. Business, industry, commerce and transportation have marched forward in a great epoch of progress. I am a relic of the past.

Ten million boys and girls cross my threshold today. They must be trained in the highest ideals of life and citizenship; they must be given the tools of the mind; they must be kept strong and stalwart in body; they must be trained for leadership if America is to grow in prosperity, in truth and in justice. I am unequal to the task.

I meet teachers who will protect and foster the health of childhood, who will bring them efficient tools of workmanship and will give them ideals of grace, culture and beauty.

I need teachers of vision, teachers with a preparation for their work, teachers with a passion for children, and with a love for the truth and the beautiful, and with a foresight of tomorrow's needs

I need a supporting public with a social vision, with a desire to render service, and with high ideals for themselves and their posterity.

I am the school home of ten million rural boys and girls looking to the nation for equality in education opportunity.

I am a challenge to thinking America.

........Flora E. Holroyd
Kansas State Rural School Supervisor

Preface

*Upon the subject of education, not presuming
to dictate any plan or system respecting it,
I can only say that I view it as the most important
subject which we as a people can be engaged in.*
Abraham Lincoln
First Political Announcement – Mar. 9, 1832

The first constitution of Missouri provided that "one school or more shall be established in each township, as soon as practicable and necessary, where the poor shall be taught gratis."

In 1820, the United States Congress made Missouri a state. This act of congress receiving Missouri into the Union provided, among other things, for the creation of a school fund in each county of the state to be used exclusively for the payment of teachers in the public schools. The Act stated that Section 16 of every township was to be declared for "school lands" and given to the state for "educational use of the inhabitants" and that "the children of the poor shall be taught free."

The earliest state laws organized school districts by townships. Township schools were put under the control of the county court on January 17, 1825 by the Missouri General Assembly.

Schools would soon be established in Jasper County, and although these rural schools mirrored those of other counties across Missouri and their histories were similar, each school maintained its own unique personality and memories.

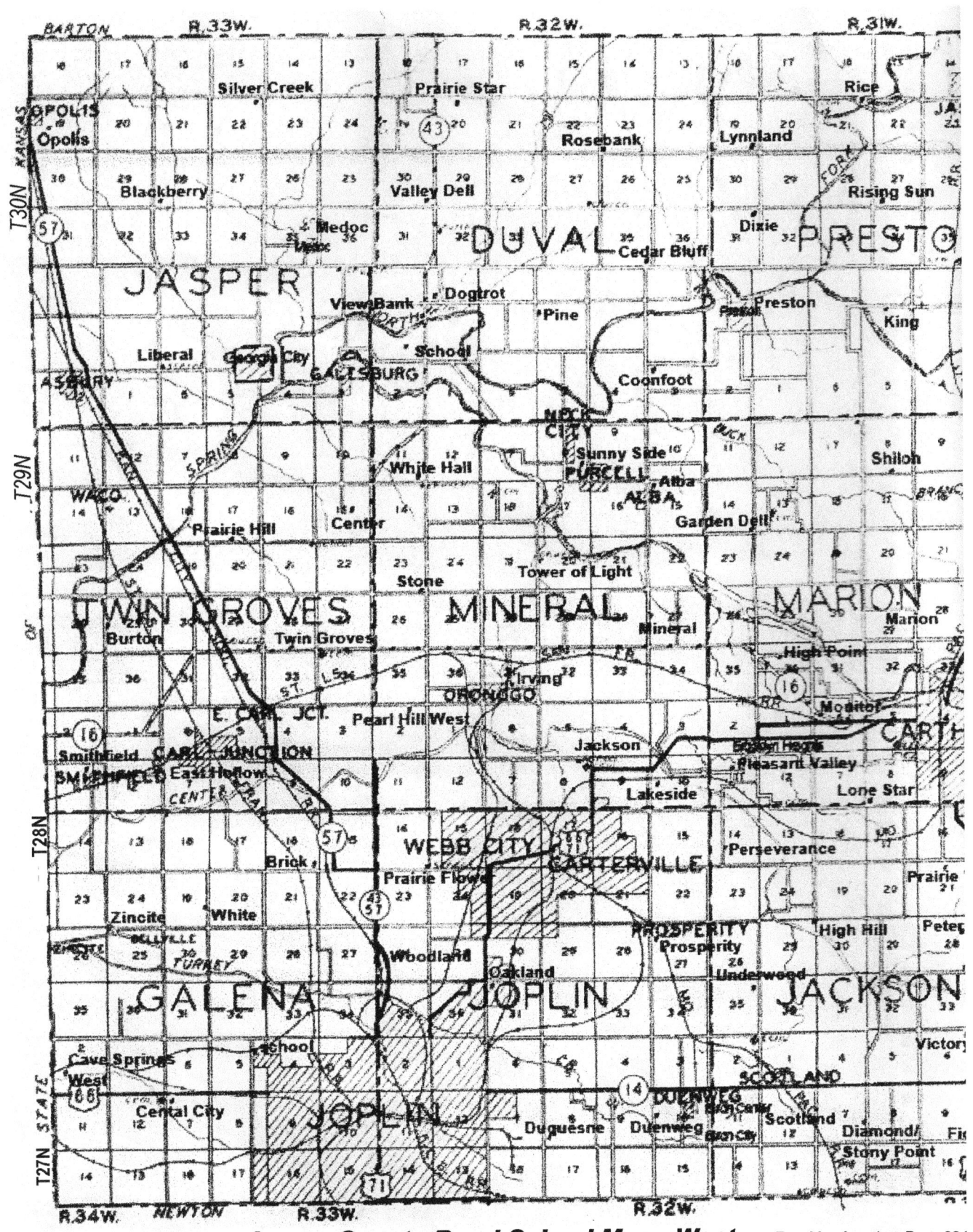

Jasper County Rural School Map - West   *East Map found on Page 334*

CHAPTER 1

1830's – Out of the Wilderness

During the 1830's Jasper County as we know it did not exist. It was wilderness with tall timbers, lush grasses, clear streams and Native Americans that few white men had ever visited. One of the few was a man by the name of Edmund Jennings.

He lived with the Native Americans, in what would become Jasper County, for fifteen years before he went back to his home state of Tennessee and told amazing stories about this area.(1) Intrigued by these stories, early settlers began moving into this new frontier in the early 1800's. Pioneers traveling west historically moved in a straight line so many newcomers were also from Kentucky.

Early Flint-lock gun

Newcomers were not limited just to these two areas and once settled, we see a blend of many ethnic and cultural backgrounds with different languages being spoken. The reasons they came are long lost to history but perhaps they were just looking for a new future for themselves and their families.

After arriving, their first priorities were to establish homesteads and businesses. Among those were a saw mill, brick yard and a general store.

In his book, *History of Jasper County, Missouri -1883*, F. A. North wrote that mills and milling was scarce; there was a small mill that ground corn on Jones Creek called Jones Mill, one was located in Sarcoxie that ground corn and wheat. He further states that times were very hard and money was scarce. Horses were worth $25 to $40; cows $6 to $10. Wheat was worth 25 cents to 50 cents a bushel. Farmers did not farm much except for their own families due to lack of demand for their product. School did not meet regularly and some settlements had no school at all. Times were hard and did not begin to get better for these settlers until the late 1840's.(2)

Native Americans, living in what would become Jasper County, were plentiful and friendly. Minor incidents with white settlers usually involved petty thievery in the smokehouse and corn crib. They could also be seen coming from the Indian Territory, visiting trading posts and using the mills.

Sketch by Steve Weldon

The Osage were the original inhabitants of this area. "The Osage are so tall and robust as almost to warrant the application of the term gigantic; few of them appear to be under six feet, and many above it. Their shoulders and visages (faces) are broad, which tend to strengthen the idea of being giants."(3)

These first settlers could not obtain title to their land because it had not been surveyed by the government. In 1836 surveying in what is now Jasper County began and was completed in 1844. A great number of settlers made their way to Springfield to secure title to their land but the trip could take a week to ten days. In order to save expense and time, people would join together and select one person to go and file all the claims on selected lands. When he returned, he would execute the proper release to the rightful owner.(4)

These early settlers, though poor, were friendly and obliging. They would travel miles to make calls on new arrivals. This trip was done on foot or by wagon and could mean many hours travel time. This was more a matter of necessity than a social call as the area was still a wilderness and settlers needed each other for protection. "Log raisings," resembling

The Osages or Wa-Saw-See Indian called Jasper County their home. This was a strong and war-like tribe. The head of each warrior was shaved with the exception of a tuft of hair the size of a man's hand. This was worn about two inches long in the center. This was the scalp lock. Laura Ingles Wilder wrote about them in "The Little House on the Prairie."

the "barn raisings" of today, were customary to help a newcomer build his home. This custom remained popular until the late 1850's.(5)

As Jasper County Historian, Marvin Van Gilder wrote, "It is clear that they were competent citizens who were fully aware of the responsibility not only to themselves but also to their immediate neighbors."

These settlers had a keen interest in education and a desire for schools. According to old records, on May 28, 1839, the county court, on petition from John M. Fullerton, ordered a section of land immediately southeast of Sarcoxie sold so that the school township could be supplied with funds. This was before the establishment of Jasper County. It is uncertain if any schools existed in the area during that time. "What little learning occurred by private instruction and the gospel was preached at intervals either in the home of some good man or at a camp meeting."(6)

Men and women both were involved in the log raising

Money was limited perhaps forcing the first schools to be subscription schools, (organized and tuition paid by parents or trustees). It is not known which ones or how many started out as subscription schools but their effectiveness depended almost entirely on the caliber of the teacher employed. Historically, these early teachers have been highly criticized. The 1876 *History of the Pioneer Families of Missouri* said:

"Now and then some pretentious pedagogue, with the title of professor, and pretending to be able to impart a knowledge of most of the languages and all the sciences, would straggle into a community and teach a three or four months' subscription school, in some disused cabin, hastily furnished as a school house, with split log benches and puncheon writing desks. To this "academy" the youth of the community would be sent, to study a little, and play a great deal more, while the teacher slept away the effects of too free an intercourse with his whiskey bottle - for they all drank freely"(7)

According to local school legend, the first subscription school opened in Jasper County near Cave Spring about 1838, as a female academy and was called Cave Spring Academy. This first school was later rebuilt a quarter mile east to be closer to the spring located below the school. A newer structure was built of brick, made and donated by William Duncan in about 1840. It had to be rebuilt again after the Civil War around 1875. This latest structure was fully restored in 2007. This school is now the oldest one-room school house in Jasper County.

A battle was being waged over control of the school system in Missouri during early statehood. Some wanted control kept at a local level and their opponents advocated upgrading the quality of education through the administrative control of schools by professionals at the state level. The latter group demanded organizational details such as type of schoolhouse and its furnishings, planned and graded curricula, careful record keeping and professional teachers.

The Geyer Act of 1839 passed by the Missouri

Cave Springs School 1903   Courtesy of the Jasper County Record Center

Legislature was an attempt to introduce greater state control. It appropriated funds for the township schools and required funding to be based on the number of white children between the ages of six and eighteen years in each township. This act also created the position of State Superintendent of Common Schools, who was charged with directing and expanding the Missouri school system. The duties also required the superintendent to report to the legislature on the condition of Missouri schools. In 1841, the legislature repealed that part of the law which provided for the office of state superintendent and transferred the duties to the secretary of state.

This repeal was viewed as a setback by educators who wanted school control handled by an office whose main focus was the organization of schools. This act was only partially effective because of inadequate funding from the permanent fund.(8) The battle between the two forces over school control would continue on into the 1840's and 50's.

(1) Joel Thomas Livingston - History of Jasper County and Its People – 1912 Vol. I - Page 4
(2) John Bradbury, Travels in the Interior of America in the Years 1809, 1810, 1811, 2nd edition
(3) F. A. North - History of Jasper County, Missouri - 1883 - Page 760
(4) Joel Thomas Livingston - History of Jasper County and Its People – 1912 Vol. I - Page 11
(5) Ibid. – Page 9
(6) Marvin VanGilder - Jasper County – The First Two Hundred Years – Page 302
(7) Tiffany Patterson - One-Teacher Public Schoolsof Missouri, c. 1774 to c. 1976
Published online at: sos.mo.gov/shpo/nps-nr/64501130.pdf
(8) Ken Luebering – Missouri Historical Review – "The Emergence of Bureaucracy" - 1980 – Page 302

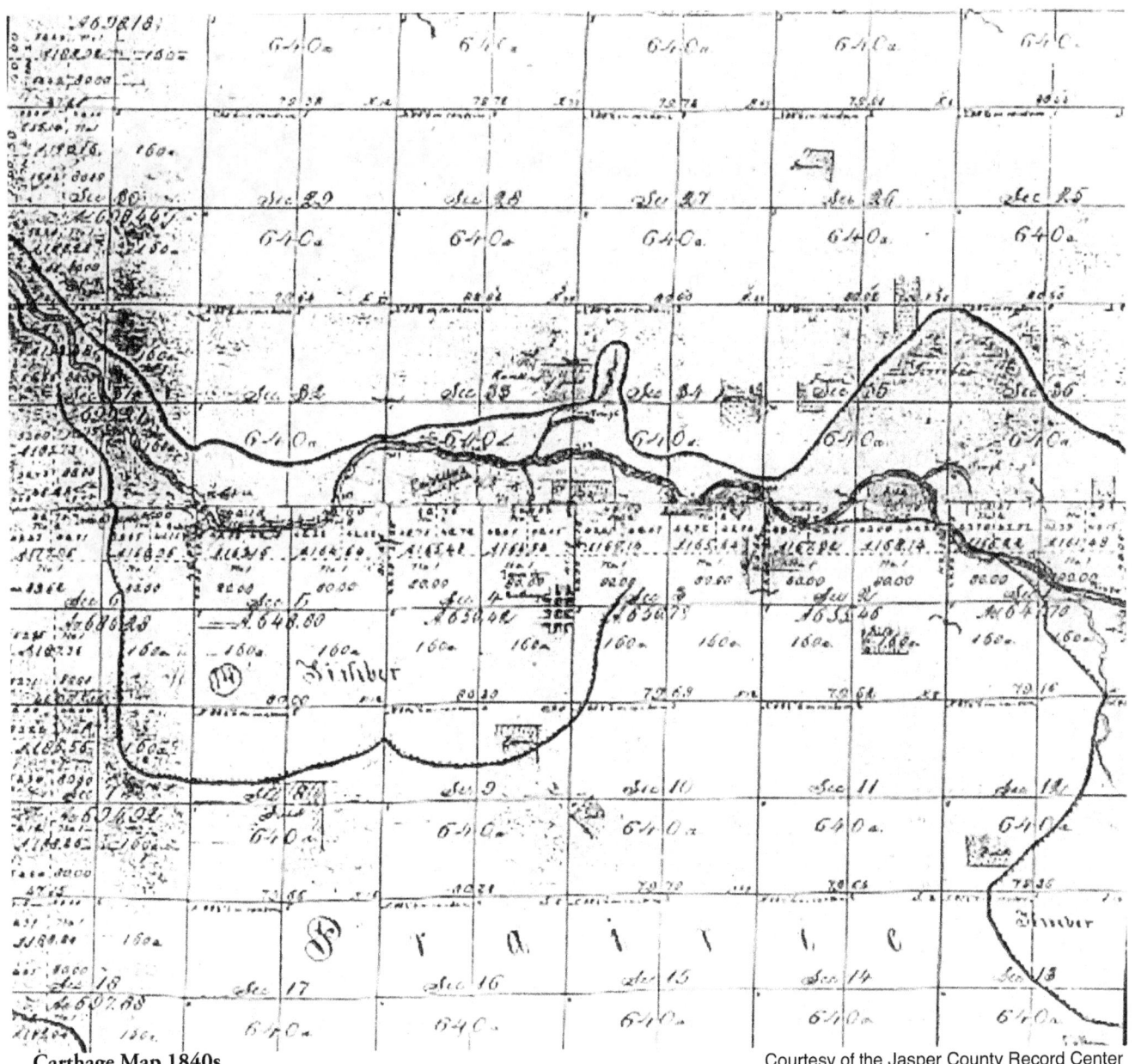

Carthage Map 1840s
Courtesy of the Jasper County Record Center

CHAPTER 2

1840's — A New County is Born

When Missouri first became a state, all of southwest Missouri was one county, Crawford County. Greene County was carved from Crawford; and then Barry County taken from Greene. Barry County included what would become seven southwest Missouri counties, including Jasper. The story goes that the old settlers of Jasper County joked that they had lived in four counties and had never moved once.(9)

The initial boundaries of Jasper County were finally established in Jan. 29, 1841. The county included what would later become Barton County and a three-mile strip on the southern boundary. In 1845, the strip was transferred to Newton County and in 1855, Jasper County contained the boundaries we see today.(10)

The first session of the county court took place Feb. 25, 1841.(11) The Justices of the Court were appointed by the governor. These Justices appointed other county officials and they soon started establishing roads, poll taxes, a county seat, townships and school districts. The first sixteenth section of school land was sold and paid for in March 1842. The land sold for $1.25 an acre and netted the county school fund $800 plus 38 cents interest. The profits went to the 'school land fund'. This money was to be used exclusively to pay teacher's salaries. Citizens were allowed to borrow money from the "school land fund" for other purposes and pay it back with interest.(12)

Leaders recognized the need to educate the young or just wanted to get the 'ruffians' off the street to prevent future lawlessness. Jasper County citizens soon turned their attention to the education of their children and schools were established as soon as practicable.

"Landowners donated a plot of land for the purpose of building the school house and adjoining yard to be built every two miles squared (four square miles), providing an average of not more than two miles for the students to walk. The land was to be considered donated as long as it was used for a school. If that status changed, the land reverted to the original owners. State-owned land was given in forty acre plots when the school was built and was farmed to raise money for school expenses. Two hundred dollars would buy forty acres." *Dorothy Shull and Nell Frost*

It is important that we look at the pioneer life of these settlers and how it affected the schools. Many times the life of these pioneers has been romanticized but we must remember these settlers had to deal

The first Jasper County Courthouse
It was reported that a fight broke out between two of the judges during the first session of the court.

Early Jasper County Seal

This is the Lincoln log home. It is typical of the log home built in Jasper County during the 1840's. Many had dirt floors and tarpaper on the windows to keep out the cold. Fireplaces were at one end of the room. There was often a loft for sleeping.

with many difficulties, an extremely high infant mortality rate, green flies would swarm and bite both man and animal making it nearly impossible to plow fields during the day. Minor accidents could be fatal due to lack of medical care. Loneliness was common because months went by without seeing anyone from outside the immediate family. Supplies could take up to two months to receive. It can be said that at best, conditions were very harsh and primitive.(13)

It wasn't until the latter 1830's or early 1840's that log homes were built in Jasper County. They were built no more than two miles from water and the oak and pine forest, although some of the best land was prairie. With no lumber available on these prairies, it was a matter of convenience to be near the timber to build homes. The log home of this period consisted of one large room or sometimes two with an immense fireplace in each. These fireplaces were used for both cooking and heating. Cornbread and johnnycakes were a staple in most homes. Nearly every family had a loom for making their own cloth. It was uncommon to see these men and women wearing any clothing that wasn't homemade. These looms wove a cloth called Butternut Jean, a durable fabric from which most clothes were made.(14)

("Butternut" refers to a dye color between light yellow to dark brown and could be made from different nuts. "Butternut Jean" material was not the jean material that we know today, but a course woven garment fabric).

The school term revolved around what needed to be done on the farms. For this reason the terms were short, averaging three or four months. Sometimes there were two short terms; one in the spring and

Baking Johnnycakes
Johnnycakes were a cornmeal flat bread often cooked on a shovel held over an open flame.

early part of the summer, and the other in autumn and early part of winter. There was very little free time for rural children. Boys older than ten years were expected to do the work of a man. Spring meant plowing and clearing brush and trees; many times this was done in sleet and snow. This work was followed by planting crops such as corn, potatoes and oats or wheat. Oxen or mules were used for the heavy work. Early summer meant hoeing and plowing followed by fall harvesting. Neighbors helped with the wheat harvest. Men and boys in the fields and girls assisting women with hearty noon meals of fried chicken, homemade cornbread, fresh butter, mashed potatoes and pies or cobblers. This was often followed by a jug of pure whiskey for the harvest help, and failure to provide it brought comments of stinginess upon the farm owner.

Women and girls were busy year-round. Quilts had to be sewn and tied. Walnuts, pecans, and hazelnuts were gathered to be roasted over a winter's fire. Persimmons were picked and dried. Meals were prepared daily, the family garden was tended and vegetables were canned.

There were strawberries, blackberries, and huckleberries to be picked in the spring and early summer. Preserving apples and peaches took place in the fall by halving or quartering the fruit and laying it on boards or sheets in the sun to dry. Some of the fruit was gathered

and put in outdoor cellars. These cellars were covered or roofed with boards, and straw and dirt thrown upon it to prevent freezing in severe winter weather. The women and young children were responsible for the apple cider press and making sweet cider. The coming of winter meant cutting and chopping wood. If not enough wood was gathered, the family could freeze to death come winter. Winter was the time for butchering pigs, processing and preserving the meat. Sausage was put away in jars or crocks. Hog fat was rendered and made into lye soap; this was usually done outdoors and in large black, cast iron kettles over an open fire. Boys hunted for squirrel or rabbit, not only for sport but a source of food to provide food. Everything was done and everyone worked for the survival of the family. Education came second. This was understood and accepted by everyone, including teachers.(15)

Even though they dealt with daily hardship, the Jasper County pioneers recognized the necessity of schools for their children. On May 3, 1843, the county court divided the county into three school districts. The first school district was organized in Congressional Township 28 and Range 29, in the far eastern part of the county, with William Maxwell as the appointed Township Commissioner. The Township Commissioner exercised supervision over the schools. He employed the teacher, mapped out the course of study, and wrote the school rules and regulations. All territory situated north of Spring River was designated District No 1 and John B. Halloman was appointed school director for the district. District No. 2 covered all the west half south of Spring River with Hiram Duncan appointed as director. District No. 3 covered the east half south of the river with Jeremiah Cravens as director.(16)

In addition, two inspectors were also appointed whose duty it was to visit the schools at least once during the school term. They reported on the performance of the teacher and progress of their students. One-room schools were soon built, the earliest made of logs or frame with fireplaces for heat. Some had dirt floors, others had hand-milled wood floors. Furnishings were few because of lack of funds and for this same reason, sometimes homemade. Joel Thomas Livingston, author of *History of Jasper County and Its People, 1912,* has written that the fireplaces were an immense affair, where great logs five or six feet long

Settlers constructed log schoolhouse very much like their own homes. Some of the later buildings were made of sawn lumber with glass windows. Paint was not often found either inside ot out. Students often sat on log benches without backs. The teacher had a desk or table on a platgform higher than the students so they could easily watch the children.

were burned. Some schools had dirt floors while others had hand-milled wood. David D. March, PHD in *History of Missouri, 1967*, referred to them as "dismal, dreary cabins." Furnishings were few because of lack of funds and sometimes homemade. The earliest desks were no more than wooden planks with the seats being a log cut in two with pegs driven into the rounded side. Students sat erect on these with their writing slates. Children brought their own slates and goose feathers for the teacher to make into quill pens.(17)

John Mason Peck, an early traveler in Missouri, wrote that a "minimum of one-third of the schools were at least public nuisances, another third did as much harm as they did good and the remaining third were perhaps an advantage to the community in various degrees."(18)

The next step and perhaps the most difficult was finding a qualified teacher for the school. Teachers in backwoods communities were sometimes hired on a catch-as-catch-can basis, and if one could not be caught, a person in the community with a little better than average education, or more specifically, one who could read, was promoted to the teaching position. The conventional wisdom of the day.

Floyd C. Shoemaker, Secretary, State Historical Society of Missouri, stated, "Virtually all it took to be a teacher in early Missouri was the ability to make a goose quill pen and to be a good judge of the toughness and durability of a bunch of hickory switches.

In his 844 inaugural address, Gov. Edwards stated, "teachers were paid poorly and very inadequately prepared for their work."(19) He also stated that teachers came from the poor.(20)

Floyd C. Shoemaker, Secretary, State Historical Society of Missouri, stated, "Virtually all it took to be a teacher in early Missouri was the ability to make a goose quill pen and to be a good judge of the toughness and durability of a bunch of hickory switches. For under the equal rights privileges enjoyed in the new land, every shoemaker or merchant was permitted to "preach the gospel, practice medicine or law, to teach school, or do whatever his heart desires."

It was difficult for good teachers to migrate to the new territory. School lasted three months and attendance was irregular. Books, blackboards and school equipment were non-existent in many places. Textbooks consisted of the Bible and any books the people of the community could gather. Schoolhouses were cold and drafty. In addition, the teachers had to put up with irregular attendance, for most fathers didn't "hold with book larnin" when there was corn to husk or ground to break and they had no qualms about keeping their children home from school when they could be useful at home. H. M. Boyd of Sarcoxie writes, "My father was a teacher in one of the earlier schools. He told stories of many happenings in the school, but the most exciting was when an older boy pulled a knife on him. He eventually settled the situation and the young man took a severe whipping. Dad said that later in life the man came to him and thanked him for straightening him out."(21)

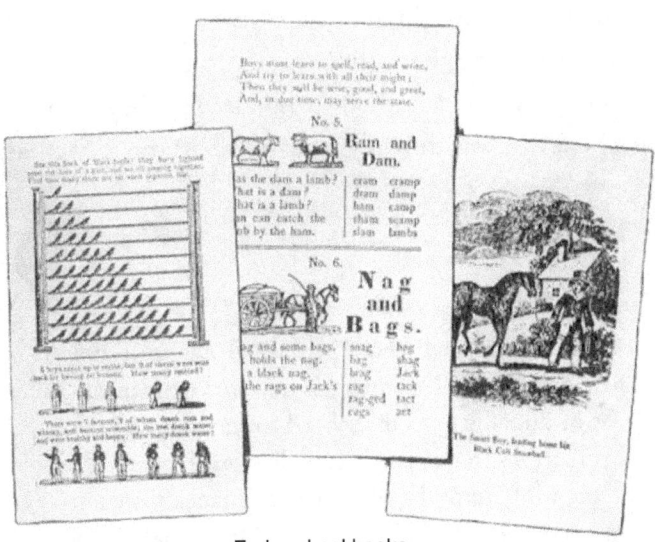
Early school books

These 'educators' were paid in kind, and perhaps the possibility of receiving their salary in corn, meat and other produce was one of the reasons that betters teachers did not appear on the Missouri scene until later. In addition to the regular fees, the teachers were boarded around a week or longer at a time by each student's family.

Nearly every parent believed in corporal punishment and "Spare the rod and spoil the child" as a form of family control. This quotation was undoubtedly the justification for many parents unmercifully beating their children. This form of control sometimes carried over into the rural schools by whipping the children with rods or switches. This form of punishment was freely used; the school authorities holding to the old-fashion theory of "no licking, no learning." Because teachers were usually men, the teacher needed muscle as much as a good certificate in securing employment. The teacher who had never heard of a school journal or a teachers' association but who heard eternal punishment preached every Sunday for disobedience cared little about kindness and used severe whippings to maintain control.(21)

Parents who were strict with their children at home did not approve of their children being brutally beaten at school, but most thoroughly believed that severe punishment for childish behavior was the only way to maintain control in school. With the advent of the "northern teacher," these views began to change and school was governed with more understanding and kindness.(22) It was generally thought that "northern teachers" were better because of a broader cultural background and were more humane toward the students.

Educators recognized the need to further educate teachers but could not decide on a specific plan. At this time, the need further educate females was view as decidedly less important than that of a male.(23)

The teacher had to arrive early in the morning to start the fire to heat the school. Some teachers were not always adept at this and required the help of an older student, usually an eighth grade boy. Some threw paraffin oil on the wood or used gun powder and striking flint to start the fire, which along with faulty flues caused some schools burning to the ground. Teachers were also responsible for keeping the building clean and sweeping floors at the end of the day.

A typical school day started with a recital of a Bible verse by each student. This could be followed by the entire school singing a selected song, usually a hymn. In some of these early schools, a course of study did not always exist. Many times the students studied whatever the teacher could teach or depended on what books they had. Penmanship was considered very important as well as spelling. Spelling matches were sometime held in these schools with students shouting out the letters. Teachers, that could, set out math problems for students. A teacher that was a good "arithmeticker" was well respected.(24)

Classes lasted until morning recess, when students played a game of deer and hounds (a form of tag), or horseshoes. Classes would resume with the ringing of the school bell. School would then last until lunch recess. Students brought their lunches from home in cloth sacks or wrapped in clothe, followed by more games played by everyone. The rest of the school day consisted of classes and another recess before school was dismissed..

School District No. 2 was the first to build a public schoolhouse, therefore, had the honor of being the oldest public school in the county at that time. Joel Thomas Livingston, *History of Jasper County, Missouri and Its People - 1912*, wrote that this first school was on Center Creek, three miles below Sarcoxie. Judge Jeremiah Cravens was one of the first school directors and Samuel Teas was the first teacher.(25)

The following des- cription of this school is written by H. M. Boyd of Sarcoxie, a student in the school in the 1840's: "The house was built of rough logs unhewn and was covered with clapboards held down

---

Hence the normal school plan was drawn to accomodate only men. This adjunct school for women was to be of direct help to the school for men as well as of instructions to women. The male school was to run in the winter months when the young men were not needed so much on the farms, and the female school in the summer when the young women would be less exposed. One of the particular functions of the female school was to be the making of clothing for the younger men of the school.

Taken from Governor Edwards' plan for a higher education school (Normal School) in 1848
— FIRST DISTRICT STATE NORMAL SCHOOL, 1905 - E. M. VIOLETTE —

on the roof with poles, as nails could not be obtained at this early day. The house had but one door; this was in the south side. In the west end one log was cut out the full length of the room for a window and this was left open summer and winter. Under this window there was a plank running the full length nailed to pins driven into the wall. This served as a writing desk. The fireplace was in the east end of the house and was wide enough to take a log a foot and a half thick and eight feet long."

"The jams on each side and the back were made of rough rock and the balance of the chimney was made of sticks daubed with red clay. The house was seated with split logs, the flat side up and the ends resting on chunks."

"In the side of the door a nail was driven into the wall and on this was suspended a little forked stick about six inches long, which every scholar took with him when he went out during the hours of study. No scholar was allowed to go out till this little fork was returned. This house stood on the east side of the road that ran from the Haskins house to the old ford on Center creek, known as the Boyd ford, and was about midway between the two. I attended this school and here I learned my A B C and received here my first flogging. The school was patronized by the Cravens, the Mills, the Boyds, the Haskins, Beasleys and Prigmons."

"Mr. Teas was regarded as a successful teacher in that day and a fine scholar. He wrote a good hand and could cipher as far as the rule of three. The school was what might be called an old-fashioned school; that is, all the students used the old blue-back spelling book and studied it aloud."(26)

Mr. Teas was mentioned as a teacher of white children in Springfield in the 1840's. It is not known whether this Samuel Teas is the same one against whom the first circuit court in Greene County returned four "gaming" indictments in August 1833.(27)

These rural schools served as social centers for the entire community and successful teachers were among the most respected members of the community as they were literate when a large portion of the population was illiterate.

> Wm. Seal, of this city, claims the distinction of having taught the first school in Jasper county in 1855.

Carthage Press 1895 article differs from other sources about who was the first teacher in the county. Article courtesy of Michelle Hansford

A later schoolhouse

Mrs. James Brummett, born in 1842 and a daughter of W. W. Shank, recalled attending a school near Carthage. "When we lived east of Carthage, I came into town and went to school in a log schoolhouse just south of the spring that later became known as the Woolen Mill Spring... The teacher of the school was Miss Susan Bowlen, whose father owned a farm east of town. The subjects taught there were reading, writing; spelling and some of the older students took a little elementary arithmetic. No advance subject could be taught because the teachers did not have much education. Two Indian boys, both Cherokees, went to the school at this time along with the white children. They dressed like the rest of the boys and, as far as I know, got along with the white children."(28)

The second township to be organized was township 29, Range 33 in the west-central part of the county. The order creating this district was made at the May term of the county court in 1845.(29) Benjamin Turner was appointed township commissioner and Samuel Bright and John R. Chenault the inspectors. Samuel B. Cooley the first teacher. It was fortunate for the schools that all three members of the court participated in the organization of the school system. (29) Other districts were soon organized and by the time the Civil War started, twenty-three school houses had been built.

In 1847, the legislature made the apportionment of money no longer dependent on county school directors filing reports with the secretary of state's office. Without these reports, that office, as acting superintendent of schools, could know very little of what was happening in the schools. This information was vital if standardization of schools was to progress.

Gradually, counties began to file reports that met the legal requirements but there were no legal means to force schools to provide the desired information.

Missouri schools also faced financial problems in the 1840's. One problem was the investment of school funds with the Bank of Missouri whose dividends had dropped from 5% to 3½% by 1842. This caused severe difficulties in townships that relied on the school fund to pay teacher salaries. Educators called for the removal of funds from the Bank of Missouri and reinvested in state funds. Action was not taken until the 1850's when the bank paid no dividends whatsoever on school money.(30)

The annual enumeration or census was taken for white children between the ages of six and twenty years of age as early as May 29, 1849.(31) The school apportionment was seven cents per child.

---

(9) Joel Thomas Livingston - History of Jasper County and Its People – Vol. 1 – Page 6
(10) Marvin VanGilder - Jasper County – The First Two Hundred Years – Page 35
(11) Minutes of County Court Jasper County Vol. A – Page 1
(12) Ibid. P 34
(13) F. A. North - History of Jasper County Missouri - 1883 - Page 760
(14) Joel Thomas Livingston - History of Jasper County and Its People – Vol. 1 – Page 9
(15) Wiley Britton - Pioneer Life in Southwest Missouri
(16) Minutes of County Court Jasper County - Vol. A – Page 80
(17) Pioneer Life in Southwest Missouri – Wiley Britton
(18) Carthage Evening Press - March 3, 1949
(19) E. M. Violette - First District State Normal School - 1905 - Page 3
(20) Ibid. Page 9
(21) Wiley Britton - Pioneer Life in Southwest Missouri - Page 216
(22) Ibid. 217
(23) E. M. Violette - First District State Normal School - 1905 -Page 11
(24) Adventures in Young America - McGuire and Phillips - 1929
(25) Joel Thomas Livingston - History of Jasper County, Missouri and Its People – Vol. 1 – Page 23
(26) Story by Boyd -Jasper County Record Center
(27) So That All May Learn – A History of the Springfield Missouri Public Schools – Chapter 1
((28) Carthage Evening Press – Sept. 7, 1922
(29) Minutes of County Court Jasper County Vol. A – Page 204
(30) Ken Lueberfing - Missouri Historical Review - The Emergence of Bureaucary" 1980 - Page 302
(31) Minutes of County Court Jasper County - Vol. A - Page 394

Chapter 3
1850's – Progress and Unrest

During the 1850's, Jasper County, still in its infancy, was becoming more populated and had a greater number of schools were being built. Churches were established and lead ore was discovered. In spite of this progress, Jasper County was still considered the frontier.

Mrs. Robinette Langley Hickman, in a press interview published in the Carthage Evening Press, September 22, 1922, recollects Indians in Jasper County in the 1850's. Her family had settled here in 1838, the year after the Osage War. ***

"One of the principal remembrances of my youth," Mrs. Hickman said, "is of the Indians; large bands of Indians would pass our house several times a year coming up from the Indian nation. There was a mill a couple of miles east of us known as Duncan's Mill and every fall the Indians would come past our house going to this mill, though what they bought there I do not know. I suppose they purchased flour or perhaps corn meal. Although the Indians passed our place to the mill, they never came back that way as all I remembered were headed east."

"All these bands were friendly and never bothered us in the least, but they were Indians and we children were very much afraid of them. When they passed, we always hid where we could watch them but where we thought they could not see us. There were men, women and children in these parties and pack ponies heavily loaded with baggage of some sort. The men wore blankets and breech-cloths and were filthy looking fellows, oftentimes with weird looking animals printed on their bare chests. I believe they generally had bows and arrows.

Every now and then they would stop and cook their meals not far from our house. The food would be prepared in a huge kettle and seemed to be some kind of soup with chunks of meat in it. When it was done, the Indians would gather around the kettle with huge wooden spoons or ladles and each would scoop up a spoonful of the soup with long strings of meat hanging from the spoon and when it was cool, would eat what they had, sucking in the long strings of meat in a most disgusting way. I never saw them do it, but I have been told that when the soup was being prepared, they would frequently catch live terrapins and throw them into the boiling liquid, laughing with glee as the animals struggled and tried to swim. The food was not done until these terrapins were cooked to pieces."(32)

The missionary Issac McCoy described the Osage as an "uncommonly fierce, courageous, warlike nation". BAE GN 4159 C, National Anthropological Archives, Smithsonian Institution

*** *The Osage War could be said to have started in 1824 when a treaty was made with the Osage and by its term they relinquished all claims to Missouri and withdrew west of the state line. The natives were unhappy with losing their land and hunting parties would occasionally return to Jasper County but caused no problems.*

1837 had not been a good year for the Osage in Kansas and the territory. Their crops had failed and they wanted to return to their old homes in Missouri. They did not desire war with the white settlers but felt they had an advantage in a conflict as they felt they clearly outnumbered the whites. They slipped across the border with guns and camped on Spring River. Militiamen were sent to battle the camped bands. Most of the renegades slipped back across the border or were captured and escorted back with threats and warnings. The Osage were astonished that the whites, of whom they had seen so few, could muster so many to do battle.

A few weeks later the natives began to slip back across the border into this county and the governor again called in troops to deal with the problem. The Osage, learning of the troops coming, fled back across the border. This bloodless affair ended what is officially known on state records as the Osage War.(26) In spite of this experience with the white man's government, the Osage were always loyal to the Union and joined the Federals in the upcoming Civil War.(31)

Even though civilization in the county had not fully developed in the 1850's (as we define it today) schools were held albeit with short terms averaging three to four months of the year. Sometimes there were two short terms, one in spring and early summer and the other in autumn and early winter. Most schoolbooks were of a religious nature, but McGuffey's Readers, Townsend's Speller and the Definer were sometimes used. (33)

On September 28, 1850, the Missouri Congress passed a law in the interest of popular education providing that where there was swamp or overflowed land in a county, that land was to be condemned and sold for the benefit of the school fund. Laws were passed during the next session establishing that swamp lands would be deeded by the state to the counties to be sold.

McGuffy Readers

An unsubstantiated story is found in Joel T. Livingston's book, *A History of Jasper County Missouri* and Marvin VanGilder's *Jasper County – The First Two Hundred Years* concerning the manner in which these lands were condemned as "swamp land." Jasper County had virtually no swamp land, but the opportunity to aid the cause of education by securing these lands was not overlooked. Spring River and Center Creek occasionally overflowed their banks during spring rains so adjacent land to these two streams was deemed "swamp land" and sold to benefit the school fund. Government agents were supposed to check on the accuracy of the claims, but perhaps they were local men with special interest. This scheme involved a little trickery involving land-seekers who placed canoes or other vessels designed for river travel upon the running gears of wagons, hitched teams of horses or mules to the wagons, climbed aboard and drove the teams over mile after mile of high and dry prairie. They then signed affidavits attesting they had ridden in boats across specific parcels of land, thus allowing them to be classified as swamp land.

Riding a canoe across the prairie

Though these testimonies were misleading at best, on December 3, 1853, county officials entered into a contract with J. M. Richardson, ex-Secretary of State, for the purpose of having these lands condemned. The commission condemned practically the entire government domain that was left unsold and the county came into possession of more than 300,000 acres of land, which was placed on the market the latter part of 1854 and sold at ninety cents per acre. A few grew wealthy from this land scheme, including the ex-Secretary of State. Future court battles would be fought over the legality of this maneuver. The amount of money secured from the sale of the swamp lands was in round numbers $200,000.(34) "Swamp Land" still appears on property deeds today, including some property within the Carthage city limits.

The Kelly Act was enacted in 1853 because of problems with school finances and the organization of the schools. This act succeeded where the Geyer Act failed. It gave power back to the state superintendent and provided for the exercise of that power. This law required that 25% of the state's general revenue be apportioned among the counties to support public schools. It stated that tax revenue would only go to organized townships. This new law required counties to file annual reports to the state as a basis for apportionment of funds. Only 39 counties qualified for the tax revenue apportionment in the first year after the new passing and by the end of 1858, all counties qualified. By this time, the state was spending $309,000 – nearly one fourth of its income for aid to the schools. Far reaching results of this law also included: administrative framework starting with the State Superintendent, the creation of the office of County Superintendent, organization and structure of schooling, state-wide use of uniform textbooks and the creation of a normal school to improve and standardize of teaching methods.(35) The state was using its power to direct the development of schools.

On Dec. 3, 1853, the county court appointed John R. Chenault the first County Commissioner of Schools(37) and on May 25, 1854 the Jasper County Court approved apportionments of state and county school money to the county's townships. The state school money was forty-two cents per child and the county was five cents per child.(38) In the 1850s, with the Kelly Act, we begin to see the beginning the unmistakable shape of the present school system.

(32) Ward L. Schrantz - Jasper County Missouri in the Civil War – 1923 - Page viii
(33) Carthage Evening Press – Sept. 22, 1922
(34) Wiley Britton - Pioneer Life in Southwest Missouri – Page 317
(35) Joel Thomas Livingston - A History of Jasper County and Its People – Vol. 1 – Page 25
(36) Ken Luebering - Missouri Historical Review – "Emergence of Bureaucracy" – 1980 – Page 307-311
(3&) Minutes of County Court Jasper County Vol. B – Page 257
(38) Ibid. Page 325

SUBPŒNA--DUCES TECUM.

STATE OF MISSOURI, County of Jasper } ss. **THE STATE OF MISSOURI:**

To Geo Blakely Co. Clk

YOU ARE HEREBY COMMANDED, That, setting aside all manner of excuse and delay you be and appear in proper person before the Judge of our Circuit Court, at the Court House, in the City of Carthage within and for said County, on instanter ~~day of~~ A. D. 18__, then and there to testify and the truth to speak, in a certain matter of controversy now pending in our said Court, wherein J W Iydings & wife Plaintiff S, and A. S. Pitcher & others Defendant S, on behalf of the Plff ; and you are further commanded to bring with you and then and there produce in evidence* "Old Swamp Land Book 1858" — "The Duplicate Certificate of Swampland Sales, 1858" + County Court Record Books "D" & "E"

and hereof fail not at your peril. And the person or officer serving this Writ is commanded to have the same at the time and place aforesaid, certifying thereon his return.

WITNESS my hand and Seal of our said Court. Done at office in Carthage

Subpoena resulting from the sell of these 'Swamp lands'

COME TO THE RESCUE!!

TO THE CITIZENS OF COOPER:

We have just arrived from Kansas, having been ordered to return home by Col. Reid, for the purpose of raising a Company, of at least SIXTY men, to join him at Westport on the 15th inst., and in order to effect this object, we propose to hold a meeting at the Court House in the city of Boonville, on

MONDAY NEXT.

Let every man attend, and give us his counsel and advice; we want men who can be relied upon, men with strong arms and patriotic hearts, to stand by the gallant REID, and those who are now with him, upon the border of our State, to resist the aggressions of the lawless bands of abolitionists in Kansas.

J. W. DRAFFIN,   H. H. BRAND,
SAM. COLE,   BOB. McCULLOCH,
JNO. HOWARD,   JNO. SHANKLIN,
AND MANY OTHERS.

Boonville, Sept. 6, 1856.

Poster from the 'Bleeding Kansas' period

Fifteen hundred Dollars Reward

~~One~~ Thousand Dollars

REWARD!

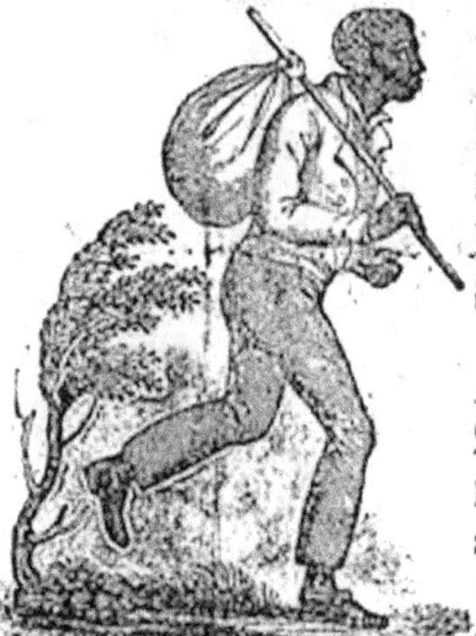

RANAWAY from the subscribers living 12 miles West of Springfield, Greene county, Missouri, on the night of the 21st ult., two negroes described as follows:

ARCHA, belonging to James L. Alexander, is a molatto man, some 21 years old, or upwards, some 5 feet 6 inches high, has grey eyes, and plays the fiddle well.

JOHN, belonging to John A. Miller, is rather a dark complected man, some 28 years old, about 6 feet high, heavy built, Weighs some 180 pounds, has rather a positive way of affirming or denying.

We will give the following rewards for the apprehension and delivery of said negroes to us in Greene county, Mo., or if confined in any jail so that we get them back to Missouri, that is to say: ~~Twenty dollars each, if taken in Greene county, Missouri; 50 dollars each, if taken out of Greene county and in the State of Missouri, and 250 dollars each, if taken in a free State or Territory, and delivered as above,~~ and $500 for legal conviction and after sentence to the Penitentiary, for the white man who has given said negroes free papers or aided in getting them off.

JAMES L. ALEXANDER, by his Agent, S. C. NEVILL,

J. A. MILLER.

November 4, 1854.

We will give five hundred dollars for the delivery of each of the above negroes wherever & $500 as above for the white man who [illegible]

[illegible] 1855

J. L. Alexander

J. A. Miller

Runaway slave poster - Courtesy of Greene County Missouri Archives

Photo courtesy of the Library of Congress

Chapter 4

1860's – Years of Pain

The county suffered greatly during the War of the Rebellion. Its most thriving towns were burned and almost depopulated. As a border state, there was general uneasiness in most family homes about a possible war and the slavery question. The question of secession was openly discussed in businesses and schoolyards all over the county. Union sympathizers were being persecuted and teachers with these sentiments felt it safer to leave and go north. Without adequate teachers, schools began to close.

In 1858 a man from Kansas was employed to teach school in Sarcoxie. He had strong abolitionist beliefs and expressed those views by reading "Uncle Tom's Cabin" telling of evils of slavery to his students. He was asked to resign his position but refused to do so. Late one night a body of citizens waited on him and ordered him to leave. Again he refused, so they escorted him to the woods and gave him a coat of tar and feathers. (39)

Events in Kansas contributed to the unrest in western Missouri and feelings about the slavery question. One such factor was the turmoil in the Cherokee Neutral Land 1853 to 1858.

The Cherokee Neutral Land, on the western border of Jasper County, was a

21

strip of land 50 miles long and 25 miles wide with its eastern boundary being the Kansas-Missouri line. It was first given to the Osage by a treaty in 1825 to serve as a barrier between the Osage and the white settlers. A treaty made between the Federal government and the Cherokee at New Echota, Georgia in 1835 reassigned this strip of land containing 800,000 acres to the Cherokee nation. Notwithstanding it was Cherokee land, white settlers began to settle the area when Kansas was organized as a territory. Anti-slavery and pro-slavery groups sent people into the area along the entire North-South border of Kansas and Missouri to influence the thinking of these settlers. Their goal was to determine how Kansas would enter the Union, as a anti-slavery or pro-slavery state.(40) This conflict lasted until 1858 and was labeled 'Bleeding Kansas' by Horace Greeley of the New York Times.

The other contributing factor to the uneasiness along the border area was a severe drought that hit Kansas in 1860 leading to crop failure, streams drying up and the near starvation of families.

Even though Jasper County was not involved in the Kansas conflict, or suffered the drought, it is very possible that people moving into this county from that affected area, in order to survive, brought with them different beliefs concerning the slavery issue. This and the simmering discontent already here caused neighbor to look at neighbor with suspicion. These conditions also made schooling almost impossible. Wiley Britten, a school student at the time, wrote in *Pioneer Life in Southwest Missouri,* "occasional disturbances and sometimes acute troubles in some of the border counties of Missouri and Kansas made the slavery question a live issue."(41)

Occasionally, a posse of men would be seen in the county looking for a runaway slave. There were between two and three hundred slaves in this county by the census of 1860. Good male slaves were worth between $1,000 and $1,500. Female slaves were worth considerably less. It was customary in this state to sell slaves publicly at the courthouse on the first day of January in each year. There was a lawsuit in the Missouri Supreme Court founded on a note given for a black girl named "Charity," who was bought at a public sale at the courthouse in Carthage on January 1, 1860. A bid of $1,380 was given and due in one year. Before the note came due, a question arose in regard to the validity of the sale, the girl having been willed by her previous owner to a daughter of his, stating that she was to belong to said daughter and the heirs of her body forever. The defense claims she was entailed property and could not be sold.(33) This is possibly one of the last, if not the last, case in the courts of the State resulting from that "peculiar institution."

Deposition taken from Tom Livingston's (the famed Confederate guerilla leader) son acknowledging he attended school during this time

25 September 1864 : Pricilla Hunter, Ozark Prairie, Mo., to Margaret Newberry
----

                                          Ozark Prairie   Sept the 25   1864

Mrs. Mag Newberry

    Dear Sister, I will commence a letter to you this morning though I dont expect to have an opportunity of sending it to the office soon. You said you reconed we had a lonesome time. You had better bet. We have nowhere to go, and if there was, no way to go, as we cant k[eep] a horse. Well Mag I would love to see you. I could tell you a good many things that I cant write. You thought we had hard times here before you left but it is ten times as hard now. Ther is men being killed every little while. There was four or five men killed over on Spring river about a week ago. The bushwhackers burnt Carthage a few days ago. The Malitia was called off from there. We heard that there was five hundred rebels at Carthage last friday. There was a company of Malitia at the School house and they left after night. I expect the troops are all called off. We are looking for a rade all the time. It may be gone north now. The bushwhackers came through this neighborhood last week. They robed old Drawin badly, then came to Mrs Clarks and cut up at a trrible rate. Made her give them what money she had and took a good many things. They are afraid of us, they go around. They went to Loves and took some things from him, he said, and then went to Mrs Seymores and robed her again. They are deth on the widow women. I am [torn page] they will call on us next time. I have bin trying to weave a little. We have a web of janes in the loom. We have cut it out twice. I do not know who will cut it out next time. I dont know how we will get our flannel wove. We are afraid to put it in the loom. I guess you have quit hiding now. We have to hide our things all the time. It is an awful job. We have bin drying apples. We have about four bushels dryed. We have had a poor chance. Pal and Ellen have bin going to school. I expect the school is broke up now. Both of Jim Crismons children was buried last friday. The babe died thursday eavening and the little girl friday morning. We heard they had the fever. We did not hear of it till after they was buried. The bushwhackers was at Dr Wilsons not long ago. They took all of his clothes. He hid in the house. They pulled a bed off of the stead and burnt it. They had shot an old man, and he could not go to see him till he got clothes. Mr Emett still stays at home. I would not be surprised no morning to hear of him being killed. Mrs Clark talks some leaveing. There has not bin any of our neighbors left yet. If a few of them leaves they will all go. Has Mr Haglers heard from Mchale lately? We heard that trane was all captured by the indians. We have never heard any thing from Robison yet that is reliable. It is strange what they have done with him. We have sold one load of apples to Emetts to take to Fort Skott. They give 30 cts per bushel for them. Mother sent for some callico and paid 65 cts per yard. About like it is at Mt Vernon. I expect goods are as hi[gh in Illi]nois as they are here.

    I have not got much finery since you left. I was at Mt Vernon last spring. I got me a Shaker bonnet. You said you had got one. I thought you would [not] have one as bad as you hated them. Mther got me a blue delane dress patron[sic]. She gave one dollar per yard for it. Well Mag I guess I will quit till some other time as I have run out of bullets.

    I will try to write a few lines more to day. The country is all in a confusion, the troops all called off. We hear that old price is within forty miles of Springfield with ten thousand men. I do not know whether it is reliable or not. We also heard that there was seven hundred down on cowskin prair-

1864 letter written by a woman living around the eastern border of Jasper County. It is unknown if the school she mentions is Cave Spring or Bowers Mill, a school just across the Jasper-Lawrence County line that also was a Union militia headquarters. There is indication from this letter that some schooling may have been taking place in the area.

When the Civil War finally erupted, it completely disorganized the county. There are no official documents indicating Jasper County schools were in session during that time. There are indications that some form of schooling took place in the county, but for how long and to what degree is uncertain.(43)

> **Cave Spring School**
>
> Cave Spring School served as a Missouri Union Militia HeadQuarters from 1861 - 1865. The Soldiers from this school killed Bud Shirley, brother of Myra Shirley, who later became known as Belle Starr.

Not only were schools closing but the office of state superintendent of schools and county school commissioner were discontinued. To compound the already existing problems, the state did not appropriate any funds from the general revenue for public school from 1861 - 1863, 1865 or 1867.(44)

During the Civil War, Jasper County was nearly depopulated except along its eastern border. The number of residents living there varies but it could have been as many as 400 families. This was because of the Missouri Union Militia headquarters and the pro-Union sympathizers living in that area. After Carthage was destroyed by Confederate forces, the Cave Spring community was selected by the governor to be the county seat and Cave Spring School to be the county courthouse. On Oct. 10, 1865, the county officials met there and resumed their duties. They began taking steps to collect interest on the school fund, foreclose on lands not paid for and collect overdue notes for swamp land with the purpose of reorganizing the county schools.(45)

The revised constitution of Missouri, known as the Drake Constitution, went into effect July 4, 1865 stating that teachers, among others, could not follow their chosen profession unless they took the 'oath of loyalty' to the Union. These individuals had to attest to their innocence of 86 acts of disloyalty to the State of Missouri and to the Union. A copy of their affidavit was filed with the County Clerk. A register was appointed to administer the oath and register 'qualified voters'. Anyone attempting to hold positions without taking this 'oath' was subject to a $500 fine and/or six months in prison. A Barry County teacher, Evaline Roberts, was brought up on charges in 1866 for not signing the oath (State of Missouri vs. Evaline Roberts - 1866).(46) It is not known what the outcome of the charge was but she appears in the 1880 census as being a servant/housekeeper. At he time of this census her age was listed as 26.

Article IX of the new Constitution of 1865 made it the duty of the state to provide free education for all between the ages of five and twenty-one. Supervision of instruction in the common schools was to be managed by a state board of education consisting of the secretary of state, the attorney general, and state superintendent of schools, who was president of the board. No township school district which failed to maintain a free school for less than three months during the year was to receive any portion of the public school fund. In case that fund did not yield sufficient income to sustain a free school for at least four months in every year, the general assembly could levy a tax on property in each county, township, or school district to provide the deficient funds.(47) We still pay a school tax today.

The Drake Constitution received its name after its chief proponent, Charles Drake

There is little doubt that a change was needed in the school system. In March, 1866, the Twenty-third General Assembly passed a set of laws recommended by State Superintendent of Schools, Thomas A. Parker. These laws came to be known as

Although Jasper County has no record of these schools this would have been typical of an early African American school

the Parker Laws. Township administration was key to his system and township districts were supervised by a County School Superintendent.(48) Although these laws were viewed as progressive, they were never fully implemented.

The Constitution also made it the duty of the state to provide education for African-American children, as it did for other citizens of the state. The legislature made it mandatory for townships to establish schools for these children and provide them with a common school education. The schools were also placed under the same board as those of other schools in the district. This was to prevent what happened in some other states (i.e. Oklahoma). The per capita expenditure for the white schools was $70.53 and the African American schools was $30.00.(49)

The need to reorganize schools became more urgent because of the number of new families moving into the county with school age children. There were so many that the local residents began to complain. This influx of people was partially due to southern sympathizers moving back after leaving or being ordered to leave the county during the Civil War. Others may have felt there was greater economic opportunity here, i.e. rich prairie land, lead mining, etc.

County school reorganization was affected in 1867 with the election of a Jasper County School Commissioner, J. C. Willoughby. Several school districts that had been organized before the war were reopened. The sales of land for the school fund began again; and by 1868 most of the available land had been sold. The County School Fund had grown in revenue from the sale of swamp lands to almost $150,000 by January 1, 1868. The revenue was loaned out at ten percent interest, earning the Jasper County $15,000 annually.

This enabled teachers to be paid fairly good wages and some of the best talent of that time entered the profession. School houses were in short supply because the fund could not be used for any building purposes; even so, the county had a fairly good school system. For the most part, the schools were one-room frame houses with few furnishings. From the close of the war until December 1869, the school system grew from 23 districts to 79 and the teaching force numbered 104, most of whom were men. The average salary was $42.75 per month. The number of school age children was 4,898; seventy-three percent were enrolled in school.(50)

> **Selling out fast!**
> The celebrated "Swamp Lands," which are not swamps, but beautiful dry prairies, are selling fast. If you want any, *buy now*, for they will all be sold before the end of Summer. Enquire of Mr. Tower.
>
> *Carthage Banner May 1868*

Rain Cascades On 1869 Fourth ---- Hogs Banned From Square

HOG ROUND-UP ON SQUARE

Enforcement of the new stock law began following passage of another ordinance establishing the office of marshal....but it seems to have been local boys instead of the marshal who made the big hog round-up on the square. "War was declared against them and like prisoners they were led to the pound,"....the town boys, ever alive to mischief, waged unrelenting war against the offending porkers. One by one (though sometimes by the dozens) they were marched off to the Andersonville (prison) of Carthage hogs. Those which were too independent to be driven were lariated, and like huge leviathans were towed unwillingly to the pound. No sooner would a hog present himself on the square than a score of boys with lariats would flank around him and try to fasten on to him."....August 12, "one of the city's dad broke open the pound the other night and let the prisoners go free. There were two dozen hogs and one venerable goat in confinement."

This article was taken from the Carthage Banner, July 1869 written by Ward Schantz. Although it is not about the schools, it is an amusing story about how times were changing. Before the passing of this new stock law, hogs were allowed to roam the streets of Carthage.

---

(39) Joel Thomas Livingston - A History of Jasper County and Its People – Vol. I – Page 39
(40) Kansas Neutral Land, Internet
(41) Wiley Britton - Pioneer Life in Southwest Missouri - Page 321
(42) Historical Atlas Map – Jasper County Missouri – 1876
(43) 1876 Deposition of Thomas R. Livingston's son – Granby Mining and Smelting Co. vs. Samual L. Long - Box 16-File 23 - Jasper Co. Record Center
(44) David D. March, PHD - History of Missouri - 1967 - Page 1081
(45) Joel Thomas Livingston - A History of Jasper County and Its People – Vol. I – Page 67
(46) ozarkcivilwar.org aarchives/3514 - Community & Conflict, Springfield - Greene County Library District
(47) David D. March, PHD - History of Missouri - 1967 - Page 1081
(48) Ibid. Page 1082
(49) Journal of Negro History - 1921
(50) Joel Thomas Livingston - A History of Jasper County and Its People – Vol. I – Page 84

Chapter 5

1870's – A Time of Rebuilding

> Every child has a right to this education, it is the interest and the duty of the State to give it to him. It is profit to the property owner, and economy to the tax tax payer to see that it is done. It is the most certain and least expensive method of reducing the annual crop of paupers and criminals, and stimulating the steady and certain development of the wealthy of the county.
>
> Carthage Banner, February 4, 1876

This decade saw Jasper County double in population and quadruple in wealth. New arrivals started enterprises such as a distillery, mills, abstract and law offices. Mining and agriculture became the focus of attention. The 1870's saw the building of three railroads in the county. This era also saw the worst flood in recorded history and a particularly severe plague of grasshoppers which ruined many farmers.

The school system was growing and becoming more important in the county. The construction of new school houses was now financed by local taxes resulting in rapid expansion. January 1, 1870, the county had seventy-nine school districts with one hundred and four teachers. By December, 1879, there were over a hundred organized schools and one hundred and sixty teachers.(51) David D. March, Ph.D. stated,"most of the new school buildings were small "box car" structures that left much to be desired, but they were superior to the dismal, dearly cabins of antebellum days."(52)

The *Minutes of Meeting of Local Directors'* meeting notes from 1870, Jasper County Record Center, show the student's age were from five to twenty-one years. At this time, the numeration included both white and African- American children. Even though the African-American children were included in this numeration, in reality they were excluded in equal education. One example of this lack of equality is in the following newspaper article.

Robert Stickney reported in the Carthage Evening Press on Oct. 13, 1934, "I remember when Jerry Garner and another 'colored' boy appeared with their books to enter school. The (civil) war feeling being what it was (in the 1870's) they were not permitted to enter but the matter was adjusted by a school for 'colored' children being provided." It is believed to be the Lincoln School. It was opened in 1881 on North Garrison in Carthage. B. F. Adams was the teaching principal and total staff.(53) This building has been restored and is still standing. Integration in Jasper County was not accomplished until the 1950's.

Jasper County was the first in the state to adopt a County Superintendent and employed that person full time. In 1870, J. W. Jacob was elected to that position. Spelling was his hobby and during his tenure, old-fashioned spelling bees were renewed.(54)

The third meeting of the Jasper County Teachers Institute was held on August 14, 1871. The event was

Stephen A. Schwarzman Building / Photography Collection, Miriam and Ira D. Wallach Division of Art, Prints and Photographs

The following are excerpts from a paper written by a rural school teacher in the Carthage Banner on Feb. 22, 1872.

"We met a sleigh-load of boys and girls the other night a few miles out of the city, on their way to a 'spelling match' in the schoolhouse of a neighboring district and the jingling bells and the merry laughter of the young folks... and the fun of a ride under the buffalo robes to the field of contest....How high we lifted our cow-hide boots as we stepped off to the corner of the room where the line of orthographical battle was to be formed! This exercise soon thinned our ranks. Four at one shot, on 'Nebuchadnezzar.' 'Our girl' let go of our hand and wilted on 'Pharaoh' and we finally keeled over on the simple word Isaac. The champion was a small boy of ten years, who was named after the son of Abraham, and the only Bible word which he would spell was that which he had won that day."

Rules For Teachers - 1872

1. Teachers each day will fill lamps, trim the wicks and clean chimneys.

2. Each morning teacher will bring a bucket of water and a scuttle of coal for the day's session.

3. Make your pens carefully. You may whittle nibs to the individual taste of the pupils.

4. Men teachers may take one evening each week for courting purposes, or two evenings a week if they attend church regularly.

5. After ten hours in school, the teachers may spend the remaining time reading the Bible or any other good books.

6. Woman teachers who marry or engage in unseemly conduct will be dismissed.

7. Every teacher should lay aside from each pay a goodly sum of his earnings for his benefit during his declining years so that he will not became a burden on society.

8. Any teacher who smokes, uses liquor in any form, frequents pool or public halls, or gets shaved in a barber shop will give good reason to suspect his worth, intention, integrity and honesty.

9. The teacher who performs his labour faithfully and without fault for five years will be given an increase of twenty-five pence per week in his pay, providing the Board of Education approves.

attended by one hundred and ten teachers. There were only one hundred and four schools at this time so this demonstrated great interest by teachers and prospective ones. U. B. Webster was elected President.

Miss M. E. Chaddle, a respected English teacher, was appointed as a critic of the meeting. At the close of each session, each participant was critiqued on their inaccuracies of speech, grammatical errors, mispronounced words, etc. By this appointment, we can see how important correct language was during that period.(55)

U. B. Webster became superintendent in 1872 and introduced the 'Superintendent's Report.' This published report was on his visitations and observations of schools. The visitations to these rural schools made teachers more aware of the condition of their school and teaching practices so the resulting superintendent's report would be favorable. During 1872 Mr. Webster made seventy-four visitations.(56)

Teachers of the Sixth Congressional district, which included nearly all the counties of southwest Missouri, met in Carthage on September 3, 1873 and organized the Sixth District Teachers' Association. U. B. Webster was elected to represent Jasper County as an officer. Several recommendations were made including the following: 1. To teach Civil Government

Lincoln School located on the southwest corner Garrison and High, Carthage

and Good Citizenship in the public schools. 2. A compulsory educational law. 3. A Southwestern Missouri Teachers' Normal.(57)

Opposition to higher local taxes, hostile feelings over the loyalty oath required of teachers directly after the War, and many incompetent county superintendents of schools brought a need for changes in the educational system. In 1874, the school laws were revised eliminating the county superintendent of schools and re-establishing the county school commissioner. The duties of this office were mainly clerical except to examine and issue teacher certificates. The office of state school superintendent continued but his duties were limited to supervising the collection of reports from the school districts. The congressional townships were changed to school districts.(58)

It was apparent that more changes needed to be made. This was slow and difficult because of the continued incompetence of those in the system. Even Governor Silas Woodson believed that an annual school term of four months was sufficient to educate children of the ordinary duties of life.(59)

Another constitution was adopted in 1875. The injunction on the general assembly to establish and maintain free school was reaffirmed in Article XI, Section I, but the minimum and maximum age limits

Peace Church, Courtesy of John and Sue Fredrickson

were changed to six and twenty years. The segregation of black and white children was made mandatory. Also, there was a legislative provision, from 1853, that stated that no less than 25% of the general revenue fund be used annually to support schools.(60) The time of electing the county school superintendent was changed from the fall election to the annual meeting in April and the name was changed from Superintendent to County School Commissioner.(61)

In 1875, the people of Lone Elm wanted a separate school organization. This would mean detaching a portion of District No. 4 and uniting it with a portion of the old Peace Church school district. In 1876, this organization took place.

"The territorial limits of the Lone Elm district included that portion of Joplin west of Joplin Creek north of "E" street, and extending north of Turkey Creek to a quarter of a mile south of old Tuckahoe. R. T. Guinn was the first teacher of the district. Mr. Guinn was paid one hundred dollars a month for his services. $1,000 was raised and a small two-roomed frame school was built. The two rooms of the school were built so that they could be combined into one room by opening the folding doors between them. On Sunday, the building was used for church purposes. It also served as a meeting place for literary societies and during political campaign, it served as a town hall."(62)

S. A. Underwood

S. A. Underwood of the East Joplin schools was elected and served as first County School Commissioner from 1877-83. He urged a uniform set of textbooks in the county and published a report of his school visits. The raising the standings of popular education in the rural districts its attributed to him. (63)

We do not know where he received his education, but W. R. McLane was the first African-American to be granted a Teacher's Certificate on August 23, 1877 and therefore was the first black teacher in the county.(64)

Uniformity in textbooks was a problem because of selection and adoption of the books. These school books could differ from school to school. The law of

1866 provided that the county superintendent and the state superintendent adopt uniform textbooks but the adoptions were made by the local school boards. The cost of these books was paid by the parents who complained that the books could change frequently, depending on the teacher or the changing school board.

Also, schools in the less populated rural areas received less tax revenue for textbooks, resulting in textbooks that were inferior or out of date.

To provide some relief, the state legislature passed the school law of 1874 that required all schools in a county to use texts selected by the presidents of school boards at a meeting at the county seat once every five years, beginning in January 1875. Publishers soon saw the wisdom in forming an agreement among themselves that no matter which publisher's books were adopted, they all shared in the profits. This ended up costing parents much more than they would have paid in a competitive market. This practice continued to be a problem for three decades.(65)

—Preston boasts of the largest singing school ever organized, in Jasper county. Our fellow townsman, E. P. Searle, is in charge. Mr. S., is a teacher of large experience and is first-class. He informs us that this school is going to run all winter, two nights each week. Good for the boys and girls of Preston township.

Carthage Banner - Oct. 4, 1877

The passing of the uniform text book law began in Jasper County due to the efforts of S. D. Carpenter through his columns in the Patriot. In 1879, the state legislature passed the uniform text book law.(66)

The Missouri State Teachers' Association held its seventeenth session in Jasper County in 1878. The result of this meeting was the organization of the teachers of several portions of the state into local associations, and the old Sixth District Association changing its name to the Southwestern Missouri Teachers' Association.(67)

It was common for music-loving people to gather at a country school and organize singing schools. These schools became very popular. The largest ever organized and attended in a rural school was Preston during the winter of 1878-79 with one hundred singers in attendance. This school became quite famous as a singing school.

---

(51) Joel Thomas Livingston - A History of Jasper County and Its People, 1912 – Vol. I – Page 96
(52) David D. March, PHD - History of Missouri - 1967 - Page 1083
(53) Carthage Evening Press, May. 26, 1977
(54) Joel T. Livingston - A History of Jasper County and Its People, 1912 – Vol. I – Page 96
(55) Ibid. Page. 98
(56) Ibid. Page. 99
(57) Ibid. Page. 102
(58) David D. March, PHD - History of Missouri - 1967 - Page 1083
(59) Ibid. - Page 1083

(60) Ibid. - Page 1084
(61) Joel Thomas Livingston - A History of Jasper County, Missouri and Its People –1912, Vol. I – P age 102
(62) Ibid. - Page 191
(63) Ibid. - Page 103
(64) Ibid. - Page 108
(65) David D. March, PHD - History of Missouri - 1967 - Page 1087
(66) Joel T. Livingston - A History of Jasper County and Its People, 1912 - Page 108
(67) Ibid. - Page 107

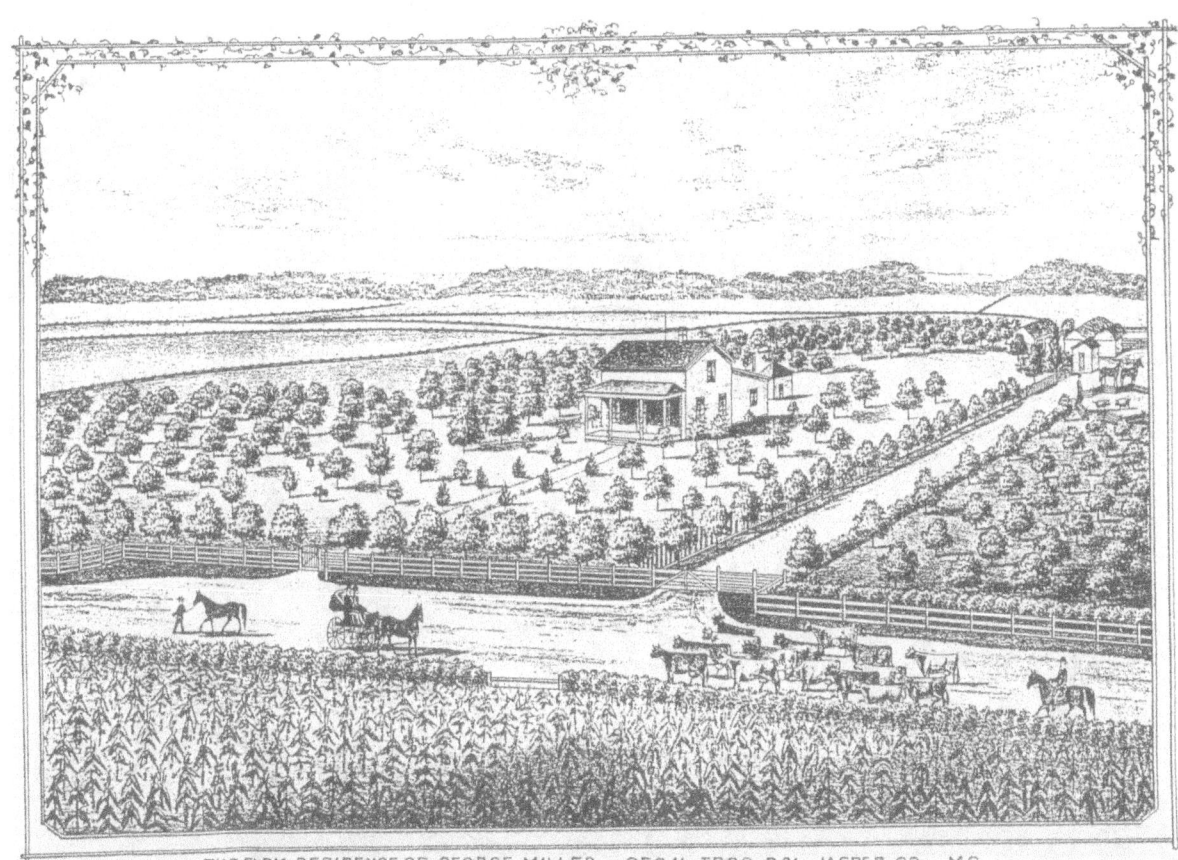

1876 Jasper County Altas, Courtesy of the Jasper County Record Center

Chapter 6

1880's – Time of Growth

There continued to be growth in the 1880's with school house construction in rural communities throughout the county. In 1880, the Missouri State Teachers Association recommended the office of county school superintendent be re-established and only qualified educators be selected for the position. It was also advocated that county commissioners be made responsible to the state superintendent of schools and have the power to supervise all public school interest in their county. It wasn't until 1889 when the legislature passed a local option for county supervision law but provisions for state-wide supervision did not happen until 1909.(68)

> County School Commissioner Stevenson gave out the following official report of the school enumeration of Jasper county, which had just been completed: Whites, males, 5026; whites, females, 6021; colored, males, 121; females, 124; Total 12,292, showing a gain of 110 over the previous year.
>
> "Twenty-five Years Ago This Week"
> Carthage Press Weekly – July 18, 1912

J. H. Franks was elected School Commissioner in 1883 succeeding S. A. Underwood. Franks was formerly a rural school teacher. Mr. Franks was known for his love of walking. It said he made most of his school visits on foot.(69)

TEACHER'S CONTRACT.

This Agreement, Made the Fifteenth day of April 1881, between John J. Pershing a legally qualified Public School Teacher, of the one part, and G. Bemrose, Hiram Dewey and S. A. Henley as School Directors of District No. 1, Township No. 56, Range No. 20, County of Chariton, and State of Missouri, of the other part,

WITNESSETH: That the said John J. Pershing agrees to teach the Public School of said District, for the term of Three months, commencing on the 15th day of April 1881, for the sum of Thirty dollars per month, to be paid Monthly and that for said services, properly rendered, and reports properly made and filed, said G. Bemrose, Hiram Dewey and S. A. Henley, as directors, as aforesaid, are to order a warrant in favor of said John J. Pershing, on the County Treasurer, for the amount of wages due.

It is further stipulated that the school house is to be cleaned, ~~fires pre~~ teacher ~~pared~~, and fires made at the expense of the ~~district, and under the direction~~

Gen. John J. Pershing began his career as a school teacher in Missouri. He then applied at West Point and was accepted. He earned the honor of being chosen first captain of the Corps of Cadets. During the First World War, he was the commander of the American Expeditionary Force (AEF) in Europe. After the war, he was promoted to general of the armies, a position held previously by George Washington. He later won the Pulitzer Prize for history in 1932 for his memoirs. (70)

Philip Arnold of Joplin was elected County School Commissioner in 1885-86. He previously held the position of superintendent of the Joplin school system at the salary of $90 monthly. He had a strong interest in uniformity of textbooks and compulsory education.(71)

These early educators deserve a lot of credit for developing the early school system. They had to be intelligent, organized and adapt in public relations in a time when the public wanted to keep any form of "government" out of their schools.

Since the 1840's, educators had urged for the establishment of a training school for continued education of teachers called the Normal School. This name came from the French word "Normal" meaning other than or beyond the norm. This higher education was needed because teachers were sometimes very young and during this time were not required to have more than an eighth grade education.

Even though there was lingering protests against paying for public education by some citizens, the Missouri State Teachers Association campaigned for the Normal School by appointing a committee to draft a proposal to submit to the Twenty-fourth General Assembly stating the reason why Missouri should provide facilities to educate and train teachers. (72) This school would offer courses of instruction to prepare teachers to teach in all the common schools.

It was at this time in Jasper County's public school history, the organization of the Normal school took place. This was a summer school for teachers of the county, instituted by J. M. Stevenson, County Superintendent, in 1887. The first session of the County Normal began July 29, 1887, at the high school building in Carthage. It was attended by 220 teachers and students. The Normal lasted four weeks and at the close, examinations were given.(46) This changed with the coming of the State Teachers College.(73)

The School Law of 1889 made it a crime in the State of Missouri for white and African-American children to attend the same school. This made it impossible for a black child living in communities where few African Americans lived, to receive an education. The law was overturned in 1954 by the Supreme Court of Brown *et al v.* Board of Education of Topeka, declaring states establish separate public schools for black and white students unconstitutional.(73)

The thirty-sixth Missouri General Assembly enacted laws that provided state colleges for white teachers. The purpose of these was to aid in the certification of teachers. The same act provided for African-American teachers, but very few of the institutes were built for these teachers. These institutes were controlled by the State Board of Education. They determined the place where sessions were to be held, length of sessions, and the appointment of directors and teachers. The compensation for an African-American teacher was not to exceed $25 a week; and $50 a week for a white teacher.(74)

(68) David D. March, Ph.D. - History of Missouri - 1967 - Page 1084
(69) Joel Thomas Livingston - A History of Jasper County and Its People – Vol. I – Page 231
(70) americaslibrary.gov/aa/ersjomg/aa-pershing.subj.html
(71) Joel Thomas Livingston - A History of Jasper County and Its People – Vol. I – Page 231
(72) David D. March, Ph.D. - History of Missouri - 1967 - P 1094
(73) Joel Thomas Livingston - A History of Jasper County and Its People – Vol. I – Page 232
(74) The Journal of African American History – Vol. 22 -1921

EARLY DAYS IN COUNTY

Late W. W. Carr Compares Present Conditions With Those in Forties

W. W Carr, an old resident of the county, whose home was on Reeds R. F. D. No. 1 told of early day experiences in Jasper county in a letter to the Press under date of January 8, 1902, as follows:

"My father came here with the first settlers from Indiana. When we arrived Carthage was not known, our county was inhabited by deer, wolves and varmints of different kinds. There were no fences, no orchards, no shops, no towns. The nearest postoffice was Springfield. Now our county ranks with the first and excels a great many counties of the state. Our county is in a high state of cultivation.

"Our early machinery was the bar shear plow and the single shovel. Our mode of harvesting was with the reap hook, then the cradle. Our threshers were men with the flail; then the next was to tramp out the grain with oxen or horses, if we had any. Our cleaning apparatus was a sheet and two men to make the necessary wind. Now the world can't beat us on anything I have mentioned. Our mail matters were different from now. It was fifty miles to the nearest postoffice and when you got a letter 12½ cents had to be paid before the letter was handed out. Now every man or nearly so has mail at his door, and two cents takes it anywhere in the United States. In place of varmints and game and Indians—for the Osages hunted here most of the time—we have the finest of stock and the best improved farms and the finest cities and the finest mines of lead and zinc and coal in the world.

"I have known Carthage since 1845. George Hornback had the first store. It stood where the First National bank now is. His dwelling house was where the Central National bank is now located and a man by the name of Miller had a grocery about where Messrs. Moore & Goucher's bank (now the Gratz Clothing Store) now stands. It consisted of a barrel of whisky and a box of tobacco. Now we have the nicest city in the state, it is filled with business houses and has the best government in Missouri.

"Now look at our freight privileges. I have hauled many a load of goods and groceries from Boonville. There was not a railroad in the state at that time. It took us from twenty-five to thirty days to make the trip. It was always with oxen, from three to six yoke. Now the same place can be reached in about eight hours by the railroads.

"Our schools were subscription schools and the teacher was often paid in corn, oats or meal—seldom in money. Our school houses were as a rule made of round logs. The floor was split puncheons and a log was cut out for a window. An old fashioned fire place gave us warmth. I never went to school a day in a frame house. Our main studies were spelling, reading and arithmetic. Now we have our county dotted all over with the best of school houses and the children can go to school at the expense of the public, or their schooling is paid for out of public funds. I mentioned the three leading studies in the old days. Now the three leading studies are: first, fix for thanksgiving, then for holidays and the third for the last day of school.

"I have been in this county sixty-four years and it has been my home all the time.

W. W. CARR.

Carthage Evening Press, March 25, 1922, This is a letter written 1902 describing the early days in Jasper County including the early schools.

Florence Miller with a friend. Courtesy of the Jasper County Record Center

Chapter 7

1890's – A Time of Refinement

In spite of the "Long Depression" of 1873-1879, Jasper County appeared to be economically stable. The Steadley Co., Keystone Hotel, Ramsey's, Carthage Ice & Storage Co. and the Club Theater are just a few businesses that were thriving. The mining industry, of which Jasper County was the center, had tripled its output by the end of the decade. Zinc's output value was $3,367,687 in 1890 and in 1899 the output value was $10,715,307.(75) Base on the 1890 and 1900 censuses, Jasper County made rapid growth in population during the nineties. Jasper county gained 33,518 inhabitants during that time.(76) There were many indications that Jasper County was ready to leave the past behind and look to the future.

During this decade, very little changes were taking place within the rural schools. Teachers were encouraged to obtain further education and certification. Attendance increased in teacher institutes by those interested in improving the quality of teachers and education in the schools. The General Assembly, soon recognizing the importance of these institutes, passed a compulsory institute law in the early 1890's that required teachers to secure a teaching degree through attendance at the institutes. "The type of teaching certificates, and the requirements for each, also changed and three grades of certificates were established. The grade of certificate limited where and how many students a teacher could teach. The higher the grade, the more opportunities the teacher had for employment and increased salary."(77)

The Normal School continued improving the quality of education of teachers. Three hundred teachers and applicants for teachers certificates attended the 1890 class. During his administration, Jasper County Superintendent W. M. Wharton, introduced a plan to issue diplomas to teachers who had successfully completed their courses. The first class graduated in 1890 having passed the same examination given to receive a five-year certificate.(78)

At the Southwest Missouri Teachers' Association in December 1890, at Lebanon, Jasper County carried off all of the honors. In the essay contest, W. M. Wharton, principal of the Medoc school, and later Jasper County School Superintendent, won the first honor.(79)

In 1899, State School Superintendent Carrington introduced a uniform course of study for the rural schools covering all eight years. County Superintendent E. D. Denison made considerable effort to make this course of study successful. The most difficult challenge was classification of the students (determining the student's grade level) this issue was resolved. At the end of the school term and completion of eight years of study, students would be required to pass a test and with a successful grade would be granted a diploma issued by the County Superintendent certifying their eligibly to enter a high school of their choice. The first graduating class numbered five, but by 1903, one hundred and twenty had passed the exam. Jasper County was one of the first of six counties to adopt this course of study that did more to raise the standards of rural schools than any other action taken.(80)

Missouri state law required the school term to be set at a period of six months in each district provided that a tax levy of forty cents on the one hundred dollars assessed value of the taxable property within the district and moneys received from the public fund is sufficient to support the school.(81)

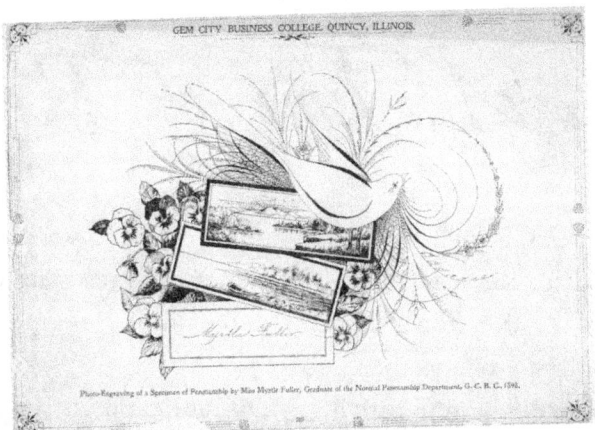

Penmanship award from a Normal Teaching School 1898
Courtesy of the Lartz family and Jasper County Record Center

(75) Joel Thomas Livingston - A history of Jasper County, Missouri and Its People, 19*12 - Vol I - Page 339
(76) Ibid Page 320
(77) Tiffeny Patterson - One-Teacher Public Schoolsof Missouri, c. 1774 to c. 1976 Published online at: sos.mo.gov/shpo/nps-nr/64501130.pdf
(78) Joel Thomas Livingston - A history of Jasper County, Missouri and Its People, 1912 - Vol I - Page 327
(79) Ibid. Page 326
(80) Ibid. Page 438
(81) School Laws of the State of Missouri. Revised Statues, 1899 - Sec. 9751 - Page 24

Revised Rules and Regulations

of the

STATE DEPARTMENT OF EDUCATION

Governing Issuance and Renewal of Certificates to Teach in Public Schools in Missouri

JULY 1, 1944

Prepared by the Director of Certification
Under the Direction
of
ROY SCANTLIN
State Superintendent of Public Schools
Jefferson City, Missouri

PART III

County Certificates:

Examinations are held in all counties in Missouri on the first Friday and succeeding Saturday in March, June and August. Applicants for first, second, and third grade certificates must present evidence of having completed four years of high school work or its equivalent. County certificates granted in other states are not valid in Missouri.

First-Grade County Certificates:

Applicants for first grade certificates must pass an examination in one branch of history, either medieval and modern, English or ancient, and one branch of science, either physical geography, physics or elementary biology, in addition to the subjects required for a second grade certificate.

An average of 90% is required for a first grade certificate and the teacher must have had at least eight months of successful teaching experience.

First grade certificates are valid in any county in the state for three years and may be renewed an unlimited number of times, provided the holder meets the requirements for renewal.

Second Grade Certificates:

Applicants for second grade certificates must pass examinations in algebra and literature in addition to the subjects required for the third grade certificate and have an average of at least 85%.

Second grade certificates are valid for two years in the county where issued and may be renewed once; provided the holder meets the requirements for renewal and may be endorsed in any county in the state.

Third Grade Certificates:

Applicants for third grade certificates must pass an examination with an average of 80% in the following subjects: United States history, civil government, including the government of Missouri, physiology and hygiene, English grammar, arithmetic, geography, spelling, reading, penmanship, language, agriculture and pedagogy.

The third grade certificate is valid for one year in the county where issued and may be renewed once; provided the holder meets the requirements for renewal.

For additional information regarding county certificates contact your county superintendent.

PART IV — MISSOURI APPROVED GRADE REGULATIONS

1. Grades made only in an approved summer or regular session of a Missouri college may be applied on the county certificate in lieu of the regular county examination. College credit earned by correspondence or extension will not be accepted as approved grades to be used on a county certificate. These grades must be certified to this Department by the college on our regulation form.

This certification of credits should be made at the close of the immediate session, and must be made within a two-year period after credits have been earned. (Section 10633 R. S. 1939, 1942 Missouri School Laws, Page 165.)

Four (4) approved grades may be earned during one term. Two (2) semester hours constitute the minimum amount of work acceptable for one (1) approved grade.

Grades earned in the following subjects may be approved:

Arithmetic	any course in advanced arithmetic
Civil Government	a course in American government or citizenship
Geography	any course in geography
Language	any course in composition or rhetoric
Grammar	any course in composition or rhetoric
Pedagogy	any course in methods of teaching, or organization and management of elementary or rural schools
Physiology and Hygiene	any course in physiology or hygiene
U. S. History	any course in American history
Agriculture	any course in agriculture
Reading	any course in the teaching of reading
Algebra	any course in algebra
Literature	any recognized course in literature
Ancient, Medieval or Modern, or English History	a course in any one
Science	any course in physical geography, physics, or elementary biology or a combination of these, such as general science

OUTLINE OF RURAL SCHOOL COURSE OF STUDY.

Classes	Grades	Quarts	Reading and Literature.	Language and Grammar.	Numbers and Arithmetic.	Geography, History and Government.
CLASS D.	FIRST.	1	Chart and Blackboard.	Lessons to develop in pupils the power to think in sentences; to describe accurately what they have seen; and to tell in detail what they have read or had read to them. Use reading and nature study as basis.	Teach numbers concretely to 10. Use rulers, yardsticks, and liquid and dry measures. Stress quick seeing and accurate telling.	Teach pupils to make record of weather changes. Field lessons on land and water forms. "Earth and Sky." "First Lessons." "Geographical Nature Studies."
CLASS D.	FIRST.	2	Primer to L. 25.			
CLASS D.	FIRST.	3	1st Reader to L. 25. "Hiawatha Primer."			
CLASS D.	FIRST.	4	Complete Book. "Hiawatha Primer."			
CLASS D.	SECOND.	1	2nd Reader to L. 15.		Numbers to 50. Use avoirdupois and apothecary weights. Introduce square measure. Put stress on drill. See Institute outline for 1901.	
CLASS D.	SECOND.	2	To L. 32. "In Mythland."			
CLASS D.	SECOND.	3	To L. 54. "Stories for Children."			
CLASS D.	SECOND.	4	Complete Book. "Thro the Year I."			
CLASS C.	THIRD.	1	3rd Reader to L. 9. "Supplement."	DeGarmo Ls. 1-20.	Teach fractions by use of weights, measures and drawings. Make and solve practical problems. Drill on seeing relations by use of blocks, geometric figures or objects.	Drainage, mountains, valleys. Relief maps on moulding board. Directions and distances. "On the Farm." "Glimpses of the World." "Corner Cupboard." "American Industries."
CLASS C.	THIRD.	2	To L. 16. "Robinson Crusoe."	Ls. 21-52.		
CLASS C.	THIRD.	3	To L. 24. "Seven Little Sisters."	Ls. 53-75.		
CLASS C.	THIRD.	4	To L. 32. "Thro the Year II."	Ls. 76-91.		
CLASS C.	FOURTH.	1	To L. 42. "Supplement."	Part II, Ls. 1-16.	Drill on fundamental processes. Study parts of one hundred. Read and write decimals. Teach long division. Drill on oral analysis.	
CLASS C.	FOURTH.	2	To L. 53. "Fairy Tales."	Ls. 17-39.		
CLASS C.	FOURTH.	3	To L. 61. "Rhymes of Wood Land."	Ls. 40-64.		
CLASS C.	FOURTH.	4	Complete Book. "Story of Patsy."	Ls. 65-75.		
CLASS B.	FIFTH.	1	4th Reader to L. 13. "Supplement."	Book II, 1-20.	Standard Arithmetic to p. 60.	Gram. School Geog. To page 25.
CLASS B.	FIFTH.	2	To L. 26. "Ten Boys."	Ls. 21-36.	To page 85.	To page 44.
CLASS B.	FIFTH.	3	To L. 36. "Field Book."	Ls. 37-54.	To page 110.	To page 65.
CLASS B.	FIFTH.	4	To L. 47. "The Odysseus."	Ls. 55-66.	To page 128.	To page 87.
CLASS B.	SIXTH.	1	To L. 60. "Old Stories of East."	Part II, Ls. 1-28.	To page 144.	To page 113.
CLASS B.	SIXTH.	2	To L. 73. "Olden Times."	Ls. 29-54.	To page 170.	To page 139.
CLASS B.	SIXTH.	3	To L. 83. "Stories of Long Ago."	Ls. 55-78.	To page 196.	To page 159.
CLASS B.	SIXTH.	4	Complete Book. "Daffydowndilly."	Ls. 79-106.	To page 220.	Missouri and Review.
		1	5th R... Apples."	Patrick, Ls. 5-11.	To page 245.	Morris' History. Parts I and II.
				Ls. 12-19.	To page 262.	Parts III and IV.
				Ls. 20-24.	To page 289.	Parts V and VI.
				...River."	Ls. 25-26.	To page 312.	Parts VII and VIII.
				Ls. 28-32.	To page 342.	Rader's Hist. Gv't. Chapters I-V.
				Ls. 33-40.	To page 368.	Chapters VI-X.
				Ls. 1-4.	To page 394.	Mo. Gov't. Chapters I-XI.
				Ls. 27 and 41.	Complete Book.	Missouri History. Chapters I-XXIV.

OUTLINE

of the

Official Course of Study

For the County of

Based largely on the State Course of Study prepared and published by the State Superintendent of Public Schools, 1899.

This Outline is formally adopted and recommended by

County Board of Education.

Missouri State Superintendent Carrington's Course of Study

Liberty School 1909　　　Courtesy of the Jasper County Record Center

Chapter 8

The 1900's A New Decade

The 1900's were the beginning of school consolidation with the Missouri legislature authorizing the formation of consolidated school districts in 1901. This would bring about many debates and consolidation proposals.

An excerpt from a report by County Superintendent W. B. Colley read: "There is excellent school sentiment throughout the entire county. The people generally desire to have good schools and desire that their children shall take regular elementary and high school courses. A large number of districts are making extra efforts to have eight month terms.... The most pressing needs of Jasper County are consolidated districts, better salaries and more permanency of the teaching profession."(81)

23,483 SCHOOL CHILDREN.

That Many in Jasper County—A School Census Just Completed.

The county clerk has prepared a census of the children of the county of school age—between six and twenty-one years. The statement is made up from the returns sent to the county clerk by the district clerks of the county and will be forwarded to the state superintendent of schools.

This statement shows that there is a total of 23,483, of which 11,630 are white males, 11,537 white females, 151 colored males and 165 colored females.

Kirksville Normal School
Courtesy of David D. March, PHD History of Missouri 1967

From 1887 to 1903, the Jasper County Teacher's Normal had been the approved summer school for teachers and during the fourteen years that it existed, it had done much for the teacher's education. In 1903, the Normal came to an end and was succeeded by the Jasper County Teacher's Association. This change came about by legislative enactment in 1903. The law required that all teachers in the county attend a three day teacher's conference before the start of each school year. This was the start of the State Teachers College.(82) Teachers could teach during the school year then go back to school during the summer for more teaching credits. They were to receive their regular pay while attending these classes. Whether or not they received this pay depended on their school board, unfortunately, not all teachers were paid for this time. One teacher stated, "I didn't get paid and it was very hard. I had a car payment and had to ask my parents for help." With each passing decade, more education was required in order to teach in these rural schools. Teaching a room of twenty to fifty students at different grade levels was a challenge to the best of teachers and most still received 'on the job training'.

It was during this time that State Superintendent Howard Gass established a program for "approved school" design. This program included points for appropriate lighting, ventilation and heating systems. Also included were maintenance of the school, education apparatus and equipment. Later in the 1920's, the state superintendent a rating system to the approval system. A rural school could get a Standard or Superior rating by having a 200 volume library and hold a minimum four community meetings during the school year. The teacher was required to have "at least four years of high school work, hold a first grade or higher teaching certificate, and be paid a monthly salary of at least $85 monthly."(83)

The County Superintendent, Luther Hardaway's report of 1904 reported that the best educated teacher in the rural schools in the county was Mr. Kennedy Brooks of the East Hollow School, west of Joplin. He had participated in post-graduate work at Ann Arbor and in Berlin. Mr. Brooks says he is actuated solely by a desire to do some good for the children of the poor miners in his neighborhood.

The report goes on to say the oldest teacher reported in these rural schools was Mr. Arthur Cooper of the Mineral school. He had been teaching in these schools for about a quarter of a century. Also, seven vacancies had occurred in the rural schools that year. One teacher bought a store, one quit to get married, one secured a position in the Carthage schools and the others quit for other reasons. Another young lady would resign in a few days, but she did not want the fact published yet.

He further stated that three of the rural schools were stone, two brick and the rest were frame structures. One school was equipped with homemade furniture. Very little work had been done throughout the county toward improving school premises and many districts needed new houses. Some buildings had stood for more than thirty years and were badly dilapidated. A child today sits in the same old room and works under the same adverse conditions that his parents contented with when they were in school and "to secure the best results from the pupil, the school house should be as comfortable and attractive as the home. He also stated that the movement for better buildings had already began and that twice as many good school houses were erected in 1903 as any year previous."(84)

By 1904, the County Superintendent reports stated there were eight thoroughly modern school houses in Jasper County. These were supplied with ventilation systems, were properly lighted and furnished with up-to-date furniture including single seats and slate blackboards. Also, in the rural schools there were forty-four male teachers and ninety-nine female rural teachers. Outside of the incorporated city and village schools, the county has 12 two-room schools, two three-room schools, one four-room school and two five-room schools.

A rigid code of conduct was set down for teachers by the school authorities, and their behavior was constantly under the watchful eye of the entire community. Many had a program at the end of the year with all the students taking part. This was a major social event and the entire community attended. A teacher's performance for the year could be graded by the students' performance. A good job by the students could mean a renewal of a contract by the board of directors: a poor showing and the teacher could be seeking other employment. This was one way for students to rid themselves of a teacher they did not like.

1915 Teacher's Code of Conduct

1. You will not marry during the term of your contract.

2. You are not to keep company with men. (Assuming that you're presuming correctly that there were no male teachers.)

3. You must be home between the hours of 8 p.m. and 6 a.m. unless attending a school function.

4. You may not loiter downtown in ice cream stores. (Now that's cruel.)

5. You may not travel beyond the city limits unless you have the permission of the chairman of the board.

6. You may not ride in a carriage or automobile with any man unless he is your father or brother.

7. You may not smoke cigarettes.

8. You may not dress in bright colors.

9. You may under no circumstances dye your hair.

10. You must wear at least two petticoats.

11. Your dresses must not be any shorter than two inches above the ankle.

12. To keep the schoolroom neat and clean, you must sweep the floor at least once daily; scrub the floor at least once a week with hot, soapy water; clean the blackboards at least once a day; and start the fire at 7 am so the room will be warm by 8 am.

Missouri passed a compulsory school attendance law in 1903. This law states that any parent, guardian or other person having custody or control of a child between the ages of eight and under fourteen must regularly attend public or private school for at least four months a year.(85)

"The Joplin Board of Education opened an experimental truant school in 1905 but it was not popular with the public and did not reopen in 1906."(86) As children we were always under the threat of this officer and what he would do if we played 'hookie' from school, but no other evidence has been found of a school truant officer operating in Jasper County.

Notes from a report by State School Superintendent W. P. Evans: "The county graduation movement has made fine progress the last four years. In 1907, there were 2,747 pupils completing the common school course in the state; in 1908, 3991; in 1909, 6,075; in 1910, 8,801. This shows an increase of 6,054 or 220 per cent in four years. The number of counties holding graduating exercises, county, township or rural district, has increased from 6 in 1906, to 112 in 1910 or nearly 1,800 per cent. It is this movement that is so largely responsible for the increase in country attendance at the various high schools, academies and normal schools. It has also brought about a more regular attendance and more interest on the part of rural pupils. As matters now stand in Missouri we have the articulated system beginning with the rural school where a pupil completes the eight grades and is given a high school entrance certificate or certificate of graduation. This certificate admits him without examination to any high school in the state. One weak spot in the system is the lack of high school advantages in some counties. Hence the pupils completing the eighth grade in these counties must go away from home to get high school privileges. The remedy for this is the consolidated school."....(87)

In spite of positive reports from county school superintendents, enrollment in rural schools continued to decline due to loss of rural population and trends toward urbanization. The Country Life Commission formed by Theodore Roosevelt to study this problem, concludes in their report of 1909, "The schools are held to be largely responsible for ineffective farming, lack of ideals and the drift to town."(88) The feeling that agriculture must color the work of rural public schools......"(89)

The Sixteenth Missouri Report of Public School, published in 1909 addressed the issue. "Heretofore, the tendency has been to educate the boys and girls away from the farm, to teach that life in town is easier than farm life. Such teaching is a great mistake. Work on the farm is just as honorable as work in town, and the teaching of agriculture will have a tendency to impress this fact."(90)

Even though this was not a new idea, very little or inconsistent classes in agriculture were being taught. Authors of Agriculture for Beginners, Ginn and

Co. 1903, stated that "this training must be taught in public schools for two reasons, I. Aptitudes are developed during the years that a child is in the public....every child intended for the farm should be taught to know and love nature. 2. Most boys and girls reared on a farm get no educational training except that given in public schools therefore the truths that unlock nature must be taught there."

Based on the findings of the Country Life Commission Report, thinking on this matter began to change and agriculture became an important course of study in these rural schools and was made part of the state's course of study. It was required that all students pass an agriculture exam when they graduated from public schools. In 1909, the Forty-fifth assembly required that agriculture be included in the course of study and examinations of teachers.(91)

Another reason rural school consolidation was advocated was the condition of roads in rural areas at times made transportation impossible at times. Jasper County is known for its rocky soil, therefore, the country roads had a rock base and were fairly decent. A road grader could be seen grading these roads from time to time in the forties and fifties. The exception to these roads were in the northwest part of the county where the rocks were fewer and therefore, could be problem in inclement weather.

> The Buford-Colley Consolidation Law was passed in 1913. The main points of this law were:
>
> 1. The formation of natural consolidation districts.
>
> 2. The schools may, as a beginning, be centralized under one board of six men without necessarily abolishing the small schools.
>
> 3. All the small schools may be abandoned and be reorganized as one strong consolidated school, if such is the wish of the community.
>
> 4. The small schools may remain intact and a central high school only be organized for the eighth grade graduates and, in particular instances, for the seventh and eighth grade pupils.
>
> 5. The patrons may decide for themselves whether or not they shall wish to make use of transportation at public expense, with this proviso, however, that when children are not transported, school facilities must be provided within two and one-half miles of all said children.
>
> 6. It provides, finally, substantial aid for erecting new school buildings, and for continued school maintenance.(92)

According to Harold W. Foght, Advisor in Rural Education, this new law will forever put an end to the box-car schoolhouse which was "dilapidated and unsightly, with its faulty lighting and ventilation, and general lack in sanitary appliances". This law had very little effect on consolidation of rural schools in Jasper County. The last rural school closed in the early 1970's.(93)

The State School Superintendent's report of 1919 reported three school inspectors were employed to investigate rural school problems and assist county school superintendents to bring schools up to desired standards. These inspectors were to show the country people that "many of their school had outlived their usefulness."..... "the great institution for the revival of country life is the reorganized and redistricted school."(94)

It is said that over its history, Jasper County had 122 functioning rural schools. By 1923, there would be an even 100 rural schools remaining.

In 1931, the Missouri General Assembly passed a school law intended to encourage consolidation. The board formed to study the counties proposed enlarged districts. The recommendations made by these boards were very slow to be implemented because most of the citizens in the districts still supported the rural schools.(95)

Also in 1931, a law was passed providing for equalization funds so that the poorer school districts so they could be brought up to minimum standards. The effect was to retard, not to encourage, the consolidation of small districts.(96)

There continued to be vast differences between the social and economic lives of the town residents and farm families during the early part of the 1900's. Many rural families still did not have telephones, indoor plumbing or other modern conveniences enjoyed by many town residents but nearly 90 percent of the urban population had electricity by the 1930's whiles only 10 percent of the rural population did. Private utility companies felt that it was too expensive to run lines to the rural areas and that farmers were too poor to afford electricity. In 1935, the Rural Electric Administration (REA) was created to bring electricity to rural areas. However, most of Jasper County's rural homes did not have electricity until the mid-40's.(97)

Dorothy and Carolyn Frost
Feed sack dresses

Photo courtesy of the Lartz family

The rural area was especially hit hard by the Great Depression of the 1930's. This was the "waste not, want not" era. There was little money for food forcing farm families to grow or raise their own eggs, chickens, milk, beef and vegetables. They made their own clothes out of feed sacks. These sacks (flour and feed) were a printed cotton material. Women got involved in the purchasing of the feed because they knew how much material it took for a garment and what pattern she found attractive. We were very proud to get and wear the pretty little dresses. In some of the school photo in this book, you will see little rural girls with feed sack dresses on who are probably in the same family.

Even though families had their own personal struggles, they also helped their neighbors through this difficult time. The rural school played a part in helping relieving the day to day struggles of the farm family. School programs, PTA meetings, pie suppers, and dances provided a much-needed diversion. These schools were also used to hand out ration cards to the poverty stricken families. The bigger the family, the more rations that family would receive.

Economic depression and the drought caused many farmers to lose their farms. to foreclosure. Many became renters of the farms they formerly owned. Others left the area to go west to find work. This caused constant turnover in the students attending these rural schools. It was sometimes difficult to make and retain friendships.

Courtesy of the Lartz Family and the Jasper County Record Center

When World War II began in 1941, more and more rural youth left for the armed services or bigger cities to work in defense factories.

One by-product of that war was it introduced new technologies that were put to use on the farms after the war. This revolutionized agriculture requiring less farm labor to produce product for market. Farms became bigger and more specialized and families became smaller. Women who went to work during the war chose to keep their new found freedom with factory jobs in surrounding towns.

With the continued rural exodus and larger schools built in towns, it became increasing difficult to provide an education for the smaller number of rural students. Rural school buildings continued to fall into disrepair. Even though rural schools remained the primary factor in public education, and had public support, serious moves toward consolidation began in the 1930's and continued to accelerate over the next three decades.

A report from the Missouri State Teacher's Association, Jan. 16, 1942 states, "From 1917 on to 1922 and even up to 1925, there was an acute teacher shortage."

Notes taken from the Feb. 29, 1942 Jasper County Educational Association meeting reports a discussion of the necessity of hiring married women teachers to meet the teacher shortage...."that teachers were becoming scarce due to the fact that defense work was paying better salaries." In the same meeting notes it was stated that Webb City has a system whereby they give credit for attending Sunday school classes. (98)

Talk of consolidation continued and even though school authorities recognized the fact that these schools served the people in the past, they felt the existing rural school program was too expensive to continue and because many students were in grades by themselves, the benefit of cross-learning and competition had been eliminated.

Richard Wardlow, a student of an eight year Diamond rural school, gives us a look at the typical school in this decade. The following description was taken his school memories found in its entirety at the end of this chapter. "There seems to have been a random pattern of locations. Roughly, one school was surrounded in all four directions by two or three square miles of land, but...with many variations and no set pattern.

In general the physical layout was the same for most one-room schools; one square acre (208.7' x 208.7') located at the corner on a square mile section. An outhouse or privy was located at each of the two rear most corners of the tract; one for girls and one for boys. The school building was usually located about 20 feet from the road front, and a few yards to the side of

NEW CLAUSE IN AGREEMENT FOR NEXT YEAR

If Teacher Marries, It Releases School Board From Its Contract With Her

Contracts to be signed by teachers for next term in the Carthage schools contain an agreement clause to the effect that if the teacher marries during the school term she automatically releases the board of education from its contract with her. This leaves the board in a position to retain the teacher for the rest of the term or not to do so, as the board may agree.

In several previous years cupid has invaded the ranks of teachers to such an extent that board members felt school efficiency suffered and this time the board decided to take measures to forestall any such condition.

In the past there was nothing to prevent a teacher marrying and continuing her school work if she chose. It is said the board was powerless to dismiss her, had it so desired. All this will be changed under the new order of things.

Carthage Evening Press April 30, 1925

the schoolhouse were the coal and woodshed for storing the fuel of the school stove. The balance of the land was for the playground and sometimes auto parking.

The schoolhouse itself was a clapboard rectangle about 20 feet wide and 40 feet long, three or four sash windows on each side, and sometimes a door (and usually only <u>one</u> door) in the center front, and a blank wall at the opposite end. Buildings usually had white exteriors and wooden shingled roofs.   Near the door there was usually a well with a pump handle type pump and a flagpole.

Immediately to the right, on entering the doorway, was the stove—a simple "pot belly" cast iron furnace, but surrounded by an embossed metal jacket. This jacket kept folks from being seriously burned should they bump against the stove while rough-housing or else wise.....much safer than falling against a red hot cast iron potbelly!! Even though the safety jacket was lined with asbestos, I have never heard of anyone contracting lung cancer from exposure to asbestos even though we were exposed seven hours per day for eight years!!

Immediately to the left, inside the doorway, and against the wall stood a wooden bench, about 1½ feet high. Students put their lunch pails on this bench and they put their overshoes and galoshes under the bench. They hung their caps and coats on wall-hooks just above the lunch pails. The central floor area had a center and two side aisles running between rows of desk toward the teacher's desk. The primary, 2nd, 3rd, and 4th grade desks were small, single seat jobs. The upper classmen had double or two-seater desks, but there was never enough students so as to require double occupancy. Behind the teacher's desk, against the rear wall was the blackboard above which hung a copy of Gilbert Stuart's "Portrait of George Washington" and a copy of Millet's "The Angelus." I went through all eight years puzzled by the two mounds of foamy white fluff rising around George Washington's chest, no teacher ever explained it. I think it took a college education to learn that the portrait was just incomplete. Also for some months I was under the impression that it was a picture of our neighbor, Theodore Mitchell. I was admittedly not the sharpest knife in Diamond's drawer of intellectuals.

Unity School

Many of the teachers were girls just out of high school (they'd had a few summer weeks of "teacher training" who wanted to accumulate a few dollars for her "hope chest' or dowry, and those usually taught only until they snagged a husband. However, there were a number of career teachers who bore excellent reputations." (See Mr. Wardlow's story in chapter 10)

Some of the schools had windows only on the left

Cave Spring School. Courtesy of the Jasper County Record Center

side of the building. This was based on the opinion that light should enter the room from the left or left and rear of the building. This was believed to be better om the eyesight of the students.

Window boards were also required by the health department. They were to be 8" to 10" wide and go the full length of the windows. They were to incline slightly towards the inside of the room to direct the fresh air towards the ceiling. All of the rural schools were also required to have the entry doors to open to the outside for safety reasons. The Jasper County Health Department had a Manual for Scoring Rural Schools. The regulations in this manual were enforced by the Health Inspector who visited each school once a year.

Each rural school was also visited yearly by the county school superintendent. This person would rate the school's performance, facilities and equipment and then file a report. One teacher told the story involving one such superintendent. His name was W. B. Colley. One day while the other children were playing on the school grounds, one young boy, sitting on a rock wall, saw Mr. Colley coming. He yelled out,, "Here Colley, Colley - Here, Colley, Colley." The teacher said, "I rushed out and grabbed him by the ear and pulled him into the school and swatted his behind. He never did that it again."

Miss Twylet Placklet, Teacher, 1928

Union School, Courtesy of Kathy Sidenstricker

The Missouri General Assembly passed the Hawkins School Reorganization Act in 1948 (Senate Bill 307) to promote the consolidation of rural school districts into larger and more efficient systems. Under this act any reorganized school district was required to have an assessed valuation or property in the district of at least $500,000 and record an average daily attendance of at least 100 pupils. This bill provided for the election of a County Board of Education whose duty it was to formulate plans for the changing of school district lines. The only thing compulsory about this law was that the people must have an opportunity to vote on a proposed district. If they voted in favor of the plan the board submitted to them, they could form a new district. If voters rejected a plan, a second was to be submitted within two years. As a result of reorganization under this law, and the merging of districts by annexation and consolidation, the number of school districts was reduced during a ten year period (1948-1958) by 65.6 per cent. (57) By 1949, because of the decline in rural population in Missouri, 2,079 of the 7,649 rural schools were closed for lack of enough students to operate. Of the 5,528 schools operating, 68% have less than 15 students and 30% have less than eight students. Jasper County schools reflected this same pattern.(99)

Also in 1949, the Jasper County board of education devised a plan to divide the county into 24 districts.

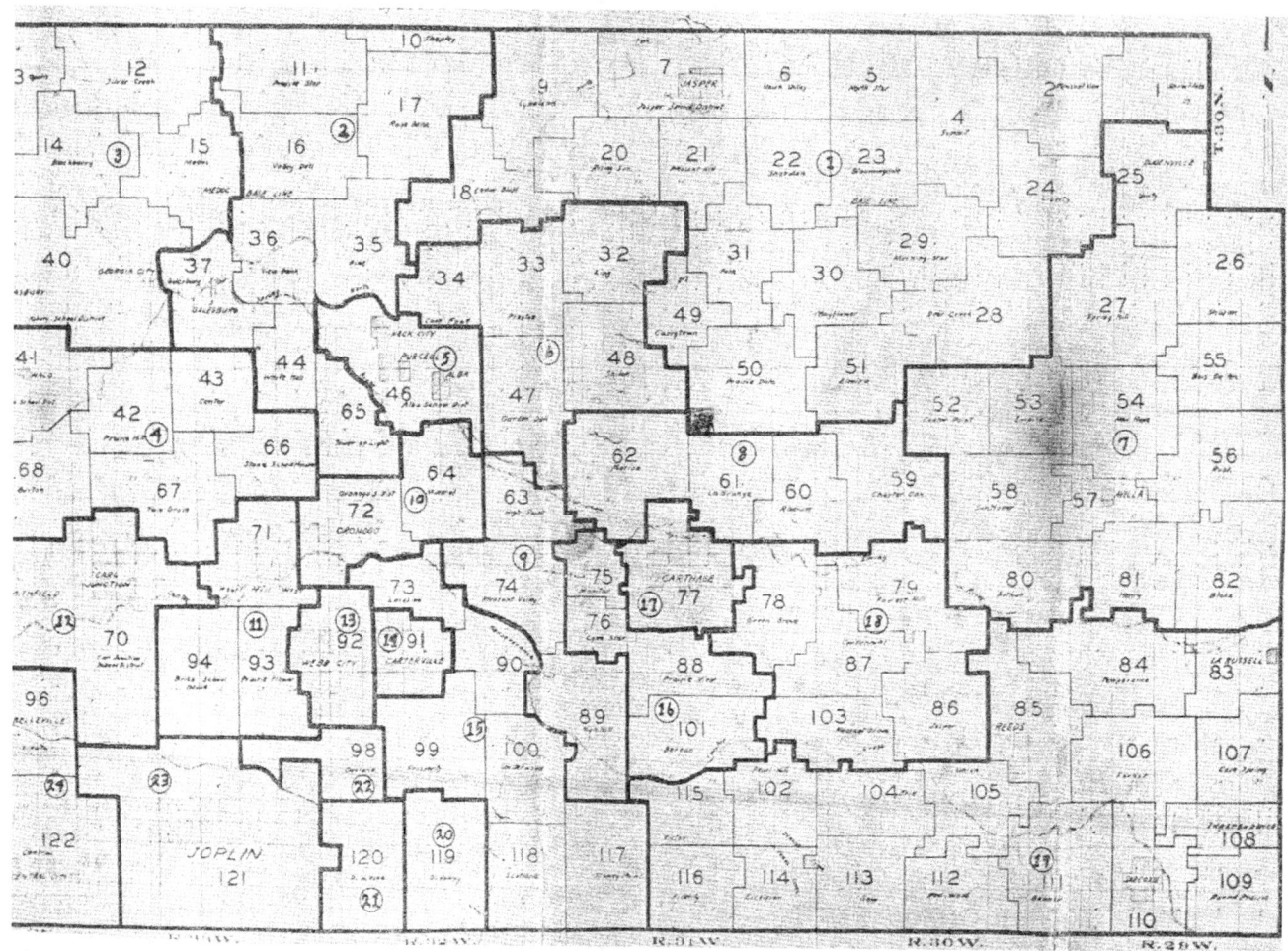

Accelerated consolidation of schools began in the 1940's and 50's. Not everyone was in favor of the reorganization.

> A delegation of approximately 150 people attended the meeting. Most all of the school districts in Jasper County were represented. 18 rural districts presented petitions to the County Board, all but one district expressed themselves that they didn't want their districts reorganized at the present time. The one district did favor reorganization.
>
> Jas. Co. Board of Education 4-30-1964

An excerpt taken from the minutes of the meeting of the Jasper County Board of Education, April 30, 1964

With the closing of these rural schools and when these rural families moved into more urban areas, the

Photo Courtesy of Benita Shields

Photo left is Miss Selma Fieker, long time and last teacher at the Cave Spring School. This photo was taken in 1930 when she started her teaching career.

Photo below is Miss Selma in 1988 trying to save the school from meeting the same fate of so many other rural schools - disappearing into history.

socialization into the new community could be difficult, especially for the children. There could be a sociality division between the "townie" and "country" child. Those from the country being considered less educated or "hicks" and often ostracized by the more urban children. Wiley Britton made reference to this taking place as far back as the 1800. He wrote, "...country boys, when starting to school in town, being made the butts and objects of jests by the town boys."(58) This ostracizing may result in a feeling of isolation for the child who formerly felt they were an important part of a close knit rural community. Parents not only could face the same sense of loss of this identification with community and place, but the loss of their culture as well. This could make it difficult to fit in or they were reluctant to socialize with their new neighbors. It can be strongly argued that education today is much improved over the education received in these rural schools. Teachers are required to have degrees, sometimes a Master's Degree, books are better and classrooms are equipped with the latest equipment. "Special needs" students are recognized and receive needed attention.

But with the passing of these schools, we have lost something valuable in our society. We've lost the

Hill Hill

togetherness that was an intimate part of these close knit communities, when parents knew each other and looked out for one another and the children. Children also knew and accepted the responsibility for each other. There was an unwritten expectation for the greater good that one had for another or "It takes a village to raise a child." (African proverb) A man's word was his bond and a handshake was a commitment and even though we know this was not always true, it was considered an ideal to be honored and trusted.

It is not to be said that these "good old days" were idealistic times. Discrimination was accepted and practiced early on and later African-American children grew up in a segregated society. Women were treated as second- class citizens with limited life choices. Electricity and plumbing were slow coming to the rural areas and survival was a day-to-day reality.

But we can be reminded of a time in the not so distant past, of the little rural schools that were our second homes. Mention these schools today and it will bring a smile to a former student's face and the stories will start with, "Oh, I remember...."

Yesterday these rural schools could be found throughout the county, but with progress, most have disappeared and are all but forgotten. It must be remembered that the rural school played an important in our educational history.

(81) Joel Thomas Livingston - A History of Jasper County and Its People – Vol. I – Page 438
(82) Ibid. - P 441
(83) Tiffany Patterson - One-Teacher Public Schools of Missouri, c. 1774 to 1973 - Section E - Page 14, 15 Published online at: sos.mo.gov/shpo/nps-nr/64501.pdf
(84) Carthage Evening Press, Feb. 18, 1904
(85) Ibid. - Aug. 30, 1909
(86) Joel Thomas Livingston - A History of Jasper County and Its People – Vol. I – Page 476
(87) Ibid. P 440
(88) Country Life Commission Report - 1909 - Page 52
(89) Ibid. - Page 54
(90) Tiffany Patterson - One-Teacher Public Schools of Missouri, c. 1774 to 1973 - Section E - P 12 Published online at: sos.mo.gov/shpo/nps-nr/64501.pdf
(91) Ibid. - Page 19
(92) Harold W. Foght - Rural School Consolidation in Missouri, 1913 - Page 4
(93) Ibid. Page 19
(94) Missouri State School Superintendent's Report, 1919 - Page 24
(95) David D. March, PHD - History of Missouri, 1967 - Page
(96) Ibid. - Page 1495
(97) Published online at: newdeal.fert.org.
(98) Jasper County Educational Association, 1942 - Jasper County Record Center
(99) Carthage Evening Press – May 13, 1949
(100) Pioneer Life in Southwest Missouri – Wiley Britton – Page 318

THE STATE OF MISSOURI

To All who shall See these Presents---Greeting:

Know Ye That, There has been deposited in the office of SECRETARY OF STATE, of said State, an abstract of the sale of TOWNSHIP SCHOOL LANDS, in the County of _Barry_, whereby it appears that in pursuance of the several acts of the General Assembly of said State, providing for the sale of the Township School Lands _Abel Gibson_ became the purchaser of _the North East quarter of the North West quarter_ of Section _Sixteen (16)_ in Township _Twenty-four (24)_ of Range _Twenty-seven (27)_ containing _Forty (40)_ acres, at the price of _Four_ dollars and _Fifty_ cents per acre, ("being land granted by the United States to the State of Missouri for the inhabitants of said Township, for the use of schools,") for the sum of _One Hundred and Eighty_ dollars and _———_ cents, which sum it further appears has been fully paid by _Alfred Pitts assignee of Abel Gibson_

Now in consideration of the premises, and in conformity with the provisions of the hereinbefore recited acts, the State of Missouri hath given and granted, and by these presents doth give and grant unto the said _Alfred Pitts_ and to _his_ heirs the land above described. TO HAVE AND TO HOLD the said tract with the appurtenances, unto the said _Alfred Pitts_ and to _his_ heirs and assigns forever.

In Testimony Whereof, I, _Herbert S Hadley_, Governor of the State of Missouri, have caused these letters to be made PATENT and the Seal of the State to be hereunto affixed by the Secretary of State. Given under my hand, at the City of Jefferson, this _Tenth_ day of _February_, in the year of our Lord One Thousand Nine Hundred and _Ten_

[SEAL.]

BY THE GOVERNOR: _Cornelius Roach_ Secretary of State.

Herbert S Hadley

A deed showing "school land" being bought from the government. Even though this individual owned this piece of property, a school could be built on it. If that happened, the property is under the control of that school. If the school closes, the property reverts back to the landowner.

Chapter 9
The Rural Schools

Out of the 122 rural schools that populated Jasper County at their peak, only 86 remain. The following pages will give you a brief glimpse of each of these original schools. The following is a list of those 122 schools.

1. Amity
2. Arthur
3. Banner
4. Berean/Peter Hill
5. Blackberry
6. Blake
7. Blood/Dewey
8. Bloomingdale
9. Bois D'Arc
10. Brick
11. Carytown
12. Cave Spring
13. Cave Springs
14. Cedar Bluff
15. Centennial/Knights
16. Center
17. Center Point
18. Central City
19. Charter Oak
20. Coon Foot/New Hope
21. Deer Creek
22. Dixie
23. East Hollow
24. Elmira
25. Empire
26. Enterprise/Peace Church
27. Erie
28. Excelsior
29. Fidelity
30. Forest/Whisner
31. Forest Mills/Magnet
32. Galesburg
33. Garden Dell
34. Gem
35. Green Grove
36. Hardscrabble
37. Hazen
38. Henry
39. High Hill
40. High Point
41. Humbard/Redwood
42. Independence
43. Jasper
44. King
45. La Grange
46. Lakeside/Jackson
47. Liberal
48. Liberty
49. Lone Star
50. Lynnland
51. Marion/Perry
52. Mayflower
53. Medoc
54. Mineral
55. Monitor
56. Morning Star
57. New Hope
58. North Fork
59. North Star
60. Opolis
61. Pearl Hill/Jones
62. Perseverance
63. Pine
64. Pleasant Grove
65. Pleasant Valley
66. Pleasant View/Magoffin
67. Prairie Dale
68. Prairie Flower
69. Prairie Hill
70. Prairie Star
71. Prairie View
72. Preston
73. Radium
74. Reeds
75. Rice/Pleasant Hill
76. Rising Sun
77. Rosebank
78. Round Prairie
79. Rusk/White Oak
80. Scotland/Diamond
81. Sharon
82. Sheridan
83. Shiloh
84. Silver Creek
85. Snowflake
86. Spring Hill
87. Spout Springs
88. Stone
89. Stoney Point
90. Stoup
91. Summit
92. Summerset
93. Sunflower
94. Swindle
95. Temperance
96. Tower of Light
97. Twin Grove
98. Underwood/Atlas
99. Union
100. Union Valley
101. Unity
102. Valley Dell
103. Victory
104. Viewbank/Dog Trot
105. White Hall

Below are names of other schools that very little is known about. It is unclear if they were mining schools, hamlet school or rural schools.

COX DIGGINGS
SUNNYSIDE
WACO
MAPLE GROVE
BELLE CENTER
WHITE
STONY POINT EAST
DIXON
SMITHFIELD
ZINITE
POSSUM CREEK
FARMER'S UNION
LOWELL
DUVAL
QUAKER SCHOOL
BLACK JACK
CHITWOOD

Chapter 10

Looking Back in Time

Those who experienced these rural schools firsthand are best suited to tell their own stories. From these schools and former students, memories and photographs are shared, allowing a glimpse into a world long disappeared but in desperate need of retrieval. A need to bring us all back, even for a moment, to a time and place undisturbed by modern conveniences. Through sharing these stories, we take a step back into the quite encompassing arms of history.

Amity School

LOCATION: SECTION: 10   TOWNSHIP: 27   RANGE: 32   DISTRICT: 120

"The two-room Amity school house was moved from Seventh Street, one fourth-mile west of Duquesne Road, to the present site about 1900. The name was officially changed to Duquesne in 1922. Two wood-frame buildings housed eight grades until 1937 when the school burned. A four-classroom brick building was built and opened in 1938."
The Joplin Globe - Our Neighbor - Thurs., April 29, 1993

"One and one-half miles east of Joplin; Henry Moore, L. B. Osborn and S. A. Hopkins, directors, L. B. Osborn, teacher, Term of six months began September 20th. District enumeration 50, enrollment over fifteen years of age 3, total 41, present 31. Building and furniture first-class. Seating capacity 28. In addition to school house and site the district property includes a good set of outline maps, a Webster's Unabridged, a nine inch globe, a teacher's desk and nineteen Victor folding desks."
1878 Jasper County School Report by S. A. Underwood - Joel Thomas Livingston - A History of Jasper County, Missouri and Its People, Vol. I - 1912 - Page 104

Early photo of Amity School, courtesy of the Jasper County Record Center

Examination Questions of November 17.

Please hand these questions to your teacher at once.

E. B. DENISON, Co. Supt.

According to announcement in the Course of Study, the following questions have been prepared by the State Superintendent for use in the rural schools of the state. Teachers should be very careful not to give the pupils any hints as to what the questions are, until the hour of examination. In case the questions cover a part of the subject not studied during the last quarter, the teacher should revise the list so as to make it a fair test of the work. This list is made to cover the last four years only, for the reason that the course of study has been in the hands of the teachers so short a time they have hardly had time to do the work in the lower grades which would justify examinations at this time.

The State Superintendent promises to have a more complete list of questions ready for the examinations on December 22.

NATURE AND CULTURE STUDY.

(These questions are prepared for both the "A" and "B" classes, based almost wholly on the work of the first quarter for the "B" class.)

1. Name two kinds of grain which are cultivated in your community; two kinds of grass; two kinds of fruit and two kinds of garden vegetables.
2. Write a short description of how to plant and how to harvest one kind of grain.
3. Is fruit-growing or vegetable-gardening more profitable? Why?
4. What are the uses of roots, of leaves? Tell how plants eat?
5. Describe a grass-hopper, a fly or a cricket as to number of parts, how it travels, what it eats and how, and how it sees and hears; What good does it do? What harm?
6. Name two domestic fowls and two wild birds that are very useful to man and tell how they are useful.
7. Name man's five senses and the special organ of each. Have insects and birds five senses? How do you know?
8. Name the zones and explain latitude and longitude.
9. Draw a map of Missouri, locating rivers, trunk lines of railroads and large cities.
10. Give three short quotations concerning something you have studied in nature.

READING AND LITERATURE, CLASS "B."

1. Tell the story of the best lesson you have read this quarter.
2. Write words and mark the vowels illustrating four different sounds of a; two of e; two of i; and three of o.
3. Write five words of three syllables each and mark the accented syllables. What rule can you make concerning long and short vowels in accented syllables?
4. Explain *emphasis* and *inflection*. Write a quotation of four lines and draw line under emphatic words and mark different kinds of inflection.
5. What are the differences in prose and poetry?

LITERATURE AND READING, CLASS "A."

1. Write Longfellow's "The Builders" in prose. (Let children have book for this question.)
2. Write in your own words the story of "A Drop of Water on its Travels."
3. Write short sentences, each giving the main thought in several paragraphs in lesson 43 of Fifth Reader. (Let children have book for this question.)
4. Write a short composition on "What Constitutes Good Reading?"
5. Scan one stanza of "My Dog Blanco."

LANGUAGE LESSONS FOR CLASS "B."

1. Write from memory "What the Bee Teaches," and draw lines under all nouns in your reproduction.
2. Write two sentences using "it" for the subject and then write same thoughts using infinitives for subjects.
3. Tell the story of "The Fox and the Crow," and draw line under all verbs used.
4. Give four rules to be observed in writing a composition or in reproducing a story.
5. Define "proper noun," "class noun," "pronoun" and "adjective."
6. Write short composition on "Uses of the Horse," or on "Uses of the Cow." (Grade on both quantity and quality of work.)
7. Write a sentence using a quotation for the subject. Abraham Lincoln. (Grade on both thought and expression.)
8. Describe his first home.
9. Tell of his education.
10. Tell of his early manhood.

GRAMMAR, CLASS "A."

1. What is a noun? Name and define the classes of nouns.
2. Write one sentence containing a collective and an abstract noun.
3. What are the properties of nouns? Illustrate and explain
4. Define pronoun: name the classes and give properties.
5. What is parsing? Parse the nouns in the sentence "William, The Conqueror, defeated Harold, the Saxon King."
6. Write one sentence containing nouns in the nominative, possessive and objective cases.
7. In each of three sentences use a noun as the object of a verb; as object of preposition; as a modifier of an object.
8. Write sentences illustrating the different kinds of pronouns and classify each pronoun.
9. "I that speak unto thee am he." Parse the pronouns.
10. Write one sentence with a noun in apposition with a pronoun. Another with a pronoun in apposition with a noun.

ARITHMETIC FOR CLASS "B."

1. Define unit, number, notation, numeration.
2. Write analysis of two problems taken from page 18 White's Oral Arithmetic.
3. Express by Roman Notation: 514; 2899. Express in words DCCCLXXXIX.
4. Add: 35; 29655; 47; 3894; 483; 769; 85; 94; 46; 324; 8.
5. Write analysis of two problems taken from page 67 White's Oral Arithmetic.
6. From 3002250 take 210596. Prove.
7. In an army of 7569 men, 388 were killed, 432 were wounded. How many remained for duty?
8. Multiply seven hundred sixty-five by nine thousand six hundred forty-three.
9. A family of three persons boarded for 6 weeks at the rate of $4.75 per week for each person. What was the cost of their board for the whole time?

ARITHMETIC FOR CLASS "A."

1. If 120 acres of land produce 2520 bushels of wheat, how many bushels will 160 acres produce?
2. Give tables for land measure and dry measure.
3. If 5-17 of a vessel is worth $17,000.00 how much is 7-8 of it worth? What is the value of the entire vessel?
4. Point out and name the mathematical terms in the above problem.
5. Write analysis of problems 18 and 19 on page 95 of White's Oral Arithmetic.
6. Define the terms used in percentage. Express $12\frac{1}{2}$ per cent in four ways.
7. Out of 350 words a student spelled 329 correctly. What per cent of the words were correctly spelled?
8. Write analysis of problems 38 and 45 on page 101 of White's Oral Arithmetic.
9. C raised 496 bushels of wheat, which was 33 1-3 per cent more than 2-3 of the wheat D raised. How many bushels did D raise?
10. A merchant who sold his goods at twenty-five per cent below cost, received 60 cents per yard for silk. What did it cost him?

HISTORY FOR CLASS "A."

1. Give brief account of Columbust and the work he accomplished.
2. Name three other exporers and tell what they did.
3. Who were the Indians? Described them as to appearance, habit, religion and government.
4. Describe the early attempts at settlement by the French and the English.
5. Tell about Virginia Dare, Henry Hudson, wampum and name five tribes of Indians.
6. Tell what you know of Captain John Smith; Pocahontas; the Starving Time; Tobacco culture in Virginia; Bacon's Rebellion.
7. Who were the Pilgrims? Where did they settle? Describe their first winter.
8. Who were the Puritans? The Cavaliers? The Quakers.
9. How did the customs and habits of the Southern Colonists differ from those of the New England colonists?
10. Tell somthing about Boston, New York, Philvdelphia, William Penn, Lord Baltimore, Oglethorpe.

Please send to me at once the best paper from each class in Arithmetic.

Exams from 1901-1902

Arthur School

LOCATION: SECTION: 2   TOWNSHIP: 28   RANGE: 28   DISTRICT: 80

"School was located on the NW corner of Incline Rd. and County Rd. 60. This school was named after Doctor Liburn Q. Arthur, resident of Avilla. "The family (Arthur) sold the Avilla neighborhood property in 1866 and moved three miles southwest of Avilla where the second Arthur School and graveyard was named in his honor.

The first Arthur School building near Avilla was used by Avilla children as the closest school building available until Avilla's first school house was erected on lots now housing the Avilla Mill. This was in the early 1870s with the exact date unknown. It is known that Rachel Williams, Sarah Williams, Libby Binney, the Stemmons brothers were pupils of Mr. David R. Melton, who was a popular and successful teacher for several terms."
Courtesy of Ed Seela - April 18, 2001

It is now a private residence.

1952 Arthur School Picture - Nellie Carter Swaim, Teacher

Alice Bowers
Very Embarrassing Moment
Arthur

"Here is my memory of a very embarrassing moment when I was in the first or second grade at rural Arthur Elementary School. I dropped my pencil and it rolled under the desk of two older boys, they coaxed me to crawl down the isle to get it. I did and the teacher saw me and said, "Alice, you like those boys so well, you may just sit between them the rest of the day!" Needless to say I was embarrassed and if I remember, I cried and everyone else laughed."

Arthur School 1952

Wayne Williams - Arthur

"I started to school in 1935. I think they got tired of putting up with me at home. I went to a rural school all eighth grades, about a mile from where I was born. When we graduated from 8th grade there were eight in the class. The school had one room there and several teachers, one of whom, was Lois Hadley, and she was pretty stern. I was left-handed and she made me write right-handed. I had her just one year. With one teacher I learned to read right off. We learned more in the 8th grade than kids do now because teacher would talk about everyday life. Parents were more involved with kids and kids were closer to each other, with older kids teaching younger kids in school. We got a good education at country school.

They had a big old stove in front of the room that burned either coal or wood the teacher was responsible for starting.

I had to walk with my sister to school, about a mile and a quarter to school. I walked to school if I couldn't catch a ride with a neighbor. My folks had an M T (Model T) and when it started it make such a racket that you could hear it in the next county.

Kids were paddled with a "keen" switch and they were paddled in front of the class over the teacher's knees. Older kids had a game called Shining (batting a tin can around). Pie suppers were used to raise money for supplies. At Christmas we cut a cedar tree out in the country near school and decorated it with cut up tinfoil from gum wrappers. I carried my lunch in ½ bucket with sandwiches and stuff. There was always a picnic on last day of school.

My first year I went to Carthage to school there was man that had his own bus. As a Senior I bought an old car (35 Ford) and hauled kids to school."

Arthur School 1926

1st Row: Glen Snyder, Valgene Mathews, Junior Jones, Vesta Snyder, Verna Bailey, Buelah Ritchie
2nd Row: Bert Bailey, Beulah Melugin, Rex Snyder, Martha Bailey, Edith Lux, (Teacher)
3rd Row: Finis Baily, Regin Mathews, Juanita Baily, Anna E. Parlor, Anna Baily

Ronald Tatum - My Memories of a One Room School
Arthur

"In December of 1948 our family moved from Carthage and Hawthorne school to a farm 10 miles east of Carthage. We had a large family with five of us in school, 4 boys and 1 girl, going to a small school was exciting. Our farm was about 1 mile from the school. We had no car so we walked to school. The teacher was Sylvia Baker. A great teacher for the five Tatums. There were 28 in the school, eight grades, and one teacher for all eight grades. In the city school they couldn't spend much time with each child, not so in the country school. The teacher had time

Ronald Tatum

for each student. The older boys came to school early in the winter to help get a fire going in the potbellied stove. There was no electric in the school. There was no bullying or fighting at the school in the country; different than in town school.

Mrs. Baker lived 6 miles from school but missed very few days during my three years there. Today, the school is still there but it stands inside a large home on the same spot.

One year we had a softball team of 4 girls and 5 boys and won most of our games against much larger schools. There were 4 of us that graduated the year I did, three girls and myself. We still are all alive and live in the Carthage area. I have only good memories of my time in the country "one-room school". The name of the school was "Arthur School".

Courtesy of the Dennison Family

Banner School

LOCATION: SECTION: 12   TOWNSHIP: 27   RANGE: 29   DISTRICT: 111

Two miles west of Sarcoxie

A. C. Stemmons, teacher. Term: 6 months. Salary, $45.00; Enrolled: Male 27, Female, 34 - Total 61 Number present to-day...51; Board: J. W. Osborn, Clerk; I. J. Almegard; President. J. W. Haggard and Jas. I. Davidson.

Jasper County Superintendent's School Inspection Report, 1893

Banner School - 1945-46
1st Row: Bill Horrell, Leroy Block, Leroy Ellingsworth, Thaine Brown
2nd Row: Norman Ellingsworth, Anna May Block, Amelia Long, Marva Lee Schaeffer, Shirley Kennedy, Mary Filarski, Agnes Filarski, Carroll Kenne
3rd Row: Gary Robb, Jean Young, Freda Mae Shore, Marie Ellingsworth, Imogene Broadaway, Billie Jean Block, Betty Jo Block, Marlin Brown Caroll Ellingsworth Mabel Gurley (Teacher)

Shirley Kennedy - Banner

"Banner School was located approximately 1¼ miles west of Sarcoxie on what is now known as County Road 52, south of Blackberry Road (old Highway 166). Church services and 'all-night singings' were often scheduled on week-ends in the school building.

I don't know when the school was founded but the Banner School District is indicated on the 1895 plat map of Jasper County. In the April 8, 1920 issue of The Sarcoxie Record, Mrs. Olive Horrell was chosen to fill a vacancy on the school board at the annual election; the article noted 'this is said to

Shirley Kennedy - 1944-45

be the first time in local history when a woman was elected to a place of this kind.' Two of my mother's brothers, James and Elmer Block, attended Banner in the mid-1920s and my father's sister, Inice Kennedy, graduated from the eighth grade there in 1930 along with Helen Kimberlin, James Lambeth and Leon Osborn.

Banner had two large school rooms, built at a right angle to each other. The classroom which faced the road had a cloakroom at the entrance, a platform at the front of the room where the teacher's desk sat and programs were staged, a big coal-burning stove toward the back of the room, and high windows on the north side. I was always fascinated by the large topographical maps of the seven continents which hung above the blackboard at the front of the room. There were two outdoor toilets, one for the boys to the north toward the woods, and one for the girls east of the school building.

As far as I know, the last time both classrooms were used was in my first year there, 1941-1942 term. Mary Grieb taught the first four grades and her husband, Ellis, taught the upper four grades. Miss Isabel Purviance taught the 1942-1943 school term and Mrs. Mabel Gurley became the teacher in 1943-1944 and was still there when I transferred to the Wildwood school in Sarcoxie in 1946-1947.

Today, I marvel at how the rural school teacher managed to keep all students interested in their class work and all the activities as well as perform janitor duties. One of the least of a teacher's worries in the 1940s and 1950s, however, was discipline. As I recall, parents instructed their children to obey the teacher in all matters in the classroom often with the added warning "if you get in trouble at school, you're in bigger trouble at home!"

As a student, I enjoyed the rural 'one-room' atmosphere where older students helped younger students and everyone participated in spelling bees, geography matches, Christmas programs and operettas; I have always believed this environment increased the learning process for all. Because I skipped the third grade, an older pupil, Billy Welde, was assigned to listen to my recitation of the multiplication tables; also apparently because I missed third grade penmanship, in my fourth grade year, I had to copy by hand an entire book, the subject of which was banana plantations. I don't specifically remember helping younger pupils at Banner but at Wildwood, the principal and 7th - 8th grade teacher, Mrs. Ruth Baker, occasionally sent me to Miss Edna Frederking's 1st - 2nd grade classroom to help a group of her students with their reading.

Other pupils who attended Banner during the early-mid 1940's included: my brother, Carroll Kennedy; our cousins, Betty Jo, Billie Jean, Leroy and Anna May Block whose father, Samuel Charles "Sammy" Block served on the school board with Paul Horrell and James Lambeth; Dorothy, Doyle and Betty Joyce Davidson and their cousin, Imogene Broadaway; Florence and Margaret O'Banion; Jim and Wayne Spence; Nadine and Billy Bricker; Laura Rose, Sonny, and Phyllis Wecker; Mildred Cobine; Patty and Billy Welde; Colleen, Anna Lee, and Bob Osborn; Phyllis, Marlin and Thaine Brown and their step-sister, Marva Lee Schaeffer; Robert and Earl Teague; Gary Robb; Clarence Wiese; and Mary and Agnes Katzfey. Bill Horrell, son of school board member, Paul Horrell, and grandson of Olive Horrell, school board member elected in 1920, was also a Banner student and was in charge of banking the fire in the stove at the end of the day and starting the fire the next day."

Berean School

LOCATION: SECTION: 26   TOWNSHIP: 28   RANGE: 31   DISTRICT: 101

Teacher: Mamie Franks; Term...6 months; Salary...$37.50 monthly; Enrolled: Male...15, Female...16, Total... 31. Present today..20. School Board: Emma Bird, Clerk; Henry Wiggins, President; Silas Rose and O. L. Bird

Jasper County School Superintendent's School Report, 1894
Courtesy of the Jasper County Record Center

Jasper County School Superintendent's School Report, 1924-25 reports that this school had an enrollment of 12 students, Water...Well; Heating...Stove

Berean school in now used as an automotive garage.

Courtesy of Kathy Sidenstricker, www.jaspercountyschool.org

Could all these Berean children be twins?

1954

1954

1959

Blackberry School

LLOCATION: SECTION: 28   TOWNSHIP: 30   RANGE: 33   DISTRICT: 14

The school was located on the northeast corner of Redbud Road and County Road 209.

Blackberry School house on Blackberry Creek, three miles west of Medoc, Miss Nora Grayson, teacher. Wages $30. Eighteen pupils on register, fourteen in attendance. Good little school house and everything in order. Good desks and teacher's desk, bell and blackboard. School doing well. Miss Grayson and Miss Pickering are both new teachers, and in their schools show good system.
1872, Jasper County School Report by U. B. Webster, Jasper County School Superintendent
Joel Thomas Livingston, A History of Jasper County, Missouri and Its People, Vol. I, 1912, Page 100

Blackberry was annexed to Asbury R-3 November 1, 1949.
Shirley Sue Fredrickson

Blackberry School - Teacher, Jennie Bell Courtesy of the Jasper County Record Center

Blackberry now being used as a community center in Waco 2004
Photo courtesy of Kathy Sidenstricker

Blackberry School, 1908 Courtesy of the Jasper County Record Center

Blackberry School
Courtesy of the Jasper County Record Center

Blake School

LOCATION: SECTION: 2   TOWNSHIP: 28   RANGE: 29   DISTRICT: 82

"**SCHOOL CAUSE OF A CARTHAGE TRAGEDY:** A neighborhood feud over the location and name of a country school house resulted yesterday in a fight in which Lee Duncan, living near Carthage, shot and killed his uncle. S. F. Duncan, and in turn was perhaps fatally wounded. The Duncans are farmers, ten miles east of Carthage. The shooting occurred on the roadway near S. F. Duncan's home. Witness say Lee Duncan was waiting for his uncle and when he drove up, opened fire with a revolver. The old man armed with a repeating shotgun returned the fire. S. F. Duncan was shot five times and the nephew three times. The nephew was taken to a hospital at Carthage and it is believed he cannot recover. The school controversy has raged in the particular locality three years and caused considerable litigation and ill feelings among friends and families. A conflagration destroyed, the old school house, and the directors desired to change the location and name of the new school. Then the trouble arose. The uncle it is asserted, accused his nephew of setting fire to the old building."
The Galena Evening Times - The Cherokee County Genealogy Library at Columbus, Apr. 29, 1913

BLAKE SCHOOL 1893
Last day of school celebration, Courtesy of Charles Chrisman

"**BUILDING BLAKE SCHOOL:** The Blake School district, located southeast of Avilla and northwest of LaRussell, is at last to have a school house. It is now on course of erection at a cost of $1,200 for the building and equipment and is expected to be completed by the end of this month so that school and can open the first of October." *Carthage Evening Press, Sept. 9, 1913*

Top Row: Lolly Funk, Ruby Chandler, Orlea Riggs, Winnie Shelton, Ovilla Wilhite, Iven Dunn ____ ____, Mitia Harper, Lena Sanders
2nd Row: Evertt Owens, Goldia Chrisman, Mable Davis, Myra Chandler, Jessie Chrisman, May Chandler, Alberta Owens
3rd Row: Freda Chandler, ____ ____, Etlon Chrisman, ____ ____, Ray Shelton, Everett Chandler, Davis ____
4th Row: Homer Chandler, ____ ____, Cletis Owens, ____ ____, Tom Shelton

Row 1: Leroy VanDyke, Rabbit Garrison, Ralph Lee, Loren Hull, Gary Culley, Larry Hood, Darrell Cline, Gary Lee
Row 2: Joe Garrison Clel Pippen, Charlene Long, Masine Long, Beverly Lee, Elvis Caster, Beverly Cochran Judy Thorn, Linda Thorn, Gene Lombard
Row 3: Kenneth Lee, Ruth Heisten, Jerry Hood, Jerry Chandler, Lenno Bishop, Barbara Cline, Lenero Culley Rodney Guinn, Darrell Lombard

Photos courtesy of Charles Chrisman

Bloomingdale School

LOCATION: SECTION: 34   TOWNSHIP: 30   RANGE: 30   DISTRICT: 23

Bloomingdale was located at the northeast corner of Redbud Road and County Road 100.

Assessed value $96,440; Teacher, Jennie Wright; Salary...$75 monthly; Officers: C. S. Johnston-Jasper, Clerk; Fred M. Johnston-Jasper, President; F. L. Stricker-Jasper & Ben Smith-Jasper, Members; Enrollment...11; Water...Well; Condition of house...Clean; Condition of out-buildings...Fair; Sanitation...Good, Blackboard...Slate; Maps...Case; Globes...1; Dictionary...1; Heating... Stove

Jasper County Superintendent's School Report, 1924-25
Courtesy of the Jasper County Record

BLOOMINGDALE SCHOOL   Miss Rosalie Petefish, teacher

Back Row: Linda Lou Lawerance, Nancy Kay Watchorn, Janelle Timble, Jim Carr, Neal Rush, Denny Pennington, Greory Baker, Jim Sherrit
Middle Row: Donna Sue Tiller, Judy Watchorn, Deloris Hood, Jo Ann Coats
Last Row: Jonnie J. Carr, Tommy Melton McGee, Dan McNary, Jackie Coats, John Serrel, Ivon Rush, Jerry Dean Tiller,

Arson destroyed the school.

BLOOMINGDALE SCHOOL, 1918   Velda Jones, teacher
Row 1: Walters children, first names unkown, Helen Bender Bowman, Bessie LeMasters, Anna Isenmann, Jack Lawrence, Verna Isemann
Row 2: Velta Jones, George Isemann, Hester LeMasters, John Zaerr, Kathryn Bender, Lee LeMasters

Bloomingdale 1919

Bois D'Arc School

LOCATION: SECTION: 10   TOWNSHIP: 29   RANGE: 29   DISTRICT: 55

Teacher: Sylvia Mason, Reeds; Grade of certificate...Regents; Officers: Walter W. Crawford-Bower Mills, Clerk; H. C. Massley-Bower Mills, President; J. T. Burgi-Bower Mills, Member; Enrollment...20; No. of pupils in Class A...3, B...9, C...4, D...4; Term...8 months; Condition of house...Clean; Condition of grounds...Clean; Water...Well: Sanitation...Good; Condition of out-buildings...Good; Blackboard...Good; Globes...1; Dictionary...1 large - 6 small; Free text books...No; Heating...Stove,

Jasper County Superintendent's School Report, 1924-25
Courtesy of the Jasper County Record Center

Moved to Section: 26, Township 29, Range: 30, being used as a Sunday school room.

Above Left: Bois 'D Arc School

Right: Bois D'Arc Children

Above Right: Bois 'D Arc today

Bois D, Arc School 1941
Back Row: Ralph Thompson, Richard Still, lloyd Burgi, Harvey Still, Codine Guinn, Carl Kilpatrick, Jr. Still, Paul Kilpatrick, Leonard Kilpatrick
Front Row: Bonibel Still, Margaret Thompson, Margaret Still, Hazel Phiefer, Vivian Briggle, Charlyn Campbell, Betty Hull, Mermyl Still

CLASS OF 1937-38

Brick School

LOCATION: SECTION: 16   TOWNSHIP: 28   RANGE: 33   DISTRICT: 94

Teachers: Mrs. Maud Cannon, Carterville; Salary...$90 monthly; Ethal Glasscock, Carl Junction; Salary...$75 monthly; Enrollment...40+25; Term...8 months; Water...Well; Sanitation...Good; Condition of outbuildings...Good; Blackboard ...Slate; Maps...1; Library: No. of vol...50; Free textbooks...Yes; Heating... Stove

Jasper County Superintendent of Schools Report, 1924-25
Courtesy of the Jasper County Record Center

Annexed to Carl Junction R-1, 1961

Now being used as a Girlfriend's fitness studio

Richard E. Sandy
Brick Memories

"I attended the Brick School for eight years (fall of 1934 - spring of 1943). I attended five school years in the old building and three in the new building. There were electric lights but outside toilets, outside hand pump with cup for drinking water and a pot-bellied coal fired stove in the back of the room. One teacher for four grades. The 1938-39 school photos reveals fifty-four students and two female teachers – Miss Southern and Miss Lett.

"Old Brick School building

As you may recall in the old school building, the 'little' room (grades 1-4) was separated from the 'big' room (grades 5-9) by some folded door panels that hung from the ceiling and could be opened or closed manually. When school was in session, the doors were pulled closed. For all school functions (Christmas program, etc.), the doors were opened.

I remember an event that occurred when I was in the 4th grade (1937-38) and seated at my desk near the folding doors that were closed as school was in session. There was a class of perhaps 3rd graders at the blackboard following the teacher's instructions and a girl was working at the blackboard near the folded doors. To the side and above the girl, I happened to notice the head of a black snake sticking out a few inches. The snake was apparently in the ceiling channel from which the folding doors were hung. I remember pointing this out to Julia Russell and soon the entire 4th grade of some eight students were aware of the situation, as well as the teacher (Miss Southern), and the blackboard students were told to take their seats.

As a 7th and 8th grader (1940-1942), we loved to choose sides and play softball at recess time. Seems those doing the choosing were always male-but once it was determined which boy got to choose first -the first pick was always Lois Shively.

Another game was 'Crack the Whip'. With heavy and strong students as the anchor(s) some eight or so students would hold hands and begin to run. Suddenly the anchor(s) would stop and turn and the light ones on the end would find themselves flying through the rock strewn play ground at a very high rate of speed. Letting go was unacceptable.

The corner stone of the new Brick Schools reads as follows: ERECTED 1938-BOARD OF EDUCATION-HUGH MAXWELL/PRES. – FRED BURCH/SECY – PETE SANDY – ARCHITECT / SIGARS &HUGES. Peter Sandy is my father and also a graduate of the Brick School. He was born in 1880 and I have two of the school photos dating back to 1891 and 1892. Peter continued to live in the area and all of his ten children attended the Brick School starting in 1910. I was the last child and graduated from the Brick School in 1942. I remember the classes contributed something (i.e. essay, etc.) for placement in the corner stone and no doubt class photos."

John Sandy - Memories of Brick School

John Sandy 1939

"I don't recall my first day at the Brick School, but I obviously walked the 1½ miles to the school and no doubt was in the company of an older sister, During my stay at the Brick, I had two teachers. Miss Southard (who became Mrs. Wyatt around the time I was in the 3rd grade) was the teacher of the Little Room (the first four grades) and Miss Lett (who became Mrs. Anderson some time after I graduated) was the teacher of the Big Room (grades 5 through 8). I have great memories of both teachers. Mrs. Wyatt started at the Brick the year I started and left the Brick the same time I left. In addition, Miss Lett started at the Brick the year I entered the Big Room and left the Brick the same year that I left. Therefore, I always gave myself credit for controlling (or at least influencing) portions of their careers!!!

One of the earliest events which sticks in my mind involved an incident I had with an older brother of a classmate, Betty Fannin. I remember that at some time during the walk home from school, Betty's older brother Eldon, was pestering my sister, Evelyn. To defend her I recall attacking Eldon with my glass milk container (this container carried about a pint of milk and as I recall, had a metal handle which allowed a small person to hold on to the handle and swing the container – thus it was a potential weapon that could be used to hit people. I don't recall the final outcome, but it apparently caused him to stop and I also stopped before getting roundly beaten up. I also recall another fight on the way home. This occurred after my older brother and sister had graduated and after my younger brother, Richard, had started school. The fight was between Richard and Jay Whisner's nephew, LeRoy Wilson (Jay and I were classmates who became close friends at school – he lived a mile west of us). I don't recall the reason for the fight but Jay and I broke it up before it became too violent.

I have memories of the lack of modern bathroom facilities that existed before the new building was built. Prior to the new building, we used the outhouses (now the idea of using an outhouse was NOT new to most of us students because that's what we had grown up with at home). These outhouses were somewhat different from those we used at our homes – as I recall they were concrete block construction and quite 'roomy'. Of course there was no running water and I don't recall any electricity in the outhouses.

Brick Children

Since the school was bordered by timbered land, we students often took trips to the adjoining timber during lunch and recess. The teachers would warn us not to do this and stay on the playground. However, when I was in the 7th grade a lot of our normal playground was being utilized by the equipment and crew of the crew constructing the new school house. In order to keep the students from getting into the construction area, the rules about going into the timber were somewhat loosened. There were wild grape vines growing in the timber and although I don't recall that we would 'swing' on these vines like Tarzan, we would bring long stretches of the vines back to the playground and play "Crack the Whip". One of us older students would grab one end of the vine and several smaller and younger students would hang on to the other end and then we'd all run and the one guy would then 'whip' the vine sending the rest of us tumbling. Since the instigators of this sport were in the Big Room, Miss Lett sternly lectured us to cease this practice before someone broke a bone. In response we students retaliated by making tags in the shape of a large bone with the words "Broken Bone Gang" which we pinned to our shirt/dress/blouse.

When I was in the 7th grade, I started going to school with my niece, when Martha Dickson started the first grade at the Brick. Now I wasn't the only student at the Brick to have nieces/nephews in school at the same time. My classmate, Jay Whisner, had his nephew, LeRoy Wilson, and Richard's classmate, Bob Maxwell, had two nieces, Ruth and Virginia Maxwell in school with him (in Bob's case, both his nieces were older than him). With Martha attending the Brick, I felt somewhat responsible for her. She lived a mile west of us and we would wait for her at the intersection, so that we could walk the final mile together. Her mother and younger sisters would walk her to the intersection and then Richard and I would take her the last mile. At the end of the day, we'd reverse the process, walking Martha to the intersection. She would then walk with Lavern Huddleston and the Adkins boys until they met up with her mother. During my last year at the Brick, one day I caused her mother considerable grief. About a quarter mile from the school house, I noticed an interesting rock sticking out of the ground in the ditch beside the road. This rock was very smooth and very different from those normally found in the area. Also, the Brick was in a community where underground mining went on on and my father, as well as the fathers of many of my classmates, were miners. I was used to my dad bringing home interesting samples of minerals that had been in the mines. In addition, our class was studying geology with particular emphasis on local geology. This smooth rock really intrigued me and I was determined to remove it and take it to school to add to what Miss Lett and others had brought to class for display in the window sill of our new Big Room.

Well, with no tools, the process of "digging out" the rock took quite a bit of time, and as a result we were delayed meeting Martha's mother. As time went on, she was getting concerned about what happened to all of us. And all of us waited until I finally got the rock out. It was an egg shaped rock, about 8 X 5 inches and quite heavy. It was the yellowish-orange color of other rocks in the area but very smooth. And it was so different from the normal that there was great speculation as to where it came from. Was it from a meteor? Did the glaciers bring it? Was it left over from the ice age?? (It turned out that it was a large geode, which isn't all that common in that part of Missouri). The rock was taken to school and displayed along with the other samples.

Another memory of the Brick dealt with my graduation. Since I was the valedictorian of my graduation class (which consisted of 4 boys and 4 girls), I had to give a speech. With Miss Lett's help, I got the speech prepared and wearing my first store-bought suit. I made my speech - chewing gum throughout the speech!!!

My first memory of the Brick was one of thankfulness. During my last year at the Brick, the school board voted to pay the tuition of all students that wanted to attend high school at either Joplin, Webb City or Carl Junction. Prior to this decision, it was the responsibility of the parent of the student attending high school to pay the tuition fees. Now since the time was 1940, the economy was not too good – most of the mines had closed down and my dad was unemployed. Of my eight older brothers/sisters, only two of them were able to attend high school (and they weren't able to finish high school), so this action of the school board opened the door for me to continue my education by my attending Carl Junction High School. From there it was Navy service in WWII, then college on the GI bill and a very happy and satisfying career as a Scientist in the US Navy Research and Development Laboratory."

Dolores (Mancy) Junge - Brick

Delores Muncy 1937-38

"The year was 1930. I started first grade at Brick School, District #96. The school was located between Joplin and Carl Junction, Missouri on Lone Elm Road and Carl Junction Road.

The schoolhouse was a one story, two-room stucco construction, light brown in color with a front and back porch made of concrete. There were woods on each side and behind the building and houses on the west. Maxwell's grocery store was near by. The first grade teacher was Frances Southard, a young, single lady. Later she married and her name was Wyatt. She taught first grade through the fourth.

The building had heavy sliding doors separating the rooms housing first grade through fourth, the south end of the building was used for grades five through eighth. A large stove with a jacket stood in the back of the south room where shelves served as our library. When we would finish our lessons early, we could go to the library. I liked to read the dictionary and world books. We had pulled down maps (like window shades) of many countries for the study of geography. There was a hand bell the teacher would ring for the pupils to enter the building after recess.

I went through all the eight grades there. Our graduating class numbered eight. I was the next highest in the class. I have fond memories of the years spent there and of all the young folk in all the classes, as well as the teachers through the years.

Lois J. Barnes - Brick

Lois Trussell Barnes

"I attended Brick for all of my eight years. I started 1st grade in 1934 under Mrs. Frances Wyatt for the first four years.

In 1938 (5th grade) plus 1939 and part of 1940, I had Mrs. Lola Letts. Mrs. Hailey was a substitute. The last of 1940 (7th grade) and 1941, I had Mrs. Ruth McReynolds.

I walked all eight years (with others) 1¼ miles each way to school. We would run from one shade tree to the next in the summer and run, when we could, in the winter.

We had an old iron handled pump for our water and would beat the erasers on the side of the pump house to clean them. Oh! The dust.

We had some outdoor classes with walks along (and in) the creek looking for and studying fossils and leaves.

In 1938, we got the new Brick School, Dist. 94. There is a time capsule under the cornerstone.

We had the usual ball diamond, swings and teeter-totters. There was a visiting nurse for all our required shots, cuts and bruises. There was an old cloak room for our lunches and coats, caps, etc.

"The Brick School at Lone Elm Road, west of present-day Stones Corner, was called the roughest in the county due to the number of children raised by coarse zinc miners. According to Jim Moss in his history of Elm Grove (Stones Corner) this poem appeared on the school grounds in 1908."

"A buzzard came flying from the south, he had Mr. Hadley in his mouth. He knew he was a fool, he dropped him down to teach the Brick School."

"One day the students went wild, grabbed the teacher by the scruff, carried him out of the building and threw him into a snow bank. Hadley caught a ride back to Joplin and never returned to the school."

History Junction
Little Schoolhouse on the Prairie
John Durbin

Memories of Brick School From 1-8 Grades - Martha (Blevins) Felkins

"Brick was a two room school with wooden desks, a pot-bellied stove in the corner, and a small table with a wash pan to wash our hands.

There was a pump outside with water with so much iron in it you could taste it. We would fill a bucket with the water and drink from the dipper.

Everyone knew each other and we all played together on the merry-go round, swings, and baseball field each recess.

This was in the 30's and everyone was poor because of the depression. Everyone brought their lunch to school in brown sacks or a metal syrup bucket. Most everyone walked to school on gravel roads. Some as far as two miles.

Mrs. Frances Wyatt and Miss Nola Lett were our teachers. Mrs. Wyatt taught 1-4 grades. She would give you a big candy bar if you learned all your spelling words and could spell them at the end of the week. The same was true if you knew all the states and their capitals.

Our tablets were red with a black Indian on the front and the pencil was brown. We called the pencils "penny pencils" and the tablets were known as Big Chiefs.

We would take turns dusting erasers and cleaning the blackboard. Sometimes it became a game to get the chalk on each other.

During the depression, W.P.A. built schools. I remember we watched them at recess. They didn't have the things to build with like today. The men used picks, shovels, and wheel barrows.

Our class was the first to graduate from 8th grade in the new school. Some of those former students are meeting each month for lunch together and have been friends for 75 years or longer.

We had a nurse come and check our hearing, eyes, and teeth. We had a man named Mr. Reed come and we would learn Bible verses and have a contest with other school on who could say the most verses when he came. We also had Sunday School in the school. Every morning we would line up to say the pledge to the flag and say the Lord's Prayer before we started class.

We also had to do a lot of memory work such as poems and other things. We would have contests on who could remember most of what we studied. We practiced writing. This was called "penmanship.

At Christmas, Mrs. Wyatt's husband would be Santa Claus and always give us candy, an apple, and an orange.

My memories of Brick School are happy memories and the teachers we had taught us the things that built character. Both have passed away this year and both were in their 90's.

Brick School year unknown

Burton School

LOCATION: SECTION: 25 TOWNSHIP: 29 RANGE: 33/34 DISTRICT: 68

Teacher, Flora Jaccard; Term...6 months; Salary...$32 monthly; Enrolled: Male...4, Female...11, Total...15; Present today...12; Board: Chas. Reinheimer, Clerk; A. D. Murray, President; D. Wise; Condition of blackboard...Good; Condition of Building...Excellent; Condition of Furniture...First class; Condition of grounds, out-houses, etc...Good

Jasper County Superintendent's School Report, 1893
Courtesy of the Jasper County Record Center

Assessed value $165,348; Teacher: Helen Amos-Smithfield Salary...$95 monthly Grade of Certificate...1; Enrollment...22, Term...8 months; Condition of house...Good; Condition of grounds...Clean;, Water... Well, Sanitation...Good; Condition of out-buildings...Good; Blackboard...Slate; Maps...Case; Globes...1; Dictionary...1; Library: No. of Vol..168 Part. good; Heating...Stove with jacket

Jasper County School Superintendent's Report, 1924-25
Courtesy of the Jasper County Record Center

Annexed to Waco R-4, November 1, 1949

Examinations for rural students and Teacher's Assoc.

MANY RURAL GRADUATES.

County Examination to Be Held at Court House March 28 and 29.

List of Schools Represented Together With the Candidates and Their Postoffice Addresses.

Superintendent E. B. Denison has made out a full list of those from the rural schools of Jasper county who have passed the preliminary examinations which entitle them to enter the final county examinations to see if they are entitled to graduate in the annual county class of rural graduates. There are over a hundred of them. The final examination will be held at the court house March 28 and 29 and will prove an interesting occasion. The date for the graduating exercises has not yet been fixed.

This will be the third annual county commencement, the first having been held in 1900 with five graduates. In 1901 there were 38 graduates and now about a hundred and thirty-seven.

Carthage Evening Press
Feb. 25, 1902

The schools along this route all closed Thursday and Friday except Pearl Hill, Green Grove and Era schools. Miss Myrtle Hout, teacher of Excelsior; Miss Cora Turner, of Gem; Miss Mina Montgomery, of Victor, attended the Missouri State Teachers' association at Springfield. They report the attendance large.

Carthage Press Nov. 21, 1912

RURAL EXAMINATION IN APRIL

Pupils of Country Schools Will Take Test for Promotion.

The annual examination of rural school pupils will be held April 17, the places where the examinations are to occur being Carthage, Medoc, Jasper, Avilla, Sarcoxie and Duenweg.

One or another of these points is easily accessible from every part of the country, so it is felt that the convenience of all rural school pupils will be well served. The subjects on which the pupils will be examined are geography, spelling, physiology, arithmetic, reading, civil government, United States history and grammar.

These matters were decided Saturday afternoon at a meeting of the examining committee at the court house. Each member of the committee has taken some of the above subjects on which to prepare a list of questions for the examination, and will submit such lists to the county superintendent for revision and adoption. The committee will meet no more until after the examination, when it will convene to grade the papers.

The committee is composed of F. C. Thompson, principal of the Webb City high school; J. E Smith, superintendent of the Carl Junction schools; J. W. Whaley, teacher at the Temperance school near Larussell; Raymond Dennis, principal of the Marion school, three miles northwest of Carthage, and County Superintendent Walter Colley.

All rural pupils passing this examination will receive a certificate entitling them to admission to any high school in the county.

Carthage Evening Press
Feb. 18, 1909

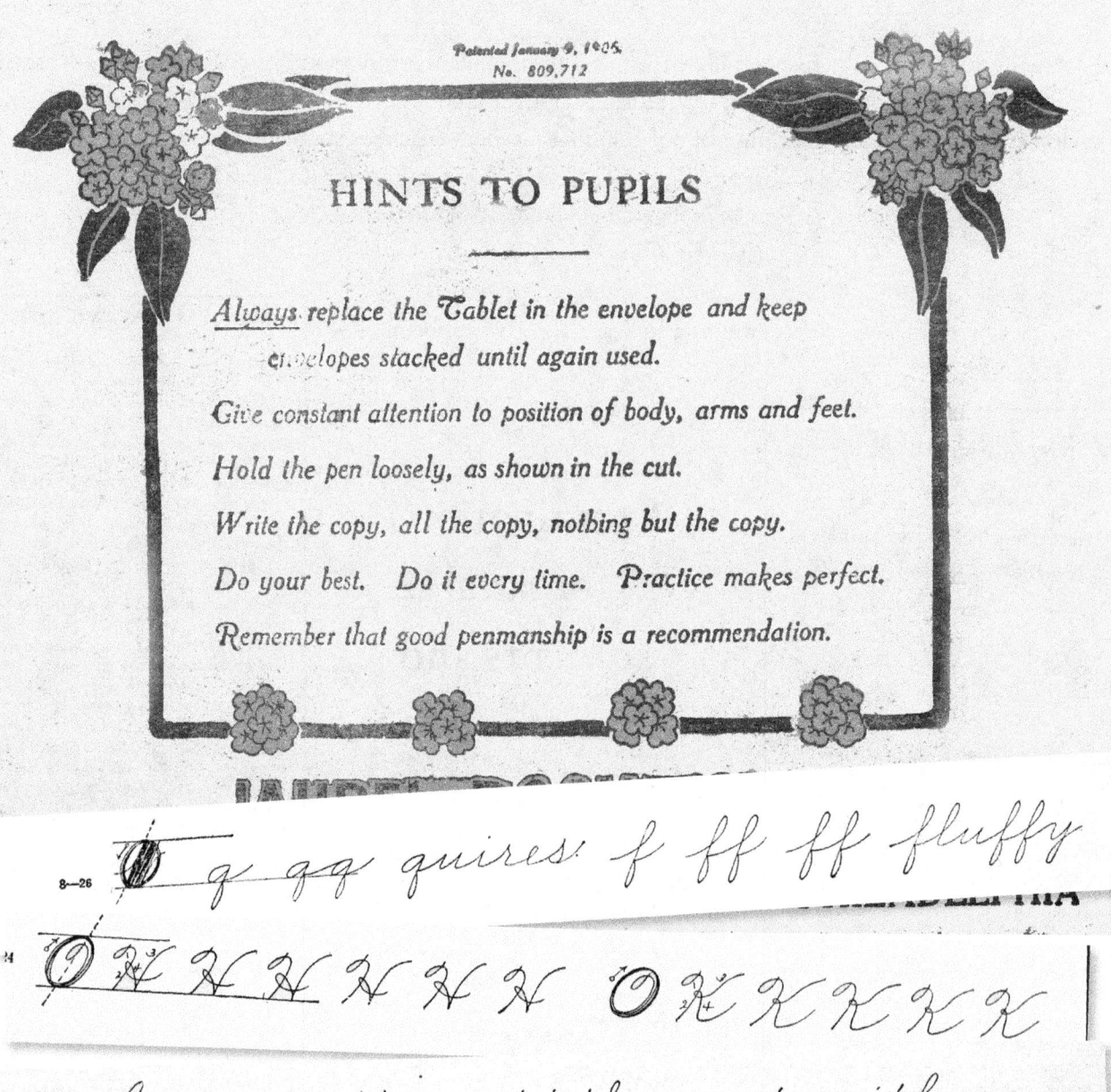

One of the writing instruction packets used in the rural schools. This came in the form of the above envelope which contained ruled paper and examples and instructions in creating each letter.

Carytown School

LOCATION: SECTION: 4 TOWNSHIP: 29 RANGE: 31 DISTRICT: 49

Esther Ballard, teacher; Grade of Certificate...3; Officers: Mrs. S. M. Replogle-Carthage, Clerk; S. M. Replogle-Carthage, President; M. J. Woods-Carthage & J. A. Gaddis-Carthage, Members; Enrollment...21; No. of pupils in Class A...5, B...7, C...4, D...5; Term...8 months; Condition of house...Clean; Condition of grounds...Weedy; Water...Carried; Condition of out-building...Good; Blackboard...Part. good; Globes...1, Dictionary...1, Free text books...No, Heating....Stove

Jasper County Superintendent's School Report, 1924-25

Carytown 1908-09

Doris (Carter) Wardlow - Carytown – 1934

"I loved to hear my mother tell about Carytown School where she went. Carytown was closed in about 1933. Old Carytown School was blessed with outstanding teachers named Dan and Vernon Matthews, both well educated in the east. Mom and her four siblings all graduated from Carthage High School and a couple went on to higher education.

The school was used by the community for Sunday morning church services where preachers held services, including my circuit rider grandfather who was also a butcher, shoe cobbler and farmer. The school hosted debates which generated lots of fun in the community, as well as holding court for "alleged crimes" by the neighbors".

Cave Spring School

LOCATION: SECTION 35   TOWNSHIP: 28   RANGE: 29   DISTRICT: 107

The first school was a log structure built by William Duncan in 1838-40. The second was built about 1/4 mile southeast of the original school, also by William Duncan, to be closer to a water source. It served as a Missouri Union Militia headquarters during the Civil War. Directly after the War, the Governor selected it to be the Jasper County Courthouse. The school was so damaged by loopholes cut into the walls by the troops, it had to be torn down and rebuilt around 1875. A porch was added in 1937. It's doors closed in 1966. It was restored in 2007 and received Missouri's Outstanding Preservation Award in 2009. It is now on the National Register of Historic Places.

Cave Spring School 1901, Courtesy of the Jasper County Record Center

Racine Palmer - My Experience at a Rural School
Cave Spring

RACINE PALMER 1962-63

"My experience at a rural school, especially a one-room school, was very rewarding with lots of memories. Small communities were very close knit where everyone knew each other and helped one another out when needed.

We always started school out in the morning with roll call, a chapter from the Bible, most of the time with a song or two from a regular song book or a hymnal. That was followed by an inspection to see if we had clean hands, ears, face, brushed our teeth, and our desk were straightened and in order.

The first class of the day was always arithmetic (math) followed by reading, history, science and spelling was always the last subject of the day. Packed in between those we had two recesses and a lunch hour at which we played games most of the time, all together or in small groups. Having class in a one room school, you not only had your class, but heard all the other classes recited from the time you started in the first grade through the eighth. By the time you got to the next grade, you had already heard the lessons, so it was easier to remember what you had to know.

Usually one or two afternoons a month after last recess we would have some kind of organized game or competition, such as spelling, math, geography, or something that would help with our learning. The games we played would be outside if weather permitted and everyone had to participate, from Run around the House, Bear, Fly and Dutchman, or Fox and Goose which was played in the snow. In the spring we would play softball and would have games with a couple of other rural schools.

Every month we would have a PTA meeting with some kind of entertainment, either from someone attending school there or from someone that one of the families had contact with outside of the community. Everyone in the community was invited no matter if they had children attending school or not. Miss Selma, the teacher would walk a mile or so at lunch to deliver them to the elderly people in the neighborhood. Almost everyone in the community attended the meetings, because the house was packed. The Highway Patrol came at least once a year and gave a talk or showed a film on safety. The PTA meetings were always followed with refreshments of sandwiches, salad, and desert of some kind.

We always had a Christmas program every year with speeches, poem recitations, songs, short dialogs, and always ending with the nativity play with all the children being involved. A week before the Christmas program we would all go at lunch and walk around the area to find a cedar tree to cut. We would get someone to cut it down and bring it to the school and set it up, and we would all decorate the tree. We would all work on some kind of project for several weeks before Christmas by making something to give our parents or mothers as a gift and exchange gifts at the end of the program.

The rural school I attended in eastern Jasper County, Cave Spring was a very historic School, being a part of the Civil War in this area. Not only being historic to this area, it was part of my ancestry since my mother, grandmother, great-grandfather, and great-great-grandfather attended school there. I was the last of my family to graduate from there before it was annexed to Sarcoxie, where most who attended school there, went to high school. I'm sure that my great-great-great-grandfather was involved in the construction of Cave Spring School.

As I look back to the graduating classes, especially at Sarcoxie, almost all of the valedictorians and salutatorians came from the rural schools, as long as they existed. This makes me proud to think rural schools made a mark in education."

Cave Spring 1933, courtesy of the Jasper County Record Center

Marjorie Dennison Bull - Cave Spring

"It was the fall of 1936. I was in the first grade and just barely six years old. My brother was four years older than I; he was already a fifth grader. Mr. Frank Massey was our teacher. He had completed some college hours toward his teaching education, and he was also a member of the 203rd Medical Detachment of the National Guard. The National Guard Armory was headquartered on the Sarcoxie Square.

One winter day when it was too cold to play outside, Mr. Massey brought a new game for us to play inside during recess. He called it Ten Pins, and it was similar to bowling. The children in the class took turns trying to knock down the pins. The big boys swaggered as they strode up to take their turns; the girls giggled and declared they just couldn't knock down all of them at one time.

Finally, it was time for my fifth grade brother to take his turn. Now, I could tell that he felt pretty good about his chances for outdoing even the older boys, for he spent as much time as they did on the chores around the farm, cutting wood and tossing it into stacks; and in the late summer he would work with his older brothers in the fields, gathering corn or the other crops that needed to be harvested. He had worked hard enough to build up a good throwing arm and he was ready to be the winner.

As my brother started to roll the ball toward the pins, his hand touched the floor and his finger rammed a long, sharp piece of wood which stuck solidly under the nail. That kind of pain was cruel and penetrating; it created shivers all over, regardless of my fifth grade brother's bravery. The children stood watching, each one beginning to feel sympathy pains in the pit of his stomach. Mr. Massey, kind and capable person that he was, assigned the biggest boy in class to be the monitor during his absence, picked up my brother, put him in his car and took him to the Armory in Sarcoxie. He knew exactly how to reassure the boy as he disinfected the area and used his medical instruments to remove the splinter. My brother and Mr. Massey returned to the school a few hours later. He was smiling and holding up a very well bandaged hand as they entered the building. The hand healed as Mr. Massey said it would. While there was soreness for some time, it was more than offset by the kindness Mr. Massey had provided.

The years went by and World War II came along. Mr. Massey was called to active duty where he served as a medical corpsman. He returned to this area after the war and opened a car dealership. Eventually he built a house south of Carthage where he lived until his passing a few years ago.

I started school when I was five years old. There was no kindergarten at that time; there were only six grades taught in a one-room school. The first four grades were taught consecutively. If you were lucky, the orderly grades would continue. Following this consistency for the first four years would be another arrangement. One year the fifth and the seventh grades would be taught. The next year, the sixth and eighth grades would be taught; but it was possible to graduate from the seventh grade.

The County Health Nurse came once each school year to check each child for head lice, to give vaccinations and to look after general health problems.

The upper grades had contests in my school. One year, the teacher strung a wire along the wall under the window. Each student had a small automobile attached to one of the wires with a paper clip. If a student had a perfect score in math or spelling, he was able to advance one car length. The student whose car first reached the end of the wire was the winner of the race. We played many games on the blackboard during the winter time. Tic-Tac-Toe and Hangman are remembered, along with others that haven't retained the popularity of those two particular games."

Cave Spring 1935, courtesy of the Jasper County Record Center

Helen K. Fullerton Hunter - Cave Spring

Helen Fullerton
1952-1953

"What I remember most about the school was the first day of school each year. I would walk through the door and encounter a smell that was a mixture of the waxed floor, ink from the duplicator and chalk. The windows would be open and a slight breeze would be blowing across the room. At the front of the room would be Miss Selma, our teacher, greeting each of us. I felt so safe there or maybe just relieved not having to do endless chores at home. Miss Selma was an excellent teacher. Maybe not because of the education we received (not that it was lacking) but because she created an atmosphere of high expectations and none of us wanted to disappoint Miss Selma. She made us feel that we were smarter than we probably were, better behaved than we were and that we could do anything if we tried. I don't remember her ever raising her voice in anger at any student. In a 1985 Joplin Globe interview she addressed this subject. "We never had any discipline problems, although we had differences and fusses." When fusses arose, she quickly squelched them with what she calls her "sermonettes".

"I stressed honesty and fair play and things like that. My students became nurses, highway patrolmen, farmers – there's none of mine on relief."

"Teaching all ages was no problem because the older ones I'd help and when they got through, they'd help the younger ones. We worked when we worked and we played when we played."

All of her students passed the final exam before entering high school. I remember taking an agricultural exam she was giving. She gave us the name and we were to tell us what it was. The one I missed was Bermuda. I did not know the answer so I put down 'shorts'. The correct answer was onions but she did give me half credit for creativity.

At one time after the school had closed; vandals cut copper wiring from the building to the utility pole. Someone made the remark, "Of course, it wasn't someone who went to school here." Miss Selma was quick to assure, "No, it wasn't. She was that sure of the character of her students.

I remember after graduating and after the last day of school, at home crying. I told my Mom that I had bit my tongue but I was feeling this tremendous sense of loss.

She was the driving force in the restoration of the school building in 2007. She had long since passed but it was something we former students wanted to do for her.

I remember giving a talk to student teachers and told them, "years from now, if the question, "Who was one of the most positive forces in your life." was asked of your former students and they put down your name, then you have done your job well.

That was our teacher, Miss Selma Fieker.

One of the unanswered questions that I still have, the school had no phone so how did our parents find out what happened at school that day before we even reached home."

Doris (Carter) Wardlow - Cave Spring

"I don't have my own personal story of Cave Spring School but there is a family story that is very dear to me. This is the best I can remember.

My great grandfather was J. G. L. Carter, from Spring River, where later Carterville would be established. He was a crippled Union man who tried to live in peace with his neighbors in this divided troubled county.

He was taken prisoner twice to the South. One time he was saved by an Indian Confederate Officer who had interred on his farm. He had one stipulation, not to burn his wood pile.

The second time he was taken prisoner with two others, Wes Rusk and Judge Stevenson. Apparently he and Judge Stevenson got out someway, ragged and hungry; they arrived at Cave Spring – the Union encampment. Somehow they got word to my great-grandmother that grandpa was there.

She and Mrs. Stevenson made the trip in the night to Cave Spring to bring them home. Grandpa learned that his guerrilla Confederate neighbor had visited his home, dumped a baby named Connie and took its blanket. (Or at least, Livingston got blamed for it.) When Grandpa heard the story, he said he could no longer live in the same county with Tom Livingston, so he loaded up his family and took them to Ft. Scott to wait out the war. Later he would sue the Livingston Estate for burning their log cabin for $1200.00."

Betty (Fullerton) Still - Cave Spring

Betty Fullerton Still - 1940

"This school served as a church in 1949-1950 and I taught the younger children's class.

The school's source of water was an outdoor pump. I remember the day I did a smart thing like walking under the handle while it was in use. The stars were not all in the sky that day!

My family walked two miles on dirt and rock graded road to school. We walked regardless of the season and have heard remarks many times from other students, "it was uphill both ways!

We played games at recess and the one I remember most was Annie-over. We also had Christmas plays. A wire was strung across the front of the school room near the teacher's desk (some of it remains there today) and curtains were hung from the wire which opened and closed after each performance. There was also a section on each side of this stage closed in by curtains where the teacher stayed and whispered forgotten lines to students and where kids waited before performing in front of their proud parents.

Paul Palmer - Memories of Our One Room School
Cave Spring

Paul Palmer - 1952

One thing I will always remember was how the older children taught the younger ones. We were also learning by listening to the other classes."

"As I look back and think on the days of my youth, my grade school years at Cave Spring School are very fond and happy years. The eight years I attended were like so many other students; all eight grades were taught in the same room by the same teacher, is Selma Fieker. Even my mother attended the same school, used the same one room and was taught by the same teacher as myself. So it was for my grandmother, only she had a different teacher, but had Miss Selma as a schoolmate.

Miss Selma, as everyone knew and called her, was the best teacher that a student could have or even hope to have. She was very pleasant yet forceful and let you know she meant business when she needed. Our years in school saw the paddle in use, which Miss Selma could handle the business end with authority. She kept a ping pong paddle in her desk drawer, which was used for big business, and carried a ruler in her hand most of the time just to make sure you were not talking or disturbing others. It also helped you concentrate on your lessons. These tools of learning were very seldom used (I did not say never) but not seldom needed. Miss Selma's kind heart and the way she expressed herself to her students made everyone work to accomplish what she asked of them. Because of the example she set, out expected goals were always placed at an elevated level. With the proper applied effort most of the students made good grades and learned the things necessary to continue education after the 8th grade. There was no such thing as grading on the curve during those years.

Cave Spring was like most one-room schools. The students that attended and the parents that supported the school considered their school as part of an extended family. Our school had PTA meeting once each month during the school year that everyone looked forward to and had nearly 100% participation by students and parents alike. These meetings included invited guest with programs with programs that were educational, informative, entertaining, and enjoyed by all. After the meetings, which were always at night, one of our favorite past times was to walk into the cemetery next to the school. The older kids would tell the younger ones that there were ghosts that would come out at night (we passed that information on as we got older). We would see how far into the cemetery we could make it before turning and running, NOT walking, back out.

My schoolmates and I would always try to get to school early to play before classes started. Miss Selma encouraged us to play games that included everyone, grades 1 through 8. She saw to it that all got treated fairly, the smallest to the largest. We had games besides softball, like Run Around the House, Annie Over, Bear, Red Rover, and Fox and Goose when snow covered the ground, just to name a few of our favorites.

Our school yard had plenty of large trees with ample shade and in the fall of the year when the trees shed their leaves we would put our engineering skills to the test (no formal teaching or blueprints to follow) by building a club house or hideout from gathering sticks covered with leaves. The doors and windows where usually top grade material of cardboard or feed sacks, precisely hung with thumb tacks, nails, wire, or even held in place with rocks. Fall was a fun time of year and we found plenty to do and always had fun doing it.

Another fall activity that all participated in was picking up walnuts. We had a couple of trees in the school yard, Miss Selma would go with us a ways down the road each direction from the school to pick the walnuts in the road. When the harvest was complete, one of the parents would take them to the market for us. The money we earned was used to help buy craft items.

Every year for Christmas Miss Selma would bring to school craft ideas for each student to make a gift for their parents. We could only work on our project during lunch time, recess, or after all our homework was complete. Each student was very proud of their accomplishment and gleamed with joy as the gifts were given to their parents each year at the conclusion of our Christmas program.

As Christmas holiday rolled around, somewhere close to the 1st of December, Miss Selma or one of the older students would get permission from one of the farmers to look on their property for a cedar tree. Usually one of the older boys would volunteer to bring a saw to school the day our teacher set to get a Christmas tree. That day after everyone had eaten their lunches, we would all go together to find the perfect Christmas tree, cut it, and drag it back to school. After it was on its stand, it was decorated with lights and all handmade ornaments from each student. The tree looked beautiful and all were very proud to have done their part.

The Christmas program was one of those special events to which all the students looked forward. Miss Selma would have three or four skits that allowed every student to participate. We would sing a Christmas song between each skit. To make this work we would stretch wire through curtains, made by Miss Selma, from each side of the room to meet in the middle. She would appoint curtain and stage people. This taught us teamwork and how to work together. The last play was always very special to me, "The Nativity". It consisted of three or four scenes. This would end with everyone in the play sing "Silent Night". It was always a proud evening. Another very special night program was the graduation ceremony. After passing eight grades you were given an examination, a test of achievement, by the county Superintendent. Your score on this test had to be passing before moving on to high school. This special evening included everyone in school helping in the ceremony. Miss Selma supported and made sure that teamwork took place and it was a good experience for all. This event saw the inside of the school transform into a stage with the colors chosen by the graduating class.

Previously, I mentioned arriving at school early to play and have fun. Our school day began with Miss Selma ringing the bell five minutes before class began. We were to stop playing, pickup everything on the playground, put up all bats and balls, toys, any trash outside was to go into a waste can, wash our hands, and get into line to march to our seats when the bell rang again. Before sitting down, everyone recited the "Pledge of Allegiance" each and every morning. When seated, Miss Selma called the roll and each student was to answer by saying "Present". Next was a health inspection that was done by different students, two at a time, each week. Miss Selma appointed them at the beginning of each week. During the year everyone got a chance to be the Health Inspector, usually more than once. Also at this time, there were two students appointed, a new crew each week, to raise the flag. Their duties also included taking down and properly folding the flag at the end of the school day. These two schoolmates had their health inspection first so they could raise the flag. This health inspection consisted of clean clothes, clean hands, clean fingernails, combed hair, brushed teeth, clean ears, and a clean, organized desk. If you neglected to do any one of these items, you received a black mark. The black mark was put on your rainbow poster that was kept on the bulletin board. That student's rainbow would be broken with a small black portion for that week. After the inspection began, Miss Selma gave us about five or ten minutes to look over our lessons. After that each class starting with the 1st grade, would go to the front of the room to go over their assignment. Usually 5th and 6th grades were combined and then the 7th and 8th grades were also. These two classes alternated each semester using different courses of study. We had a fifteen minute recess in the morning which was always a good time then back to class with a different subject. Noon was lunch time with everyone bringing their own lunches in a pail or sack. Most everyone went outside to eat their lunch, even if it was raining, but not hard. We usually would sit under a tree or eat in the coal shed. We had one hour for lunch and most lunches were eaten very fast or sometimes could be downed while choosing up teams so the games could begin sooner.

After lunch class resumed with a few minutes taken for current events, a student reading a short story or poem and sometimes Miss Selma would read us a book, doing a chapter a day. One of the books that come to mind was "The House of Seven Gables." After this short quiet time, we had our Spelling, then a solid subject for all classes until our last recess for which everyone was waiting. After recess it was back into the school for our last subject of the day. Our school day was over at 4:00 PM unless your homework for the day was not complete, which usually was a privilege to stay after school to finish. With our school day over, everyone grabbed the books they needed for homework, lunch pails and coats and walked home. Even our time walking home was filled with stories, games or plans for the next day.

Fridays of each week were a little different after our health inspection. We were to have memorized a new Bible verse each week and stand up to recite them when called upon. Miss Selma would record your verse by verse, chapter, and verse to make sure you didn't say the same verse twice. After our verse we would all stand close to the piano to sing a few songs that the students would pick out while Miss Selma played the piano.

Another enjoyment of the students was one Friday a month, or sometimes every other Friday closer to the end of the school year, we were permitted to have a contest during the last 30 minutes of the school day. These contests were spelling bees, math competitions, or an outdoor game. One of my memories was a head-on-head contest, you against another student, doing the usual addition, subtraction, multiplications, and division. The exception was if your competitor was Ronnie Fullerton and he had his choice so he always chose Roman Numerals. This really made me learn the Numerals better in an effort to win the contest but I could never seem to win that completion.

To obtain the privilege of having our games and contest, after our last recess and before class began, a student would have to stand and address Miss Selma as Madam Chairman. After she recognized the student, they would ask if we could have a game or contest that day. If we received a favorable answer "yes, you may", the other students moved to motion the choice of the games or contest, with each motion requiring a second and also a motion for nomination to close with a second. The nomination then had to be passed by the vote of the students and then the games nominated were voted on. Miss Selma would write the nominated games on the black board and call for a vote on each game. She would count the votes and tally them on the board. The games with the most votes were the ones to be played at the time Miss Selma set.

Those attending a meeting at the Cave Spring Community Club at the Cave Spring School, 4 1/2 miles northeast of Sarcoxie, are shown in the above picture.

Photo courtesy of Betty (Fullerton) Still

At the time we did not realize we were learning parliamentary procedures and the way our voting system worked. This was just one of the many ways Miss Selma incorporated learning with fun.

Field trips were another favorite. Even today we might not know how the Joplin Globe or the Carthage Press operated if not for these educational field trips. Other trips included George Washington Carver Monument, Harry Truman's birthplace, Jasper County Courthouse and Jefferson City. Every experience was a lesson taught by Miss Selma.

Finally, with the advent of the late Missouri Reorganization Education Program, all one-room schools were consumed by larger city schools. Cave Spring, along with Reeds and La Russell, were ushered into the Sarcoxie R-II School District. The doors of Cave Spring School finally closed in 1966. The closing of all the one-room schools also ended the time when you would hear people say, "They live at Bethany," "That family grew up at Forest Mill," or "I went to school at Round Prairie." These and many others went by the wayside are not even mentioned today. It was a sad time for every community when the doors of their school closed. It is my opinion that we have lost an educational experience we will never see again.

These days were some of the best and most treasured days of my life."

Cave Springs School

LOCATION: SECTION: 8   TOWNSHIP: 27   RANGE: 34   DISTRICT:
2 1/2 miles southwest of Zinite

"One district maintains two separate schools. This district lies west of Joplin and includes the two mining camps, Central City and Cave Springs. Each camp has its own school.
Jasper County School Superintendent's Report
The Carthage Evening Press Thursday. Feb. 18, 1904

Sept. 30, 1915, Delpha Stone King - teacher   Courtesy of Kathy Sidenstricker & Karen Oheim

Cave Springs 1914   Photos courtesy of Kathy Sidenstricker & Karen Oheim

Jasper Co. Mo. March 9th 1867

Mr. N. C. Hood County Treasurer

Pay ~~Due~~ Mr. Miller Ingram for Services rendered in Teaching a Public School in District No. 1 Township 28 Range 33 Jasper Co. Mo.
The Sum of $50 fifty Dollars

John Bentley Clerk of
Township Board

Teacher Payment

Courtesy of he Jasper County Record Center

Courtesy of the Jasper County Record Center

Cedar Bluff

LOCATION: 35   TOWNSHIP: 30   RANGE: 32   DISTRICT: 18

Cedar Bluff was located about 4 miles north of Alba. It was built in the 1860's

"Cedar Bluff, two miles west of Preston. Henry Hubbard, teacher. Wages $35. Forty-six pupils on register, average attendance twenty-seven. Small boxhouse, cold and uncomfortable; good seats and maps, but insufficient blackboard. School just about average. Cannot be much improved without a new house, which is much needed."

1872 Jasper County School Report by U. B. Webster, Jasper County School Superintendent
Joel Thomas Livingston, A History of Jasper County Missouri and Its People, Vol. 1, 1912, Page 101

The school closed in 1950.

CEDAR BLUFF-1937
Row 1: James Hegar, Paul Hegar, Rose Ann Bennett, Luke Heger, Walter Bell, Patricia Flesher, Barbara Flesher, Charles Ball, Don Baker
Row 2: Doris Wood, Ester Nell Baker, Betty McConnell, Doris Jean Sellers, Bob Barkley, Erma Wood, Standley Hall, Martha Baker, Juanita Hall
Row 3: David Buxton, John Phillips Hall, Edith Gladys Baker, Doris Buxton, Betty Buxton, Barbara Ball, Leo Heger, Orville Buerge, Gerald Barkley, Teacher-Rose Ann Heger

Margaret Manley - Teacher - Cedar Bluff, Pleasant View

"The first school that I taught was Cedar Bluff located as you come north from Alba to the Baseline road. I started teaching in January 1947. At that time you could take a test at the County Superintendent's office. If you made a good enough grade, you could get a certificate to teach one year without any college hours. I took that test and got a certificate but didn't get a school.

The Superintendent told me to let him know where I was working and that every year he'd have to find a teacher to finish out a term. At Cedar Bluff the teacher got pregnant and wasn't allowed to finish the year. He called me at work at the S.H. Kress Store and said he had a school for me in January. I taught that half year out, plus one more year.

We always had the Pledge to the American Flag then all said the Lords Prayer together. Then the health inspection; they were supposed to have clean hands and fingernails and a clean a handkerchief. Lessons were next; Reading was usually first for the first four grades, for the older ones it was History or Science.

We always played games at recess and noon. Before we ate our dinner we always washed our hands while someone poured water over them and each had their own towel. After the lunch hour was over I would read a book to them, like Tom Sawyer, Uncle Tom's Cabin, Dog of Flanders, Old Yeller or Black Beauty, stopping in an exciting place until the next day.

We had an old cold stove that had to have coal put in it to keep warm. During the day I usually had to add some buckets to it and the older boys loved to go get extra if we needed it, to get out of school for awhile.

Most every year we played a lot of softball during recess. We called it work-up unless you caught a ball and then you were batter.

I was paid $100 a month to teach that half of a year. If I would go to college in the summer I could have $150 a month the next year. I went to Bolívar Junior College that summer and got eight hours.

An excitement that happened the next year was that a family got the "Itch" and came to school with it. It was one of the Director's family and the mother was so embarrassed that they had it. Yes, you guessed it; we all got it before we got it stopped.

We always had decorated posters up for health inspection; this was done so each could place a star by their name. We always had what was called Writing. You made circles close together and marks up and down. One day I heard one of my students say "Oh yes, we must cross our T's and dot our I's, that's what Miss Margaret always says."

We always had a Christmas program and sang Christmas songs, had a recitation by some, dialogue, Rhythm Band and Twirling acts by girls that had batons. After the program there was always the passing out of presents to the one whose name you had drawn.

As a teacher I always had a box of Life Savers that had ten rolls of Life Savers or a sack of Christmas candy for each student and a big dish and platter of home-made candy to pass out to the families that came. We always took down the Christmas tree after the program. As there was no more school until after Christmas and as the tree was a real one it was getting pretty dry. I remember one time when we had strung popcorn and put one on the tree. When we went back on Monday, the popcorn was gone. The mice had eaten it all.

Every year the school had a pie supper with a program by the children. Pretty boxes were decorated by the girls and the boys would bid on them. The one who paid the most for the box got to eat with the girl. Pieces of pie or whole pies were sold. You were lucky if you made $300 at the supper. Pop (bottled) was fixed up to sell at 5 cents a piece in ice in the old wash tubs that different ones brought. The auctioneer usually did it for nothing as he was a good friend of the Directors.

There were always four to six Directors. One was the President of the group and one was the Treasurer (the guy you wanted to see at the end of the month).

I taught the Pleasant View School, about eight or ten miles east of Jasper, for five years until it closed because of consolidation. It was a great community and was always behind the teacher one hundred percent. But one winter day when I got to school all six Directors were there. Yes! I thought something bad was wrong. I spoke to each one and asked them inside. The day before we had a bad snow storm and as I was driving a Jeep to school, I pulled the children around in the yard and then up the road. Now nothing happened and no one got hurt but it could have. Now all the children thought that was so great of the teacher doing that at the noon hour that they excitedly told Mom and Dad what had happened. It was a dangerous thing to do but the teacher was so stupid she never gave it a thought that a car might come along and couldn't stop as the road was slick.

Each Director told me what they thought about it. I told them I was very sorry and you know I never started that Jeep again around when the children were around. What a dumb thing to do. I'd have a fit if a teacher had done that with my child.

One great thing they did for me after I taught at Pleasant View the first year, was have a meeting with me and told me that they knew the school was going to have to close in a year or so and if I would go to college that summer and get 15 hours, they'd pay me $300 a month as they had extra money and I just as well have it as to turn it back into the system. I did what they asked the next summer.

When I was asked to teach the school I told the Directors I wouldn't as I was going with one of the boy's brother and I'd have to make him behave. They went back and told his father and mother what I said. They came to me and told me to go ahead and sign the contract. He would do as I said or else. During those five years I did marry the boy's brother and did make him do what I said. Sometimes he didn't like me but always did what I said. We had one of the old globes that hung from the ceiling and I'd told the children never to play with it without my permission. You got it, one pie supper we had, he let it down on the head of the auctioneer. I put him in a chair the rest of the evening. Dad and Mom never said a word.

We had what were called community meetings once a month. The first one that I went to at Pleasant View, a game was being played was to have a suit case of clothes for the man and one for the lady. The person in charge picked out one of each. I was picked to dress like the woman, and as I was picked I heard a lady whisper to her husband, "I bet she won't do it." She didn't know me as I was there to make an impression. I walked right up there and got my suitcase, put on the outfit and got the prize for getting dressed so quick. That lady was a grandmother of three of the children I taught and what a good friend she was. I always felt I made my brownie points that night. Each family took turns being the host and hostess at the monthly meeting telling you if it would be sandwiches, cookies or whatever the next time they met.

All teachers remember the old courses of Study Books we had. It was instructions for daily teachings for all the classes from one to eight. What they must be taught from Art to Social Studies, materials to use and anything you could think of.

I remember that in the winter time instead of sending the children's lunches, the mothers would once a week bring a big pot of some kind of hot soup to feed us all and then end up with delicious cookies or cake.

So that everyone from first grade to eight would get to play a game they liked, we had a decorated shoe box that on Monday everyone was to write down a game that they wanted to play. Some of the older pupils would help the younger ones write down their game and talk them into playing bigger games. We had a box for sunny days and rainy days.

We had a cemetery to the East of the school yard and the children would play hide and seek. Many times someone would come up with Poison Ivy.

The last hour on Fridays, sometimes we would choose up sides and have a ciphering match. It was interesting to see a younger one beat an older one.

On Valentine's Day we always had a big box all decorated up. One year we worked on making a big heart out of paste board boxes. At noon and recess they would work on that and each one made a heart to decorate the sides.

Our desks were all screwed on the long boards so if there was even a fire we could get them out sooner. We had one little fellow that he loved to get out of his desk and crawl down under everyone else telling them he was a snake. Finally, I broke him of it by tying him in his seat. Then the folks were behind me, now I'd be in trouble if I tried anything like that.

One boy that I had at Cedar Bluff was about six feet tall and was in the 7th grade. When he moved to my school his mother said to me, "Where we came from the teacher we had wasn't interested in teaching my son to read.

This year if you don't do anything else please teach him to read." I told her that she would have to help also. I'd send her things to help him do some homework. My first thought was he wouldn't try. Was I ever wrong! He truly did want to read. If he had his lessons and he saw some other one had their lessons, he would ask if they could help him read. He didn't care how much younger they were, he'd let them help him. He loved school that year and read a lot of books. To this day I get a Christmas card from he and his wife and was invited to his 25th wedding anniversary.

I always tried to play with my students or be where I saw what they were doing. One winter we had lots of snow and at recess and noon they had they had built two forts. I was on the side with the weakest side. I stepped out from behind the fort to say, "Time to go in," and just as I stepped out a snowball hit me in the face. You could hear the oh's. I guess they thought they'd have to stay in the rest of the school term, but I said "Well, next time I'd better throw up my hat first before I tell you it's time to go in." The boy that hit me still thinks I was a great sport to say that.

When I left Cedar Bluff School to go and teach at Pleasant View School, one of the ladies told me, "You won't like that community, they are stuck-up." Another lady told me later that it was a wonderful community and she was right. I still have good friends out there.

There were three little girls in that community and when one lady made a last day of school dress for the program and dinner for her daughter, she would make all three of them alike. They were always so cute in the program. It was so nice of her to do that as this little girl's mother loved to sew and the other mothers didn't know how, but I always thought they bought the material.

The 8th graders always had to take a big test their last year in school. There was to be no school that day, only for the teacher and the 8th graders. One year I had five eighth graders. That really cut the school when they graduated. We had two first graders the next year.

Each school had what they called a cloakroom. All coats, hats and overshoes were put in there. There was a storage box for basketballs, bats and other games, etc. Sometimes the boots were wet so they were set around the old coal stove to dry on old newspapers. The ashes from the stove had to be taken out everyday or so. They were spread on the walks to the outside toilets. If you needed to go to the toilet, you would hold up your hand with two fingers. It was no-no for the girls to be out around the boy's toilets and the same for the boys to be around the girl's.

These are few of the things that happened as I taught the six and a half years. I loved every minute of it and it was a dream of mine to be a teacher and as my folks couldn't help pay for my college, it was all up to me to pay my way. Now I'm the one of my brothers and sisters of twelve that ever went to college."

Cedar Bluff 1903

Centennial
a/k/a Knights

LOCATION: SECTION: 18 TOWNSHIP: 28 RANGE: 30 DISTRICT: 87

Centennial School, also known as Knights School, opened in 1876.
Building specifications taken from a contract taken from a Directors' Proceedings, 1876 for Centennial School.

"The size of the house is to be 26 feet wide and thirty six feet in length with 14 feet walls with roof rise of 10 feet from square with braces on the corners.....with 10 window frames. Two door frames in size 2 feet 8 inches in width by 6 feet 8 inches in length...wainscotting to be 3 feet high from floor with a moulded cap...the framing to be of white pine except the sills and sleepers which are to be of oak...the sheeting to be rough edge oak."

The school house was to be built for the sum of $85 labor.

Signed 29th day of May, 1876

Jacob Heistand, builder

Courtesy of the Knight family and the Jasper County Record Center

A. D. Henry - Centennial

I went to school at Centennial from grades one thru sixth. We played ball and raveled to different schools such as Radium, Forest Mills and Green Grove to play other kids.

Our parents would load us up and take us to the games.

The school held pie suppers with the girls furnishing the pie in a nice box. We would sneak a peek at the pie. We were more interested in getting a good looking pie more than we were the girls.

A. D. Henry 1959-60

The outhouses were cold and we had to watch out for the snakes. We played the usual games outdoors and sometimes musical chairs indoors.

The worse experience I had was new teachers. We had a new one about every year, some good and some had no business being teachers. Teacher turnover and I wanted to play baseball was why I transferred to town school my seventh grade year.

I remember a littler store called Knights' Station across the road from the school run by an older woman. When President Kennedy was shot she let us watch the event on the TV in the store.

I had always heard that a Civil War battle or Indians that had escaped the reservation were captured in the area of the school. **

My dad and a neighbor are the only parents left from my grade school years.

Photo courtesy of A. D. Henry

Row 1: Bobby Wicker, Mike Vanway, Gary Henry, Mike Bayless, Brenda Cole, Christine Bayless
Row 2: A. D. Henry, Karen Wicker, Debie Vanway, Ricky Good, Mike Hensley, Ricky Cole
Row 3: Beth -------, Connie Cole, Janet Wicker, Jimmy Bayles,

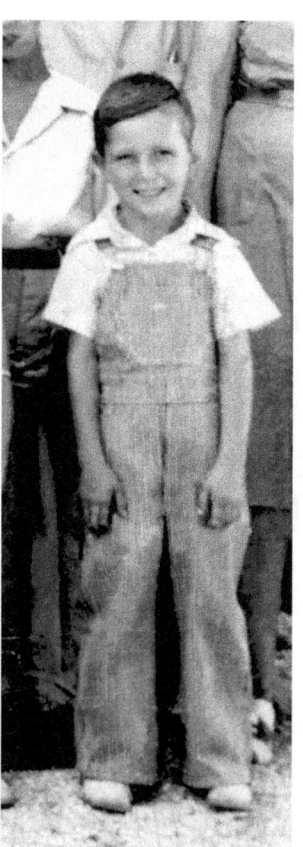

Danny Hensley

**The area where the school was located was called Knights Station. According to Jasper County history, Sigel's troops passed through that area. Perhaps there was a skirmish. Knight family history, rejected Union volunteers were coming home from Springfield. Renward Napper, one of the group, stopped overnight at the home of Thomas Buck near Axilla. Bushwhackers, perhaps looking for returning members of this company, surrounded the house and summoned Napper to surrender. He broke for liberty instead and was brought down, wounded with five bullets. His captors placed him on a horse and took him as far as Wildcat Grove in the vicinity of present-day Knight's Station where they decided he was going to die and so abandoned him. He recovered, however. During the Osage War in Jasper County, the Osage left their servation and some would have been captured in that area.... Editor*

Rules and Regulations Adopted.

To govern the term of School commencing Nov 5th 1877

Rule 1st No partiality to be used
" 2nd no romping in School house
" 3rd no profane language allowed
" 4th no fighting at or going to or from School
" 5th no wrestling
" 6th no taging
" 7th no nicknaming

The above rules are to be strictly observed by order of the Board of Directors

The above to be read by the Teacher to School once a week

G. H. Burkhart
B. J. Parker

Rules for government of School at Centennial School house in Dis No 9 T 28 R s 30 & 31 Jasper Co Mo

First School shall commence 10 min befor 9 Oclock A. M. and a received of 10 min A M at twelve 50 min recess 10 min recess P. M. dismiss at 4 P. M.

Centennial School Rules

Center School

LOCATION: SECTION: 15 TOWNSHIP: 29 RANGE: 33 DISTRICT: 43

Teacher: Edna Ault; Term...6 months; Salary...$30 per month; Enrolled: Male...16, Female...16, Total...32; Board: S. S. Ladd-Oronogo, Clerk; Issac Ault-Galesburg, President; Jacob Harmon; Condition of Blackboard...Poor; Condition of Building...Poor; Condition of furniture...Fair; Condition of Apparatus... Very poor; Condition of grounds, out-houses...Good.
Jasper County Superintendent's School Report 1893
Courtesy of the Jasper County Record Center

Assessed value $112,733; Teacher: Isabelle Stover-Orongo; Salary...$65 monthly; Grade of Certificate...3, Officers: B. H. Uaryan-Oronogo, Clerk; A. W. Poundston-Oronogo, President; Wm. Leggett-Oronogo, Member; Enrollment...11; No. of pupils in Class A...3, B...4, C...1, D...3; Term... 8 months; Condition of house...Fair; Condition of grounds...Moved; Water...Well; Sanitation...Good; Condition of out-buildings... Good, Blackboard...Slate; Maps...Case; Globes...1; Dictionary...1; Library: No. of vol...100; Suitability of books...Good; Free textbooks...No; Heating...Stove
Jasper County Superintendent's School Report 1924-25
Courtesy of the Jasper County Record Center

Annexed to Waco R-4, November 1, 1949
Building now sets at 10195 County Rd. 284, Carl Junction. It is used for storage.
Shirley Sue Fredrickson

Center School Courtesy of Sue Fredrickson
Center School Today

"Center school District - Ira Gray, Amos Atherton and J. A. Wilson, directors; Miss Josie Culpepper, teacher. Term began October 14th and continues five months. District enumeration 103, enrollment over fifteen years of age, total 25. Building and furniture first-class. Seating capacity 34. School is supplied with out-line maps and charts. Miss Culpepper succeeds unusually well in teaching mental arithmetic.

A class of young ladies in civil government acquitted itself creditably. Good order and thoroughness in all the work gone over characterizes this school.

S. A. Underwood - 1878 Jasper County School Report
Joel Thomas Livingston - A History of Jasper County Missouri and Its People, Vol. 1, 1912, Page 106

Center Point School

LOCATION: SECTION: 16   TOWNSHIP: 29   RANGE: 30   DISTRICT: 52

Center Point School stood on the northeast corner of Locust and County Road 80.

Assessed value $89,430; Teacher: Geneva McMahan-Carthage; Salary...$57 monthly; Grade of Certificate...T. T.; Officers: U. A. Riffie, Clerk; Harry Carr, President; H. Hickler, T. J. Hawkins, Members; Enrollment...14; No. of pupils in Class A...5, B...3, C...4, D...2; Term...7 months; Condition of house...Poor; Condition of grounds...Good; Water...Carried; Condition of out-building...Good; Blackboard...Painted; Maps...Old case; Globes...Planetarium; Library: No. of vol...100; Value...$100; Free textbooks...No; Heating...Stove in center.

Jasper County Superintendent's School Report 1924-25
Courtesy of the Jasper County Record Center

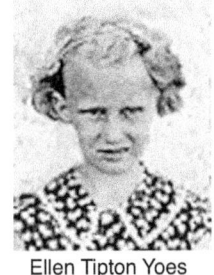
Ellen Tipton Yoes

Ellen (Tilton) Yoes - Center Point

"In the fall of 1936, a very frightened little girl began her elementary school career at The Center Point School located at the intersection of Locust and County Road 80. My parents were middle-aged when I was born and there were no brothers and sisters to play with, so getting used to other children was a new experience. My first grade teacher was Ruth Gipson Heisten. During my years at Center Point some of the teachers were Evelyn Martin, Virginia Hyde, Harriet Holmes Dyer McBain and my eighth grade teacher was Lucille Spencer.

The ladies had eight grades in one room. They were to follow a book which I think was called a "Course of Study" issued by the State of Missouri. That was certainly very different from our Curriculum Guides of today. Each county had a Superintendent who visited the rural schools to see if they were following regulations. When I graduated from the eighth grade, Jasper County Superintendent Bertha Reed came to my school and gave a test to each eighth grader to see if they were ready to enter high school. I wanted to attend Carthage High School but they didn't have a school bus coming out in the country so it was necessary to go live with my grandmother who lived in Carthage.

When I was small my father took me to school in his pickup and came after me when school was out. After

I grew older there was a mile and half walk to school in the morning and the same back home that evening. Before going to school mornings, and after arriving home evenings, there were chores to be done.

We didn't have a lot of money in those days. Lunches were mostly fried egg sandwiches on homemade bread. My father was a farmer and we lived on what little income we had from the farm and grew most of our food in the garden. Some of the men in the community had jobs in town and their children had little cans of Vienna sausages and various other goodies in their lunch boxes. If there was enough money Mom might go to the "Cash Store" and buy a little cardboard carton of peanut butter from the wooden barrel and then I had peanut sandwiches. My lunch bucket was an old syrup can. It even had a bail on it!

We had few library books. I read them till I had memorized them. We did have a nice blackboard. The only playground equipment was a teeter-totter, a jump rope and a ball and bat. We played a lot of tag and Andy-over (Annie Over) the school house.

In the winter, it was part of the teacher's duties to arrive early and build a fire to warm the building. Usually some of the older boys carried the coal in from the coal shed the day before. We had a large coal stove in the corner of the room with a metal jacket around it. The purpose of the jacket was to keep children from getting to close to the stove and being burned. The metal jacket usually got as hot as the stove! The jacket was good for hanging wet gloves or socks on to dry.

There was a well with a hand pump out North of the schoolhouse. The teacher pumped a bucket full of water, put a dipper in it and set it at the back of the room on a small table. Every one drank out of the same dipper when they were thirsty. In warm weather, we usually went outside for drinks and cupped our hands under the spout on the pump and someone pumped while we drank. One time the pump broke and we had to go across the road to the neighbors to get water. They didn't have a pump. They had a hand dug well with a rope and pulley and a bucket on the end of the rope. We lowered the bucket into the well and pulled up a bucket of water. Our bathroom was a little house out back of the school, one for the boys and one for the girls.

During World War II, we were able to buy savings stamps for a dime. It was a big deal to have the mail carrier stop out in front of the school and buy a savings stamp. Little books were supplied in which to stick the stamps. A full book was worth $25.00 after ten years. The only social event of the year was the annual pie supper. The girls decorated boxes with such things as crepe paper, construction paper or some kind of flowers, put a pie in it and sometimes sandwiches and brought it to the pie supper. An auctioneer came and auctioned off the boxes to the highest bidder. Then the purchaser was supposed to eat some of the food with the girl that brought the box. Pieces of pie were sold to others. The pie supper money was the only fund raiser the school had.

I can't complete this article without mentioning the clothing we wore. Everyone usually bought a new pair of shoes at the beginning of the school term. Boys mostly wore overalls if they could get them. There was a shortage of overalls. Everything, even material to make overalls and dresses went to the war effort. Girls wore dresses.

During the war many people bought laying mash for their hens. The laying mash came in sacks of print cotton suitable for sewing. Everyone tried to get enough sacks of the same print to make a dress. Some feed came in white sacks and they were sewed together for sheets, etc.

My husband attended Empire School. He mentioned several teachers including Elizabeth McDaniel, and Charleton and Zelda Mers. Some of the older boys took Miss Mers rabbit hunting one night. They chased the rabbits down out in the field with a car. They skinned the rabbits and sold the hides so they could have some spending money. He recalled how he and another boy in his class used to get in fights all the time just to liven things up. One day the teacher made them go outside and cut switches off a tree so she could switch them.

They walked home together that evening the best of friends! One year the teacher asked him to go to school early and make the fire so the building would be warm when school began for the day. She gave him a key to the building and he lost the key. He didn't want anyone to know about losing the key, so he fixed a window so he could crawl in through it. Someone going to work in town saw him crawling in the window, so he was in trouble!

Melba Hansen McCune - Center Point

"I was fortunate enough to attend Center Point School the last two years that it was opened in 1950-52. Center Point School was located 5 miles east of Carthage then 2 miles north on BB Highway. After it closed it stood there several years as a barn full of hay then it was finally torn down a few years ago.

It consisted of one large room and a cloak room. There was a garage on the northeast corner of the property and two outhouses in two different corners. Our desks were in single rows connected together and our books and supplies were under the desk top. The coal stove was in the back of the room to keep us warm. The coal was stored in one side of the garage and the teacher parked her car in the other side. The school faced south with one door and there were windows on the east and west of the building but none on the north side; which helped to keep the room warmer. In the front of the room was the teacher's desk with a globe on it and pictures of George Washington and Abraham Lincoln on the wall. There was a blackboard going all the was across the front of the wall and maps of the World and the United States attached to the top of the blackboard that could pull down whenever the teacher the teacher needed to for a geography lesson. There were some pictures on the side walls but I'm not sure what they were. It seems like one picture was of a wheat field with a person standing in the center of the field. We had a partly enclosed porch where the front door stood. There were swings and teeter totters out back. The school house didn't have running water in it. We had a pump outside where we had to go to get a drink.

As a first grader starting out in my first year of school I was excited but a little scared too. That changed pretty quickly because I was surrounded by older students that made me feel part of a family that only a one room school can create. We only had ten to fourteen students but that made it even better, Most of the time I was the only one in my grade. It was more fun when there was another student in my grade.

We had a U.S. flag in the front of the room and we would start the day by standing and saying the pledge of allegiance. Lucille Spencer was my first and second grade teacher. In the winter she had to get to school early and load the coal stove so it could warm up the school room before we all got there. The teacher had to teach all eight grades unless there wasn't anyone in a certain grade. She would have the first and second grades do some flash cards and learn all and subtraction facts and vocabulary words. She would help us with reading and Think and Do workbooks and we had to do a lot of studying on our own while shed worked with the upper grades. I can remember going to the back of the room at a table and using small colored sticks to learn to count and do Arithmetic problems. Also, I remember Mrs. Spencer making me a big pink pig out of construction paper and whenever I learned to spell a word, I got to put the word inside the pig. It seemed like a big thing to me at that time. She had some of the older students help the younger ones at various times. She put some of the grades together when she taught various lessons: such as geography, history, arithmetic facts, etc. I can remember one time when she drew a big circle and put numbers from 1-10 around it and a number in the very center. She would take a yardstick and point to one of the outside numbers. I never could figure out how 9 and 4 would equal 36. I thought it should be either 13 or 5 since I was either in first or second grade. It was much later when I learned the multiplication tables and understood what the teacher was teaching.

The cloak room was not only used for coats but lunch boxes, bucket of water and a dipper. It was a place to play in bad weather, a place to practice flash cards, etc. The teacher would set up a store inside the cloakroom and students would take-turns pretending to sell various items with play money. This was a fun way to learn Arithmetic and the value of money.

At recess when it was raining, we could play out in the enclosed front porch. I remember one time we were playing a game when someone had a broom and it flew out of their hands and came across the porch and hit me in the eye. Needless to say, my eye swelled shut in a very short time. Mrs. Spencer had to keep me at school because she had no way of getting hold of my mother. We had no phone and the school didn't have as phone either. The teacher put a cold rag on my eye and had me put my head down on my desk and I fell asleep. That was about all that she could do until the end of the day when my mother came to get me. Usually my mother would take me to school and pick me up afterwards because I lived one and a half miles from school so I would have to walk home alone by myself. When we had to play inside we would sometimes play board games, jacks, up set the fruit basket, etc. When ever it was warm, we went outside and sit on the grass in the shade and ate our lunch. Everyone sit together including the teacher and it was like a picnic. Sometimes the older boys would go out to the garage and go up in the loft to eat. They had fixed it up so they could sit up there by themselves. Whenever it was cold or bad weather we ate inside at our desk or at a table or on the floor in the back of the room. Since we didn't have running water in the school house; one person would have to go outside to the well and pump some water into a bucket and bring it back and put it in the cloakroom for us to dip water and put in our cups. There was a dipper in the bucket for us to use to fill up our cups but I have a feeling that some of them just used the dipper to drink out of instead.

We always had a lot of fun at recess playing various games such as Dare Base, Blackman, softball, anti-over and Red Rover, etc. I can remember watching the older kids play softball more than playing it since I was little. Sometimes I would get to be out in the field and go get the ball. We also had swings and teeters. The boys would try and swing as high as they could. It was a game to see who could swing the highest. The teeter totters were extra long boards so we could get up to 3 kids on the end of each one. One thing I remember was the teacher would come outside with her hands behind her back and have the school bell in her hand. The best part was that sometimes she would hand the bell to me and I would get to ring it signaling that recess was over.

If it was a very hot day everyone would run to the water pump to get a drink of water. Since we didn't have our cups with us we would just cup our hands together and reach down and get a drink from our hands. One kid would have to pump while another got a drink. If you were out there by yourself and wanted a drink; you would have to pump real fast then quickly put your hands under the faucet to get a drink. You might have to pump two or three times to get a good drink of cold water.

We rarely had art or music but one time the teacher had us draw an art picture and color it. I made a pumpkin. One of the older girls drew a girl in a very pretty dress. It was very good. We voted on the best one and she won. She got a prize but the rest of us got to choose a piece of candy out of a big glass candy jar. We rarely got candy so this was a big treat for all of us.

The school was a place for the community to gather whenever anything came up that needed to be discussed and taken care of in the neighborhood. Also, the school would have pie suppers to raise money for the school. Everyone in the community would come and take part. The ladies would bake pies and cakes to be auctioned off and the young girls would decorate a pie supper box with all kinds of fruit, pie, sandwiches, fried chicken, etc. in it to be auctioned to the highest bidder. The young lady and the person that bought the box would get together and eat the contents of the box. You never knew who was going to buy your box. It was all done in fun.

The one room school was quite different from the one where I started my teaching career. I taught in Carthage R-9 schools for 31 years. I had 33 fourth graders my first year but I was glad that I didn't have to teach all 8 grades. I do feel that some things were lost from the close family atmosphere in the one room school where everyone helped each other. It was an experience I will never forget.

Center Point School consolidated in 1952 and so in the third grade I had to attend Sunflower School which was another one-room school.

Central City School
LOCATION: SECTION: 12   TOWNSHIP: 27   RANGE: 34   DISTRICT: 122

Teachers: Mrs. S. G. Hamley-Joplin; Delpha Doke-Joplin; Mary Amos-Smithfield; Enrollment...85; Condition of house...Clean; Condition of ground...Clean; Water...Carried; Condition of out-buildings... Being modernized; Blackboard...Good; Library: No. of vol...170; Free textbooks...Yes; Heating...Waterbury

Jasper County School Superintendent's Report, 1924-25
Courtesy of the Jasper County Record Center

Edith Pugh - Teacher
Central, Prairie Star and Silver Creek

Edith Pugh

"It is a pleasure to write about the early days in the one-room rural schools. Many memories flood my mind as I think back about how I began my teaching career. I was a senior at Minden Mines, Mo. high school in 1936. One day while I was in my typing class someone knocked on the door and asked if he could speak to me. It was Mr. Tom Farader, the fifth grade elementary teacher. He told me that his father was on the school board and they were looking for a teacher and would like for me to come to a meeting with the board members and apply for the position. He encouraged me to go. I went to the meeting the next evening and after talking with me the board hired me. The only requirements were to go to summer school and take a teacher's test at the County Superintendent's office. I taught my first year at Central School, four miles west of Lamar. There were thirteen pupils through first and eighth grade. What a learning process! The State of Missouri had adopted "Courses of Study for the Elementary Grades." It was a complete outline of what children in the elementary school should be taught. I was so thankful for that book. I know I learned as much as the children did that year. My salary was $50.00 a month. I was driving 30 miles to school and 30 miles back home.

In the spring or 1937, a school close to my home asked me to apply for the teacher position. The school was Prairie Star School in Jasper Co. With mixed emotions about leaving 13 children I had grown to love, I decided to accept the Prairie Star position. I wouldn't have far to drive plus a raise in salary, $70.00 instead of $50.00 a month. There would be 29 pupils - what a change.

School's Daily Program:

The school bell was rung at 8:55 A.M. The children would line up outside on the school steps – the girls on one side and the boys on the other side. They would march in and take their assigned seat. We would then stand, pledge the flag, have Bible reading and prayer. A child would be chosen by the other children to lead the class in the morning activity. A Bible was presented to the school by the Gideon organization. If a child wanted to read from the Bible and have prayer, they could, however, they were never forced to do it. There was a piano in the school so they would sing <u>America</u>, <u>America the Beautiful</u> or <u>The Star Spangled Banner</u> as they began the day.

Classes would begin with first grade reading. I used phonics in teaching the alphabet and the sounds each letter and letter blends made. Flashcards with pictures plus the chalkboard were used a lot. The children in the other grades would hear the teaching and this was great reinforcement for them. The reading books being used were <u>Dick and Jane</u> and <u>The McGuffy Readers</u>. The older students would help the first graders with letters and numbers while I went on to the other students.

This was the beauty of the one room school – "Students helping Students." Reading was covered in all eight grades. Each student had an assignment to read silently before class time, then I would stand by their desk, listen to them read orally and ask questions to check their comprehension. After reading class would be arithmetic then spelling. Recess followed spelling and it lasted about 15 minutes. This gave the children time to go for a break to the "outhouse," get a drink of water or run around the school building before the bell rang indicating it was time to line up, come in and get ready for another session. English and Penmanship classes were held before lunch time.

Lunch time would be spent outside if weather permitted. All of us brought our lunch. We would set on blankets, the swing sets or the merry-go-round. Lunchtime usually lasted about 20-25 minutes. Everyone was expected to clean up the eating area and not leave anything on the playground. The remaining time of 30-35 minutes was left for supervised play. One of the favorite things to do was a game of softball.

After lunch I always read a chapter or two from a book to the children. I remember reading <u>Little Women</u>, <u>Little Men</u>, <u>Heidi</u>, <u>Uncle Tom's Cabin</u>, <u>Rebecca of Sunnybrook Farm</u> and <u>Anne of Green Gables</u>.

Afternoon sessions were spent studying history, geography, agriculture, civics and science. We alternated history and geography every other day and the same way with agriculture and civics. Science was scheduled everyday. Children loved doing experiments. Collecting wild flowers and butterflies was another activity they enjoyed doing. Other activities were geography matches, spelling bees and arithmetic matches at the chalkboard. Every Friday evening we had an - "evening off" - that is from the books. The children chose up sides and had a spelling match or arithmetic match.

One year we had a very unique activity. There was a peach tree in one corner of the school yard that had so many peaches the children suggested we can them. The older girls and boys peeled the peaches. I borrowed my mother's pressure cooker and we canned several quarts. Later on we opened the jars and had peaches for our lunch.

In order for the children to learn poetry, we would pick a poem to learn orally and recite it in front of the other children. The children had access to books on our library shelves. I would order books in the spring for the next school year. The School Board always had money available for books. In the 50's a traveling library would come to our school. It was called "The Bookmobile." The children could check out books or other resources. Extra Curricular Activities – Music was part of our everyday life. I played the piano, the children played different instruments such as the tambourine, bazooka and drums. "What a band." One year the mother's made band capes and hats for each child. Several songs were learned so we could perform for the annual pie and box supper we had each fall. The parents always looked forward to seeing and hearing their children sing and recite poems for the program. The mother's made pies and cakes to be auctioned off; the girls decorated a box filled with lunch enough for two, hoping a good looking boy would buy it so she could eat with him. Also in the room were places for a country store, a cake walk and a fish pond. Several merchants donated many items to put in the store and fish pond. We made enough money to buy a swing set, merry-go-round or whatever we needed.

There were several one-room schools in the area. Most were five-ten miles apart. The teacher got together and organized a "play day" for the schools. In the spring each year we would go to one school and have indoor and outdoor activities. The indoor activities consisted of spelling tests and arithmetic tests for each grade. These tests were graded by the mothers. Outdoor activities were high jump, broad jump, 50 yard dash and sack races. A softball game between the two schools ended the day's activities. Everyone went back into the schoolroom where the winners were awarded blue, red or white ribbons. We always had a picnic lunch and Kool-Aid prepared by the mothers. An enjoyable time was had by all. I spent six years at Prairie Star. Then Silver Creek hired me. "Uncle Sam" called my husband into service, WW II in 1942. When he got back from overseas I stopped teaching so I could stay home and have a family.

A pencilled notation on the back of this picture reads as follows: "Central — No. 5 — Miss Lowen. 1892-1893." A notation on the front says "Central School, Room 5."
There are no other identifications and the photograph has been on hand in The Press for a long time with no record of from whence it came.

Ten years later because of the drought, money was very scarce so we decided perhaps I should look for a job. My husband took care of the children and I got in our car to go look. I had to have gas for the car so I stopped, went into the station and guess who was in there? The School Board from Prairie Star. They were looking for a teacher. They asked me if I would take the job and I told them I wasn't sure if I could since I had not got any more college hours. We went to Carthage to see the County Superintendent and he said if I would take college classes one night a week or on Saturday morning and take a teachers test in his office I could accept the job. I taught Prairie Star for five more years. During that time I completed my elementary degree. As the country schools were being consolidated we had to close Prairie Star. The next year all of us went to Jasper R-5 School. I taught 5th grade for 22 years, retiring in 1982."

Robert L. Rader and Nellie - 1925

Rural school children were expected to do chores before leaving for school in the mornings. This meant feeding and milking the cows. There were always farm kittens around hoping for a stream of milk to come their way. There was feeding chickens, making sure the horses had water and harnessed for the day. After school, they had an equal amount of chores to do. After the chore; supper, homework, then bed. The next day it started all over again. This was necessary for the survival of the family.

Charter Oak School

LOCATION: SECTION: 28   TOWNSHIP: 29   RANGE: 30   DISTRICT: 59

"Charter Oak School, five miles northeast of Carthage, was the scene yesterday of the third annual reunion of its former pupils and teachers.

For historic interest, Charter Oak is outstanding among Jasper county rural schools. The first schoolhouse was built in 1852 by a Mr. Whitehead, one-half mile south of the present location. J. N. U. Seela, the county's oldest pioneer, still living in the Charter Oak neighborhood, assisted in its construction. About four years later the building was moved to the present site. At this period Miss Lena Riffee, now Mrs. Lena Jewell, 1011 Grant Street, Carthage, and John C. Crawford taught several terms. The original building was sold and moved away, and the present structure was built in 1875.

Among the Charter Oak teachers from that time until about 1890 were Nathaniel Harry, Hiram Harry, John Wolf, Mollie Adams, Mr. Giterly, Mr. Wealty, Freeman Lucas, George M. Jacobs, John Bryan, A. B. Callison, Lizzie Hemphill, Emma Randall, C. H. Briggle, Mamie Biffee, J. C. Tidball, John Atkinson, O. D. Bleam, Mrs. C. Briggle, Miss Wallace, and W. G. Fassen."

Carthage Evening Press, June 5, 1926 - Page 5

"Charter Oak closed after the 1967-68 school year. The building was converted into a home, but has since been torn down."

Kathy Sidenstricker - www.jaspercountyschools.org

Charter Oak 1956

CHARTER OAK OLD SCHOOL

FIRST BUILDING CONSTRUCTED IN 1852

History Recalled Yesterday at Third Annual Reunion—H. L. Hornback Heads Association

Charter Oak school, five miles northeast of Carthage, was the scene yesterday of the third annual reunion of its former pupils and teachers.

For historic interest Charter Oak is outstanding among Jasper county rural schools. The first schoolhouse was built in 1852 by a Mr. Whitehead, one-half mile south of the present location. J. N. U. Scela, the county's oldest pioneer, still living in the Charter Oak neighborhood, assisted in its construction. About four years later the building was moved to the present site. At this period Miss Lena Riffee, now Mrs. Lena Jewell, 1011 Grant street, Carthage, and John C. Crawford taught several terms. The original building was sold and moved away, and the present structure was built in 1875.

Among the Charter Oak teachers from that time until about 1890 were Nathaniel Harry, Hiram Harry, John Wolf, Mollie Adams, Mr. Citerly, Mr. Wealty, Freeman Lucas, George M. Jacobs, John Bryan, A. B. Callison, Lizzie Hemphill, Emma Randall, C. H. Briggle, Mamie Biffer, J. C. Tidball, John Atkinson, O. D. Beem, Mrs. C. H. Briggle, Miss Wallace, and W. G. Fasken.

Several of the older persons present yesterday recalled these bits of the school's history. The program included also the reading of a letter and a poem entitled "Fifty Years Ago," from Mrs. Belle Paul, now living in Illinois, who was a Charter Oak pupil half a century ago. Readings were given by Mrs. Daisy Kyle Raine and I. M. Jacobs, both former pupils. There was a talk by James Wininger, and the assembly sang, "America," led by H. L. Hornback. A sumptuous dinner was served at noon.

Next year's reunion will be held the first Friday in May, 1927.

During the business session H. L. Hornback was elected president of the organization, and Mrs. J. A. Largent was elected secretary and treasurer.

Charter Oak's foundation, courtesy of the Jasper County Record Center

Back Row: Teacher, ____, Silas Sanders, Robert Thorn, ____, Floyd Pennington, Winston Carter, Sanders____, David Thorn, Noah Thorn
Third Row: ____, ____, ____, ____, ____, Virginia Williams, Thelma Clubb.

Coon Foot School

LOCATION: SECTION: 3 TOWNSHIP: 29 RANGE: 32 DISTRICT: 34

"The school was located two miles north of Alba on the east side of the road. The building was constructed on land donated by John Harbison."
Kathy Sidenstricker - www.jaspercountyschools.org

Assessed value $84,611; Teacher: Lela Smith-Alba; Grade of Certificate...3; Officers: C. J. Smith, Clerk; J. J. Weir, President; J. E. Smith & Moses McWilliams, Members; Enrollment...18; No. of pupils in Class A...6, B...6, C...4, D...2; Term...8 months; Condition of grounds...Grassy; Water...Carried; Condition of out-buildings... To be sanitary; Blackboard... __ of slate; Maps...Case; Library: No. of vol...50; Free textbooks... Yes; Heating... Stove
Jasper County Superintendent's School Report, 1924-25
Courtesy of the Jasper County Record Center

Coon Foot closed in 1945

Coon Foot 1944-45

Coon Foot 1937　　Couresy of Kathaleen McClanahan

L-R: Harold Mackey, Mary Lon Dodson, Bud Jenkins, Teacher, Miss Vivan Frazar, Jack Dodson, Kathaleen McClanahan, Laurence Leggett
Front Row: John R. Luman, Ruth Ann Jenkins, Charleen McClanahan, Vistor, Edith Dodson

Coon Foot 1938-39　　Courtesy of Kathaleen McClanahan

L-R: Charleen McClanahan, Laurence Leggett, Mary Lon Dodson, Kathaleen McClanahan, Harold Maky, Roberta Hood
Front Row: John Richard Luman, Ruth Ann Jenkins, Edith Dodson, Teacher-Miss Viva Frazar

Deer Creek School

LOCATION: SECTION: 2 TOWNSHIP: 29 RANGE: 29 DISTRICT: 28

"The Deer Creek school closed the doors to its 1-room frame building in the spring of 1960, joining in the halls of history a growing list of other similar institutions of learning which were a hollowed part of an earlier, less competitive day.

Students who live in what was Deer Creek district now travel via school bus, the symbol of the dramatic changes in educational methods during the last 50 years, to the town of Jasper and the modern, superably equipped plant of the sweeping R-5 district.

But the old Deer Creek school, 11 miles northeast of Carthage, remains a living part of the heritage of Jasper county. Having served its purpose well for many decades, during a period when its methods and facilities were admirably suited to the needs of the people of the community, the school remains a fond memory in the minds of many. The building which still stands, now converted to use as a residence for the family of Joe Frerer, Jr., was sparking new.....in the fall of 1902......teacher that year was Lawrence Daniels. Mrs. Pearl Kentner was the last teacher in the Deer Creek school.

The building was the successor to an earlier frame structure which stood for many years on the same 2-acre plot of land midway between Dry Fork and Deer Creek."

Carthage Evening Presss, Oct. 29, 1926

Deer Creek School is still standing

Dick Sunderland - Deer Creek

"I started school in 1940 at the age of six years. I had to walk 1½ miles to school and some kids walked two miles.

Mrs. Patterson was our 1st grade teacher. There was around 25-30 kids in the school. The teacher had to carry coal from the north side of the school house and build a fire before school started. The building would be warm when we got there.

Wilma Jean Palmer was the 2nd grade teacher and she was only seventeen years old. She boarded with a family in the community during the two years she taught.

Another teacher was Mrs. Helen Clouser. She rode the Jasper School bus and they would pick her up after school and take her back to Jasper where she lived.

For some reason, I got a spanking the first three years at school and my mother always seemed to know about it because I always got another when I got home.

One day Mrs. Clouser told us that when it snowed there was to be <u>no</u> snowball fights after school. Just as soon as we thought we were out of sight, the fight began. Mrs. Clouser came outside and caught us and made us all go back to school and sit until her ride came to pick her up.

I remember Mrs. Clouser reading Bible stories to the students daily.

We played ball games during recess in the morning and afternoon. There was a cable on each side of the school where the older kids would get on each side and swing the younger kids back and forth. One day they were swinging me and threw me on the ground and broke all the bones in one of my arms. There was a tall concrete wall at the school. We boys invented a contest to see who could pee the farthest over the wall. The winner is a well kept secret.

DEER CREEK SCHOOL - 1930

In the early 1940's, Carl Flenniken drove a hay wagon pulled by mules to pick up all the kids at Deer Creek School. They were to attend a ball game at Mayflower, a distance of six miles. The teacher and Clara Sunderland accompanied them.

Mrs. Clouser and I remained close friends for the rest of her life."

This is a report card from 1934. Take note of the categories in which the students are to be evaluated.

This may be what was considered at the time to be "Home Work".

Dewey School
a/k/a Blood
LOCATION: SECTION: 36   TOWNSHIP: 29   RANGE: 31   DISTRICT: 31

Teacher: Lula Emery; Salary...$30 monthly; Board: Wm. Simmons, Clerk; D. Matthews, President; Daniel Goff, Term...7 months; Enrolled: Male...12, Female...9, Total ...21, Condition of blackboard...Good; Condition of building...Medium; Condition of furniture...Fair; Condition of apparatus...Fair; Condition of grounds, out-houses, etc...Good

Jasper County Superintendent School Report, 1894
Courtesy of the Jasper County record Center

Assessed value 112,170; Teacher: Aretha Flowers-Carthage; Grade of Certificate...3; Officers: T. A. Flowers, Clerk; Hiram Rush, Member; Enrollment... 24; No. of pupils in Class A...4, B...8, C...6, D...6; Condition of house...Good; Condition of grounds...Weedy; Water...Well; Condition of out-buildings...Fair;Blackboard...Fair; Maps...Set on tripod; Globes...0; Dictionary...1; Library: No. of vol....80; Free textbooks...Yes; Heating...Stove with jacket

Jasper County Superintendent School Report, 1924-25
Courtesy of the Jasper County Record Center

Dewey School

Phyllis (Bull) Probert
Dewey, Bloomingdale, Rosebank and Rising Sun

"As I remember, Dewey had a large attendance. I started there in the second grade because my Mom taught me before and there wasn't another first grader. Jennie Wright was my first teacher. There were more students there than any other school I attended.

When I was in the third grade my sister, Marybeth, fell out of a swing at school. Her hip was broken and I went to live with Grandpa and Grandma Fasken while Mom was with her for a while at Shriners' Hospital for Children in St. Louis. While there I went to Bloomingdale, since my Aunt Ruby was the teacher.

I didn't like going to the outhouse; I just knew there would be a snake. Old catalogues were used for toilet paper and if we had to go during class time, we held up two fingers to be dismissed.

These were only two or three classmates, probably a total of eighteen or twenty students. The room was heated by a big coal stove in the middle of the room. The older boys kept the bucket filled from a coal house near the school.

Everyone walked to school. The farthest was about a mile.

Once a year we had a pie supper and program for extra school money. The girls brought decorated boxes filled with a lunch that was auctioned off and we ate with the highest bidder.

At Christmas time, we drew names and bought a gift for that person. There was a set price for the gift. There was a program and gift exchange and then we were out for a short vacation.

County schools were always out in April with a last day school dinner with each family bringing food. The afternoon was spent playing games and visiting."

Marybeth Denton - Precious Memories How They Linger
Dewey, Rising Sun and Rosebank

"First memories of attendance in rural schools takes me back to 1930 and Dewey School, eight miles northeast of Carthage. I was in first grade and Miss Fern Flowers was my teacher. I also knew her from Salem Church and was very fond of her. It was early September when an older schoolmate was pumping me on the swing and we were going high. I flew out of the swing and never returned to Dewey but had tutoring in Shriners' Hospital in St. Louis for seven months while healing a dislocated hip.

In the meantime, my parents, Vance and Lora Bull, moved to the Sandhills. That area is southwest of Jasper and our school in that district was Rose Bank. Mr. Herbert Moser was our teacher. My only memory is that it was a rock school house and I still remember some of the student's names.

Dewey School - 1946-47

About a year later we moved to the district of Rising Sun, five miles southwest of Jasper. I entered there in the third grade and graduated from the eighth grade. My teachers were Miss Blanche Rice, Miss Kathryn Berry, Miss Maurine Mink and Miss Helen Dyer.

When the first bell rang students would go to their assigned desk and stand beside it; on the second ring we would sit down. Dewey school had an outside rooftop bell that rang over the countryside and children from all four directions would know to hasten their steps when the bell rang.

The day would begin with the Pledge of Allegiance to the Flag. We learned early that the flag is an important symbol of the country and should be treated with love and care.

We also had an opening prayer. Looking back today, maybe the teacher had that for her own benefit.

Study time was quiet time. This was enforced and there was no gum chewing. That wasn't a big problem for there usually wasn't extra money to buy gum. The Course of Study was followed and County Superintendent, Miss Bertha Reed, visited school often.

We were taught to respect and obey our teachers even if we disagreed with them. I was really upset over losing in the Friday spelling match when the teacher refused to accept the spelling of stationery (writing material) for she thought it was stationary (not moving) and would not consult a dictionary. Teacher was eighteen years old, so in later years I realized she just wasn't that knowledgeable.

DEWEY SCHOOL-1933

Favorite recess games: Marbles – remember those circles in the dirt? Annie-over – we tried (and tried) to throw a ball over the school house roof.

Baseball – the dreaded baseball (to me) game. When I was at bat the kids from the field would gather in close for they knew the ball would be batted only a few feet. So embarrassing!

Searching for Clover – Four Leaf Clover of course. In the spring the search would begin and munching on sheep shire. Of course, this was a girl's thing.

Ice skating – Our pasture joined the school yard and was separated by a barb wire fence. On the east edge of the yard was a slight incline and a path worn under the fence which led to a small shallow pond. After a hard freeze the pond made a good skating rink and during recess, we were allowed to slide under the fence, run down the hill to the pond to slide on the ice. A grove of trees were nearby and kids would find sticks for clubs and a chunk of wood or an old can, and voila', a hockey game was in process.

In winter the room was heated by a coal stove centered in the middle of the room. My Dad was on the School Board and he banked the fire at night and often got it started early in the morning. We lived near the school and sometimes during bad weather teachers would board at our home.

Our school house was old and there were initials carved in most desks. I think older boys carried pocket knives. Also, there were ink wells built into the desks and some desks were ink stained. Coats hung on hooks at the back of the room and galoshes were piled on the floor under them. Somehow there were funds available to get new desks and a closet built across the back of the room with a shelf. This enclosed our coats, galoshes, lunch buckets and there was storage for books.

One repair remains a mystery to me. I believe every one-room school had windows on both sides of the building. A new ruling was made for schools to board up on one side of windows so light would come in over our left shoulder. Maybe this rule came out of Jefferson City. Anyway, Rising Sun kept up with the times and followed the rule.

In the fall of the year there would be a pie supper which was open to the public as it was a fund raiser. Boxes were decorated to represent something, or to just be inviting. Mom would fix a feast-like fried chicken, potato salad and chocolate cake. Fellows would bid on the auctioned boxes, pay a nice price, and eat with whoever brought the box.

Valentines Day – As I recall the teacher would provide a large box and we would decorate it with red and ruffles and frilly things. The valentines were either home-made or from the S.H. Kress Store. We brought one for every schoolmate and our teacher. No valentine today compares to the one in the 1930's. I still have all of my grade school cards and the oldest is 1929.

I'm not sure if the photographer came every year but when he came it was an event. It was always an outside group picture. Invariably, some kid ended up with a twisted face or some undesirable grimace. The Kodak was perched on long wooded legs and covered with long wooden legs and covered with a long black cloth. The photographer would get us lined up and then disappear under the long black cloth. That always brought on snickers and giggles.

Programs – We all enjoyed preparing for a program for we had practice instead of studies. The programs were almost always held at night so the fathers could attend.

Friendships – We all had our spats and disagreements but they were short-lived, and many grade school friends have been life-long friends.

I feel blessed to have grown up in the country where hard work and school was just a way of life – no questions asked – and love of God and Country foremost."

Dewey School Interior

The photo above is believed to be Dewey's school year 1958-59. The pupils attending that school year were:
Kathy Sue Bull, Loyd K. Sloan, Gale L. Knight, Kenda Betts, Shirley Powell, Sarah Ann Bacon, Charles A. Rice, John J. Mansfield, Jeanette Rice, Dale Powell, Claude B. Jones, Carten E. Jones, John R. Bacon, Peggy Jones, Ralph Powell

Dixie School

LOCATION: SECTION: 32   TOWNSHIP: 30   RANGE: 32   DISTRICT: 19

District No. 6 was created in 1886 from parts of districts 2 and 5. The District encompassed parts of Township 29 and 30, Range 31 and 32 in northern Jasper County. The school, known as Dixie School, was first located four miles northeast of the town of Alba. In September 1886, a new schoolhouse was built one mile north of Alba. Dixie was closed about 1920.

"Uriah Smith Resigns"

"Uriah Smith who was recently elected representative by voters of the eastern district of Jasper county has resigned his position of teacher of the Dixie school near Preston and in his stead Miss Gertrude Etter of southeast of Jasper was named by the board. Mr. Smith has hired a substitute for some time but did not resign until after the election."
The Jasper News, 26 Nov. 1908

"Miss Mary Curtis has been employed to teach the Dixie school this coming winter."
The Jasper News, 16 Jun. 1910
Courtesy of Kathy Sidenstricker - www.jaspercountyschools.org

The school building is gone.

THREE TEACHERS "LOSE OUT"
Due Solely to Religious Beliefs, Joplin Board Member Says

Charges that three women of the present teaching staff of the Joplin schools were refused reelection by the teachers' committee of the board of education simply because of their religious beliefs were made by Clark Craycroft, a member of the board, at the regular meeting last night, when the general staff of teachers were reelected for the year.

A motion to include the three teachers in the list of those to be reelected was voted down, four to two, Craycroft and Jesse Zook voting for the resolution and Dr. A. B. Clark, J. T. Haggart, John Emerson and Roy Breazeale voting against it.

Three Carthage women are among the teachers reelected for the coming term. They are: Miss Ethel Masters, Mrs. J. B. Cochran and Miss Pearl Vermillion.

Carthage Evening Press May 8, 1924

Prayer and the memorization of a Bible verse was the usual and expected part of a rural school's daily and weekly routine.

Webb City Sentinel - May 7, 2010

WHEN PRAYER WAS ALLOWED IN SCHOOL

Before 1963, prayer was a standard, and seemingly accepted, activity in America's public schools; heads were bowed en masse at assemblies and other school gatherings without protest. Group prayer was a routine part of the school day for many children, just as standing with hand over heart to recite the Pledge of Allegiance to the flag in their classrooms each morning.

But a lawsuit filed by activist/atheist Madelyn Murray O'Hair in 1963 led to the United States Supreme Court ruling that deemed public school children should have the freedom "from" religion, and that coerced prayer would no longer be allowed in government sponsored schools. Although some organized groups of students still gather in selected areas to pray together today, the court's ruling ended "forced" prayer in school for all children across America.

But BEFORE all that, the May 14, 1954, Webb City Sentinel printed a front-page report that enumerated the success of Webb City school children who had memorized Bible verses in their public classrooms.

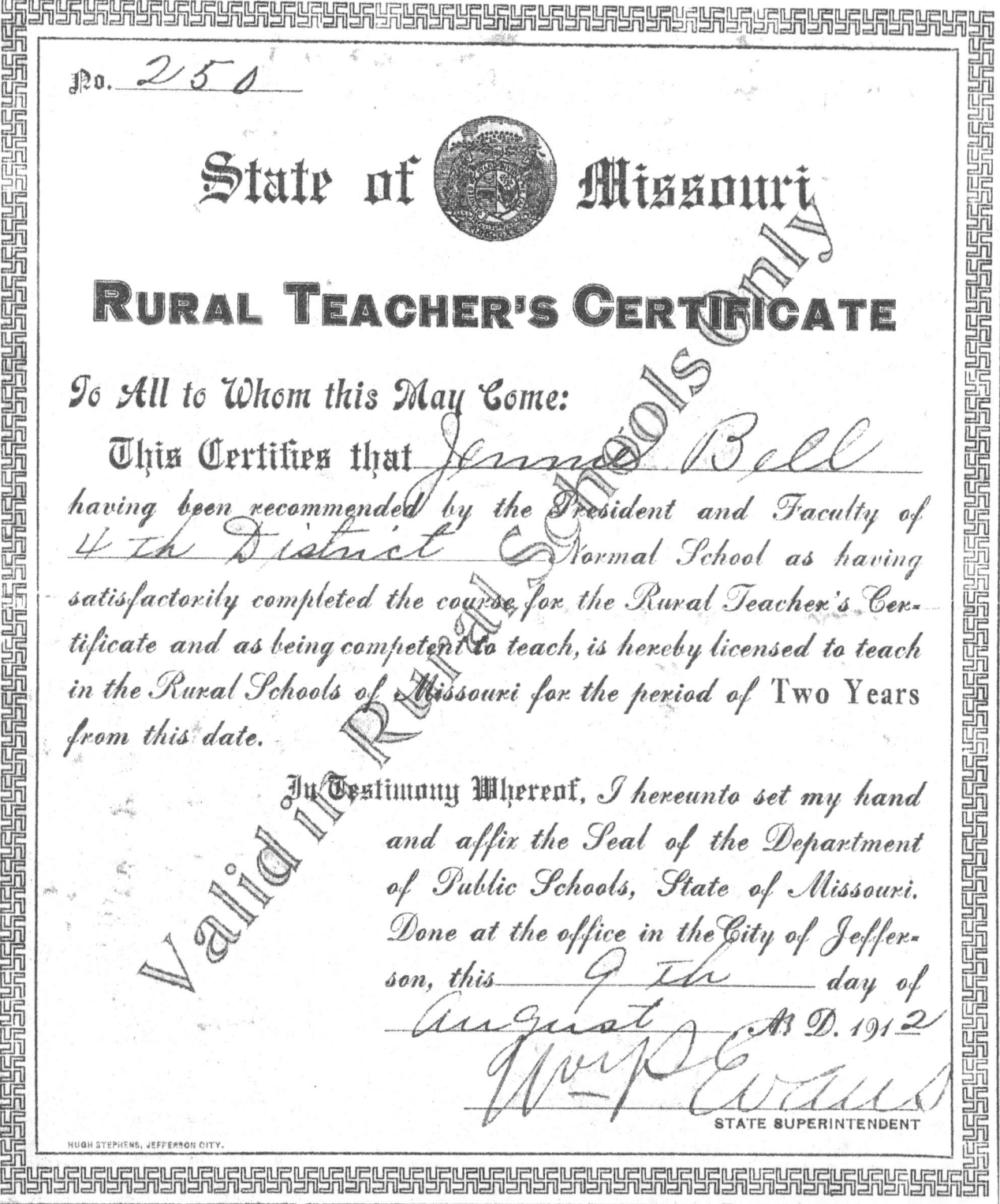

Above is a rural teaching certificate from 1912. How did these certificates differ from what a teacher teaching in town would have had?

Elmira School

LOCATION: SECTION: 17   TOWNSHIP: 29   RANGE: 30   DISTRICT: 51

"Elmira School was built in 1888 and its last class was graduated in 1949. Elmira received its name from a prominent farmer with the last name of Schooler. He donated the land to build the schoolhouse and made it a condition of the agreement to name the schoolhouse after his wife. Elmira was originally located on Road 10 northeast of Carthage. It was moved by Lowell Davis to his Foxfire Farm property northeast of Carthage in 1988."
Carthage Evening Press, June 6, 1988

Assessed value $118,798; Teacher: Florence Carter-Carthage; Grade of Certificate...1; Officers: C. Cottingham-Clerk; Wm. Wilson-President; W. Underwood & Mrs. N. Darral-Members; Enrollment...13; Term...8 months; Condition of house...Clean; Water...Well; Blackboard...Good; Heating...Stove
Jasper County Superintendent's School Report, 1924-25
Courtesy of the Jasper County Record Center

Elmira School today

Do you know or recognize any of the students or teacher in this old photograph of Elmira School? Marjorie Bull, a volunteer in the Jasper County archives office, said a book of old rural school photographs, including one from the 1880's, is being compiled for the archival records. More photographs and identities are needed. The Elmira School was located on County Road 110, northeast of Carthage. The building itself was moved to Red Oak II. Bull said the name Sylvia Binney may be associated with the photo, although it is unknown if she was a teacher, a student or a descendant of one of those pictured. Any information about this photograph, or photographs of other rural school groups would be appreciated, Bull said.

Empire School

LOCATION: SECTION: 23   TOWNSHIP: 29   RANGE: 30   DISTRICT: 53

Teacher: Retta Magoffin; Salary:...$35 monthly, Enrolled: Male...16, Female...20, Total...36; No. present today...33; Term: 7 months; Board: P. C. Bowman-Avilla-Clerk, Chas. McDaniels-President, Chas. Bastin

County School Superintendent's Report, 1893
Courtesy of the Jasper County Record Center

Assessed value $87,260; Teacher: Margaret Carr-Reeds; Salary $65 monthly; Grade of certificate...TT; Officers: T. D. Holmes-Reeds, Clerk; C. B. McDowell-Reeds, President; Ed Holderman-Reeds, Member; Enrollment...16, No. of pupils in Class A...5, B...3, C...5, D...3; Term...7 months; Condition of house... Clean; Water...Carried; Condition of out-buildings: Girls...Good - Boys...Poor; Blackboard...Poor; Maps... Case; Globes...Planetarium; Dictionary...1; Library: No. of vol..221; Value $165; Suitability of books... Good; Free textbooks...No; Heating...Stove

Jasper County School Superintendent's Report, 1924-25
Courtesy of the Jasper County Record Center

Building made into a hog house

Memories of Attending School in a One-Room School
Empire, Deer Creek
Bobby Compton

Bobby Compton 1942

"It was the year of 1935 that I started to school at Miller, Mo. My sister and I walked two and one half miles, one way, to school. I finished the 1st grade when my family moved to Jasper county on a farm 10 miles NE of Carthage. My 2nd grade was at the Deer Creek school. It was a 1 1/2 mile walk to school. We later found out that our farm was in the Empire school district. The next year (1937) I started attending the one room school of Empire. The building was about 24 X 50. There was 13 students and the teacher was Elizabeth McDaniel - Pauline (Yoes) McCormick and I visited our 1937 school teacher at the Sarcoxie nursing home last year (2009). Elizabeth is 102 years old. Her comment to us was that she did not plan to live this long. It was at Empire that I completed the 8th grade. My mother also attended Empire school in the early 1900's.

Classes would start at 9:00 a.m. That would give the students time to do farm chores, feeding animals, milk cows, before it was time to be at school. In season the boys would set traps for rabbits and other fur bearing animals. We would check our traps before school. If a skunk was trapped, we would be late for school, and sometimes sent home to cleanup.

About all the food that we had was produced on the farm. School lunches was sandwiches made with homemade bread, fried eggs, meat produced on the farm, and garden vegetables. If we didn't like what was sent with us, we would try trading with another student. Water was drawn from a hand dug well. A bucket of water was placed at the rear of the room for everyone to drink.

Recess was our favorite time at school. Lunch was 1 hour. We would choose sides and play ball or a completive game. In the winter when there was a good wet snow we would choose sides and have a snowball battle. Each side would build a wall made of snow for protection. The object of the game was to hit a member of the opposing team, he or she would have to move to the other side. The game would end when one side gained the larger members and would charge on the smaller group. The coal fired stove, that heated the building, was a good place to dry gloves and wet clothing.

Once a year there would be a pie supper for a fund raising project. The girls, with the help from their mother, would bake a pie and place it in a colorful box along with other goodies. The boxes would be auctioned and boys would bid trying to buy his favorite girls box. After the auction was over, the boy and girl got together and shared the contents of the box. It was suppose to be a secret who the girl was that owned the box. Most brought a dollar or less but sometimes there would be strong competition and price went up to as much as five dollars.

I consider it a privilege to attend a one room country school and I am grateful for all the teachers, and the education that I received. There is also friendships that was made that has lasted a lifetime."

EMPIRE SCHOOL 1937

Front Row: Bobby Baldwin, Austin Yoes, Kenneth McVey, Frank Knell, Bobby Compton, Delores Knell

Back Row: Morris Gene Bowman, Boyd Carter, Gladys Baldwin, Dorothy Womack, Elizabeth McDaniel, Teacher Pauline Yoes, Bobby Bastin, Fred Knell

Enterprise School
a/k/a Peace Church
LOCATION: SECTION: 15   TOWNSHIP: 27   RANGE: 30   DISTRICT: 53

"Among the historic old churches of Jasper county was the Peace church in Galena township southwest of the Snapp farm........was built by the congregation, each man furnishing a certain number of logs. The church building served for a time also as a schoolhouse."
Joel Thomas Livingston - A History of Jasper County Missouri and Its People, Vol. 1, 1912, Page 30
Courtesy of the Jasper County Record Center

" The first school house was erected near Peace Church in 1845."
F. A. North, History of Jasper County, Missouri, 1883 - Page 1053

"Enterprise school was first called "Peace Church" school. The Peace Church building served for a time as the schoolhouse when the district was organized. The old church log church building was torn down in 1909. Enterprise school was closed in 1944 after consolidating with Carl Junction schools."
Kathy Sidenstricker - wwwjaspercountyschools.org

Based on the information above, it has not been determined if this church was used as Peace Church or Enterprise School.

Teacher: Guy E. Henry-Carl Junction, Salary...$100 monthly & Mildred Thomas-Carl Junction; Salary... $75 monthly; Grades of Certificate...TT; Enrollment...38+34; Term...8 months; Condition of house...Good; Condition of grounds...Clean; Water...Carried; Blackboard...Fair; Dictionary... Old; Free textbooks...Yes; Heating...Modern (Smith)
Jasper County School Superintendent's Report, 1924-25
Courtesy of the Jasper County Record Center

Consolidated to Carl Junction, March 16, 1926
Shirley Sue Fredrickson

Building is now gone

Erie School

LOCATION: SECTION: 6   TOWNSHIP: 27   RANGE: 30   DISTRICT: 104

Teacher: Otis Underwood-Carthage, Salary..$75 monthly; Officers: H. W. Bradley-Carthage, Clerk; P. J. Shipman-Carthage, President; T. A. Roper-Carthage, Member; Enrollment..24; Term..7 months; Condition of house..Clean; Condition of grounds..Clean; Water..Well; Sanitation..Good; Condition of out-buildings.. Very Poor; Blackboard..Fair; Maps..3; Globes..1; Library: No. of vol...100; Free textbooks..Yes; Heating.. Arlington

Jasper County Superintendent's School Report 1924-25
Courtesy of the Jasper County Record Center

ERIE SCHOOL - 1937

Front Row: Alma Edwards, Evelyn Turner, Madge Roper, Anniece Turner, Laura Beth Underwood, Helen Grenninger

Middle Row: ____, ____, Lilian Ogle, Edna Ogle

Victor Turner - Erie

" I recall that in April of 1937 while I and Helen Turner were attending Erie School, a really big snowstorm came along. Drifts were as high as four feet. I remember that Mr. Harris (Evelyn Turner's future father-in-law) came to school with a team of mules and wagon piled high with quilts. The purpose being to take the pupils living east of the school home.

Mr. Harris later said the trip was very strenuous for the mules. They were so wet from perspiration that they had to be dried off in order to prevent pneumonia."

ERIE SCHOOL - 1952-53

ERIE SCHOOL - 1959-60

Excelsior School

LOCATION: SECTION: 14 TOWNSHIP: 27 RANGE: 30 DISTRICT: 114

Teacher: Ella Lambeth-Carthage; Salary..$60 monthly; Officers: J. R. Warden, Clerk, Joe Greninger, President, W. T. Hunter, Member; Enrollment..16; Term..8 months; Condition of house..Clean; Condition of grounds..Clean; Water..Carried; Blackboard..Small; Globes..Broken; Dictionary..1; Library: No. of vol..15; Free textbooks..No; Condition of school records..Good; Heating...King heater

Jasper County School Superintendent's Report, 1893
Courtesy of the Jasper County Record Center

EXCELSIOR SCHOOL

Teacher: Anna Dodson
Pupils in the 1955-56 class: Terry Moss, Charlotte Howard, Erpil Lovelond, Steve Lovelond, Helen Finley, Linda Sue Spor, Barbara Howard, Judy Ann Long, Linda Kay Meyer, Brenda Fay Meyer, Della Southard, Jerry Lovelond, Carl Goodnight

EXCELSIOR SCHOOL - 1952-53

REGISTRATION AT SCHOOLS OCT. 21, 22 AND 23 FOR RATION BOOK NO. 4

Announcement that registration would be made at school houses Thursday, Friday and Saturday, October 21, 22 and 23 for war ration book 4 was made today by J. G. Callaway, Kansas City, district OPA director.

Distribution of the books will be through a procedure similar to that used in distribution of book 2.

Arrangements are being made through the state department of education and with local school authorities for the use of schools and for assistance of teachers.

Every applicant for book 4 will have to present book 3 to a registrar at a schoolhouse and sign a simple application form to be filled out by the registrar. There the registrar will mark the book 3 to indicate the book 4 has been issued. The registrar will place the name and address of the book recipient on the new book.

There will be no registration of any supplies on hand and there will be no tailoring of coupons from the books.

There has been no announcement as to what use will be made of book 4. However, it is presumed that one purpose will be to take the place of earlier expiring books.

Distribution of the books to OPA district storage centers and from those to schools will be under direction of OPA district officials.

The three registration days will be the same throughout Missouri. The registration will be completed nationally between October 20 and 31.

Carthage Evening Press, 1943

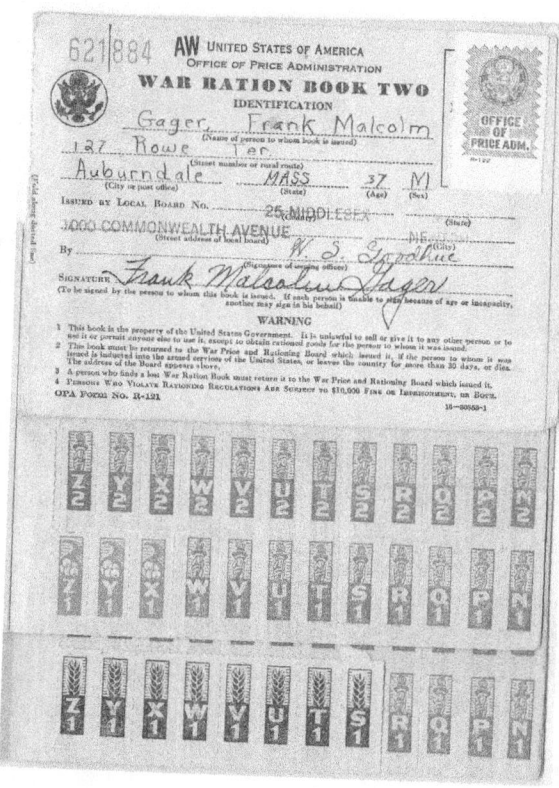

War rations book and coupons were given to each American family, dictating how much gasoline, tires, sugar, meat, silk, shoes, nylon and other items any one person could buy.

Families would trade rations with each other to get the product they needed.

Fidelity School

LOCATION: SECTION: 9 TOWNSHIP: 27 RANGE: 31 DISTRICT: 116

"Report for the term ending the 20th of June 1884. Number of pupils enrolled 42; number of day's attendance of all pupils 1086; average number of days attended by each student, 42; number of days taught 60; The pupils having the highest average of scholarship during term, Matilda Woods. The following are the names of those having 100 in punctuality and deportment during the term; Victoria Grubb, Gabie Corwine, Myrta Cupp, Nettie Young, Cara Bardoe, George Shivley, Rachel Shivley, Bertie Cupp, Andrew Hopkins, Joseph Lundy, Vilah Newton and Thos. Smith.
Thanking all patrons and pupils of this district for their kindness toward me and recommending this school to teachers. I close this, my third term at this place. CLARA B. LUNDY, Teacher."
Carthage Banner, June 1884

"Founded in 1922, the Fidelity schoolhouse, on U.S. 71-Alt, Fidelity, still stands, through its time as a one-room schoolhouse from 19-22-65, to its time as the residence of a family from 1965-79, to its time as another family's residence from 1981 to the present."
The Carthage Evening Press June 24, 1987

FIDELITY SCHOOL - 1960
Ruth Carter, teacher

SCHOOL HOUSE BURNS

FIDELITY BUILDING, A LAND MARK, IS DESTROYED

Children Save Books But Library is Lost—Not to be Rebuilt at Once and School Sessions to End

The Fidelity school house, seven miles south of Carthage on Grand avenue, one mile south of the W. N. Haggard store, was destroyed by fire which broke out in the roof at 2 o'clock yesterday afternoon. There was no means of fighting the flames.

The children and teacher saved their books and small equipment. The school library was burned.

The fire was discovered by H. G. Frame, an insurance man, of Carthage, who was driving along the road. He went to the school door and told the children to get their books and march out of the building as the roof was on fire. They did so without mishap.

Saved the Coal Anyway

One small boy ran home screaming. When he was overtaken and told not to cry he complained that he had left his pencil in the school house and that it had burned. Another pupil rescued a half bucket of coal that was sitting beside the stove and after dumping the contents of the bucket into the road went back and hurled the bucket into the burning room.

The school has been taught by Miss Dolly Jeans. The directors of the district met last night and decided not to make an attempt to rebuild the structure immediately. No suitable place for holding school was obtainable and no school will be held in the district the remainder of this term, it was decided.

Structure Built 40 years ago

The school building was an old land mark, having been built 40 years ago. The frame was of timbers hewn from the native forest. The building was insured for $500. It would cost about $2,000 to replace it new. The structure was 244 by 36 feet in size. A defective flue is believed to have caused the fire.

Carthage Evening Press
Feb. 4, 1922

Carthage Press file photo
The old Fidelity Schoolhouse as it appeared around 1964-65 as its years of service were being phased out as part of the rural school consolidation program of that period.

Top: Fidelity School in 1967
Bottom Right: Fidelity School building today
Left: Article about the school

Forest School

LOCATION: SECTION: 32　　TOWNSHIP: 28　　RANGE: 29　　DISTRICT: 106

Founded in 1893 and was also known as Whisner and Webster.

Assessed value $97,370; Teacher: Mrs. Pearl Evans-Sarcoxie; Grade of certificate..3; Board: Roscoe Henry-Sarcoxie, Clerk, J. R. Southern-Sarcoxie, President, Chas. Begley-Sarcoxie, Member; Enrollment..6; No. Present..41; Term..8 months; Condition of house..Clean; Condition of grounds..Clean; Condition of outbuildings..Fair; Blackboard..Slate; Maps..1; Free textbooks..Yes; Condition of school records..Fair; Heating.. Hart

Jasper County School Superintendent's Report - 1924-25
Courtesy of the Jasper County Record Center

Forest was moved and is now a home.

FOREST SCHOOL - 1950-51

Back Row:　Marjorie Bull, teacher, Robyn Lewis, Linda Ross, Altha Jo Dauray, Sue Kaylor, Marvin Williams Gary Coates

Front Row:　____ Kaylor, Tommy Grace, Frankie Greathouse, Billy Lewis, Roy Greathouse, Don Coates, ____ Broadway, Jackie Dilworth, ____ ____, Gaylen Ross

Forest School 1928

A School Reunion, 500

"Despite the rain approximately 500 persons attended the home-coming Sunday at the Frorest school, formerly known as the Whisner school, three miles north of Sarcoxie.......

John W. Dennison, Carthage jeweler, and a form teacher of the school, presided. He was teacher at he school during the years of 1902, 1903, and 1904. His brother, Jess M. Dennison, who now lives in that community, taught six terms at the school and their father, the late W. M. Dennison, was a teacher there four terms.

An interesting feature of the program was a history of the school district read by a former teacher, Vernie Whisner, a grandson of the late S. D. Whisner at whose home the first meeting to organize the district was held May 8, 1884. Mr. Whisner was the contractor on the first two school buildings erected. The first petitioners were S. D. Whisner, John Deck, William Coates, Jacob Rimmer, T. W. Johnson and John Meador. Directors elected at that meeting were T. W. Johnson for a 3-year term and S. D. Whisner of one year.

On June 2, 1884, voters of that district met at the Whisner home for the purpose of voting bonds to build and furnish a school house. After a bond of $700 had been voted for the building expenses, another bond of $40 was voted for incidental fund. The building was erected at a cost of $475. A 6-month term began November 3, 1884, with 39 pupils attending.

In the spring of 1888, a cyclone wrecked the school building making it necessary for the remains to be torn down. The school was rebuilt at a cost of $240. In April 1899, this building was totally destroyed by fire. The present school building was completed in August of that year at a cost of $449."

The Carthage Press, Thursday, August 24, 1933

Forest Mills School
a/k/a Magnet
LOCATION: SECTION: 9   TOWNSHIP: 28   RANGE: 30   DISTRICT: 79

Magnet school preceded Forest Mills in District 79.
"Magnet, the first school to serve this area, was located in the same square mile as Bethany Baptist Church. This site was about 3/4 mile south of the present school. In 1890, Magnet Mining Company sold the land by warranty deed to the school district.
The teachers of the school from 1894 to 1920 were Grace Swain, Ada Stanley, Mabel Swingle, and Valeara Seela.
In 1920 Magnet School burned. From 1920 to 1924 some of the students went to Jasper Rural School. School was also held in a log cabin on what then was known as the Greenwood farm. Mrs. Mona Edwards was teacher at this time. She taught a total of 16 pupils.
There was a great deal of controversy over the location of the new school, but finally school began at Forest Mill in 1924. The teacher was Opal Ferguson. the first graduate of Forest Mills was John Wickstrom.
Some school property of earlier years included a coal house, one chair, 35 desks, a Victrola (still at the school and in working condition) and a globe (which was stolen before the end of that year).
Some additional property purchased was a circulating heater and piano in 1936, a duplicating machine and new coal heating unit in 1945, a telephone installed in 1958 and a refrigerator in 1960. Electrical service was installed at the school about 1938.
School was held in two rooms for seven years. The largest enrollment recorded was in 1952 when there were 55 pupils."
Courtesy of Carthage Evening Press May 13, 1972

FOREST MILLS SCHOOL 1940

Lillie (Thorn) Tatum
Forest Mill, Empire and Reeds

I went to 3 rural schools. My first 3 grades I went to Forest Mill. My 4th grade I went to Empire. My 5th, 6th & 7th I went to Reeds. Then my 8th grade I went to Forest Mill again. I had some cousins and brother & sisters that went to the same school. My 8th grade teacher was Mrs. May Cochran. She was very nice and a very good teacher.

Something very bad, but also funny (now), happened when I was in the 8th grade. We had gone to church one night and when I went to school the next day I had forgotten to take some matches that I used the night before to light the lamp with (we didn't have electricity in those days.) I took the matches out of my pocket while we were at recess. My cousin wanted to see the matches (it was a book of matches). I didn't want to give them to her, but she kept insisting and so I gave them to her. She proceeded to light a piece of paper that was sticking out of a piece of siding on the school building. Some of the rest of us put the fire out with our hands. Then she went into the toilet which was an outside toilet and set some toilet tissue on fire and kicked it in the stool. It caught the paper down there on fire. The toilets had vents coming out of the roof. The smoke was boiling out of the vent. We ran in the school to get some containers to carry water in to put out the fire. Eugene Lindsey ran in the school and told Mrs. Cochran that the girl's toilet was on fire. She came out and got a water hose and put the fire out. We didn't get to have recess for 4 weeks.

> The new Forest Mill school opened yesterday in the house fitted up on the Franklin Greenwood farm. There were 13 or 14 students who answered roll call the first day. The enrollment is expected to total about 16. The school is a subscription school, there being no regular school funds available in the newly organized district, and in reality is not a part of the state or county public school system but Walter Colley, county superintendent of schools, has agreed to supervise the school and it will be conducted strictly along the lines laid down for the rural public schools.
>
> **Carthage Evening Press 9-19-1923**

Front Row L-R: Johnnie Dumm, Russell Long, Marty Lasiter, Steven Lee, Duane Pennington, Johnny Wickstrom, Valerie Pennington, Marcia Cowan, Robyn Willoughly, Gene Lambeth

2nd Row: Eugene Lasiter, Peggy Mitchell, Debbie Holland, Dennis Lasiter, Allen Lee, Teresa Wickstro Karen Holland

3rd Row: Teacher: Mrs. Ruth Sneed, Susan Wendleston, Diana Cowan, Brenda Howell, Carol Cowan Peggy Curry, Ginger Mitchell, Steven Tilton, Brent Curry,

Galesburg School

LOCATION: SECTION: 10   TOWNSHIP: 29   RANGE: 33   DISTRICT: 37

"Located 4 miles NW of Neck City. Built in the middle 1800's. Second time built in 1893. The school consolidated with Asbury in 1940. Closed July 21, 1964."
Courtesy of Kathy Sidenstricker

"Term began September 23rd and continues six months. Building and furniture second class. Seating capacity 46. District enumeration 48, enrollment over fifteen years of age 7, total 40, present 32. Here we find order, the movements of the pupils to and from recitation regulated, and pupils who recite do not depend upon the teacher to perform that duty for them. Too many teachers hold their pupils up and lead them through the recitation. Remember that what the pupil does not recite independently is not recited. Mr. Booton is bringing the Galesburg school up to a level with other leading schools of the county. It pays to employ a good teacher even if to do so requires the payment of a reasonable sum for his services."
Jasper County School Report by S. A. Underwood, 1878
Joel Thomas Livingston, A History of Jasper County, Missouri and Its People. Vol. 1, 1912 - Page 103
Courtesy of the Jasper County Record Center

Galesburg Girls 1925

Unkown Galesburg Boys 1950-51

Assessed value $96,306; Teacher, Bess McMullen, Oronogo; Salary..$75 monthly; Grade of Certificate..2; Board: D. L. Hancock, Clerk, C. R. Mitchell, President, Mrs. Jessie McMullen, Member; Enrollment..26; No. of pupils in Class A..5, B..8, C..5, D..7; No. present..25; Term..8 months; Condition of house..Clean; Condition of grounds..Clean; Water..Carried; Condition of out-buildings..Good; Blackboard..Old slate; Maps..Case; Globes..1; Dictionary..1; Free textbooks..Yes; Condition of school records..Good; Ventilation..Good; Heating..Smith
Jasper County Superintendent's School Report 1924-25
Courtesy of the Jasper County Record Center

Galesburg School 1950   Courtesy of Kathy Sidenstricker & Judy Crutcher Hughes

GALESBURG 1951-52 - Erma Allen, teacher   Courtesy of Kathy Sidenstricker & Jeanne Newby

Front Row: Vernon Masters, Marietta Smith, Larry Miller, Mary Leggett, Sue Smith, Catherine Howard, Carl Landes, Rosemary Davis

Middle Row: Carolyn Smoker, Rosalie Smoker, David Miller, Judith Troyer, Arthur Landes, Mary Smith, Beverly Miller, Albert Landes, Carlene Gunlock, Robert Miller

Back Row: Carol Gunlock, Shirley Gully, Ethel Howard, Herbert Miller, Donnie Lucas, Phyllis Dobbins, Erma Allen, Ronnie Gunlock, Gary Minkler, George Landes,

Garden Dell School

LOCATION: SECTION: 14   TOWNSHIP: 29   RANGE: 32   DISTRICT: 6

Assessed value $196,435; Teacher, Verna Fox-Carthage; Salary...$94 monthly; Board: R. C. Wright, Clerk, C. A. Billingsley, President; Mrs. R. Wright and Mrs. Frank Potter, Members; Enrollment...35, No. present...33; Term...8 months; Condition of house...Good; Condition of grounds... Clean; Water...Well; Condition of out-buildings...Not very good; Blackboard... Good; Maps...Case; Globes...1; Dictionary... Old; Library: No. of vol. 100; Free text books...No; Condition of school records... Good Ventilation...Good; Heating...Smith
Jasper County School Superintendent's Report 1924-25 Courtesy of the Jasper County Record Center

GARDEN DELL SCHOOL
Courtesy of the Carthage Evening Press - 1964

"The district was first called No. 6 and formed in 1870. J. W. Johnson, S. W. Johnson, John Hendricks were elected to the first Board of Education. Hendricks contributed an acre of land - the northwest corner of Route D and County Road 18 and a building was erected to serve as the first school.
Taxpayers became aware the building was not larger enough for the growing enrollment and proposition to finance construction of a large building was considered in the 1876 election. It was defeated abut two years later a similar measure was adopted. The first building then was sold and a larger one was constructed.
In 1879, the district purchased an adjoining acre of land to the west and north and a fence was installed to enclose the entire two-acre campus.
It was used for educational purposes and today, in converted condition, serves as a residence."
Marvin VanGilder - The Carthage Evening Press, Sept. 6, 1972

Trouble at Garden Dell - School Directors Under Arrest for Helping Chastise an Unruly Pupil.
"There is quite a commotion out in the Garden Dell school district, northwest of Carthage, three miles this side of Alba. The trouble grew out of the whipping of Frank Stuckmyer, a 17-year-old boy who is one of the big students of the school, and as a result two of the directors are under arrest charged with assault.
According to the story of B. A. Shuper, the teacher, Stuckmyer had been boasting that he had "his knife sharpened for the teacher." Accordingly the teacher was on his guard and when young man was guilty of alleged impertinence soon afterward he demanded of him that he apologize to the school or take such punishment as the teacher saw fit to inflict. The boy declined to accept either of these propositions, and the teacher went to the school board for advice. The directors were unanimously of the opinion that Stuckmyer was acting the part of a bully and should received a thrashing. After procuring an elm switch five feet nine inches in length, they placed it in the hands of the teacher and proceeded to the school house to see that the chastisement was

properly administered.

The teacher waded into his task heroically, but the pupil was not disposed to meekly submit, and a fierce struggle ensued in which the switch had to be laid aside. Seeing that the teacher was not meeting with unqualified success, two of the directors, Messrs., Charles Ferree and Robert Ross, stepped in to give him a lift. Just what they did is not clear, but it is presumed they joined in the wrestle, as it is declared they did not strike the boy. Mead Hickman, the third director, did not get into the encounter.

GARDEN DELL SCHOOL 1915

As a result of the difficulty a warrant was sworn out for Messrs. Ferree and Ross on the charge of assault, and a constable served the papers on them the next day. They will have a hearing later. Sentiment is said to be considerably divided on the question, some sympathizing with the boy and some with the teacher."
Carthage Evening Press Mar. 20, 1900

"Report for third month, ending Dec. 23: Who number of days attended by all pupils, 618; average attendance each day ___; days taught 18. The following pupils received 100 in attendance and punctually:

Ora Cupp, Olive Folger, Anna Weeks, Mary Folger, Emma Gause, Maud Cupp, Jennie Folger, Fannie Bryant, Bertie Owens, George Weeks, Atba Green, Frank Folger, Arde Owens, Noah Hall and Owen Weeks.

Alice E. Scantlin, Teacher

The Carthage Banner

JASPER COUNTY SOFTBALL TOURNEY FINALS PLAYED

Carthage, Mo., Aril 18.—The finals in the Jasper county rural softball tournament were reached today as Garden Dell squeaked past two opponents to gain the championship trophy in the one-room division.

Garden Dell edged Green Grove, 13-12, in the semi-final tilt and defeated Arthur, 7-6, in the championship game.

Arthur outscored Green Grove, 6-2, in the consolation finals.

In the two-room division, Zinc-Ite mauled Lakeside, 40-10, for the championship trophy. Although winning second place Lakeside was not awarded a trophy.

Carthage Evening Press

GARDEN DELL SCHOOL - 1956-57

Gem School

LOCATION: SECTION: 6   TOWNSHIP: 27   RANGE: 31   DISTRICT: 113

Assessed value $102,908; Teacher: Mrs. Myrtle Cloud - Sarcoxie, Salary: $85 monthly; Grade of certificate: 1; Board: G. E. Kinney, Clerk; H. S. Winder, President; R. E. Grieb and G. E. Kinney, Members; Enrollment.. 24; Term: 8 months; Condition of house..Good; Condition of grounds..Dry; Condition of out-buildings..Good; Blackboard..Good; Maps..0; Globes..1; Dictionary..Old; Library: No. of vol..200; Value $50; Free text books:..No; Condition of school records:..Good; Heating:..Coal stove

Jasper County School Superintendent's Report - 1924-25
Courtesy of the Jasper County "Record Center

Grand Concert at the Gem School House

GEM SCHOOL

"We are glad that it is our privilege to give a favorable report about the concert held at the Gem School House, March 7th, under the direction of Pro. Graham. Early in the evening we saw several young men, with their better halves, winding their way to that hallowed spot; I being a Granger, you know, could not get there before eight o'clock. When we arrived friend D. assured me the exercises were nearly over and that had better save our quarters. Upon entering we found it had not yet commenced. The house was packed, crammed and running over, and not withstanding the limited latitude, all seemed to enjoy the music hugely. The stage was beautifully ornamented with evergreens and pictures, and when the class occupied it it was a beautiful scene, but hardly large enough to accommodate the class well. It would have been better if they had placed the larger ladies and gentlemen near the edge of the stage, as we noticed some of the smaller ones were pushed off during the performance.

The time having arrived for the exercises to commence, the class took their places and the Professor with his magic Wand in hand led us in that good song, "There is always a Welcome for Thee." The music was all good, among the best was the "Helping hand." "Mother,, watch the little feet." "Lift up your heads." "Beautiful Home." "Glory to God in the highest." "Beautiful Dewdrops." "Summer Morn." "Truly Yours." "Go to work on the farm." "Sunday Night." "What will people say." "We will have to mortgage the farm," best of all. This coincided with our views exactly, and we think it did with all who were present, from the cheers that came from the audience-even a little dog that was in the rear of the house said, "amen to that." We hope this song will have its weight and that those young men will not have to mortgage their farms to the merchants for yellow ribbons for their better halves.

After the "Good Night" song was sung a vote of thanks was given Mr. Graham for his services as a teacher. The class also gave a vote of thanks to Mrs. Mollie Hood for her services as organist, which she rendered so successfully. We now returned home, feeling that the concert had been a grand success and that all had been "muchly" benefitted. The good people of Jenkins Creek shall ever have our best wishes-especially the young ladies that sung in the concert-as they travel "along the river of time." *Editor -Carthage Banner, Mar. 19, 1874*

Charlene Purviance - Teacher
Gem, Union, Monitor Schools

"When I was nineteen I taught at Chapman School south of Pierce City, south of Hwy. 60, Jolly Mills. Now they have moved that school house to where Jolly Mill Park is now. I was just there one year. I taught for $50 a month and paid $10 for room and board, so I had $40 a month left. An elderly lady lived there, Mrs. Belle Baldwin. She was born back east (near where Henry Wadsworth Longfellow hung out) and they had a big farm.

> New School at Parshley
> The Gem school house at Parshley is to be torn down and moved away as soon as a new building has been erected on the ground. Contract for the new building has been let to Wilbur Cale of Sarcoxie and work has already begun. The old Gem school building has stood on its present site for nearly 50 years and is in a bad state of repair.
> Carthage Press Aug. 19, 1920

They knew I had just graduated from high school and was single. There was no contract that I could not marry but they didn't need one…I had enough to do. I had 27 students and had never taught a day in my life. The one stipulation for teaching in a rural school was that I had my first eight years in a rural school. Dry Valley School was part of that and it was a large rural school. I think there were sometimes fifty or sixty students.

Mrs. Lee Dumar was a sports person and rather mannish. There was a big woods back of the school house so one day at noon she said, "I brought my rife, let's go squirrel hunting". This was her first year of teaching and incidentally it was her last. With all the kids behind her, we went down in the woods. I cannot remember her firing the gun but it was on ready. We were looking for squirrels down in that timber, about forty of us. People would die now.

The boys would get the game up of Fox and Hounds. The game was sort of a race for the hen and they didn't stay on the school grounds. They roamed and were gone too long but no causalities.

The first school I taught in was down by Pierce City, Chapman School. It was south and west of Pierce City. I didn't get the school until the next year. There were applications from everywhere for those school so I failed to get a job. The woman who took my place offered to take it for $75 dollars a month, which was the beginning of the Depression. You could probably do their grocery shopping for that so I went home with no school to teach.

I had saved about $100 dollars, how I don't know. How do you save $100 from $50 a month and help your folks buy groceries? So, anyway I had enough to pay tuition to go to Carthage Junior College. If you know about it, it belonged to the City of Carthage. The first and the second semester I didn't have the money to pay tuition so I was going to stay home and try to get me a school and they called and said the school had been turned into a WPA school and there would be no tuition. I could work in the library the dean had permission to hire a librarian, you know, someone for the library each hour. I could work several hours for $16 a month. I wasn't going to miss that! I spend it for my room and I did my own cooking so I got to finish out that one year of college.

The next year I taught at Union School. It was south of Reeds and east of Dudman. I had twenty students and bless their hearts; some of them came from homes where there wasn't much money and I was just about as bad off. There was a settlement of people back in some woods north of the school; I don't know what they called that, Pumpkin Center or Rabbit Town. There was a little girl in the second grade that came to school one morning and said, "Well, I have a new baby brother," I said that was sure nice. Nothing nice ever happened to those kids, you know. I said "I know you're sure proud and I bet your daddy and mother are proud." She said, "Oh, Daddy doesn't know anything about it, he hasn't seen the last three kids."

I taught at Union two years. There I had a boy, I won't tell names, who caused trouble in school south of there and the Director said they would give him a job doing chores for me and he was janitor. When I started to explain a session or something, he would get up and stoke the stove and make all kinds of noise. Well, to get along with him, I put up with some of that in a nice way. One day he caused trouble on the play ground and I told him to come in and take a seat. He said, "I won't do it." I think I was eighteen or nineteen and it was unexpected when I shoved him into one of those double seats and he was lying down and I slapped his face just awful. You know he never resisted and the rest of the year he didn't give me any static. Four years I heard from that boy. After he was a grown man, he would write and send me a valentine signed "From Your Bad Boy".

After Union I went to Gem. Parsley was a different community entirely with well-to-do farmers and many of them were members of that Christian Church west of the highway, Center Church. There was a store that adjoined the campus. They played together summers and they were good kids and good families, which was a little bit of a change. I taught there five years.

We had a tornado one morning. I was allowed on days that I gave the county test to the 5th through the 8th grades (the older kids) to let the other kids have a holiday. The parents knew about it a day or two before. The papers were laid out on the desk with reference material and the kids were coming in and The sky was getting dark. One child came in when the wind started blowing nd said "the wind turned me upside down coming up that hill and blew me over." Nothing would stop me from giving the test and about the time we were ready to start the sun got away from the window. I said let's all get back here in the corner. No one got hurt but it blew the coal house away and turned the outhouses over. Mrs. Miller was the custodian and her daughter went to school there; she said her mother fainted when the storm was going on.

A lot of damage, but not one of the kids got hurt, but one girl who was not quite as bright as some of the others didn't come to the corner very fast and she was looking out the back window and saw the coal house blow over. She called me Miss Charlene. She said. "Oh! Miss Charlene, the coalhouse is blown over, it is not over yet." The next day was Election Day and I dismissed school because that was the rule then. That day the custodian came and examined the windows and said that bank of windows was hanging just by a hook and a big nail.

After Gem, I went part of a year west of Carthage, a three-room school called Monitor School. I was teaching the first and second grade and at Christmas time.

A little after we declared war with Germany I was concerned because I didn't know what the principal was doing, he was driving from Sarcoxie and I was riding with him. They kept that school open for me.

Sarcoxie had built a grade school, Wildwood; four nice rooms and a big auditorium. Starting with two teachers for each grade. I don't think there was a change in that staff for a long time. When the time came around, one of the Directors said, "You need to go talk to the Superintendent. We had a meeting last night and I told them about you and your experience." I am sure others knew me too that were on the board. I went over and talked to Mr. Evert Thomas, the Superintendent. It was sometime that evening or the next day, they said they wanted me to teach out the rest of the year there. It was a long drive I was making every morning beyond Carthage and back, I was going to retire or resign from school. Wildwood was three miles from my home, so I felt I could not turn that down. I felt sure it would be a lasting job and it was. I taught there, I think six or seven years and then married and we moved to Joplin.

A typical day in a rural school. We usually had a Bible verse or two, the Pledge of Alliance and the Lord's Prayer. It was good in those days. Then I would have Reading classes in groups with the first, then second right on through eight grades, but not every year. They would teach the 5th and 7th one year and the next year they would teach the 6th and 8th. Some kids took 6th grade work and then went back and took 5th grade work, but they were so near alike that there wasn't any problem and that was the way the county had it set up. When the teacher went with them, she had no school for the rest of them. I hadn't thought of that.

At Gem, we raised money for the school with pie suppers and it wasn't very much money, but it went a long way.

We had a Christmas program at night so the parents could come. At the three rural schools I taught, everyone brought dinner, laid it out and everyone would eat on the last day of school."

GEM SCHOOL 1952-53 Twyla Arnett, teacher   Courtesy of the Jasper County Record Center

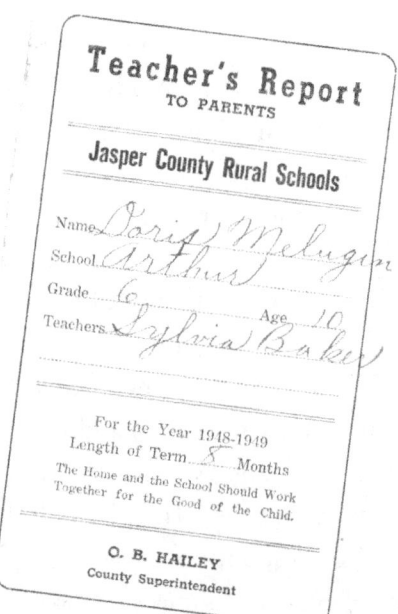

Report cards from the 1940's

Georgia City School

LOCATION: SECTION 5   TOWNSHIP: 29   RANGE: 33   DISTRICT: 38

"Georgia City District: Jacob Myers, J. M. Woolomes and Thomas Enos, Directors; Miss Sue Gray, teacher. Term of five months began September 29th, District enumeration 103, enrollment over fifteen yeas of age 8, total 50, present 20. Building second-class and furniture first-class. Seating capacity 50. Miss Gray has taught eleven terms in the county and is now teaching her third term in this district. An in phonetic spelling witnessed showed that the pupils had been patiently and thoroughly drilled in orthoepy which, though essential and interesting, is overlooked in some of our schools. The district is the owner of a large and well bound bible, the only one, I believe, owned by any district of the county. Georgia City pays her teachers liberally and invariably has good schools."

Jasper County School Report by S. A. Underwood -1878
Joel Thomas Livingston - A History of Jasper County, Missouri and Its People, Vol. I, Page 106, Pub. 1912

Teacher: Anna Sailer; Salary: $30 monthly; Board: J. P. Eilway, Clerk; G. A. Bridgewater, President; H. W. Enis; Term: 8 months; Enrolled: Male...11, Female...18; Total...29; No. present today...22; Condition of Blackboard.. Not very good;   Condition of building...Very good; Condition of furniture..Good; Condition of apparatus.. Maps only; Condition of grounds, out-houses...Good.

County School Superintendent's Report - 1893
Courtesy of the Jasper County Record Center

Georgia City consolidated to Asbury, 1919
Courtesy of Sue Fredrickson

Georgia City No More

"Georgia City, in the northwest part of Jasper County, yesterday was wiped off the map-not by fire, storm or flood-but by a brief order of the county court granting a petition presented by Mrs. Guinn Young asking that the streets and alleys of the platted village be vacated and the land formally returned to farm acreage.

Georgia City, platted March 23, 1868, by the late John C. Guinn, at one time was a thriving country trading point with two stores and a blacksmith shop. A school stood there and as officials could best recall today there at one time was a post office. However, with the advent of the motor car the need for the trading village passed and some years ago the school which had been a center of activities was consolidated with Asbury district and the school moved.

It was following this that Mr. Guinn, objecting to certain features of the consolidation which wiped out the school, moved to south of Carthage, thus withdrawing the tax support which his large personal tax assessment previously had given the district.

Mr. Guinn's removal was the final death blow to the small village and only the wreckage of some former buildings now remain. The land around the city belongs to Mrs. Young who inherited it from her father's estate."

The Carthage Evening Press, Feb. 11, 1930 Page 1, Column 3

Rural School teachers - Names Unknown

Green Grove School

LOCATION: SECTION: 2 TOWNSHIP: 28 RANGE: 31 DISTRICT: 78

"Dating her report June 5, 1882, Mrs. Alice E. Scatilin filed the teacher's record for the term's third and final month at Green Grove School near Avilla, revealing enrollment of 38, with average daily attendance of 33.
Perfect attendance awards were earned by Belle Franklin, Ina Hatten, Cora Hatten, Maggie Pine, Hettie Franklin, Annie Smith, Mattie Smith and Belle Carson."
A Brief For History-Marvin L VanGilder - Aug. 15, 1977
Courtesy of the Jasper County Record Center

Green Grove School Today

Assessed value $158,243; Teacher: Sylvia Jones-Carthage; Grade of Certificate..TT; Board: E. C. Sherrill-Carthage, Clerk; J. D. McRae-Carthage, President; Mrs. Laura Baker-Carthage, Member; Enrollment...40; No. present..39; Term...8 months; Condition of house...Good; Condition of grounds...Clean; Water...Well; Sanitation...Good; Blackboard...Slate; Maps...Case; Globes...0; Dictionary...Small; Library: No. of vol...100; Value...$50; Suitability of books:..Fair; Free text books...No; Condition of school records...Good; Heating...Stove; Remarks:..All news seats
Jasper County School Superintendent's Report 1924-25 Courtesy of the Jasper County Record Center

Green Grove School 1954-55
Front Row L to R: ____, ____, ____, Claude Ralston, ____, ____, Butter Baugh
Middle Row: ____, J. W. Gandy, ____, Ben Allen, Steve Hoover, Larry Fox, Mary Ann Lovecamp
Back Row: Velma Case, teacher, Nadine Wheat, George Heiston, Larry Potter, ____, ___, ___

GREEN GROVE SCHOOL 1940

Henry School

LOCATION: SECTION: 32   TOWNSHIP: 28   RANGE: 29   DISTRICT: 81

Teacher, A. J. Keeling; Salary: $33 1/3 per month; Board: W. H. Williams-Avilla, Clerk; Peter Fishburn-Avilla, President; Bev. Henry & Walter Tremble; Enrolled: Male...10, Female...8, Total...18; No present today...14

Jasper County School Superintendent's Report 1893
Courtesy of the Jasper County Record Center

Assessed Valuation: $80,683; School Officers: F. E. Melin-Reeds, Clerk; J. E. Henry-Avilla, President; Harry McFaddon & ___ Dilley-Avilla, Members; Teacher: Myrtle King-Avilla; Salary...$65 monthly; Grade of Certificate...2; Enrollment...19; No. of pupils in Class A...6, B...1, C...6, D...6; No. present...18; Condition of house...Poor; Condition of grounds...Clean; Water...Carried; Condition of out-buildings...Fair; Blackboard...Fair; Globes...1; Library: No. of vol...25; Value...$10; Free text books...No; Heating...Stove

Jasper County Superintendent's Report 1924-256
Courtesy of the Jasper County Record Center

Henry 1944-45

Henry photos courtesy of Kathy Sidenstricker
wwwejaspercoutyschools.org

Henry School 1940

Henry School 1942-43

High Hill School

LOCATION: SECTION: 19   TOWNSHIP: 28   RANGE: 31   DISTRICT: 89

"The new High Hill school, five miles southwest of Carthage, erected on the site of the old building destroyed last January by fire, has been completed.

The structure, which cost approximately $9,000, is modern in every detail for a rural school. Equipment is expected to be moved into the building this weekend and classes will be held in the new structure beginning next week.

A formal opening will be held Friday night, November 9, under the sponsorship of the High Hill Parent-Teacher Association. The public is invited to attend. It is planned to have a kitchen shower for the school at this time.

Since the other structure was destroyed by fire, classes have been conducted in the three-car garage on the school grounds. Members of the board made ready the garage immediately after the fire and the pupils have been comfortably situated there since. There are 14 pupils enrolled at High Hill. Mrs. Marguerite Lown is the teacher.

HIGH HILL   Courtesy of Kathy Sidenstricker & Karen Oheim

The new structure was financed through bonds voted by the High Hill school district and the insurance from the former building. It measures 30 by 40 feet and the exterior is on concrete blocks.

The large main room for the classes, has a stage at one end, to be used for entertainments., Five modern tables are hinged to the west wall so they may be raised or lowered to be used by the pupils during study periods for drawing or for studying. Chairs also have been installed for use at the tables.

On the north and east walls are three tiers of book shelves, sufficient to hold about 1,000 books. The shelves are placed near enough to the floor that the smaller children can reach the books without assistance. The room has 22 feet of blackboard space and the same amount of bulletin space above that. The cloak room is spacious and there are two rest rooms, eight by six feet each.

The structure also includes a modern kitchen and utility room. The kitchen is equipped with a sink, with hot and cold water, and a stove and metal cupboards are to be installed. The furnace and water heater are in the utility room. Butane gas will be used for heating.

The school directors are Rex McNew, president; G. W. Southard and Maurice Salsbury, T. B. Hood of Carthage was the contractor for the building."

The Carthage Evening Press Nov. 3, 1951

HIGH HILL 1955-56

High Hill 1959   Teacher, Marguerite Lortz

High Point School

LOCATION: SECTION: 36   TOWNSHIP: 29   RANGE: 31   DISTRICT: 63

Assessed value $127,273; Teacher: Elton Kirksey-Carthage; Grade of Certificate:..TT; Board: Walter P. Brown, Clerk: Raymond Lambeth, President; F. B. Leidy, Member; Enrollment:...17; No. of pupils in Class A...4, B...1 C...7, D...5; No. present...17; Term begins: Sept. 15; No. Months...7; Condition of house... Poor, Condition of grounds...Grassy; Water:..Well; Sanitation...Good; Condition of out-buildings...Rebuilt; Blackboard..Poor; Maps..Case; Globes...1; Dictionary...1 large; Library: No. of vol...100; Value...$75; Suitability of books...Good; Free text books...No; Heating...Stove

Jasper County School Superintendent's Report, 1924-25
Courtesy of the Jasper County Record Center

"High Point is one of the old districts of Jasper County. It first was part of the old Monitor district, formed not too many years after the ending of the Civil War. Because of the long distances pupils were forced to travel, it was decided to form a new school district and High Point was born. It was organized in 1875. School was held there until 1945, when it was decided to transport pupils, some going to Carthage, Carterville and Mineral grade schools. High Point students of the area selected their own school........

"High Point school building was located on a 2-acre tract on Highway 96 about four miles west of Carthage.

The High Point district voted in 1958 to merge with the Pleasant Valley school district by a vote of 23 to 5. The merged district would be known as Pleasant Valley.

The new district built a modern school on a new site, one block south of Highway 66."
Courtesy of Kathy Sidenstricker - www.jaspercountyschools.org

"High Point school, four miles northwest of Carthage, will celebrate the fiftieth anniversary of the erection of the present school building with an all day meeting and dinner at the school house on Sunday, May 3. Erection of the present school house was begun on May 3, 1875. The two acres of round on which it stood was purchased from J. F. Humickhorn for $25. Prior to that the High Point school had been conducted in a small log building. Among the early directors who served High Point were J. F. Ellison, Jonathan Loveless, Judge J. M. Hickman, Judge Marion Brown, W. E. Smith and Perry Finn. The first clerk of the district was G. B. Walker. Most of these men have now passed away. Only three persons who were residents of the district fifty years ago still reside in the neighborhood. These are: Mrs. G. B. Walker, Mrs. J. M. Hickman and James Herrell.

The school has been served by some 55 or 56 teachers, there being at first spring and summer terms as well as those in winter. Miss Elton Kirksey is the present teacher. It is planned to have present on Sunday, May 3 as many of the old teachers, patrons and pupils of the school ass possible, and those in charge of the arrangements ask that this news item be made an invitation to any and all such to be present. The teacher who taught during the longest period at High Point is W. S. Brown, now residing at 421 Walnut street in this city. He taught there four years.

A program for the meeting and dinner on May 3 is being arranged and it is planned to have it include an address by Phil Callary, a former pupil, who is now a lawyer in Pittsburg. There will also be short talks by other former pupils, teachers and patrons. The Lyric male quartet, of Carthage, has promised to be present and sing." *The Carthage Evening Press March 24, 1925 - Courtesy of the Jasper County Record Center*

STABBED DEEP INTO LUNGS

Wentworth Waters Lying Critically Wounded from Assault Last Night

Mother of Assailant Tried to Shield the Victim—Was Going Home from Revival

What may prove a tragedy occurred last night about 9 o'clock near the Radium school house, three miles east of Carthage, on the Avilla road. In a bed at the home of J. W. Bennett, near the scene of the affray, lies the victim, Wentworth Waters, pale from loss of blood and suffering from knife wounds in his lungs and on one hip.

For some time a revival has been going on at Radium school house and it has drawn a crowd of young persons every night. Among those attending was Wentworth Waters, who boards at the Bennett home, while working on a farm nearby. Perhaps it was not altogether the themes of the preacher that drew Wentworth, for the fair Annie Spencer was also a regular attendant.

Wentworth's attentions to Miss Spencer, although the young people were usually accompanied by Miss Spencer's mother, aroused the enmity of rivals. Amos Mehan, who lives in that vicinity, resented it to the extent that he is said to have appealed to Tom Spencer, the young lady's little brother, aged about 14 years.

Secret threats were heard by other young men, it is said, and trouble was not unexpected. It came with a suddenness that made the assault spectacular. In company with Miss Annie and Mrs. Spencer, young Waters was going home from the revival last night. About midway between the school house and the store at the corner where the mill road leads south, Tom Spencer in company with Amos Mehan appeared and started a quarrel. Spencer drew near Waters and called him the fighting name and was promptly knocked down. As Waters straightened himself for an attack from Mehan, he saw young Spencer springing up with a long-bladed knife in his hand.

He attempted to get back out of the way and Mrs. Spencer ran in between her son and Waters, in an effort to shield young Waters. Tom is said to have rudely pushed his mother to one side.

Just what Mehan was doing all this time has not been made clear, but some witnesses say he was crowding Waters toward the youth with the knife. Others declare he took no active part. Mrs. Spencer says Mehan attacked Waters when her son was knocked down.

With a sudden spring, Tom Spencer jumped onto Wentworth Waters and made two wicked slashes with his knife. The blade first cut a deep gash in Waters' hip and the second blow struck him in the left side, near the lower border of the lungs, making a wound several inches long and almost through the ribs. The base of one lung is involved and from this serious complications may arise that will end fatally.

Young Spencer and Mehan ran. Mrs. Spencer and daughter hurried home and Waters walked unsteadily to his room at the Bennett residence. As he entered the door, he fainted from exhaustion. His wounds were bleeding so profusely that he left a trail of blood glaring in the moonlight.

He was assisted to disrobe and was put on the bed. Dr. Baker, of this city, was called and responded quickly in his auto. He dressed the wounds, and made his patient easy for the night. This morning he visited him again and found him resting well. The doctor learned nothing of the particulars of the affray, being too busy with his patient to ask questions.

For several days it will be impossible to determine the result of Waters' injuries. If septic poison does not develop, or other complications arise, he will recover.

The Spencers, Mehans and Waters are well known old families in that neighborhood. Wentworth's father, Henry Waters, resides about 10 miles east of Carthage. Mrs. Spencer visited the bedside of the stricken young man this morning and spent some time at the home of Mrs. Bennett. No warrants had been issued up to 3 o'clock this afternoon.

Carthage Press Nov. 29, 1912

Incidents in Jasper County rural schools show that problems did occur in the schools.

GIRL WHIPPED THE TEACHER

A correspondent sends the following the Sarcoxie American Tribune this week:

"The teacher at the Cave Spring school house is having troubles of its own. One of the young lady scholars became stubborn the other day, on being ordered to change her seat and refused. The teacher proceeded to force the order and the re-result was a pugilistic encounter, which was warm and furious. In the short space of a few seconds the books, slates, desks and other intruments of learning were scattered over the building in promiscuous heaps. When quiet had been restored the teacher emerged from under the coal scuttle, and bruised and battered countenance slowly wended his way home—an overpowered but still an unconquered individual. From all appearances and rumors, She must have whipped him."
The Carthage Evening Press
December 21, 1901

Forest Boy

Independence School

LOCATION: SECTION: 4 TOWNSHIP: 27 RANGE: 29 DISTRICT: 108

Independence School

Assessed value $77,970; Teacher, Elina Ruth Nagle-Sarcoxie; Salary...$80 monthly; Grade of Certificate..1; Officers: Mrs. V. F. Palmer-Sarcoxie, Clerk; G. S. Marshall-Sarcoxie, President; V. F. Palmer, Member; Enrollment...21; Term...8 months; Condition of housed...Clean; Condition of grounds... Clean; Water...Carried; Condition of out-building...Fair; Blackboard...Good; Maps...Old case; Globe...0; Dictionary...2; Library No. of vol...180; Value:..$75; Suitability of books... Good; Free text books...No; Condition of school records...Poor; Heating...Stove

Jasper County Superintendent's School Report, 1924-25
Courtesy of the Jasper Country Record Center

Independence School has also served as a church throughout most of its history. Services continue to be held there today.

INDEPENDENCE SCHOOL

INDEPENDENCE SCHOOL 1899-1900

Teacher, Loren Seneker
Front Row L to R: Emma Cramer, Nora Lamb, Neta Berry, Mary Lunderman, Homer Brown

Second Row: Berenice Berry, Zelpha Cramer, Myrtle Taylor, Stella Edwards, Iva Edwards, Charlie Cramer, Andy Palmer

Fourth Row: Nelly M. Taylor, Hattie Brown, Ella Downer, Lizzie Cramer, Clarence Palmer, Crayton Brown, Volly Palmer, Nick Lunderman

Jasper School

LOCATION: SECTION: 21   TOWNSHIP: 28   RANGE: 30   DISTRICT: 86

Assessed value $ 108,050; Teacher, Mrs. Jeff Swingle, Reeds; Grade of certificate...2; Officers: A. Willoughby, Clerk; J. T. Kennell, President; John McGowern & Wm. Wickstrom, Members; Number present...26; Term...8 months; Condition of house...Clean; Condition of grounds...Clean; Water...Well; Condition of out-building...Fair; Blackboard...Good; Maps... Case; Free text books...Yes; Condition of school records...Good; Heating...Stove

Jasper County School Superintendent's Report, 1924-25
Courtesy of the Jasper County Record Center

Jasper School

"A patron's report printed during the first week of June 1882, marking the conclusion of typical three-month spring term.

The patron's report described festivities held in observance of the last day of school for the term at Jasper School southeast of Carthage. Miss Blanche Pratt, a Carthage resident, was the teacher.

"The first thing on the program" for the community feat "was a richly and bountifully spread table. It is of no used to try to tell what all we had to eat; suffice it to say that all did eat and were filled and the fragments were gathered up which filled several baskets.

"After dinner came the literary exercises by the scholars, from a six-year-old boy to a 16-year-old girl.

"Then came speeches by S. M. Smith, S. G. Whitlock, Charles Bissell and others who expressed themselves freely, congratulating the teacher and scholars...."

Marvin L. VanGilder,
Carthage Evening Press, August 15, 1977

Jasper School tocay

Jasper Schoolroom

Jasper School 1959-60

Teacher-Mrs. Faye Neil
Attending Students: Sherry Alumbaugh, Billie Black, Patty Black, Ramona Black, Sherye Black, Connie Dixon, Danny Dixon, Jerry Good, Jimmy Good, Ricky Good, Linda Goodson, Tommy Goodson, Aline Hendricks, Larry Hendricks, Sue Hendricks, Ann Lawrence, Jane Lawrence, Joanne Mazur, Denny Mac Neil, Jerry Neil, Barbara Stamp

King School

LOCATION: SECTION: 32   TOWNSHIP: 29   RANGE: 31   DISTRICT: 61

"KING DISTRICT: Isaac N. Johnson, James Pitts and Orville Frost, directors; Miss Alice Peterson, teacher. term began November 4th and continues four months. District enumeration 72, enrollment over fifteen years of age 8, total 21, present 23. School house third-class. Seating capacity 24. This is Miss Peterson's third term and her school compares favorably in deportment and recitations with any in the township. The reading recitation witnessed was excellent."

KING SCHOOL-1964   Courtesy of the Jasper County Record Center

This is apparently the second King School building. "The Doughty brothers attended classes in an earlier building which stood on the same site and was similar in appearance." *Carthage Evening Press - Feb. 18, 1964*

Ruby Knight 1954

Ruby (Blasé, Knight, Liles) Canup - Teacher, King

"Well, children, grandchildren, this is Ruby Knight Liles Canup talking to you as some of you have asked me to tell of my life.

I was born May 19, 1912 and was named Ruby Pearl Blase. Pretty precious name, wasn't it.

I suppose I remember some things before going to school, but not anything too important, I guess. I was six in May and I started to school the following September. I went to the same country school that my brother and sister attended, King School. They were out of school by then. I'll describe the school to you first of all. It was a one room school with a stage built along the entire end. It was about a foot higher than the regular flooring and then back of that stage, back toward the other end of the room, was a recitation bench. Back of the bench were all the desks. They were assorted sizes to fit little, medium, or large bodies. Then back at the other end, in a corner, was a big old coal burning pot-bellied stove with a large steel jacket around it on three sides. The front side was open to put your coal and use the poker and stir the coals around, but the sides were to throw the heat out into the room. It was at the back of the room as I said. Also at the back of the room there was a door and it opened out into a hall that was not heated. Here were kept our coats, our caps, our overshoes, and lunch buckets. We could bring our lunch buckets in and put them under the stove or around the stove if we wanted.

The first three or four years I attended this school, I rode in a horse drawn buggy with three neighbor boys. They were Aaron, Clarence and Cy Frost. The horse's name was Old Babe and she drew the buggy. Later on Old Babe died and I walked. We lived about a mile and three quarters from the school house. During snowy weather, we'd always walk in the ditches to see how deep the snow would get. We had high topped overshoes, and five buckle overshoes that kept our feet from getting wet. I'm sure it didn't help any when we walked in the ditches. When I was riding with the boys, I'd watch out the dining room window to watch for the barn door to open, and when it did, I knew that I should walk down the lane, to the road to catch my ride. It was a distance of about two city blocks.

In school, each child had a desk according to the grade and size of the child. First I'll describe a typical day. First thing we did was we had the flag salute, then we said the Lord's Prayer and then we had a song or two or three according to the kind of mood the teacher was in. Then business started. Usually reading was first. It was first taught in the morning or else math, whichever one the teacher preferred. But if it was reading, the teacher would say first grade reading and that was the one that was first called, and the first grade would rise and go to the recitation bench up front and stand until the teacher would say, "Be seated, please." They had to stand there until she said that. One by one, she'd call their names. The children would rise and read. If it was an arithmetic class, they'd be sent to the blackboard to work problems. Whatever class was called always went to the recitation bench until further orders.

I had three teachers during my years at King. One of my teachers taught five years and I just loved her dearly, and she was a wonderful, wonderful teacher. I think she was my second to seventh grade teacher.

My mother made me repeat the eighth grade as she thought I was too young to go to high school as I would have had to have driven our car. We lived about eight miles out of Carthage. I was hurt to see the other two in my class go to high school and I stayed behind, but as it turned out it was really fun. The teacher that year had a lot of ear trouble and she'd sit back at the stove hurting and she'd let me teach, even my own grade. I felt pretty smart, and I learned a lot about teaching that year.

Do you know what a ciphering match is? Two older students were chosen as captains and the teacher wrote a number on paper and told what number it was between. She would say this number is between 10 and 50. Each captain would guess a number, and the one guessing the closer chose the first student for his side. Then the other captain got to choose one and so on and so on. You know the first ones chosen were the best students. This went on until all the kids were chosen. Then the two smallest, one from each side, would go to the board and the teacher would give a simple math problem, as 1 plus 9 take away 2, or whatever. A child had to write the problem on the board, write the answer, and call out the answer. Problems were given until a child had three right, and the one ciphered down, went back to his seat and the next one on his side went up. The one who went to board got to choose what she wanted to do, addition, subtraction, multiplication, or division. Then as you went up higher in the upper grades they could choose fractions or decimals or percentages.

In a spelling match, sides were chosen as before and the words were given out and if a child misspelled a word he or she sat down. Another kind of spelling match was where the teacher would give a word to the smallest child on one side. She would say, bag, and the child would spell b-a-g. Then the opposite side child would pronounce and spell a word that started with the last letter of the one the child had spelled, as in this case, would be 'G'. This went on until a child could not think of a word starting with the letter of the previous word.

In the seventh and eighth grade in our geography books they had double-paged maps of the United States in regions. We would choose a region that we wanted to look for towns. The captain would go to the board and write the name of a town in a selected region. We searched for that town and the student that found it would yell out the answer and then go to the board and write a city and who ever found it yelled out the name of the state. We looked for towns on that map until we had found so many and then the maps were changed. It would then begin all over again. Points were given for each city found and then the side with the most points won the match.

I'll describe some of the games that we played. One was Black Man. A child was chosen to be it. We said rhymes to get the person. I don't know what all these rhymes were, Hickory Dickory Dock or something. Once that child was chosen, they stood in the center of the play area and others stood at lines on each side of the area. We had to run from one side to the other and not get caught. I was usually the first one caught as I never could run very fast. I just waddled along. After all the children were caught a new game started. The first one who had been caught was 'It'. Lots of times it was old Ruby. I'd finally catch one or two little ones and finally all of us could gang up and catch the bigger ones. Loren Knight and Aaron Frost were the fastest runners of the school, and they were always the last to be caught. They would never be it unless they'd volunteer. When they did volunteer, kids were caught just real quickly.

We played charades dare-base. Here again were two sides and each stood about three feet behind the line that was the dare-base. One side would start toward the other side saying, "Here we come" and the opposite side would say "Where are you from?" The first side would say, "New Orleans" and the second would say, "What's your trade?" The first side would say, "Lemonade." The second side would say then, "Show us some if you are not afraid." The first would stand on the line that was out in front of the other. Four feet out in from the side that they were nearing, they would pantomime an occupation, deed or something like changing a tire, climbing a tree, or whatever, and the second side would guess until they got the right answer. The first side then would dart for home base and anyone caught before getting there had to go to the other side. Then we played Run Sheep Run and I'll explain that a little bit. There was a shepherd who was the shepherd of the sheep. Then there was somebody who was it. He'd hide his eyes and the sheep would go run and the shepherd would see where they were. When the person who was it would get close to where the sheep were hiding he would say "Run Sheep Run", and they would all try to get home and get in 'free'.

We played Steal the Flag and that was two sides again and behind the line where people stood was an object. Each side had an object like a rag or something. The kids from one side would run to the other side and while they were running the other side would try to run and steal the flag.

We played another game called Rover, Rover, Let Nathan Come Over. In this game, each side held hand tight and called for someone to come over and try to break hands apart. If Nathan was the runner, he would run as hard as he could. He would hit the other side and try to break the hands loose from each other. If he could do so, he could choose someone from that side to take back home with him. If he couldn't break, he had to stay on the side that he tried to break free.

We played Annie Over too. This was throwing the ball over the school house to the other side. The ball used for this was usually a soft rubber ball, tennis ball, or something that didn't hurt because when you threw the ball over the house you'd yell "Annie Over" and the others on the other side would catch the ball. They would come running around and try to tab the runners on the other side and throw the ball and catch them that way. Sometimes they fooled you and the very last one coming around had the ball. If when you threw the ball over the house, and it didn't go over, you would yell "Pigtail" so they would know that it wasn't coming over.

Later we played baseball and volleyball. We had races, but in these I was a failure. Always coming in last, as I have told you before, I was no runner. In baseball I was a good hitter, but as I said a poor runner. One time, much, much later, when I was teaching school at Lone Star, a boy said to me, "Teacher, you run just like a duck." I guess that was a carry over from childhood. But, I could play volleyball.

We had county spelling bees, ciphering matches, and when I was in the eighth grade I was the last one standing from King, our school. A girl from Rising Sun, where we were visiting, on the other side. I was given the word Parallel, and I spelled it P-a-r-a-l-e-l instead of Parallel. The minute I did it I knew it was wrong.

So, down I went and the girl from the other school spelled it correctly and Rising Son won the match. I was pretty sad.

I graduated from grade school and went to high school in Carthage. I drove our car and had to leave it at a filling station. My Dad had made a deal with the owners of that station that the car was to stay there, I was to drive it in there no late than 8:30 of a morning and it was to stay there until school was out at 3:30 in the afternoon. Then I was to go to the station and get the car and drive immediately home. I did, because I knew what would happen if I didn't. My Dad would have taken me out of school. I drove the first three years and then the last year I lived with a family and worked for my room and board. Country people had to pay $60 per year tuition as they weren't in the city of Carthage. I graduated from high school in 1930. I was number five from the top on the honor roll. I wrote the class song that was sung at graduation exercises.

At the end of my senior year I took the State Board Teachers Examination and made a high enough grade to get a three year teaching certificate. I went right from high school in May to teaching in September. I didn't go to college then. I applied for King School, my home school, and I was hired and I taught three years.

I taught 1930 and 31 for $70 a month. For 1931 and 32, they raised me to $75 a month. But in March of '32, the school house burned. The school was moved to Mrs. Annie Knight's home. So, 1932 and '33 they cut my salary back to $70.

One morning, I kept hearing funny noises up in their attic, like birds walking around or something, and it started in about 11:00. At noon, as I went out to go to the outside toilet, I just looked up at the top of the school and there was smoke coming around the chimney. Not out of the chimney, but around it. I ran back in and told Paul Knight to go get Loren. It was a distance of probably a half a mile for him to run. Loren ran up to the school and went down through the aisles and jerked those school desks that were bolted down, free from the floor, and he got all the school desks out. I got all the books out of the library out and the children got their books and I put them out by the coal house and we watched it burn.

Loren and I were married December 15th, 1932 and I wasn't hired back as a married teacher because they didn't want married teachers at that time. So, April 1933 ended my first three years of teaching school at that time. I didn't go to the college the first summer, but the next summer I went to Tulsa University and stayed with my brother. The next summer I attended Southwestern Missouri State Teachers College in Springfield.

Now we'll go back to my childhood days. When attending the country school, I had chores to do when I arrived home. I had to change my clothes, bring in cobs or chips to start the fire for the next morning, fill the wood box, gather eggs, and help get supper and then do dishes. I studied my lessons by a kerosene lamp that burnt coal oil. Then later we had an Aladdin Lamp that burned gasoline and somehow, you pumped air into the base of the lamp and little girl's stockings made the light. It was a much improvement over the coal oil light that we had. My folks didn't have electricity until after 1930.

There was always a pie supper at the first of the school year. Usually around from the first to middle of October, and these pie suppers were held to raise money to buy books or whatever the school needed. You'd buy a good book like Black Beauty or Little Women or Mark Twain stories for probably 50 cents a book. The books wore out of course because the kids usually liked to read. Preparations were made by the people who brought boxes to be sold at the pie supper. They were made quite a while before the pie supper was held. The pie supper was announced, oh, a month ahead of time. Then we girls would get a box, maybe four or five inches high and a foot and a half square. We would get crepe paper and trim it in our favorite colors. I suppose mine was either pink or purple. Maybe we'd make paper roses and trim it, or ruffles all around and just make it as pretty as we possibly could, so the boys would like to buy our box. There was an auctioneer and he held a box in his hand and asked what you would bid for it and the bidding would start. Start probably at a quarter and the boxes sold for 75 cents to maybe $3.00. If a boy was found bidding on a certain box, they knew it was his girlfriend's box and the other men in the congregation or in the audience would run that box up on him and he'd have to pay maybe three or four dollars for the box. Then when they'd bought the box, they'd go forward and give the auctioneer the money, and a number was given to them. At the end of the auction or at the end of the pie supper when it was time for supper, he would take that number up and the number would correspond to a box. He was given the box and told who brought it and he would have to look for that person and they would eat supper together. If we didn't want our pretty boxes to be seen, we wrapped them in newspaper and took them to the pie supper that way so nobody could see them.

We had contests at these pie suppers. There was a jar of pickles for the most lovesick couple, and oh how the couples hated to get that. If John and Mary were put up, they would vote for someone else. Voting was a penny a vote and these contest would bring quite a bit of money sometimes. There was also a bar of soap for the man with the dirtiest feet, a pair of socks for the man with the biggest feet, a cookbook for the best cook in the district. One time when I was teaching, I wanted that cookbook cause it was a real good cookbook and I spent three or four dollars on myself so I'd get the cookbook. There was a box of chocolates for the prettiest girl, and as I told you votes were a penny a vote, and the pickles and the box of chocolates usually were the best. Some pretty girl, some boy that liked her really well, he'd spend quite a bit on her to see that she got that box of chocolates.

We always had a Christmas tree and a Christmas program. The teacher prepared the program and here again I was a shining star. As I said, I loved to be in dialogues and songs and I really did my best. We drew names, put our names in a basket or a hat, and then we would draw names. If we got our own name, of course, we had to throw it back into the hat, but the name we drew was the one we bought a gift or to be put on the Christmas tree. Then we'd take up a donation to buy the teacher a gift too. The Christmas tree was usually provided by one of the men in the community and they'd go out into their pasture or into the woods and the tree was usually cedar, and oh how good it made the school house smell. The lights on the tree were real candles. They were in candles holders and then the candle holders clipped to the branches of the tree. You had to be awfully careful because if the candles got the tree afire that tree went up pretty quickly. Fortunately Kings School never had a fire with the candles that they put on their Christmas tree. The teacher always gave a treat of candy and a piece of fruit, like an orange, to each child. When I was teaching, I made my own candy. I made homemade candy. I made fudge, divinity, peanut brittle, penuche, fondant, and I dipped this fondant and made dipped chocolates. I gave each child a pound of homemade candy and I put it in cellophane sacks and then gave an orange, a banana, or a big red delicious apple.

I always knew that I wanted to be a teacher and I didn't play with dolls. I didn't like dolls but I did have cats. I used to tie my cats up and put them in doll clothes and tie them in a chair and act like I was teaching them. I'd read to them and ask them questions. Of course, I answered my own questions. I really spend a lot of my time doing that because I like to teach.

So, this is Mom, Grandma, Great grandma, and Friend signing off until we meet again.

Ruby Knight
Comments from Jeannie Hill

"Ruby Knight was born in 1912. She is 90 years old. She was a school teacher and loved her students like they were hers.

The Jeffers family lost their mother. There were four children; Mrs. Knight gave one girl a home permanent.

Her church had a revival and she took all her students one evening. She was taking painting lessons and taught Ruth Ann and she painted a wonderful sunset scene.

King School today

She went all out and made treats for her students at Christmas. She would pick up children and make sure they got to school. When they had lunch and offered thanks, one little boy wanted to be a preacher so Mrs. Knight would always ask him to say the prayer."

Carolyn (Frost) Johannes - Grade School in the 1930's-1940's
King

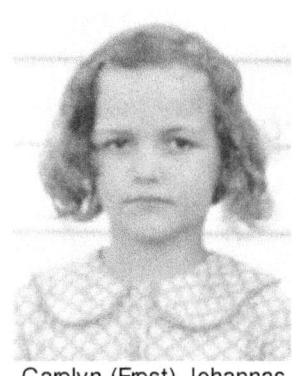
Carolyn (Frost) Johannas
1939-40

"King School was not an ordinary country grade school. It was extraordinary!!! We had one of the best teachers in Jasper County (Miss Glenna) and a picturesque setting. All of us pupils walked to school and that was a valuable experience. My siblings and I walked a mile and one/half to get there and we were always anxious for school to start in the fall. None of this, "Aw gosh, school is going to start in two weeks." No, we anticipated what we would see walking that distance and any new kids in class. Most children weren't lucky enough to experience the foot bridge spanning Dry Fork Creek. My grandfather build the swinging bridge that was about 80 feet across, held up by tall poles on each end and a huge cable above. Fish, frogs and turtles swam beneath us. Twelve steps took you to the "double lane" (two 2 X 12 oak boards) walkway, though we didn't know to call it a double lane "road" then. The bridge would swing right and left, if you were daring enough to cause that to happen. Boys liked to do it just to see if we girls would get scared and scream; none of that silly stuff for us. Our parents told us we could do anything any ole boy could do.

At the second curve on the road to school, there was a hazelnut bush and it gave us much needed protein as we walked home after a day at school. Miss Glenna drove to school. We talked and saw fox, skunks (although we didn't mean to see them, but if we did, everyone at school knew it) ducks, geese, beaver and many other animals. We never saw deer or wild turkeys. They weren't migrating in this area then.

The morning bell would ring at 9 o'clock and we all took our prescribed seats, according to the grade we were in. First graders sat at the front and 8th graders sat at the back. I sometimes thought it should have been the other way around because 8th grade boys could be boisterous and 1st graders were often shy. We began by reciting the Pledge to the Flag, followed by the Lords Prayer, and then sing a few songs. Sometimes she read from the Bible, especially when a student needed a biblical lesson. Then it was time for the first graders to go to the recitation bench. It sat just in front of the teacher's desk and was kind of like a short church pew bench. It was interesting to watch the first graders learn to read and do math. The great part of all grades being in the same room was if you didn't learn a particular lesson, say when you were in the 4th grade, as a 5th grader, you could view that subject all over again. After we came in from playing at noon, Miss Glenna would read a chapter from a book. She taught us to love to read. I remember when she had her 25th birthday. I thought she would be an old maid forever, that there must not be any hopes of marriage for her. A decade earlier, a teacher lost her job when she got married. Miss Glenna made her own clothes and some real pretty ones, too. She won a prize at the Jasper Fair with the blue and yellow one that had a circular skirt and trimmed with wide blue rickrack. I thought it was her prettiest dress and loved for her to wear it.

I started school when I was five years old. I wasn't six until the next summer. Now you have to be six years old near the beginning of the school year. At that time, the County Superintendent of Education or the State of Missouri thought it would be easier on the teacher if she only had to teach four grades, so next year I was to start at the age of six, the teacher was teaching the 2nd, 4th, 6th and 8th grades. Then next year I would have to take the 1st grade lessons, and go backwards every other year. That didn't make sense to my parents so I was sent to school when I was five years old so I could take all the grades in order. I might have made better grades if I had been older, but I didn't suffer any. I graduated valedictorian of my class!!! There was only one other boy in the 8th grade that year and to put it mildly, he just wasn't too smart.

We had two recess periods, one in the morning and one at mid-afternoon, each lasted 15 minutes. Lunch was one hour long. Of course, we took our lunch in a home-made bucket. Mother made good lunches. One mother didn't and when her child brought lard and cocoa sandwiches, I would pretend that I liked them and would trade one-half of my sandwich for one-half of hers. We used recess and lunch time playing softball, Annie-over (or ante-over) or Blind Man's Bluff. Two of the boys wanted me to play "horse", but I didn't know what that was, so I promptly told them, "No". We didn't have a basketball hoop at our school. Later, that is how you played horse, but I wasn't taking any chances then.

We had a water pump just outside the back door. In the winter time, boys would want you to stick your tongue on the cold pump, but we sisters had been told by our parents about not doing that and not going snipe hunting, Two toilets were at the back edge of the school ground, one for boys and one for girls. There was a garage for the teacher's car.

One year, it was October and the presidential election was coming up in November and Miss Glenna being a Democrat, and T. J., Jimmy and I being Republican kids, got to school early one day and wrote in chalk on the driver's side of the garage, "MISS GLENNA LOVES WILKIE". She didn't think that was as funny as we did and she promptly gave us a rag, a bucket and pointed to the water pump and said, "Wash it off, all of it." We did. That was the only trouble I got into at school. My sister, Dorothy sang alto and I sang soprano and Miss Glenna would teach us songs and mother would make us costumes and we would go to organizations and sing. The one that I remember distinctly was when I was dressed as the Statue of Liberty and Dorothy was Uncle Sam. It was well received, as it was during World War II.

Friday afternoons would be spent at the blackboard doing spelling, arithmetic and geography matches. I loved that time, naturally, as spelling and geography and music were my best subjects. Miss Glenna didn't believe in giving an "E", as she said no one was excellent. But I did get E's in music and spelling. I didn't miss a single spelling word from the 3rd grade on and she told my mother that she thought she should give me my first "E". Mother said she thought so, too.

In the winter time all the teachers kept the potbellied stove going. Our feet would usually be cold when we got to school and we would take off our shoes and sit in a chair and put our feet on the foot rest on the side of the stove. If our feet were real cold and we said so, Miss Glenna would come over and rub our toes. She was a good teacher. I had her all eight years of grade school.

We had school eight months of the year. School was out the first week of April. We had a big dinner at noon and we usually played softball in the afternoon, all of us. I remember one last day of school very well, as someone found a black snake and big Jim Tullis picked it up by the tail, swung it around and around above his head and "crack", broke its neck, much to we kids relief. School being out meant going barefoot as long as it was over 80 degrees Fahrenheit. Older ladies told us if we went barefoot before that, we would get the measles. We didn't test that fact.

Dorothy Shull - King

Dorothy Frost Shull
1939-40

"To attend a one-room school in Jasper County was a very special experience. Living in the country and sharing everything with a large family made it a lifetime of understanding human nature and developing a positive attitude for everyday living. This was my past history and development as a child. Most rural schools were started by a community land owner giving a plot of land to construct a school building to provide a place for children who lived in the four-mile square area to acquire a well balanced education. The school in our neighborhood was a mile and three-quarters away across a footbridge over North Fork of Spring River. The footbridge was the only crossing to reach the other side of the river and was well anchored at both ends with a double set of planks supported by an overhead giant cable and hanger cables about every ten feet throughout the span of seven twelve-foot planks. Oh, that bridge could swing and sway with the wind, and bounce a bit as we kids walked across it. Sometimes a "meanie" would jump on the planks to ripple those planks up and down and make it feel like you could fall at any minute. But an edging of wire fencing kept us safe and sound. Every morning and every evening we walked to and from school, crossing the river and seeing everything as we went. Sometimes there we saw wild animals and snakes. Only one time do I remember encountering a copperhead snake in the middle of the road just beside a big water puddle..which made it difficult to give the snake a wide berth for us to get to school on time. Nine o'clock was bell time to take up school studies. Our teacher Miss Glenna was always early and had the building open and made the big round heater's fire in the cold weather. That heater burned coal from the little coal house in the northeast corner of the school yard. A big metal coal bucket held the next stoking of the fire. Usually the oldest pupils brought in the filled coal bucket and carefully sat it by the south door for its next needed use. As I remember it, the one-room school was warm and comfortable during our school day... The fire went out overnight and needed to be built each morning. No one stoked it for overnight heating.

The classroom was the entire interior. A south door for getting a drink at the hand pump, or going to the outhouse at recess or lunch time. The east door was for entering the room or putting out the American flag each morning....Which was taken down each evening. The first thing was to say the pledge and then sing a song and say the Lord's Prayer. Our teacher could play the piano which was against the west wall. The north wall was entirely covered with "first class" slate for the blackboard. We used that blackboard for a lot of things. A test might be written on it...then we were sent to the board for practicing our arithmetic lesson and chalk art was special class and a fun time. Every other Friday evening we had ciphering matches, geography matches or spelling bees. The best spellers were not always the best math pupils. It was fun as a lower grade pupil, to watch the best ones try to be the winner of each match. It was even more fun when we became those bigger pupils and could win a match ourselves.

There was a RECITATION BENCH at the front of the room just in front of the teacher's desk, and when it was time for your class to report for their lessons, we sat on that long bench and answered questions and told of our geography lesson or orally spelled our daily list of words, or any of the many lessons we had daily. The smallest desks were located just behind the recitation bench and the size of the desks became larger as the students became older and larger. The largest double desks were for the seventh and eighth graders and were divided for two persons to put their books, papers, pens and pencils in. It happened when I was in the seventh and eighth grades the number of persons attending school were so small that there was no other student to share the double desk that was mine. I got to choose which side to sit in...which was the left side and the right side remained vacant and clean! I do remember how slick those wooden seats were from the many, many years people slid in and out of those big desks.

King School was the name given to our school because Mr. King gave the land free and clear as long as the land was used as a school. The building sat on the south side of the dirt road and had no house on either side

KING SCHOOL 1938-39
Teacher-Glenna Gresham,
Attending Students: T. J. Frost, Carolyn Frost, Anamae Rush, Dorothy Frost, Agnes Rush, Charlotte Frost, Wayne Robinson

of it for half a mile. There were only three homes on the way to school and no other school age children. Most of us were related and it was unusual for new pupils to move into the district. School programs and pie suppers were a big event. Boxes were decorated by the girls and young ladies and were auctioned to the highest bidder. In the 1930's a $5.00 box bid was a huge amount. Penny votes for the most popular young lady totaled for the gift of a box of candy to the lucky winner. There were other penny votes given for the reddest hair, biggest feet, tallest boy, most love-sick couple, etc. The money was used to purchase school equipment. Another special event was the Jasper School Fair. Each rural school brought their brightest pupils and the best exhibits for notebooks, art work, music participation and recitations or skits. I remember singing a little song solo and getting a blue ribbon for my performance. That was a very big thing for a six year old.

We also had a Last Day of School picnic dinner and graduation ceremony for the eighth grade graduates. All the parents and district residents came, brought a basket dinner to share and the pupils provided a short "program" to preface the graduation exercises. It was a noon and afternoon affair and enjoyed by all.

One thing I should mention is that our father Walter Frost also attended the same school but it was named HARMONY SCHOOL in the 1890s. His eleven brothers and sisters also attended the same school. Grades one through 12 were included. He attended the University of Missouri after the 12th grade graduation, and received his degree from MU in 1907. Our family of six children attended school up through grade eight then we continued our education at Carthage or Jasper High Schools.

It was most unusual for teachers to be married. Most lived with a district family while teaching in their school. Our Miss Glenna Gresham lived very close to our school and she drove a car and provided transportation for students who lived on her way to school. I remember she was a well dressed person with a good personality. She also wore a very special finger ring that had a pretty lady with a diamond necklace on it. Pant suits were not invented then, and we all wore dresses. If the weather was very cold, we put on overall but took them off when we arrived at school, as they were added over our dresses and long cotton socks. There was no cloak room, just hooks on a wooden strip at the back of the room. Our lunch ails were set on a shelf and when noon came we ate what was packed in them. Some students had homemade biscuits and butter, with sometimes jelly; others had lunchmeat which seemed extravagant to us.

On some Friday afternoons we would play softball with the closest school which was Rising Sun School. Their teacher was a very good friend of our teacher and it was fun to go to another school ground to play our type of softball game. I don't remember who won those games, but it was a big trip to go the four miles to their school on our Friday afternoon "off". Another big thing was our annual Christmas Program. It was at night with all the Christmas trimmings. Big natural tree with glass birds and beads, popcorn strings and pasted rings made a colorful garland. We saved little bits of tinfoil and covered small items and they were hung on the tree. A student program was held with song, ducts, and solos as well as whole school plays and songs. Santa came at the end of the program and provided gifts for each one as well as the gifts we gave to the name we drew earlier. We were very secret about whose name we drew so it would be a surprise on Christmas Program night.

To get our final graduation certificate, each eighth grader went to the County Superintendent's office to take the final examination. I remember our teacher was very anxious about the results of each of her students. It was a reflection of her teaching if any of her students "flunked" the county exam. It was very different going to town to have the final exam. A lot of other eighth graders were there too and you did not know them. All of us went to Carthage. I was among 309 students. It certainly was a very scary first few days to have such a big place and so many students in my grade.

The years we spent in that one-room school house was a super education. Of course we all thought Miss Glenna was the best teacher anywhere!! The added educational tool was that when we started school, all the other students' lessons were heard and observed by the younger classes. Which meant by the time we were in the 8th grade, we had heard their lessons for 8 years, had observed their geography matches and ciphering matches and spelling bees and learned as we observed. Older students assisted in helping younger students learn t spell correctly, add, subtract, and read, which gave them experience in the teaching field. Times may have been in a depression economically, but we didn't know about it. A time for us was not to waste ANYTHING and to be happy with what you had."

King School 1952   Teacher, Ruth Thomas

ERIE SCHOOL - 1952-53

Many times children's pet would follow them to school and wait for the school day to be over. I think they saw it as their duty to make sure the children got to school and back home safely.

La Grange School

LOCATION: SECTION: 26 TOWNSHIP: 29 RANGE: 31 DISTRICT: 61

La Grange School

"La Grange was used as a school for more than 105 years District No. 1 in Jasper County. Under the terms of the original deed, when Samuel B. LaForce gave the land, it was to revert to his heirs if the property ceased to be used for a school. In June, 1973, when the little school was consolidated with Carthage R-9, Miss Arria Murto and Sam Murto, her brother, obtained the buildings.

Samual B. LaForce was their great-grandfather. He had homesteaded land north of Carthage, having come from Breckenridge County, Ky. The land was rolling; the prairies were high with native grasses and LaForce and his neighbors realized there was a need for a school.

In 1850 a little one room log school was built. The school was adequate for the needs of the time. It was an isolated community situated on one of the highest points in Jasper County.

One of the first teachers was Thomas Jenkyn, a Welshman. It wasn't too long before he married one of his pupils, Martha LaForce, daughter of Mr. and Mrs. LaForce. it was their daughter that married James Murto, with Miss Murto and her brother becoming their heirs.

During the Civil War, when feelings ran high among the citizens, the log school burned and no classes were held until after the war.

A new school was built in 1868, this time of rock which LaForce and his neighbors dug from the nearby hills. They call the stone "cotton rock." Cotton rock was a white or slightly buff variety of limestone that had a soft, somewhat chalky or porous appearance. Technically it is not called that but just a local name for a fine grain limestone. Part of that old school is still standing. For years it was called the Stone School, because it was built of rock, but it was deeded to the Jasper School District No. 1 in 1869."

Saga of a Small School, Dot Smollen - The Ozark Mountaineer

"The old building was modernized during the summer of 1938.

The latest improvement came in 1956, when a $16,000 concrete block addition was erected just south of the old stone structure and connected to it by a hallway. The project resulted from an overcrowded condition, when school age population outgrew the space available in the old building. The addition consisted of a 30 X 46 foot addition and full basement and 17 X 17 foot connecting hallway. When school opened that fall, thirty-eight pupils were enrolled."

La Grange School, Rich in History, Readies for Another Term, by Marvin VanGilder, Press Staff Writer
Courtesy of Kathy Sidenstricker

Piercy's View of the Past
Ralph M. Piercy

"The first Piercy to come to Southwest Missouri was Uncle Henry who arrived in the Carthage area in late 1832. In 1833 Uncle Henry built a cabin on the slopes above Spring River's south bank at a spring that ran clear and fresh just east of present North Main Street. Now, Uncle Henry isn't listed in the genealogy of those who purchased farming land four miles north on North Main street road in 1866 but they shared a common origin of Gilford County, North Carolina.

Pleasant Piercy brought two tracks of land one on each side of what is now Route D which runs east and west across North Main street road or what was known at that time as the Carthage to Jasper Road. The Piercys were twelve in number when they arrived: Pleasant, his wife, Virginia and ten children - four were 12 years and older, already considered educated for the school of the area, three were of school age (11, 8 and 6) and three were too young for school. The family lived in the La Grange School District, a school that opened its door to students in the 1843-44 school year. The Piercy children lived three and one-half miles from the school and walked or traveled on horseback, spring or buckboard to and from school.

The school was a one-room structure with one entrance door at the west end and a fireplace in the east wall. There was a vestibule inside the west door and two entries into the classroom. The walls were constructed of limestone, outcroppings gathered with a mile of the structure, the walls were approximately three feet thick, the mortar holding the stones in place was of sand, lime and horsehair. The ceiling was embossed tin squares with a plank floor. Some slave labor was used in construction. Water was hauled from a spring one-half mile to the northeast and stored in a 30-gallon wooden barrel in the vestibule. The students brought individual lunches usually in a syrup bucket or several students from the same family would use a lard bucket. Usually, the ants found their way into the lunch by entering through the air holes punched in the lids. Each student had an individual water cup hanging from a nail in the vestibule where the coats and caps were hung. The toilets or chitsails were located in the corners of the playground opposite the west door of the school. The boy's toilet was a two-holer and the girls' was a three-holer. There was a fuel storage shed just east of the school. Each child performed an assigned chore according to age; carrying fuel, dusting erasers, carrying out the ashes, sweeping the floor, etc. Discipline was dispensed by the teacher or if necessary the school board will take corrective action. Discipline was seldom a problem since every school board member knew each child and his dog on a first name basis.

The La Grange (Stone) School District was taxed according to the number of students attending school prorated by the school board. It encompassed an area north and south from Spring River to Buck Branch; east and west from North Main Street Road to what is now County Road 10. When Radium School was built to the east, the district was revised from County Road 10 to County Road 12.

These rural schools also served as social and community centers. For the Christmas program or an occasional pie supper, the community would turn out bringing their kerosene or gas lamps or lanterns and fun was had by all.

I was the last Piercy to attend La Grange (Stone) School from 1932-1937. Some noticeable improvements when I started were a drilled well with a pump and a depot stove rather than fireplace and a fenced playground. La Grange (Stone) school is presently owned by Barney Scott. It is in a reasonably good state of repair-conditioning. It is an antebellum structure. Located one mile off Highway 96 on County Road 13. Go look it over."

Lakeside School
a/k/a Lakeview
LOCATION: SECTION: 10 TOWNSHIP: 28 RANGE: 32 DISTRICT: 73

"The school opened its doors with an enrollment of 63 and Miss Myrtle Ford of Duenweg as it teacher."
Webb City Register, Sept. 15, 1914 - Courtesy of Kathy Sidenstricker

"A fire was discovered about 7:15 AM after the janitor had build a fire to warm the classes. This was determined to be a flue fire. The blaze burned a hole of considerable size in the roof and through the ceiling, also damaging the floor. There was also water damage. Lakeside has two large class rooms and a large hallway. Classes will be dismissed and repairs will probably take two weeks."
Carthage Evening Press Jan. 8, 1929
Courtesy of Kathy Sidensticker
www.jaspercountyschool.org

Lakeside School

Lakeside School 2010

Lakeside School 1952

Lakeside School 1956-57

Liberal School

LOCATION: SECTION: 6   TOWNSHIP: 29   RANGE: 33/34   DISTRICT: 39

Teacher: F. R. Burns; Salary:... $40 monthly; Term...8 months; Officers: N. Olson - Waco, Clerk, Geo. Havens, President; Enrolled: Male..12, Female..16, Total:...28; No. present today..25

Jaspedr County Superintendent's School Report 1893
Courtesy of the Jasper County Record Center

"There was a mild sensation at the Liberal school last Saturday. Prof. Clark, the teacher, was holding an extra session to make up for a day lost the week before. Walter Varney, Tobe Toomy and his brother-in-law fired two shots in the road, disturbing the peace of the school. They were requested by the teacher not to shoot any more, but they deliberately fired two more shots. Warrants were issued for them. Walter Varney was arrested, pleaded guilty and paid his fine, but the other two disappeared and at this writing have not been arrested."

News From Nearby Points, Carthage Evening Press, Dec. 17. 1904
Courtesy of the Jasper County Record Center

A student's award for perfect spelling lessons. These were also given out for perfect attendance and deportment. Sometimes the award was just a gold star placed on a heart or car strung on some string. Believe me, we kept count of those stars.

"JASPER COUNTY NEWS"

THURSDAY, April 6, 1939

RURAL SCHOOL FAIR GREATEST EVER

Eighteen Rural Schools Participated in Annual Event

The rural school fair held at the Jasper high school Monday and Monday night was the biggest event of the kind ever held here. Eighteen rural schools with about 180 students took part in the athletic, scholastic and program events.

The rural school fair is an annual event and is looked toward eagerly by the students who are anxious to compete with other schools in the different events. The largest number competing from any school was 32 and the smallest number was three.

The grand trophy which was furnished by the chamber of commerce was awarded to the school that compiled the greatest number of points during the day. This was won by Prairie Star school ten miles west of Jasper. Rosebank, also west of Jasper placed second and was awarded a trophy.

The night session at which time each school put on a short program, was attended by the largest crowd that has been in the auditorium in the past several years. Every available seat was occupied and standing room was at a premium. With each succeeding year these programs have improved.

The management of the fair and others received many compliments for their efforts in making the fair possible and the fine way in which it was carried out.

Besides the trophy winners the schools entering the display and programs were given a framed diploma stating the ratings given them.

The following is the ratings on display and program:

Display ratings:
  Farmer's Union, Excellent
  Pleasant View, Excellent
  Rosebank, Excellent
  Bloomingdale, Excellent
  Summit, Superior
  Prairie Star, Superior
  Rising Sun, Superior
  Dewey, Good
  Lynnland, Good

Program ratings:
  Mayflower, Excellent
  Bloomingdale, Excellent
  Marion, Excellent
  Rising Sun, Superior
  Rosebank, Superior
  King, Superior
  Summit, Superior
  Pleasant Valley, Superior
  Pleasant Hill, Superior
  Farmer's Union, Good
  Dewey, Good
  Prairie Star, Good
  Pleasant View, Good

50 yd dash, boys 8 yrs—Kenton Boyer, Rosebank; Kenneth Zaerr, Lynnland; J. C. Bauer, Prairie Star.

50 yd dash, girls 8 yrs.—Bonna Mae York, Wanda Fae Crutcher, Maxine Pryor.

50 yd dash, boys 10 yrs.—Ray Dell Coss, Norman Thomas, Wayne Thomas.

50 yd dash, girls 10 yrs—Evelyn McWilliams, Alene Coss, Donna Lee Schell.

50 yd dash, boys 12 yrs—Lynn Brown, Leonard Brown, Floyd Youngblood.

50 yd dash, girls 12 yrs—Carrol Wilson, Betty Maples, Emma Marie Hain.

50 yd dash, boys 14 yrs—Jerry Bailey, Murrill Wakefield, Harlan Hain.

Rural School Fair

50 yd dash, girls 14 yrs—Caroline Garrett, Lillie Stiles, Jaunita Hall.

50 yd dash, boys 16 yrs—Floyd Rice, Preston Waggoner, Cecil Bauer.

50 yd dash, girls 16 yrs—Lois Bauer, Martha Etcheson, Delmas Nixon.

Baseball throw, boys—Cecil Bauer, Raymond Seeber, Preston Waggoner.

Baseball throw, girls—Lois Bauer, Martha Etcheson, Lillie Stiles.

Broad jump, boys—Preston Waggoner, Cecil Bauer, Jerry Bailey.

50 yd shuttle relay—Prairie Star, Rosebank, Pleasant View.

Soft ball tournament—Prairie Star.

Scholastic Events

Reading, grade 2—Betty Fenner, Virginia Lee, Carolyn Frost, Barbara Moser, Avanell Scott, Elvin Achey.

Reading, grade 3—Dorothy Harvey, Emma Mae Rush, Chas. Hernany, Luella Stiles, Wanda Crutcher.

Reading, grade 4—Lorin Griggs, Gordon Wilkes, Maxine Winder, Lydia Jane Earl.

Reading grade 5—Geneva Crutcher, Norman Thomas, Helen Dorsett.

(To be continued next week)

Liberty School

LOCATION: SECTION: 32 TOWNSHIP: 29 RANGE: 30 DISTRICT: 24

Teacher: A. B. Callison; Salary..$50 monthly; Term..8 months; Officers: Ed Conray, Clerk; J. C. Cartwright, President; Geo. Binney, Member; Enrolled: Male..16 Female..12 Total..28; No. present today..25; Condition of blackboard:..Excellent; Condition of building:..Good; Condition of floor:..Fair; Condition of furniture:..Very good

County Superintendent's School Report, 1893
Courtesy of the Jasper County Record Center

SideView of Liberty, (Was used as a hay barn)

Assessed value: 154,309; Teacher: Lena Wiseman-Jasper; Salary...$85 monthly; Grade of certificate...2; Officers: G. R. Lowry-Golden City, Clerk; J. S. Conder-Jasper, President; A. B. Conder-Jasper & Carl Keeppes-Jasper, Members; Enrollment...21; No. of pupils in Class A...4, B...7, C...7, D...3; No. present...21; Term...8 months; Condition of house...Fair; Condition of grounds...Clean; Water...Well; Condition of out-buildings...Good; Blackboard...Slate; Maps...Case; Globes...1; Dictionary... Worn out; Library: No. of vol...200; Value...$60; Care...Case; Free text books...Yes to 6th; Heating...Stove; Heating...Stove

Jasper County School Superintendent's Report, 1924-25
Courtesy of the Jasper County Record Center

LIBERTY SCHOOL TODAY
Photos Courtesy Jasper County Record Center

Liberty's Original Blackboard, (Still in Building)

Liberty 1952-53

Barbara Bock, teacher
Students attending school at this time: Bobby Everhand, Judy Cook, Marcia Payne, Jackie Vaught, Jonnie Johnston, Nina Beth Everhand, Allen Hill, Max Payne, Peggy Payne

Lone Star School

LOCATION: SECTION: 8   TOWNSHIP: 28   RANGE: 31   DISTRICT: 76

Teacher: Mahala Thacker, Carthage; Salary...$90 monthly; Grade of Certificate...1; Officers: W. R Robertson, Clerk, W. G. Hodges, President, B. F. Bensing, Member; Enrollment...28; No. present...23; Term...8 months; Condition of grounds...Clean; Water...Well; Blackboard...Good; Maps...Case; Library: No. of books...100; Value...$80; Free text books...Yes; Condition of school records...Good; Heating...Stove

Jasper County Superintendent's School Report 1924-25

Courtesy of the Jasper County Record Center

LONE STAR SCHOOL

"In recent years, the rural schools have dwindled rapidly in number as the result of district mergers and reorganizations.

Some buildings formerly used as educational centers now have been converted to other uses and some have been or are being razed.

One example is the building of the former Lone Star district, southwest of Carthage, now in the Carthage R-9 district.

Lloyd Rush purchased the building at auction from the R-9 Board of Education and sold it to Clarence Baugh.

The structure, long an important part of the Jasper educational scene, now is being razed."

The Carthage Evening Press, Aug. 18, 1966

Lone Star being torn down after being declared no longer useful for educational purposes. Only eight rural schools, with estimated enrollment of 400 and total faculty of 17, will operate during the coming term in Jasper County. Carthage Evening Press Aug. 18, 1966

**Ruth (Hill) Beckett
Random Thoughts
Lone Star**

Lone Star 1956 - Ruby Knight, Teacher

"I attended seven years...had the same teacher all seven years, Ruby Knight. Outdoor toilets were really, really cold when it was cold outside and as the weather got warmer, it was fragrant. Most of the time during school hours we could just get up and go if we needed to and then sometimes we would have to raise our hand and indicate if we had to go "1" or "2". One of the older kids would be appointed each week or month to put up and take down the flag and they would have one younger child as the helper. We played the usual games at recess. I could never get it over playing Annie Over and so it was pigtails for me. We had two or three swings and they were big so we could go really high. We also had teeter totters, two I think. Most of the time they played baseball at recess, but I did not like to play, so sometimes I would get to play with the lower grade kids. When they played baseball and it was time to come in for recess, they would write the stats down on the blackboard. Jim was pitcher, Mike was on 3rd base, etc. and at the next recess they would resume. I don't remember how they determined who pitched/caught, etc. but I am sure she had a plan. Sometimes the teacher would play with them and sometimes she would pull her car over and sit on it and watch them. I don't remember how long the recesses were, but I do remember we had an hour for lunch. We would pray before we got our lunch, which was brought from home. We could bring toys from home, like our dolls or whatever, I guess it was mostly the girls that did that, as I don't remember what the boys brought.

When you walked in, there was a general purpose room with a sink, refrigerator and a bench on either side of the room. The girls hung their coats on the left hand side of the room and the boys on the right. The lunch boxes sat on a bench beneath our coats. It seemed like we put them in order from left to right according to grades. There was a cabinet where they kept the ball, bat and gloves and they took really good care of them. There was a door on both sides of this room that went into the school room. There was a big heater in the back, so it was much warmer back there. The teacher sat at the front of the room and the desks were arranged in rows; the older kids sat on the left hand side and then the got younger as they went over. The windows were on the west side, so that was the only way we could see out. Back of the teacher's desk was the blackboard and then we had one wooden table that could be used for small groups. On the side of the room was a long bulletin board and we always did art work to put on them. We said the Lord's Prayer and saluted the flag after the bell rang in the morning. After lunch Mrs. Knight would read to us, I don't know how many books she must have read to us during those seven years. The younger kids could sit with the older ones while she read. At Christmas-time we always put on a big program and we had curtains we could pull, but the "stage" was not elevated. We always had lots of art; Mrs. Knight was very creative. One year she had taken oil painting lessons and we all learned to paint, I think she must have done a lot of them for us. I still remember the picture, it was a house, winter scene and a creek, I remember how she would try to show us how to shade the paint. We always made items for our families for Christmas, Mother's Day, etc. I remember some of them, one year we took a large juice can like tomato or pineapple and cut it down the side all the way around and then bent the "spokes" and took yarn and wove it around and they were "hot pads' you set on the table and put a hot dish on. We made a lot of corsages, I think it was from something fabric like, but it was called wood fiber or something, we cut them in squares with pinking shears and the flowers were pink or lavender, maybe white, but pastel colors. One year I remember we took the part of egg cartons that did not have the dividers and covered them in really nice fabric, made a little cushion and covered it with satin material and I gave one to my Grandpa and one to my Grandma. They were little "boxes" to set on the dresser and put jewelry or keys or something in. I think a casket company donated scraps of material. Some years we could order things from a company, I believe it was called Lee Wards. They were leather and they were little key chains, coin purses, etc. and we would put them together with a plastic like thread. We also had Weekly Readers too, but not sure if had them every year. We would sign up and get something in the summer also and that was really something to look forward to. When it rained or it was too cold to go outside, we would play games at noon. I remember we watched the inauguration of Pres. Kennedy and the funeral later, I guess all schools did. Mrs. Knight brought a little TV.

In May, the 8th graders would graduate, each class would have a program, color, phrase, flower and the usual things that are said and done at a graduation. Mrs. Knight would make corsages for the girls and I guess the boys got boutonnieres. We would make programs and they would be made in the color for that year of students. I did not get to "graduate" because at the end of my seventh grade year, they closed the school and we had to be bussed into Carthage. I believe that year the 6th and 7th grade students were honored so they would not feel so left out. I believe the 7th grade was three kids, I and two boys, and the 6th grade was four girls. I have a picture of the girls with Mrs. Knight, I believe we sang. It was quite a shock going from eight grades being together and about thirty kids in all grades to three grades with several hundred kids. My sister went to Long Star that last year they were open and I was in 7th grade, but I have no memories of that year except how sad it was that we had to change our way of life. I surely must have had interaction with her, taking care of her as she is six years younger than me. She remembers that she cried every day at the first and then when she got home that Mom would spank her if she had cried. I really don't remember that. We had so much fun and it seemed almost everyone had a huge imagination. There were kids that did get a spanking though and what I remember about that was I was scared to death. About the only time I remember someone getting a spanking and punishment, was when a boy pooped in his pants. After his spanking, he had to take his underwear and wash them out and she had some of the kids watch him so he would be embarrassed. I am pretty sure that he never did that again, he must have been at least ten, if not older.

We had a piano and Mrs. Knight would play and we would learn songs for our music education, I don't remember if we learned much about music. I do remember Mrs. Knight would write songs. One time, she made up some words to go along with the Missouri Waltz, don't remember if she submitted them or not. We had a small library, like a bookcase, each month someone would be "librarian" and we checked them out. We had a small file box with all the books listed and whoever was librarian would check them in and out. We had to keep a list of all the books we read. I believe it was in the spring we would have spelling bees at the various different country school, I believe the two years I went that we went to Pleasant Valley for them. I placed the two years I went but never got first place. I don't remember how we determined who went. All seven years I was the only girl with two or three boys in my grade. That was always my dream to have a girl in my same grade, but the boys were really nice to me and always told me how smart I was. We had really great parties at the holidays, at Valentines Day we would cover a box (usually a shoe box) and then the day of the party we would all open them and we had party food that I guess was supplied by Mrs. Knight. At Christmas time we would draw names and exchange gifts and we always had a big program... whoever had missing front teeth got to sing "All I want for Christmas Is My Two Front Teeth. We sang and did plays; I cannot even imagine how she put it together every year. We would have a big tree, I don't remember if it had lights or not, but we all made ornaments for it. I remember one year, it got knocked over and Mrs. Knight was really upset and the girl that knocked it over cried. I remember when I was about 4th or 5th grade; we had to have a door put in at the "front" of the room, which was really the back of the school room. I am sure it was fire code or something. There was a telephone on a stand by the teacher's desk and that was our only communication with the outside world. It hardly ever rang though as that would have caused a disruption in class.

I remember we could have "extra" desks, if we had too much stuff to fit in ours. I always had an extra desk, but don't know why I had so much stuff. There was one boy who was a few years younger than me and he was so messy, it just drove me crazy, every now and again I would attempt to straighten him out by cleaning out his desk and boy did he ever get mad! He would mutter under his breath about "durn women". I always got to help the younger kids with their lessons and I really liked that. We hardly ever had homework that I can remember, except I do remember studying at home for the spelling bees. Imagine eight grades of children, they were taught all subjects and we rarely (if ever) had homework. One organized teacher! Of course we did not have art, music, etc. every day, don't know what criteria she used for that, but I do remember when we had art, sometimes it would start one day and finish the next for everyone to get their projects done. We didn't have P.E. as such, but I remember in the sixties, Pres. Kennedy passed some kind of law or something and I guess we did some sort of exercise then. But really, with all the activity we had outside playing games and then of evenings and summer time we were always outside playing, riding bikes, etc. we got plenty of exercise. Most all of the kids were in good shape and not overweight, there were one or two over the years, but not really obese, in thinking back they must have had some medical reasons for that. No bus would pick us up and deliver us at home, either we walked or our Mom's took us. I don't remember any of our Mons that had a job outside the home or don't remember any of the kid's parents getting a divorce. It was totally different than it is now.

Sometimes Mrs. Knight would get us all together on a sunny afternoon and we would go for a "hike". It was never far, but can you imagine taking thirty or so kids on a walk down Fairview?? Of course the older ones helped by looking out for the younger ones. I believe that one time we walked down to a house and they had a bonfire built and we roasted wieners, maybe it was a birthday party?"

Lone Star 1952-53, Courtesy of the Jasper County Record Center

Lynnland School

LOCATION: SECTION: 19   TOWNSHIP: 30   RANGE: 31   DISTRICT: 9

Teacher: Mrs. Frank Buston; Jasper; Grade of certificate...2; Enrollment..17; No. present...15; Term...8 months; Condition of house...Clean; Condition of grounds...Mowed; Water...Well; Condition of outbuildings...Good; Blackboard...Painted; Maps...Case; Dictionary:..4 small; Library: No. of volumes:..180; Value...75; Suitability of books...Part. good; Free text books...No; Condition of school records...Good; Heating..Hart

Jasper County Superintendent's School Report, 1924-25
Courtesy of the Jasper County Record Center

Lynnland 1936-37 Marie Hannah, Teacher

First Row: L. to R. Bonnie York, Dean York
Second Row: Patsy Patterson, Jene Henderson, Johnny Henry, Orie McCune, Jess Zaerr, Jr, (Pete) Brice Henry
Third Row: Evelyn Lorenz, Celia Zaerr, Willa Bird, Marie Hannah, Darrel Patterson, Eugene Henry, Eugene (Ted) Henderson, Bruce Lorenz

Lynnland School 1940-41

Lynnland School 1947-48   Courtesy of Doris Wardlow
Back Row: L to R - Ethel Wardlow, (teacher), Frank Burgi, Marvin Wescott, Richard Wescott, Buster Edwards
Front Row: Velma Wescott, Frankie Kling, Mary Thetge, Susan Thetge (holding slate), Kathryn Wescott

Marion School

LOCATION: SECTION: 29   TOWNSHIP: 29   RANGE: 31   DISTRICT: 62

School Wins Fame
"A rural schoolhouse near Carthage was winning note. It was to be featured at the St. Louis World's Fair. The following is from The Press April 16.

"The fame of the Marion schoolhouse located just across the river north of Carthage has no equal in the rural school areas of Missouri.

"The cozy little building has been selected out of all the country rural schoolhouses to be the one which will posed in pictures and written description as the one approaching the nearest to the model structured for rural schoolhouse purposes.

"County School Superintendent, Luther Hardaway yesterday received a letter from G. W. Buchanan, in charge of the World Fair educational department, asking for a negative picture of the building to be used as a transparency in the facade of schoolhouse pictures which will be part of the school exhibit."

"In his letter to Mr. Hardaway, Mr. Buchanan says that the picture of the Marion schoolhouse, displayed at this fair, will make it the most noted school building in the whole world.

"The building is a small frame structure costing about $1,500. The cost and size are not the points which makes it sought after as a model structure but it is the arrangements of the design, both interior and exterior, which has won for it the reputation daily becoming more widespread."....

The Carthage Press 1904
Courtesy of the Jasper County Record Center

"The present schoolhouse is a modern two-room structure build in 1903 on the same ground the old building occupied at its completion soon after the Civil War. The old schoolhouse was destroyed by fire."
Carthage Press, Thursday, August 16, 1923
Courtesy of the Jasper County Record Center

"Marion school has nearly fifty scholars enrolled, and nearly all in regular attendance, which speaks well for the teacher." *Carthage Banner Dec. 10., 1885*

Carolyn L. Wyatt
Marion Elementary School

"I attended Marion Elementary School for all eight grades, walking, riding my bicycle or being picked up and delivered by my parents the mile and a half or more from our farm house to the school.

My father was on the school board most of those eight years, but that didn't curry favors for me. From first grade through the eighth I had a total of six teachers. The most students that attended Marion during that time were thirty-two, but that number dwindled to about twenty.

Being an avid reader, there wasn't a book in the school library that I hadn't read. This also placed me in the position of helping those in the younger grades read. Our school house had two rooms and a stage, so I would take those students in the unused room, which we used as a lunch room and rainy day room, and have them read aloud.

Thinking back I remember the smell of wet wool coats and rubber boots being stowed in the closets of the entry hallway, as we played outside whenever possible. The few things that we had for playground equipment were for baseball and dodge ball. We would play Red Rover, use the swings or giant stride (which caused me to have a black eye just before grade school pictures were taken). Using your imagination to make up games, like cowboys and robbers, was important and necessary.

On rainy days we would play Simon Says, the whole school participating together no matter the age differences. Someone might play the piano, (sometimes that would be me) and we would sing together. Every Christmas we would put on a play for the PTA, it might be the Christmas story or some other play our teacher had found. We would find costumes at home for our parts and practice on our stage.

We were fortunate that our school house had a forced air heating system. There were electric fans used when it was hot and the windows were open. My last two years there we were blessed with indoor bathrooms, no longer having the outhouses to contend with.

When we started out in the first grade there were five of us, but only two of us were left when we graduated, going on to the Carthage Junior High School."

Marion School 1954-55
3rd Row: Mrs. Dorothy Landers (Teacher), Ferman Clyde Beaver, Charles Patterson, Raymond Peters, Mary Ann Cribbs, Judy Hobbs, Barbara Bowman, Barbara Cribbs, Mary Ellen Simmons
2nd Row: Margaret Anne Patterson, ____, William Weatherman, David Simmons, Chris Moore, Larry Hoofnagle, Jimmy Melvgin, Marvin Dean Beaver, Janice Sue Patterson
1st Row: ___ Lee, Wydonna Mitchell, Janet Melvgin, Peggy Moore, Danny ____, ____, Carolyn Largent, Glenda Grimes, Gloria AHobbs, Edwin Madsen

Mayflower School
LOCATION: SECTION: 6   TOWNSHIP: 29   RANGE: 30   DISTRICT: 30

"Report of Mayflower school for second month ending October 31, 1902. Enrollment 32, number attending everyday 24, number absent five or more days 5, total number of days attendance by all pupils for the month 505."
The Carthage Banner

Assessed value $120,570; Teacher: Opal Brooks, Carthage; Salary...$70 monthly; Grade of certificate...1; Board: Alfred Burnett, Clerk, Low ___, President, Thos. McCall & G. W. Baker, Members; Enrollment...11; No. of pupils in Class A...2, B...2, C...1, D...5; No. present...11; Term...8 months, Condition of house...Clean; Condition of grounds...Weedy; Water...Well; Condition of outbuilding...One poor; Blackboard...Good; Maps...Old case; Globes...1; Dictionary...1; Library: No. of volumes...120; Value...$75; Suitability of books...Good; Free text books...No; Condition of school records...Good; Heating...Stove

Jasper County Superintendent's School Report 1924-25
Courtesy of the Jasper County Record

Mayflower Boy

Bonnie (Tiller) Earl - A Young Girl's Memory
Mayflower School - 8th Grade Graduate - 1960

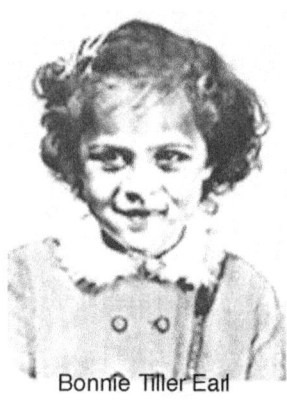
Bonnie Tiller Earl

"Oh, I am too sleepy. I can't go to school today. Please let me sleep a little longer." Nothing would work with Mother today. I had to get out of this warm snuggly bed, get dressed in my very warmest clothes, get my lunch and into the car for Mother to take me to school. When we got there I went into the little white framed building and into the front hall. That is where we keep the water cooler and out lunch boxes and on the other end of the hall I hung my coat.

When I round the corner to go into the classroom, I am met with a cold burst of air. The coal stove hasn't warmed the room yet, so I went back to get my coat and gloves. Mother says, that my teacher gets here really early to get the coal into the big aluminum colored stove that sets in the back corner of the room. She tried to get it warm and ready for us, but it is too cold outside and the wind is howling in and around the windows. Brrrr! I can't wait for lunch. Mother packed my favorite today. She fried a hamburger for me and it is very thin and very well done. She put relish and mustard on it and wrapped it in aluminum foil and now I will put it on the stove to keep it warm. By lunch time it will be crispy and wonderful. Mother also gave me potato chips and yummy cookies that she made and a wonderful piece of chocolate cake, my favorite. My thermos is filled with warm hot chocolate. I am so hungry; I wish we could eat now.

I better get my mind off of lunch. What did the teacher just say? Oh, yes, it must be 9:00 AM, she wants us to stand to say the Pledge of Allegiance to the Flag and then close our eyes and say The Lord's Prayer. We do that every morning and I like it. It is a nice way to start the day. Usually the teacher has two of us go to the flag pole in the front of the school and raise the flag, but it is too stormy out today.

I am still very cold, even though I have on my coat and gloves. My teacher said we can circle around the stove to try and get warm. Oops! I stayed too long and too close and the whole back of my coat is burned. I hope I don't get into trouble when I get home. I was just so cold.

I love my big school desk. Everybody has great big desks. They are very old. My Grandma, Faye Bruffett Tiller and my Dad, Emerald "Pete" Tiller went to school here. I bet they sat at my same desk. The desk is big enough for two students, with a pencil holder on each side, and an ink well in the center. We don't have enough students to have two in each desk and I am glad I don't have to share, because I fill the whole desk with my important papers. I love having all eight grades in the same room because I can hear the classes from all grades and it is like a refresher course in every class every year. I think it must be harder to go to a town school and only hear what you are learning for that grade and not get the refresher classes like in a one room school.

It is morning recess and we can't go outside today, because it is too cold. We are going to play Upset the Fruit Basket. I love that game. Sometimes it is really fun to stay inside. When we go outside the boys always want to play ball and I get so hot and tired and I don't like running around the bases and I don't like standing in the field waiting for somebody to hit a ball to me, because I always miss it anyway. When we play White Man or Black Man or just get to swing or play on the teeter totter, which is fun. Red Rover, Red Rover is also a lot of fun, but I am really tired of playing ball. Recess is over and back to work.

I will get out my beautiful tablet that I bought in Kansas City before school started. Every summer before school we go to visit my aunt and uncle and buy my school supplies. They have really neat lunch boxes and tablets and it is hard to choose which movie star I want on the tablet or what kind of lunch box to buy. It is always so much fun to buy my new supplies and a new outfit for school. I love every September when I go back to school. But, it is now in the midst of winter and next August seems a long time away, so I have to stop dreaming and get my tablet out of my desk and get to work.

I really can't wait for lunch now. Mother gave me snacks for recesses and lunch but I want my hamburger. Lunch is finally here, but first I have to go to the bathroom. The girl's bathroom is in the corner by the field. Even though it is winter, I always look up above the door before I go inside, because I am afraid there will be a snake up there. It is very cold in here and it always smells awful. I sure don't want to take a book and sit there to read. Back to the classroom and lunch. Oh, wow, it is as good as I expected. The hamburger is just right. It is a little crispy and even the bun is crispy. I love the relish on it and the potato chips are the best. Now for the chocolate cake. Mother bakes really good chocolate cakes. She really likes chocolate and so do I. Even my hot chocolate is wonderful.

Now the teacher said we can go outside for a short time. I think the older boys are getting a little too rowdy to stay inside very much longer. I don't want to go outside, so my teacher said I could stay inside and read. I can't decide what to read today. I love Donna Parker and Trixie Beldon mystery books and I love the Boxcar Children, but I think my favorite is all of the books written by Grace Livingston Hill. I'm off in another world, the world of books, when the boys start coming back into the classroom.

The teacher rang the bell and told everybody to get a drink of water before we settle down and listen to her read. The water cooler is in the front of the school. The older boys filled it from the pump before school started this morning. It is very cold and tastes very good. I am going to lay my head on my desk and listen to the teacher read to us today. She always picks the very best books to read. I love this time of the day.

Back to more studies. I don't like arithmetic. My Dad helps me almost every night, and he makes it seem very east, but when I start to do it by myself, it doesn't seem that easy. I'm glad arithmetic is over for the day and it is time for another recess. We are all suppose to stay indoors this recess because it is beginning to snow outside and the teacher thinks it is too cold for us out there. I hope it snows ten feet and we don't have school tomorrow. After we play more games we will do our spelling and then it will be time to go home.

Sometimes the School Superintendent comes to visit our school and I like it when he visits. He brings films for us to watch on our projector. They are almost always interesting, but the very best time is when the Bookmobile comes. We don't have very many books in our little library at school, but the Bookmobile brings a whole bus full. When you open the doors to get on the bus, you can smell the books and I love to smell them. I can choose books that I get to keep for one whole month, until the Bookmobile comes to visit us again.

Yesterday, it was a really nice day outside and when we were playing, one of the bigger boys said he was going to kiss me. Ugh! I didn't want that to happen, so I went to the road and started walking home. When the teacher saw me, I got into bad trouble. She made me go inside and stay. I told her why I did it, but she was still upset with me. I don't care, because I didn't want him to kiss me. I hope he got into trouble too.

Well, it is almost time to go home for the day. I need to get an "outside reading book" because I always get my Reading Circle Certificate. Every year you read a certain number of books from Category A, B and C. Category A is the best, because it is fiction reading and there are always more of those to read than others. Category B is history and that is a good category too, but Category C is always hard for me to read. It is the Science books and I almost always leave them until last. If I get all of my books read every year, when I graduate from the 8th grade I will get a Lifetime Reading Certificate and I can't wait.

I hope tomorrow is Art and Music. We don't have a special room for those classes but I love our Art Class because there is a special paper on every other page to protect the page with the beautiful art work by the Masters. The Sunflowers picture by Van Gogh is very pretty. We learn about the artist and then the hard part is to try and draw the same picture. I am a terrible artist. Usually during music, we all choose an instrument from our band instruments and try to play a song. We don't sound very good. Sometimes our music time is to practice our programs for our parents and the community. We have great productions. The boys bring in the stage and put it together and then we hang the big, heavy canvass, white curtains, all across the front of the school. Our school production is outstanding. Everybody participates, not just the best actors and singers but we all get parts and the night we present the program it is a magical, wonderful night.

It is finally 4:00 and Mother is out front ready to take me home. We don't have school buses like town schools, and I would like to ride on one, but I really like for Mother to bring me to school and pick me up. I don't even have any homework for tonight. Yeah!

2002 – Recently, I took my grandchildren to see my old school. They said, "Where is the cafeteria, the library and the gym"? I explained to them that the little library was in the corner and that the gym was the yard outside and when it was too cold we would play games like Upset the Fruit Basket. The cafeteria was a metal lunch box. I visit my grandchildren's school and am in awe of the cafeteria, the gymnasium, a beautiful library filled with books and lots of windows, the playground equipment, the computers, the very qualified teachers, the monies spent on each child's education, and I wonder are they getting a better education than I did. They are learning to be more social because of the hundreds of students they interact with on a daily basis, but I am not sure all of that equates to a better education, maybe just more money being spent. They don't have the programs and the community support that I had and I am sure the school cafeteria doesn't come close to those hamburgers my Mother fixed. I wouldn't trade my experience in a one room school for the best rated schools in the USA.

Nelle Hoenshell - Teacher
Mayflower

Nelle Hoenshell
1952-53

What a wonderful way to begin the fall of 1952. I was newly married, away from home for the first time, but eager to teach children. I rode the Jasper School bus, leaving home at 7:00 AM to arrive at this quaint little school eight miles from town. My first thing to do was unlocking the door, and make sure that the big stove in the corner of the room had held its fire all night (in the winter months). After seeing that all was ready for classes, I'd run next door to spend some time with the nice neighbor lady. I didn't admit it at the time but I was scared to stay there by myself. And here I was supposed to be an adult and entrusted with children. Anyway, this was a wonderful time of my life.

My first year I had eleven students; seven of them were Baker's. The children were all very sweet and helpful. I had four first graders and five in the seventh grade.. They were so eager to learn. I wouldn't have made it if they hadn't been so helpful. Those big boys carried in coal and helped in any way I asked them.

I remember the programs we put on. I loved music and it soon became evident that the children did too. I can remember Helen Baker singing "Singing in the Rain" all dressed up and strolling across our make believe stage carrying an umbrella. She thought she was quite the star. Then one Christmas, Charlotte Baker, with two missing teeth, sang" All I Want for Christmas is my Two Front Teeth". She was a first grader and so cute.

One day, I missed first grader Charles Leaming. I knew he was unhappy, but couldn't find him. I was so scared that he had run home. But no, he was hiding behind the door in the entryway. Well, I am afraid he got a swat. He never did that again. It was hard to punish a boy with such big black eyes.

One of the highlights of the springtime was playing ball against other schools. We would practice hard and since we had four big boys, we usually did pretty well. I guess in these days you would say we had PE. Anta-0ver was one of their favorite games.

We did study. As I said, these kids were eager to learn. It didn't seem hard at all for them to get their lessons. I was proud of Sharon Bruffett because she was valedictorian of her senior class at Jasper, beginning in my first grade class at Mayflower.

We had to do our own janitor work, carry water from the well (sulfur water), and go to the out houses at the back of the school yard. The school days were from 9:00-4:00 each day, but only eight months.

I can't close this without mentioning how helpful the parents and all in the community were in whatever we did. You would think we were on Broadway. Rural schools had a lot to offer. The closeness that we felt, the commitment to each other, and the love they shared was very important to the children's overall development. Those were happy days.

Lester Roper conversing with Marcella Sweet-Roper – Teacher
Mayflower School

Marcella Sweet-Roper

"Do you remember when you taught Mayflower School?

It had rained all day. You started home that evening. When you came to the branch just north of our house, your car drowned out right in the middle of the branch. You waded in water above your knees. You came up to our house. I took the tractor and pulled your car up to the house. Stella got you some dry clothes. We talked you into staying with us that night. You called your folks in Carthage to tell them you wouldn't be home. When your brother Buddy heard about it, he and your sister, Mildred (which is now my wife), immediately came after you.

Plesant View Children 1948

Rising Sun

Mayflower

Pleasant Vally Girls 56-57

Unkown children

Medoc School

LOCATION: SECTION: 35 TOWNSHIP: 30 RANGE: 33 DISTRICT: 15

Located 6 miles NW of Alba. Closed around 1951

Medoc School

"The town of Medoc was founded in 1848 but not platted until after the Civil War. William Allison laid out the new town of Medoc in the spring of 1867, erected two stores and sold out. He entered into partnership with George L. Bell and they built a business building and continued business for many years.

In 1868, the town had a population of 200 with one saw mill, two dry goods stores, one general store, two hotels, one meat market, one grocery store, one copper shop, and two blacksmith and wagon shops. Medoc Lodge No. 335 A.F. and A.M. was organized June 18, 1869. At this time there were four churches. The Medoc district school taught by William J. Sailor, had a 5-month term and 71 enrolled. A Mr. Askins taught the first session after the $1,975 brick building was erected, with 80 in attendance.

Though a vigorous schoolhouse campaign by the temperance people, the vote on forbidding the sale of liquor won a majority of 1,514 in the county. The people of Medoc voted 40 for license and 59 against."

The Carthage Evening Press
Courtesy of the Jasper County Record Center

"Having a day's lecture Jan. 22nd, found me at the Medoc School under the care of Mr. U. B. Webster. There are about 73 pupils enrolled, 52 in attendance that day--absenteeism of almost one third. This is one of the worst for the district school teacher has to contend. The exercises of the afternoon were reading and arithmetic. Opening exercise, singing, which was creditable to both teacher and scholars. The exercise in reading was conducted as is usual, in district schools, excepting that it was interspersed with spelling phonetically all difficult words, which were then defined. The classes in arithmetic, showed that they had had the care of one who was thoroughly versed in teaching.

To the people of Medoc, we would say, "wake up" to the interest of yourselves and your children, or you will find out, when too late, that you have lost a treasure. --your present teacher"

Carthage Banner Feb. 15, 1872

Assessed value $126,380; Teacher: Frances Flesher, Alba; Grade of Certificate...2; Board: A. B. Callison, Clerk, J. D. Motley, President, G. W. Bower, Member; Enrollment...24; No. of pupils in Class A...0, B...5, C...10, D...9; Condition of house...Good; Condition of grounds...Weedy; Water...Carried; Condition of out-buildings...Poor-needs repairs

Blackboard...Slate; Maps...Old maps; Globes...0; Library: No. of vol...100; Value...$50; Suitability of books...Poor; Free text books...No; Condition of school records...Good; Heating...Modern-Waterbury

Jasper County Superintendent's School Report 1924-25
Courtesy of the Jasper County Record Center

1935-36   Photo Courtesy of Kathy Sidenstricker & Bob Thurman

Medoc School 1933-34   Photo Courtesy of Kathy Sidenstricker & Charles Floyd

Mineral School

LOCATION: SECTION: 27　TOWNSHIP: 29　RANGE: 32　DISTRICT: 64

"Mineral School was located two miles south of Alba on O Highway. It was built in 1894. The school was closed between 1938 and 1947 with students being transported to other school districts. In 1961, Lakeside, the original Pleasant Valley, Mineral, Garden Dell and Shiloh school districts consolidated to form the New Pleasant Valley R-6 School District. Students were transported to the Pleasant Valley school building located in Brooklyn Heights.
Mineral school was sold at auction, August 26. 1961. The building is now a residence."
Kathy Sidenstricker - www.jaspercountyschools.org

Mineral School 1952-53

Bonnie Stevens, Teacher Students: (not in order) Billy Ray Stour, Shirley Stauffacher, Thomas Joe Stevens, Gary Lee Nelson, Billy Vasco Payton, John Elwood Stevens, Marjorie Stauffacher, Margaret Wright, Thomas Edward Lee

Mineral School 1954-55

Mineral School 1956-57
Inez Wimsett, Teacher
Student (not in order) Glenda Williams, Donnie Williams, Darlene Page, Ray Robinson, Billy Nichols, Patricia Nelson, Dianne Page, Carol Stevens, Violet Beavan, Alice Williams, Shirley Stauffacher, Tommas Stevens, John Robinson, Barbara Black

Monitor School

LOCATION: SECTION: 6   TOWNSHIP: 28   RANGE: 31   DISTRICT: 75

"When Miss Lena Russell was the teacher at old Monitor school, classes were held in this building, a frame structure erected in 1894 on the site now occupied by a later brick school. the 1894 building replaced an earlier one which stood on the site farther to the south in what now is known as Morgan Heights.

Frame Monitor School 1894   Courtesy of Kathy Sidenstricker

Monitor district annexed about 1955 to Carthage and the last public school classes were held in the building during the 1955-56 term.

"Friday Feb. 26, 1960, Monitor School west of Carthage on the Oak street road, became a training center for mentally handicap children. R. W. Shepherd, director of training centers for the state board of education made the announcement and has been in Carthage working with Lester Gillman, Carthage superintendent of schools and John Wilson county superintendent of schools.
Monitor has not been used by the Carthage system since September 1957."
Courtesy of the Jasper County Record Center

The old school now serves as a Knights of Pythias meeting hall.

Monitor building today

Monitor School 1927
Back Row: L-R: Helene Horton, Carolyn Tubbs, Garnet Butcher, Robert Hawkins, Neva Haggler, teacher, Evan Bridges, Wayne Joslin, Vertile Nixon, Leonard Daggy
Row 2; Marie Coats, ____, Ellen Huntley, Rose Butcher, Martha Butcher, Genevieve Huntley, Betty Jane Thompson, Leona Daggy, Mildred Coats
Row 1: Bob Zinn, Bill Huntley, Bill Scantlin, George Huntley, Pete Horton, Charley Coats, Walter Butcher

Monitor School 1934

Morning Star School

LOCATION: SECTION: 4   TOWNSHIP: 30   RANGE: 30   DISTRICT: 29

"Morning Star was located 5 miles southeast of Jasper. In operation from the fall of 1879 to 1949. Student were then transferred to Bloomingdale School. The Morning Star building was later sold to Fairview Friends Church to use as an annex to the church."
www.rootsweb.com

Teacher: Gus Hout; Term...6 months; Enrolled: Male...15, Female...10, Total...25; No. present today...16; Board: E. P. Reed-Carthage, Clerk, H. R. Schooler-Carthage, President Wm. Gray, Citra;
Jasper County Superintendent's Report 1894
Courtesy of the Jasper County Record Center

Assessed value $88,342; Teacher: Mounte King-Jasper; Salary...$60 monthly; Grade of certificate...2; Officers-Ethal Probert-Carthage, Clerk, H. G. Sherrel-Jasper, President, Thedaway Yoes-Carthage, & J. L. Probert-Carthage, Members; Enrollment...15; No. present...15; Term...8 months; Condition of house... Fair; Condition of out-buildings...Being rewired; Water...Carried; Blackboard...Slate; Maps...Jasper Co.; Globes...0; Dictionary...Old; Library: No. of vol... 40; Value...$20; Suitability of books...Fair; Free text books...No; Condition of school records...Good; Heating...Stove
County Superintendent's School report 1924-25 - Courtesy of the Jasper County Record Center

Morning Star 1930-31
Seated: O'Neill Tubbs, Clifford Ashley, Golda Jones, Lavina Ashley, Mary Louise Sherrell, Leota Tubbs, Lois Jones
Standing: Chalmer Dunn, Charles Sample, Owen Jones, Melvin Jones, Miss Monte King (teacher), Thelma Jones, Boyd Sherrell

Morning Star Pupils

George Baker

Marvin Earl, Ferris Baker,
George Baker, Alvin Achey

New Hope School

LOCATION: SECTION: 29   TOWNSHIP: 29   RANGE: 29   DISTRICT: 54

Teacher: Maggie Jackson; Salary...$30 monthly; Term...8 months; Enrolled: Male...18 Female...13 Total...31; No. present today...26; Board: Robt. Teague-Alba, Clerk; Tillman Fox-Alba; President; Condition of blackboard...Good for this year; Condition of building...Excellent; Condition of furniture...First class; Condition of apparatus...Maps only; Condition of grounds, out-houses, etc...Good

Jasper County School Superintendent's School Report 1893
Courtesy of the Jasper County Record Center

Assessed value $121,726; Teacher: Eva Burgi-Bower Mills; Grade of certificate...TT; W. B. Wheat-Reeds, Clerk, D. A. Chapman-Reeds, President, Ralph Veills, Member; Enrollment...15; No of pupils in Class A...6 B...4 C...4 D...1; No. present...12; Term...8 months; Condition of house...Good; Condition of grounds... Weedy; Condition of out-buildings...Poor; Blackboard...Slate; Maps...Case; Globes...1; Library: No. of vol..235; Value...$200; Suitability of books...Good; Free text books...Yes; Condition of school records... Good; Heating...Arbygust

Jasper County Superintendent's School report 1924-25
Courtesy of the Jasper County Record Center

MAYOR AND CLASSMATES — When the students of New Hope School posed in 1915 for a student body picture with their teacher, it is unlikely any of them suspected one of their number would become mayor of Carthage. Carthage's current mayor, John Sheldon, known to his teacher and fellow students as Johnny, readily is identifiable here as the only male student adorned with necktie and button-down collar. Several businessmen and at least one banker also are among those pictured. The photograph is property of Mrs. Floyd Meador, 1211 Hazel St., who at the time of this pose was Miss Effie Earnst, the teacher. The unidentified but innovative photographer added a somewhat unusual touch by displaying three boys in the front row apparently partaking of a meal from their lunch pails. The pupils are identified tentatively as: front — Clarence Chapman, Ollie Ziler and Paul Sheets; second row — Cloyd Chapman, John Sheldon, Russell Bastin, Myrtle Wheat, Aletha Ziler and Romaine Kollenborn; third row — unknown; Lavina Kollenborn, Eva Rush, Kenneth Wheat, Orville Ziler, Clay Youngblood; back — Annabell Youngblood, Gayreet Kollenborn, Miss Earnst, Jim Young, Zeta Chapman, John Wheat, — Maxwell, Freddie Youngblood, Earl Bastin.

New Hope - Year Unkown

NEW HOPE SCHOOL, A MILE AND A QUARTER SOUTH OF AVILLA

Front row, left to right, Jackie Brooks, Bobby Evans, Hubert Kahl, June Buster, Faye Kahl, Max Kahl, Martha Bell Letsinger, Doroth Kahl, Betty Buster, Lloyd Kahl, Bobby Baldwin.

Second row, Charles Kahl, Billy Kahl, Robert Brooks, Warren Wilson, Gladys Baldwin, James Kahl, Eugene Evans, Kenneth Earl Gipson Thelma Evans, Leon Evans, Mrs. Sylvia M. Baker, teacher.

Third row, Chester Gipson, Lester Gipson, Mildred Spangler, Olah Belle Adams, Mary Alta Kahl, Helen Baldwin, Virgil Burton.

The Carthage Press Tues, March 23, 1937

New Hope 1919
John Sheldon-Carthage, Kenneth Wheat-Carthage mail carrier, Rex White-Deceased; Cloyd Chapman-Fulton Street, Ross White-Mail carrier, Myrlin Wheat-Now MrsRaymond Rhodes; Altehta Holmes-Not known, Frances Viele-Wichita-name unkown, Myrtle Wheat-Mrs. William Neely-Avilla, Beatrice Byon-Deceased, Paul Sheets-Sheets Truck Lines, Joplin Stockyards, Clarence Seta Chapman-California, Robert Holmes-Maple Street, Sylvia Mason (Baker)-Avilla,

North Fork School
LOCATION: SECTION: 21   TOWNSHIP: 30   RANGE: 31   DISTRICT: 8

North Fork, a log structure, was located just west of Jasper.

"North Fork District: J. W. Underwood, Joseph Cather and Isaac Herring, directors; J. W. Spaid, teacher. Term began September 16th and continues five months. District enumeration 50, enrollment over fifteen years of age 15, total 43, present 28. Building and furniture first-class. Seating capacity 48. This is Mr. Spaid's second term in Jasper county; he has thus far secured employment in our best districts and receives the highest wages paid in Preston township. North Fork directors have "a number one" school."
Jasper County School Report by S. A. Underwood
Joel Thomas Livingston - A History of Jasper County, Missouri and Its People-1912, Page 105

Teacher: Nora Fox; Salary...$30 monthly; Term...6 months; Enrolled: Male...17, Female...6, Total...23; No. present to-day...17; Board: Jas. Bird, Clerk, Joseph Cathers, President, John Waller & Geo. Wagner
Jasper County Superintendent's School Report 1894
Courtesy of the Jasper County Record Center

North Star School
LOCATION: SECTION: 22   TOWNSHIP: 30   RANGE: 30   DISTRICT: 5

Teacher: Daisy Lane; Salary...$22 monthly; Term...7 months; Enrolled: Male...13, Female...8, Total...21; No. present to-day...5; Board: M. A. Mitchell, Clerk, Saml. Holdeman, President, Geo. Wade
Jasper County Superintendent's School Report 1894
Courtesy of the Jasper County Record Center

Assessed value $85,330; Teacher: Elmo Maize-Jasper; Salary...$65 monthly; Grade of certificate...3; No. of pupils in Class A...1, B...5, C...3, D...4; Term...8 months; Condition of house...Fair; Condition of grounds... Grassy; Water...Carried; Condition of out-buildings...Fair; Blackboard...Good; Maps...Case; Globes...Old; Dictionary...1; Library: No. of Vol...200; Value...$50; Suitability of books...Poor; Free text books...No; Condition of school records...Welch; Heating.,...Stove
Jasper County Superintendent's School Report 1924-25
Courtesy of the Jasper County Record Center

North Star School 1936
Back Row Ilene Stump, Paul Isenmann, Elsie Wilson, Dorothy Isenmann, Mary Lee Greenlee, teacher, Gene McClintock, Swely Wilson, Kenneth Earl

Middle Row: Berniece Stump, Elaine Hubhard, Carol Wilson, Virginia Stump, Doris Isenmann, Carolyn Hubhard, June Wilson

Front Row: Harlan Stump, Eugene Foster, Robert Earl, ____ Keith, Floyd Stump

North Star School 1954

Opolis School (East)

LOCATION: SECTION: 19   TOWNSHIP: 30   RANGE: 33   DISTRICT: 64

Teacher: A. E. Taggart; Salary...$40 monthly; Term...7 months; Enrolled: Male...14, Female...12, Total...26; No present to-day...19; Board: A. A. Barrett-Opolis, Clerk; Jos. Davis-Opolis, President; Dr. Lyngar & David Everet

Jasper County Superintendent's School report 1893
Courtesy of the Jasper County Record Center

Asssessed value $84,034; Teacher: Geneva Ohler-Carterville; Salary...$65 monthly; Grade of certificate...1; Officers: George Fingerle-Carthage, Clerk; F. S. Fosclick-Oronogo, President; Harry Davis-Oronogo, Member; Enrollment...19; No. of pupils in Class A...4, B...__, C...__, D...__; No. present...18; Term...8 months; Condition of house...Fair; Condition of grounds...Clean; Water...Well; Condition of out-buildings...Good; Blackboard...Fair; Maps...Case; Charts...1; Globes...1; Dictionary...Old; Library: No. of vol...150; Suitability of books...Good; Free text books...Yes; Condition of school records...Good; Heating...Modern

Jasper County Superintendent's School Report 1924-25
Courtesy of the Jasper County Record Center

Opolis School (East) 1907 Jennie Bell-teacher

RURAL SCHOOL CHORUS OF 1,200 AS IT APPEARED IN MEMORIAL HALL

—Photo by Steward

The chorus of 1,200 pupils of the rural schools of Jasper county gave a program Saturday afternoon before a crowd which filled Memorial hall to capacity. It was probably the largest chorus of rural school children ever assembled in Missouri. The program was arranged under the direction of Walter Colley, county superintendent. Miss Vanna Patterson of Carterville acted as director and Miss Helaine Johnson as accompanist. The above picture shows the huge chorus as it appeared in Memorial hall.

Carthage Evening Press Wed. March 30, 1932

Pearl Hill School (East)
LOCATION: SECTION: 2 TOWNSHIP: 28 RANGE: 31 DISTRICT: 102

"Report of Pearl Hill School for the term commencing November 5, 1883, and ending February 22, 1884: Number of day taught: 78, number of pupils enrolled: 37, number of days attendance of all pupils: 1,682, average number of pupils attending each day: 20 12-13; average number of days attendance by each pupils: 44 4-37. The names of those who came every day are Albert Stoner, Daisy and Linnie Warden. The following are the names of those placed on the roll of honor for progress, conduct and attendance: Sarah Stoner, Rebecca Hicks, Alice, Daisy, Linnie and Herman Warden, Emma, Cora and Albert Stoner, Myrta Moss and Oliver Jones. The one having the highest average of scholarship is Sarah Stoner. Clara Lundy, teacher."
The Carthage Banner Feb. 28, 1884

Teacher: Tresa Daugherty; Salary...$30; Term...6 months; Enrolled: Male...17, Female...9, Total...26; No. present today...19
Jasper County Superintendent's School report 1894
Courtesy of the Jasper County Record Center

Assessed value $169,033; Teacher: Ruth Utter-Carthage; Salary...$63 monthly; Grade of certificate... TT; Officers: J. E. Wilks-Carthage, Clerk; George Williams-Carthage, President; A. Hoofnagle-Carthage, Member; Enrolled...21; No. of pupils in Class A...2, B...5, C...5, D...9; No. present...21; Term...8 months; Condition of house...Fair; Condition of grounds...Clean; Water...Well; Sanitation...Good; Condition of out-buildings...Fair; Blackboard...Fair; Maps...Old case; Globes...0; Dictionary...Old; Library: No. of vol...50; Free text books...No; Condition of school records...Fair; Heating...Wood stove
Jasper County Superintendent's School Report 1924-25
Courtesy of the Jasper County Record Center

Pearl Hill School 1956-57
Marjorie Landers, Teacher
Pupils in school during the 1956-57 term: Rebecca Ann McWilliams, Allen Lee Ross, Jerry Ray Marlin, Linda Marie Hicks, Janice Ann Potter, Linda Kay Stewart, Gloria Jean Pace, Stephen Snider, Nancy Hoofnagle, Carolyn Aubrey, Carolyn Marlin, Gary Dean Hoofnagle, Michael Cline, Weslen Gilbreath, Russell Lee Hoofnagle, Gerald Harrison

Perseverance School
LOCATION: SECTION: 14   TOWNSHIP: 28   RANGE: 31   DISTRICT: 90

Two miles east of Johnstown

Teacher: Ella Clubb; Salary...$30 monthly; Term...5 months; Enrolled: Male...17, Female...16, Total...33; No. present to-day...17; Board: Alpheres Hummel-Carter, Clerk; A. M. Osborn-Carter, President; I. J. Wood-Carter, Condition of blackboard...Good
Jasper County Superintendent's School Report 1894
Courtesy of the Jasper County Record Center

Assessed value $170,318; Teacher: Miss Loveta Kennedy-Duenweg; Salary...$70 monthly; Grade of certificate;...3; Enrollment...19; No. present...19; Term...8 months; Condition of house...Clean; Condition of grounds...Clean; Water...Well; Condition of out-buildings...Indoor toilets; Blackboard...Fair; Maps... Case; Charts...1; Globes...0; Dictionary...Old; Library: No. of vol...100; Value...$100; Free text books...No; Condition of school records...Good; Heating...Modern
Jasper County Superintendent's School Report 1924-25 - Courtesy of the Jasper County Record Center

Perseverance School 1955-56

Perseverance School 1959-60   Marguarite Lortz, Teacher

Pine School

LOCATION: SECTION: 5   TOWNSHIP: 29   RANGE: 32   DISTRICT: 35

This sweet photo from long ago illutrates "back to school" in its purest form. Pine School closed in 1956 Webb City Sentinal
Photo couresy of John Honey

"Pine school was located two miles west and three miles north of Alba, in Duvall Township, Twp. 29, R 32.
Built in the late 19th century, the earliest records for the school noted by the Jasper County Record Center in Carthage are from the 1893 school year. That years's term was seven months long, with 15 boys and 22 girls enrolled.
Miss Nellie Potter was the teacher and her monthly salary was $30. The following Carthage Press news story about the end of the 1914 school year gives a warm picture of the close connection between that farming community in northwest Jasper County and Mary Harbison, the teacher in charge of its children.
North of Neck City, May 13, 1914-Miss Mary Harbison closed a most successful term of school at the Pine school house Friday, May 8th and as a token of their appreciation for Miss Mary's efforts toward making the school the success that it has been, the patrons of the district gathered at the school with well filled baskets and a sumptuous dinner, such as only farmers' wives can prepare, was enjoyed by all...The scholars presented Miss Mary with a nice water set. (A decorative pitcher with matching glasses used in formal entertaining).
The accompanying early photo of the Pine School, 1915, is unusual as it is not the ordinary school group shot. Instead, it captures a familiar childhood exercise known to anyone who ever went to grade school: the lineup. That was the time for the students to collect himself and prepare for the business of the classroom. This photographer was wise to capture such a moment from this turn-of-the-century, rural schoolhouse and preserve it for us. The girls in their dresses are in a separate line from the boys. The back straps of the little boys'

overalls stand out, as do the bare feet of the little girl who is last in line.

Their columns are straight and their arms are at their sides as they wait obediently for the command to enter from the teacher in the doorway; all charming details of that time and place. One can imagine the interior with the mud-room entryway where the teacher is standing with her hands on her hips, the hooks lining the walls to

receive caps and coats (cloak room was another old term for that area), the creaky wooden floor, rows of desks, a wood or coal stove in the back of the room, the teacher's desk in front and chalkboards all around. An open window served as an air conditioner. Drinking water had to be carried in, and there would have been separate outhouses for the boys and girls. These children went to school without IPods, PCs, backpacks or cell phones, and the only blackberries they knew about grew in the pasture."

Webb City Sentinel, Aug. 21, 2009

Pine's last school term
Pupils attending school during that term: Connie Boling, Sharon Nally, Richard Capps, Alvin Nally, Nancy Capps, Joyce Capps, Vera Edwards, Gary Nally, Pauline Barley, Teacher

Pleasant Grove School
a/k/a Brush College
LOCATION: SECTION: 30   TOWNSHIP: 28   RANGE: 30   DISTRICT: 103

Teacher: Wayne Bistline; Salary...$30 monthly; Term...7 months; Enrolled: Male...30, Female...29, Total...59; No. present to-day...44; Board: J. W. Batton-Carthage, Clerk; T. A. Royer-Carthage, President; B. R. Watson-Carthage.
Jasper County Superintendent's School Report 1894
Courtesy of the Jasper County Record Center

"The Pleasant Grove or Brush College school in "the Neck" is enjoying a new location this year. The Carthage & Western railway now crosses the old site."
The Carthage Evening Press, Thursday, Feb. 18, 1904

Assessed value $98,443; Teacher: Frank McKelvey-Carthage; Grade of certificate...1; Officers: R. L. Dodson-Carthage, Clerk; F. E. Jones-Carthage, President; Alva Oldhan-Carthage, Member; Enrolled...36; No. present...34; Condition of houses...Fair; Condition of grounds...Clean; Water...Well; Condition of outbuildings...Good; Blackboard...Fair; Maps...2; Globes...1; Dictionary...1; Library: No. of vol...15; Free text books...No; Heating...Stove
Jasper County Superintendent's School Report 1924-25
Courtesy of the Jasper County Record Center

Pleasant Grove 1952-53   Nell Davis, teacher

Pleasant Grove 1956-57   Pauline Barley, Teacher

Pleasant Grove 1959-60

Pleasant Hill School
a/k/a Rice
LOCATION: SECTION: 36   TOWNSHIP: 30   RANGE: 31   DISTRICT: 21

Assessed value $117,070; Teacher: Mrs. Roy Fenner-Carthage; Salary...$65 monthly; Grade of certificate...3; Board: E. L. Maxwell-Jasper, Clerk; Earl Loudenslayer-Carthage, President; J. B. Edwards-Carthage, Member; Enrollment...10; No. present...10; Term...8 months; Condition of house...Clean; Condition of grounds...Mowed; Water...Carried; Condition of out-buildings...Fair; Blackboard: Slate; Maps...0; Globes...1; Dictionary...1; Library: No. of vol...120; Value...$50; Suitability of books...Good; Free textbooks...No; Condition of school records...Welch; Heating...Stove

Jasper County Superintendent's School Report 1924-25
Courtesy of the Jasper County Record Center

PLEASANT HILL SCHOOL, NORTH OF CARTHAGE

OBJECTED TO A SCHOOL RULE

Dr. Whitney Thinks Sick Pupils are Forced to Attend.

Board Has the Matter Under Consideration and Physicians Disagree—Christmas Holiday Dec. 24 to Jan 5.

At last night's monthly meeting of the board of education, Dr. Whitney appeared and protested against the rule requiring pupils to take examinations because they may have been absent a certain number of days. This, he says, is detrimental to the health of children because by it they are oftimes constrained to attend school when they are sick and should remain at home. The matter was discussed by the board as a matter of greatest importance and was laid over till next meeting. Superintendent Holiday went around town this morning and interviewed eleven other physicians on the question, and all of them disagreed with Dr. Whitney's views on the matter.

The board ordered that the annual Christmas holiday shall begin on the evening of Dec. 24 and end the morning of Jan. 5, a total of eleven days.

The superintendent is to purchase $15 worth of kindergarten supplies for the primary departments.

Carthage Evening Press
Dec. 2, 1902

Ballot To Abolish Office Of County Supt.

Tuesday, August 6, voters will be asked to cast a ballot to abolish the office of county superintendent of schools.

Charles Goll, county clerk, said the office has been vacant of a superintendent since the resignation of Leo Sanborn in 1969.

Mrs. Blanch Probert continued in the office and served as secretary to the county board until her retirement one year ago.

At that time the county clerk assumed the responsibility of records and other duties that are required by the office.

For many years John F. Wilson served a county superintendent of schools, having charge of all rural schools in the county. To date there are no three-director rural school districts in operation.

Voters are requested to vote yes or no, to abolish the office of the county superintendent of schools.

JASPER COUNTY
COUNTY SCHOOL SUPERINTENDENTS
1855-1974

Years	Name	Years	Name
1855-1856	Archibald McCoy	1899-1902	E. B. Denison
1857-1858	Ben E. Johnson	1903-1904	J. T. Livingstone
1859-	Archibald McCoy	1905-1906	Walter Colley
1860-	John J. Williams	1907-1908	Luther Hardaway
1866-	A. J. Shepard	1909-1910	Walter Colley (R)
1868-	J. C. Willoughby	1911-1918	L.W. Kost (R)
1870-1872	Wm. J. Seiber	1919-1934	Walter Colley (D)
1873-1874	U. B. Webster	1935-1936	G. P. Campbell (D)
1875-1876	S. D. McPherson	1937-1944	Bertha H. Reed (D)
1877-1882	S. A. Underwood	1945-1946	John F. Wilson (R)
1883-1885	J. W. Franks	1947-1950	O. B. Bailey (D)
10/85-1888	Philip Arnold	1951-1966	John F. Wilson (R)
1888-1894	James M. Stevenson	1967-1970	Leo Sanborn (R)
1895-1898	W. M. Wharton	1971-1974	Blanche Probert (R)

August 6, 1974: The Office of County School Superintendent was abolished.

Pleasant Valley School

LOCATION: SECTION: 11   TOWNSHIP: 28   RANGE: 32   DISTRICT: 74

"Pleasant Valley school, west of Carthage has served as an educational center at three different sites in the same general area for more than 96 years.

"Earliest records available indicate the original school site, was some distanced south of the present site and was purchased by the first Pleasant Valley Board of Education July 20, 1868 for $105.

The school got its named because it lay in a peaceful valley, accented by a winding little stream known as pleasant Valley Creek.

Pleasant Valley

The first building, made of rough-hewn logs, was constructed by men and boys of the community. Some milled lumber was hauled from Baxter Springs, Kansas and points in Arkansas, while limestone for the foundation was taken from the farm of Tom Ferguson, a pre-Civil War settler in the community. Sand for the mortar came from the banks of Center Creek.

Work on the building was started in July, 1868, but it was several months before the structure was ready for use. The building was composed of a single large room with seating capacity for 65 to 70 persons. Classes were held initially for grades one through five and school terms were brief. For several years classes were conducted during two terms, a winter term of three months and spring term of two months. The teachers were paid $35 to $40 per month for their services as educators and custodians.

Water came from a well dug across the road and south of the school building and was carried to the school by pupils. Later, a well was drilled on the school grounds.

In addition to its educational function, the school building was used as a community center and worship services.

In the spring of 1870, the Pleasant Valley Union Sunday school was organized there by a Mr. Simon. Services were held there by ministers of different faiths, many whom were traveling evangelists.

A form of adult education was provided via the "Lyceum," a general community meeting held one night each week. Activities included debates and spelling bees, as well as social events.

The population of the community gradually increased and, in 1878, the original district was divided at Center Creek. The southern portion and the northern portion continued as Pleasant Valley.

In 1890 a new building site a short distance west of the original school was selected but the purchase was not made until 1896.

According to a deed completed July 7, 1896, the district trustees purchased the new site for $95. Lumber was hauled from Carthage for the construction. The 2-room structure was completed at a cost of $1,000. Later a third room, plus a basement kitchen, was added for $1,800.

In that building classes were provided for grades one through eight and properly classified textbooks were used.

Longer terms were provided and modern playground equipment was installed. First classes in that structure were held in Sept. 1896, when Hardy Davis was the teacher.

A history compiled in 1946 relates:

"About 9 o'clock on Monday morning on the date of moving, the teacher opened school in the old building. The janitor opened the doors of the new building and rang the bell. Mr. Davis led his pupils, carrying their books and lunch baskets and singing "School Days.' They marched up the hill to the new schoolhouse."

The original building was rented for a time for non-school purposes. After being damaged by a storm, it was sold at auction. The original site was sold in 1898 for $70.

The second building served until 1958, when the present modern brick and stone building was completed. It was expended in 1962. The new building was erected following a merger, voted April 1, 1958, of the Pleasant Valley and High Point districts."

The Carthage evening press, Thursday Sept. 24, 1964

Pleasant Valley 1956-57

Pleasant View School
A/K/A Magoffin
LOCATION: SECTION: 17 TOWNSHIP: 30 RANGE: 30 DISTRICT: 2

"Magoffin District - W. F. Stemmons, Geo. McCormick and Peter Schell, directors; Hiram Harry, teacher. Term of five months began October 7th. District enumeration 45, enrollment over 15 years of age 5, total 39. Building second-class and furniture third-class. The directors will during the term supply the school with patent desks sufficient to accommodate 40 pupils. Willingness and promptness were noticeable merits in the classes examined and the recitation and deportment."
Joel Thomas Livingston - Jasper County Missouri and Its People - Vol. 1 - 1912, Page 105
Courtesy of the Jasper County Record Center

PLEASANT VIEW

Pleasant View - Assessed value $132,110; Teacher, Glen Magoffin-Jasper; Grade of certificate...2; Board: Pearl Hale-Jasper, Clerk; R. W. Hale-Jasper, President; V. Pickering & J. A. Probert-Jasper, Members; Enrollment...20; No. of pupils in Class A...5, B...5, C...4, D...6; No. present...20; term...8 months; Condition of house...Clean; Condition of grounds...Clean; Water...Carried; Condition of out-building... Good; Blackboard...Fair; Maps...Case; Globes...1; Dictionary...1; Library: No. of vol...168; Free text books... No; Condition of school records...Good; Heating...Stove
Jasper County Superintendent's School Report 1924-25
Courtesy of the Jasper County Record Center

Pleasant View 1941-42

Pleasant View 1948-49

Back Row L-R: Jerry Probert, L. A. Potts, Geraldine McIntyre, Teacher-Margaret (Still) Manley, Arlene Probert, Loy Hale Trimble, Doris Probert

Front Row: Joyce Trimble, Marilyn Storbeck, Richard Manley, Karen Storbeck

Pleasant View 1950-51

Margaret Manley-Teacher
Joyce Trimble, Richard Manley, Doris Probert, L. A. Potts, Loy Dale Trimble, Jerry Probert, Karen Storbeck

Prairie Dale School

LOCATION: SECTION: 14   TOWNSHIP: 29   RANGE: 31   DISTRICT: 50

"Report for month ending January 6: Pupils enrolled, 43; days attended by all pupils, 731; average daily attendance, 36; average days attended by each pupil, 17; days taught, 20. The following pupils having merited 90 per cent in deportment, punctually and lessons, are entitled to a place on the roll of honor: Euphemia Potts, Mattie Petefish, Mona Fosdick, Mattie Branson, Johnnie Potts, Flora Shippen, Tommy Fosdick. The pupil receiving the biggest general average for the month was Euphemia Potts. Parents are earnestly solicited to visit our school.   J. W. Barson, Teacher"

Carthage Banner 1877
Courtesy of the Carthage Library

Assessed value $191,500; Teacher: Ida Fleshes-Avilla; Grade of certificate...2; Officers: E. S. Wheeler-Carthage, Clerk; Elvis Smith-Carthage, President; John Houseman-Carthage. Member; Enrollment...23; No. present...22; Discipline...Good; Condition of house...Clean; Condition of grounds...Mowed; Water...Well; Sanitation...Good; Condition of out-building...Good; Blackboard...Slate; Maps...Case; Globes...1; Dictionary...No good; Library: No. of vol...30; Value...$50; Suitability of books...Poor; Free textbooks...No; Condition of school records...Good; Heating...Arbogast

Jasper County Superintendent's School Report 1924-25
Courtesy of the Jasper County Record Center

Prairie Dale 1923

PRAIRIE DALE SCHOOL, NORTHEAST OF CARTHAGE

First row, left to right, Mary Jean Shields, Billie Baker, Donald Law, Nancy Ann Shields. Second row, left to right, Weldon Means, Harold Baker; Mrs. Mahala Thacker, teacher. Absent when this picture was taken, Dorothy Law, Darrell Shields.

Class of 1936-37

Prairie Flower School

LOCATION: SECTION: 14   TOWNSHIP: 28   RANGE: 33   DISTRICT: 93

Teacher: Eddyth More: Salary...$33 monthly; Term...6 months; Enrolled: Male...12, Female...23, Total...35; No. present to-day...14; Officers: M. C. Rickman-Webb City, Clerk; H. J. Jones-Webb City, President; J. O. Rusk-Webb City; Condition of blackboard...Very good; Condition of building...Fair; Condition of furniture...Good; Condition of apparatus...None; Condition of grounds, out-houses, etc...Good

Jasper County Superintendent's School Report 1893
Courtesy of the Jasper County Record Center

Prairie Flower School — Courtesy of Kathy Sidenstricker

The Old Prairie Flower School Bows to Progress

"The old Prairie Flower school building, at the west edge of Webb City on Highway 57, is being razed to make way for aviation progress. The one-room frame structure is located on a small tract which was purchased recently by the airport board form the Webb City school district. The property was sold following abandonment of the building, so far as school usage was concerned about five years ago.

The abandonment came after patrons of the former Prairie "Flower school district voted to merge with the Webb City district. Since that time Prairie Flower district youngsters have been brought by bus to schools in Webb City.

The exact age of the building now being razed could not be ascertained by this writer today. However, Prairie Flower is one of the older school districts in the west part of the county and a school was in operation on that approximate location and with the same name, since at least as long ago as the 1860's or early 1870's, before the existence of Webb City. Including among his students there and at Franklin school, further to the south were members of the Webb, Rothenbarger, Cox, Dale and other pioneer district families.

Since being closed as a school, the building has housed a church congregation, since moved to another building, a short distance south and the Prairie Flower 4-H Club."

The Webb City Sentinel, May 31, 1955
Courtesy of Kathy Sidenstricker - www.jaspercountyschools.org

Chuck Surface
Prairie Flower School

"I grew up in Webb City and was eligible for a city school but I wanted to attend with all my buddies from my neighborhood. They were 6-8 months older than I and were ready to go to first grade. My dad checked and I could not enter early but I could transfer from another school. Dad arranged for me to go to Prairie Flower School which was one room and I believe 5 and 6 grades in one room with each grade having a row. The one recollection from that year that it was not very productive for me and we did a lot of tracing. My mom worked with me after school and I was in fine shape academically. After one half year, I was able to transfer back to the Webb City School System and did fine. The school was located at the north end of Prairie Flower Road on what is now the property of the Joplin Airport."

Graduation Programs

Prairie Hill School

LOCATION: SECTION: 17   TOWNSHIP: 27   RANGE: 33   DISTRICT: 42

Teacher: W. W. Scantling; Salary...$40; Enrolled: Male...8, Female...15, Total...23; No. present today...22; Board: J. P. Merker-Carl Junction, Clerk; Jas. Yaryon-Carl Junction, President; J. A. Lumbattis-Carl Junction; Condition of blackboard...Excellent; Condition of Building...Fair; Condition of floor...Very good; Condition of apparatus...Need dictionary; Condition of grounds, out-houses, etc...Good

Jasper County Superintendent's School Report 1893
Courtesy of the Jasper County Record Center

Assessed value $151,208; Teacher: John Dick-Oronogo; Salary...$85; Grade of certificate...3; Officers: G. E. Fullmer-Carl Junction, Clerk; J. Zergler-Carl Junction, President; C. Frederickson-Oronogo, Member; Enrolled...29; No. present...28; Term...8 months; Condition of house...Good; Condition of grounds... Weedy; Water...Well; Condition of out-buildings...One good; Blackboard...Slate; Maps...Case; Globes... Broken; Dictionary...Old; Library: No of vol...100; Free text books...No; Condition of school records... Good; Ventilation...Good; Heating...Arbogast

Jasper County Superintendent's School Report 1924-25
Courtesy of the Jasper County Record Center

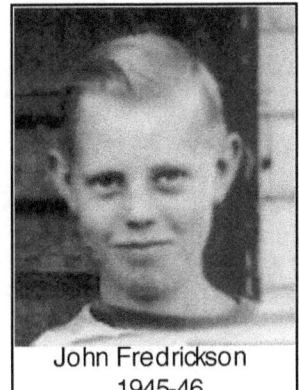

John Fredrickson
1945-46

John Fredrickson - Prairie Hill

"I started to Prairie hill in the fall of 1940. I lived 3/4 miles from the school and rode my bike home for lunch.

At the start of the school day, we lined up in lines to enter school, from 12 to 24 kids, to say the Pledge of Allegiance. The teacher taught starting from the youngest to the oldest. I don't remember the teacher having any help teaching all those kids. I did have some very good teachers. One of my teachers was a student in the 8th grade when I was in the 1st. When I was in the 6th grade, she was my teacher. She finished high school and went to summer school at Pittsburg to get her teaching certificate. Years later she told me how intimidated she was that first year. She shouldn't have worried, she was a very good teacher. The teacher was Joan Johnson-McCune.

My first three years I had Mrs. Gladys Warnick, and she was an excellent teacher especially in teaching penmanship. Her husband was a carpenter and he would build the scenery and props for school plays. We put on plays at Christmas time and the end of school. The parents were all invited and most came to see our hidden talent. For Christmas, I think the teacher brought the tree and we decorated it with handmade decorations. I remember some were chains made from construction paper.

During recess we played softball if the weather was nice. We did not play ball with other schools. During poor weather, we stayed in and did artwork.

For our drinking water, we had a well with a hand pump. We did not have electricity until about 1944. There were two outhouses, one for the boys and one for the girls. These were located behind the school. For heating, we had a big coal stove with a metal jacket around it so we would not burn ourselves.

One snowy day in winter, the snow was too deep to ride my bicycle home after school on Friday so I put it in the building for the weekend. Monday morning, the bike still has snow on it. Is this an indication of our heating system? One cold morning a little girl came to school with her hands so cold that the teacher had to put them in a pail of cold water.

The one thing that stands out in my memory was when the teacher sent an unruly boy outside to cut his own switch from a tree and then had him stand up in front of the whole school, reach behind himself and give himself a whipping.

Some years the Coke Cola truck would stop and give each of us free cokes, pencil boxes with a ruler and pencil sharpener.

Occasionally, parents would bring the ingredients to make soup to school. That would mean we would have hot lunches. I am sure some of the ingredients they grew themselves.

Many Valedictorians came out of these rural schools attesting to the quality of education we received in the little schools. I was fortunate that the school lasted long enough for me to attend all eight grades before it was consolidated into Waco."

Joan (Johnson) McCune-Wilson
Prairie Hill

Joan Johnson
1945-46

"I was teaching rural school right out of high school. (I was 17 years old) My father was on the school board when he and Mr. Peterson decided I would be a good prospect to teach school at Prairie Hill the fall of 1945. Daddy would have to go off the board if I was the teacher, which didn't make my father feel a bit bad. I was the oldest of three girls and my father wasn't ready for me to go to Joplin to St. Johns Hospital to live to become a nurse. Joplin was so far away (12 miles). My salary was $75 a month for an 8 month term. That included the janitor work also (carrying in drinking water, sweeping the floors and building fires in a big coal stove that sat along the west wall, about 1/2 way along the side of the room.)

I had taken the test at the Carthage Court House in Carthage. If you passed the test you received a Teacher's Certificate to teach one year. I also started summer school at Pittsburg, KS. Teachers College to qualify to teach one year. The teacher they had at Prairie Hill had gotten married so she was going to follow her husband who was in the service. I taught and went to summer school for three years - then I got married and my new husband didn't want me going to summer school - so if I would take the test again I could teach one more year, which I did.

Mr. Pete Peterson, who was the president of the board (there were 3 board members) lived on the other side of the section. I don't remember ever calling school off because of weather before I was married, but one time after I was married. (I was 1 1/4 miles from school before I was married and 13 or more miles after marriage). My husband had taken me to school and built the fire for me and Mr. Peterson came and called school off - no telephones at the time - (1945 thru 1948).

Mr. Peterson wanted me to teach that 4th year, because he had a son that was starting the 1st grade. (He had a daughter that was an A student). Well, that son didn't believe in studying. I told him to do something one day and he just "sat". I came up behind him, picked him up out of his seat and gave him one swat on the bottom and he did what I had told him to do. Of course, the older sister couldn't wait to tell her father what had happened. Mr. Peterson had been injured in the mines and couldn't work so he brought his children to school everyday and came in to see if I needed help with anything like starting the fire. He didn't come in to check on me for sometime after that. Then one morning he came in and told me that was the best thing that had ever happened to Larry. I always said that was the best compliment I ever received during my 4 years of teaching.

I had my youngest sister in the 8th grade the first year I taught school. She called me Miss Johnson at school and Joan at home and never missed.

My mother always said I learned more the 1st year I taught school than I had the 12 years I had been in school.

I had attended Prairie Hill from February of my 3rd grade until graduating from 8th grade. There were years I was the only one in my class (grade) so I really didn't know how to study in high school. I didn't make the honor roll the 1st two quarters of high school, but I did after that. I finished 6th out of a class of 33 students in high school.

Prairie Hill was one of the first school to consolidate with Carl Junction.

There was a Rural School Superintendent that came around to check on you (not very often) during the school day.

I had a little boy that wasn't quite normal. One morning I was ready to leave for school (that last year after I was married) and my husband ask me to tell him when a skunk would be coming around the house. He had his gun and was going to kill it. I did as I was asked, got in the car and went to school. Two different times during the day, "this little boy" was next to me and said he could smell "opossum". I didn't notice anything and I just let him smell opossum. He was the only student that said anything.

The second year I taught, I had twenty some students in all 8 grades - that really kept me busy.

I had taken piano lessons while in high school, so I could at least play the piano for the programs I was expected to produce. This was for Christmas and the last day of school. I had no discipline problems during my 4 years of teaching!! Those children would come to school and tell all that had happened at home - Oh Me!! I just thought I knew our neighbors.

I only had one child, a daughter and I always said, "I didn't want a 17 year old as her teacher.

One morning, John Fredrickson came to school laughing. I asked him what was so funny. He said his dad had lost his glasses. He had them on the top of his head, but John didn't tell him where they were.

I've always said, the behavior of a child goes back to their home life. I'm 85½ years old and I still believe it.

Mrs. Gladys Warnick, our grade school teacher, while I was in grade school always said we were an, "Example to someone, rather it be Good or Bad. There is someone watching you at all times". I've used that saying many times. (teaching a Sunday School class, also)

Mrs. Warnick was a married woman and she had a mother dog that had puppies. My father liked bird dogs and he went hunting on our own place. Louise, my other sister, came home and said the teacher wanted to give her a puppy that was 1/2 Airedale and 1/2 German Shepherd and would turn out to be a bird dog . She got the dog.

Once a week in the winter time, one family would furnish the meat and the other families would furnish a jar of vegetables and we would have vegetables soup for lunch. It smelled so good simmering on the stove. So we had a hot meal during cold weather)

The first year I taught school, the children kept telling me-every time I did something - that wasn't the way

Miss Canfield did it - I finally convinced them my name wasn't Miss Canfield.

I almost had some of them convinced I had, "eyes in the back of my head," by the end of four years."

Teacher's Certificate.

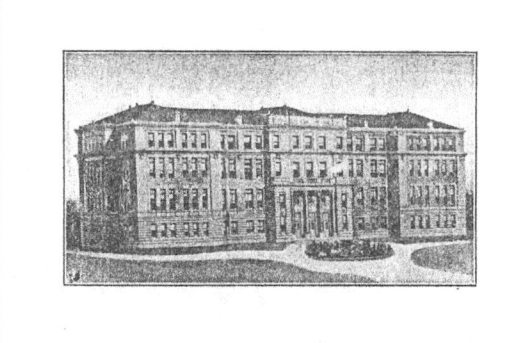

This Certifies, That *Jennie Bell* has been in attendance at the

State Manual Training Normal School of Kansas

twenty weeks or more, and has, in the manner required and prescribed by the Board of Administration, passed examination in all of the subjects required for a one-year State Certificate, and has also given satisfactory evidence of the other qualifications necessary to teach a good common school.

Pittsburg, Kan., Aug. 26 1914

President of the Faculty.

Secretary.

In accordance with Section 13 of "An Act to organize the State Manual Training Normal School" and Section 1 of "An Act relating to the powers of the Board of Regents of the State Normal School," approved March 4, 1905, this is a legal Certificate to teach in the public schools of any county in the State. It is good for one year from date, and will not be renewed.

Done at Topeka, this 28 day of Aug 1914

No. 746.

State Superintendent.

Teaching Certificate from a State Normal School

Prairie Star School

LOCATION: SECTION: 20   TOWNSHIP: 30   RANGE: 32   DISTRICT: 11

Teacher: Myrtle F. Davey; Salary...$30 monthly; Term...8 months; Enrolled: Male...21, Female...18, Total...39; No. present to-day...27; Board: R. C. Thomas-Nashville, Clerk; R. Williams-Nashville, President; Thos. Ferguson-Nashville: Condition of blackboard...Good; Condition of building...Good; Condition of floor...Very Good; Condition of apparatus...Maps only

Jasper County Superintendent's School Report 1893
Courtesy of the Jasper County Record Center

Assessed value $98,830; Teacher: Hattie Flesher-Jasper; Salary...$75 monthly; Grade of certificate...2; Officers: Mrs. Minnie Rudy-Medoc, Clerk; John Bauer-Medoc, President; B. Hedworth-Medoc & R. C. Armstrong, Members; Enrollment...23; No. of pupils in Class A...9, B...2, C...5, D...7; No. present...21; Term...8 months; Condition of house...Clean; Condition of grounds...Mowed; Blackboard...Good; Maps...2; Globes...1; Library: No. of vol...250; Value...$100; Suitability of books...Good; Free text books... No; Condition of school records...Poor; Heating...Stove

Jasper County Superintendents's School Report 1924-25
Courtesy of the Jasper County Record Center

Prairie Star 1955-56

Prairie Star 1956-57

Prairie View School

LOCATION: SECTION: 21 TOWNSHIP: 28 RANGE: 31 DISTRICT: 88

"We had the pleasure of attending an entertainment and spelling match on last Friday night at the Prairie View schoolhouse, which was given by Miss Higgins, at the close of the school at that place. The exercises were commendable and show the careful drill the pupils have had during the winter. The Prairie View Herald, a paper edited by the school and "up with the times." In spelling the Prairie View school did nobly carrying off the honors, as it does on all such occasions. An essay read by a young lady at the close of the exercises left a good impression on the minds of all present. Everything undertaken was successful. The teacher, we congratulate and wish her to be crowned with happiness as her success deserves."
Correspondent - Carthage Banner March 13, 1873

"Prairie View School District No. 88. Etta Spencer, teacher; No. months in present position, 1; Salary paid, $40; Vols. in library, 100; Value of library, $30; Assessed valuation, $70,750; Estimated value of school property, $1,200."
State superintendent's representative school report 1910
Joel Thomas Livingston - Jasper County Missouri and Its People - Vol. 1, 1912 - Page 101

Prairie View 1946
Teachers: Marjorie Heckert - 1st thru 4th
Hazel Brock - 5th thru 8th

Prairie View 1952-53

Joyce (Bowman) Carter
Prairie View

"Mrs. Reed was my 1ˢᵗ & 2ⁿᵈ grade teacher at a large country school, Prairie View, before she became Superintendent.

My two sons, Steve & Doug remember some things about their days there. The county furnished ½ pints of milk, chocolate or white, for each child for 1 cent each. One year they started charging 2 cents, I thought doubling the price was a lot, which seems ridiculous now.

My husband, Gene, was on the school board and when they hired a new teacher (Mrs. Gordon Lee) they warned her about one of the big boys that caused trouble. She just said, "I won't have any trouble," and she didn't. The first time he acted up she boxed his ears and sent him home. When he came back he was a model pupil that liked his teacher. Imagine teachers doing that now! I remember the rest of us thought we sure didn't want to get slapped like that and of course, no one did."

Prairie View School 1962-63

Preston School

LOCATION: SECTION: 2   TOWNSHIP: 29   RANGE: 32   DISTRICT: 33

"Preston school. Whitmore, teacher. Wages, $40. Sixty-five pupils on register, thirty-five in attendance, average forty-two. This school still retains its old name of being a hard school to manage. It is, and requires a teacher of experienced and a thorough disciplinarian. Directors should employ some of the old "Wheel horses" of the county, who would enforce discipline. Whitmore is a good teacher but this is his first term. He is doing well, considering all things. This house has blackboard enough, for every available space is covered with good wall black board. Houses well seated with cherry desks. Directors present. A good school but lacks that great essential, discipline. An $85 bell crowns the building. With good discipline this school would be all right. Good singing."
U. B. Webster - Jasper County Superintendent's school report 1872
Joel Thomas Livingston - Jasper County, Missouri and Its People,. 1912 - Vol. 1, Page 101,
Courtesy of the Jasper County Record Center

Teacher: A. Cooper; Salary...$45 monthly; Term...7 months; Enrolled: Male...20, Female...29, Total...49; No present to-day...42; Board: S. N. Worst-Brest, Clerk; Travis Wingfield-Brest, President; Frank Mink
Jasper County Superintendent's school report, 1894
Courtesy of the Jasper County Record Center

Assessed valuation $122,644; Teacher: Opal Presley-Purcell; Grade of certificate...3; Officers: C. O. Barkley-Alva, Clerk; Louis F. Mink-Alba, President; J. G. Berry-Carthage & Fred Powers-Carthage, Members; Discipline...Good; Enrolled...15; No. of pupils in Class A...2, B ...6, C...3, D...4; No. Present...12; Term...8 months; Condition of house...Good; Condition of grounds...Clean; Water...Well; Decorations...3 pictures; Condition of out-buildings...Poor, need repairs; Blackboard...Slate; Maps...0; Charts...0; Globes...1; Dictionary...1; Library: No. of vols...163; Value...$100; Suitability of books...Good; Free text books...No; Condition of school records...Good; Ventilation...Good; Heating...Smith
Jasper County Superintendent's School report 1924-25
Courtesy of the Jasper County Record Center

Doris (Carter) Wardlow
Preston School

"Another major factor for any country school was the Directors and their devotion to the cause. My sister-in-law, Lorena Frost Carter, who taught part of her years at Preston Country School, remembered the Mink family with fondness. Their house was close to the school and she was supported by them in anything she tried.

Though theirs was a large family, she was always welcome at their table, which usually consisted of one large pot of food. Their devotion to education showed in their children. One received his Doctor's Degree in Education, and one became a nurse. All the boys were in the service of their country."

Preston School 1921
Teacher: Miss Jennie Couard
Back Row: Augusta Powers, Odell Howell, Oma Howell Eliason, Elma Myers, Lawrence (deceased 1980) Paul Clark; Gaylon Henry
Middle Row: Maxine Mink Williams (deceased 1973), Paul Myers, Lila Griffith, Ruth Henry, Maurice Mink Leansing. Gerald Barkley
Front Row: Orie Scott, Earl Myers, Louis Howell, Roy Scott

Radium School

LOCATION: SECTION: 25   TOWNSHIP: 28   RANGE: 30   DISTRICT: 60

Radium School 1964

Assessed value $156,958; Teacher: Mrs. Ruth Shackelford-Carthage; Salary...50 monthly; Grade of certificate...3; Officers: E. B. Wittenmans-Carthage, Clerk; E. F. Paugh-Carthage, President; John R. Carr-Carthage & Geo. Fadler, Members; Enrollment...23; No. Present...22; Term...8 months; Condition of house...Fair; Condition of grounds...Clean; Water...Well; Condition of out-buildings... Good; Blackboard...Good; Maps...Yes; Globes...1; Dictionary...1; Library: No. of vols...100; Value...$50; Suitability of books... Good; Free text books...No; Condition of school records...Poor; Ventilation...Good; Heating...Modern

Jasper County Superintendent's School Report 1924-25
Courtesy of the Jasper County Record Center

Doris Carter Wardlow with Snowball and Kittens 1942

Doris (Carter) Wardlow
Radium School 1934

I only went one month to a county school. I can truly say we walked through rain, snow and sleet 2 or 3 miles to get to old Radium School, or at least my brothers did. Dad sure didn't crank up the old car to take us there.

I must say, I was one scared little first grade girl, even though I had three older brothers to take care of me. Part of the reason was an incident from the year before. Mom and Dad were very supportive of education and teachers, but one went too far.

I don't know what my youngest brother, Gene, had done, but his punishment was to wear his shoes on the wrong feet all day long. This raised Mom's Scottish ire and the teacher learned what a real reprimand was. She only lasted one year.

Anywhere, the success of their school year depended on the unselfish devotion of the teacher. Such a teacher could have a lifelong influence that changed their lives. A "bad" teacher could be cause for a miserable year that had to be overcome from other sources.

Radium School today

Raduim School 1954-55

Redwood School
a/k/a/Humbard
LOCATION: SECTION: 16 TOWNSHIP: 27 RANGE: 30 DISTRICT: 112

HUMBARD - Teacher: W. N. Burbridge; Salary...$40 monthly; Term...6 months; Enrolled: Male...19, Female...20, Total...39; No. present to-day...30; Board: N. C. Motley-Sarcoxie, Clerk; Jas. Wyatt-Sarcoxie, President; J. A. Waight-Parshley & W. R. McBride
Jasper County Superintendent's School Report 1894
Courtesy of the Jasper County Record Center

REDWOOD - Assessed Value $103,874; Teacher: Mae Michael-Carthage; Grade of Certificate...TT; Officers: Wm. G. Willoughby-Sarcoxie, Clerk; W. R. McBride-Sarcoxie, President; Henry Hirshey-Sarcoxie & L. E. Houk-Reeds, Members; No. pupils present...27; Condition of house...Old; Water...Well; Condition of grounds...Clean; Blackboard...Good; Heating...Stove
Jasper County Superintendent's School Report 1924-25
Courtesy of the Jasper County Record Center

Redwood School 1928

Teacher: Harris Moss, Clyde Bass, Cren Moss, Cecil Hill, Gene Moss, Carl Moss, Florence Kiser, Crystal Moss, Wanda Bass, Velma Hill, Dorothy Hill, Freda Simmons, Edward Simmons, Lemoine (Calvin) Hill, Freddie Kiser, Everett Kiser, Doris Moss, Billy Simmons, Lee Bass, Floyd Taylor, James Dension, Lorra Kiser, Cleo Walker, June Moss, Ruth Dension, Martha Carmical, Aline Garber

Redwood School 1952-53

Redwood School 1956-57

Reeds School

LOCATION: SECTION: 36   TOWNSHIP: 28   RANGE: 30   DISTRICT: 85

Reeds school house is now a private resident and is located just north of Reeds on Hwy. 37.

"Reeds' school house, in sub-district No. 7, township 28, range 30; Miss Carrie Ditto, teacher; wages, $33; small new house, and first term of school in this district. The people of the district have long needed a school. Thirty-two pupils on the register; term three and a-half-months. Miss Ditto is doing well, I think. I heard in this school the most perfect recitation in Geography that I have heard this winter. It was perfect--even to the exact locating of St. Petersburg, Russia."

Jasper County Superintendent's School Report by U. B. Webster, 1872
Joel Thomas Livingston - Jasper County Missouri and Its People, Vol. 1, 1912, Page 100

"The school board at Reeds called for bids to build a new brick one story, two room building."
Courtesy of Kathy Sidenstricker - www.jaspercountyschools.org

Teacher: C. W. Carter; Salary...$50 monthly; Enrolled: Male...41, Female...31, Total...72; No. present to-day...48; Board: John Stevent-Reeds, Clerk; Frank Melugin-Reeds, President; Andrew Duty
Jasper County Superintendent's School Report 1894

Reeds School today

Courtesy of the Jasper County Record Center

Assessed value: 187,992; Teachers: Mrs. Bertha Reed-Reeds & Olive Duty-Reeds; Grade of certificate...1 & 1; Officers: C. L. Spencer-Reeds, Clerk; Geo. H. Bragdon-Reeds, President; W. H. Nowell-Reeds & Chas. Marrett-Reeds, Members
Jasper County Superintendent's School Report 1924-25
Courtesy of the Jasper County Record Center

"Report of Reed's School, for the fifth and last month, beginning January 26, ending February 20th.

Reeds Class before 1921   Photo courtesy of Kathy Sidenstricker

Number of pupils enrolled, Male, 33; female, 25; total, 48. Average number pupils attending each day 37. Average number of days' attendance by each pupil, 17

Names of pupils present every day during the month as follows:
Vina Van Coren, Idea Hine, Cora Hine, Mary Alombaugh, Manda Alombaugh, Cora Smith, Ada Whitaker, Laura Whitaker, Effie Carpenter, Sam Alombaugh, Mary Hine, Lee Sprouse, Elmer Sprouse, Oscar Stevens, Harry Van Curen, Geo. Hine, Jas. Phillips.
We wish to return our thanks to both scholars and patrons for contributing largely to the pleasures of the closing exercises. Maggie Ely, Teacher"
Carthage Banner

I found my mother in the above picture I had not seen this before. She is in the 3rd row up and 6th girl from the left. She has a black bow in her hair and her arms crossed. She never did like her picture taken. Her name was Lela Whitaker.......Editor

Reeds Class 1921   Photo courtesy of Kathy Sidensricker

Rising Sun School

LOCATION: SECTION: 27 TOWNSHIP: 30 RANGE: 31 DISTRICT: 20

"Rising Sun School was established prior to 1880 on a small plot adjoining the Ruddick Cemetery. In the summer of 1883, the building was moved almost a mile to the west. In 1884 the building was repaired and enlarged, but was sold at auction on September 15, 1884. It was moved to the Fred Gresham farm and used as a smokehouse. A new school site was purchased on December 19, 1885 from Samuel and Naomi Patterson.

"The new building was constructed at a cost of $387. In 1905, a cloakroom was added. In 1920, the Dixie school district closed and some of the Dixie students were sent to Rising Sun School. New windows were installed in 1939. The Rising Sun and Pleasant Hill school districts merged for the 1951-52 school year. Classes were held in the Rising Sun building. Rising Sun's final term was 1960-61."

Rising Sun 1921

Jasper City, Hometown USA, by Marvin L. VanGilder
Courtesy of Kathy Sidenstricker - www.jaspercountyschools.org

Teacher: Eva Busby; Salary...$30 monthly; Term...7 months; Enrolled: Male...16, Female...13, Total...29; No. present to-day...18; Board: Jasper Owings-Jasper, Clerk; T. Kauffman-Jasper, President; Ed. Owen-Jasper
Jasper County Superintendent's School Report 1894
Courtesy of the Jasper County Record Center

Assessed value $126,470; Teacher: Mary Joice-Joplin; Grade of certificate...3; Officers: Jos. E. Rice-Jasper, Clerk; Fred R. Gresham-Carthage, President; T. F. Weber-Jasper, Member; Enrolled...17; No. of pupils in Class A...7, B...5, C...3, D...1; No. present...17; Term...8 months; Condition of house...Clean; Condition of grounds...Mowed; Water...Well; Condition of out-buildings...Good; Maps...Case; Globes...1; Library: No. of vols. 75; Value...$25; Free text books...No; Condition of school records...Good; Ventilation...Windows; Heating...Stove
Jasper County Superintendent's School Report 1924-25
Courtesy of the Jasper County Record Center

Rising Sun 1935-36

Rising Sun 1953
Back Row: Richard Tilley, _____, Larry Heaps, Clifford Shubert, Larry Tilley, Kay Garret, Ethel Wardow-Teacher, Jaunita Heaps

Front Row: Ricky Garret, Jerry Gresham, Ruth Garret, Stanley Garret, Kathleen Conroy, _____, _____ Conroy, _____, _____, (Holding Slate)

Rosebank School

LOCATION: SECTION: 23   TOWNSHIP: 30   RANGE: 32   DISTRICT: 17

Rosebank School is located west of Jasper. It opened in 1876 and closed in 1960.

"Rosebank School report for term of five months ending March 1, 1884: Average monthly enrollment, 23; average daily attendance, 16. The following constitute the roll of honor for the last month, for their effort to attain to the highest rand in deportment and scholarship: Ella Graber, Clarence Bradford, Clayton Bradford, Charlie Rudy, Billy Graber, Cary Armour and Geo. Foley. Ray Bradford, having received the highest general average for the term, is entitled to Cahn Bros.' prize book. L. L. McCormack, Teacher"

The Carthage Banner March 20, 1884

Assessed value $118,226; Teacher: Nellie Hane-Jasper; Grade of certificate...2; Board: T. C. Ozburn-Medoc, Clerk; L. A. Waerf-Jasper, President; L. R. Ross-Jasper & F. Kinney-Jasper, Members; Enrollment: 25; No. present...21; Term...8 months; Condition of house...New roof; Condition of grounds...Mowed; Water...Well; Condition of out-buildings...Boys poor; Blackboard...Poor; Dictionary...1; Library: No. of vols...200; Value...$100; Suitability of books...Good; Free text books...No; Condition of school records...Good; Heating...Stove

Jasper County Superintendent's School Report 1924-25
Courtesy of the Jasper County Record Center

Present interior of Rosebank School. In the first schools, the teacher's desks was put on a platform so he could better see the children. Rosebank has such a platform.

A new concrete coal house has just been completed at Rose Bank school house.

There was no school at Rose Bank on Thursday and Friday on account of our teacher, Miss Stella Mick, attending the state teachers' association, which was held at Springfield the latter part of last week.

Carthage Evening Press Nov. 21, 1912

Rosebank School 1959

Round Prairie School

LOCATION: SECTION: 11   TOWNSHIP: 27   RANGE: 29   DISTRICT: 109

Teacher: B. F. Scroggs; Salary...$37.58 monthly; Term...7 months; Enrolled: Male...26, Female...23, Total...49; No. present to-day...42; Board: H. N. Scroggs-Sarcoxie, Clerk; S. B. Staples-Sarcoxie, President; W. H. Jones & J. T. Standley; Condition of blackboard...Fair; Condition of building...Very Good; Condition of floor...Good; Condition of furniture...Good; Condition of apparatus...Maps only; Condition of grounds, out-houses, etc...Good
Jasper County Superintendent's School Report 1893
Courtesy of the Jasper County Record Center

Round Prairie

Assessed value: $95,296; Teacher: Ina Landers-Sarcoxie; Grade of certificate...3; Officers: Fred W. Stebbins-Sarcoxie, Clerk; J. B. Oliver-Sarcoxie, President; J. W. Allen-Sarcoxie & J. C. Rosebaugh-Sarcoxie, Members; Enrollment...31; No. present...28; Term...8 months; Condition of house...Good; Condition of grounds...Clean; Water...Well; Condition of out-buildings...New; Blackboard...Slate; Maps...0; Globes...0; Free text books...Yes; Condition of school records...Welch; Heating...Coal stove
Jasper County Superintendent's School Report 1924-25
Courtesy of the Jasper County Record Center

Round Prairie 56-57

ROUND PRAIRIE SCHOOL 1908

Rusk School
a/k/a White Oak
LOCATION: SECTION: 28   TOWNSHIP: 29   RANGE: 29   DISTRICT: 56

"White Oak-Other districts soon were organized and when the war came on twenty-three school houses had been built. Among the districts organized in the 'forties were Franklin school, near Castle Rock on Turkey Creek, with Charles Harris as its teacher; Peace Church school, later called Enterprise; Spring River school, Carthage; Black Jack in McDonald township; the Duval in the northwestern part of county and White Oak school near Avilla."
Joel Thomas Livingston - A History of Jasper County Missouri and Its People, Vol. 1, 1912 - Page 24
Courtesy of the Jasper County Record Center

Left: Warren Campbell
Rt: Elmer Rush, Teacher

Rusk - "The journey from home to school and return during the early years of the century was "nearly always by shanks pony," according to Warren Campbell, rural Avilla, who remembers with fondness his years as a student at the old Rusk School two miles east of Avilla.

There were no buses, no bicycles or other modern contrivances to ease the wear and tear on the students' feet. Some walked as far as 2 1/2 miles and may walked at least a mile each way.

To meet his daily responsibilities as teacher in 1907, Elmer Rush drove a one-horse Banner model buggy more than six miles from his farm home near Maple Grove, taking his own two children along as passengers.

Fuel for his vehicle was a bundle of oats and four or five ears of corn daily and the journey was made through mud, cold, snow or dust at about six miles per hour. When rain or snow was falling the riders were protected to some extent by side curtains and a large apron attached to the dash. During periods of severe cold, a stack of hot bricks, a kerosene lantern or a jug of hot water were placed near the feet of the teacher and his passengers.

In winter, garments included ear muffs, flap caps or stocking caps, heavy overcoats, long and thick stockings, high-button shoes for the girls and felt boots or high leather boots for the boys.

In addition to his educational responsibilities, Rush did the janitorial work and tended the pot bellied stove which used wood or coal to heat at least the center of the one large classroom which was utilized by all eight elementary grades.

Few students had any opportunity to attend high school or college and many remained in the rural school until they approached adulthood., Some teachers therefore often were confronted with the necessity of disciplining "children" who were larger and stronger than themselves.

Campbell remembers one teacher, J. K. Jones, handled the problem effectively. Handsome and of giant size, as Campbell recalls him, Jones opened the term by placing a long "hickory persuader" atop the blackboard at the front of the room and writing beneath it in large letters, "DO RIGHT," said Campbell. "We all agreed--and we learned.

The original Rusk building was destroyed, July 4, 1898, by fire and the last structure, currently used for hay storage, was constructed shortly by Ralph and Irwin Bawbell, who also were the builders of the New Hope and Deer Creek school buildings....

For many years, water for drinking and washing was carried by two boys from the well of a neighboring farm or a spring east of the school on the

Rusk School 2001

property of Charley Perkins. The water bucket was placed on a bench, accompanied by a dipper, a wash pan and a rolled cloth towel.

Campbell's memories include the occasion when Clay Stemmons was the teacher and one of the older boy pupils was directed to eliminate a large yellow hammer woodpecker which was attempting to drill a hole in the wall of the building. The bird was dispatched with a large chunk of coal thrown with considerable force by the student.

Tom McKelvey was described as an excellent teacher who occasionally found respite from the pressures of his work by taking a lunch-time stroll through the nearby timber to explore and study trees, squirrels and birds and search for arrowheads.

One day a student was inspired and led the remainder of the student body to perform a disappearing act during the teacher's absence. Two of the larger boys mounted the porch roof and, one by one, lifted the other pupils through an opening in the ceiling, which then was closed. All remained silent when the teacher returned and rang the bell for resumption of class work. Campbell neglected to describe the exact nature of the resulting punishment.

The Rusk graduate remembers several other teachers that included Chauncy Briggle, about 76 years ago; Bertha Hood, who later was Jasper County superintendent of schools, and in later years Mrs. Sylvia Baker, who taught six terms, and Mrs. Allen Holmes, last teacher before the school was closed and the Rusk District became part of Avilla Reorganized District No. 13.

The world has undergone a total change since the era when Elmer Rusk taught a six-term with 30-40 pupils enrolled for a salary of $50 per month.

The work done there had a significant impact, however, producing a number of successful citizens and community leaders, and should not be forgotten."
Marvin VanGilder, Press Historian
Carthage Evening Press Sept. 22, 1973

The Rusk School is now gone.

Sharon School

LOCATION: SECTION: 3 TOWNSHIP: 29 RANGE: 29 DISTRICT: 26

Sharon School — Courtesy of Matile Lafon Wilson

Assessed Value: $137. 890; Teacher: ____ Withers-Golden City; Salary...$90 monthly; Grade of certificate...1; Officers: A. Lofan-Golden City, Clerk; Warren A Stiles-Bowers Mill, President; J. C. Alexander-Bowers Mill, Member; Enrollment...21; No. present...21; Term...8 months; Condition of house...Clean; Condition of grounds...Mowed; Water...Well; Condition of outbuildings...Fair; Blackboard...Good; Maps...Case; Globes...1; Dictionary...1; Library: No. of vol...100; Value...$100; Suitability of books...Good; Free text books...No; Condition of school records...Good; Heating...Arbogast

Jasper County Superintendent's School Report 1924-25
Courtesy of the Jasper County Record Center

The Adams Family

"Five of us went to school at Sharon--Darius, Louise, Russell, Wallace and Olah Belle. We were not in Sharon District. The school that we were supposed to go to was 2 miles across the field and the distance to Sharon was one mile across the field.

We walked across the field most of the time when the weather was suitable. When the weather was bad, we would go in the buggy pulled by our horse named Old Nig. Old Nig was a very patient horse to put up with some of the monkeyshines the boys were guilty of.

Darius didn't go very long before he graduated from the eighth grade. I am sure the most vivid memory he would have was he and Pauline Alexander holding hands across the aisle.

Louise remembers all the games we played: Blackman, Ante Over, Blindman's Bluff, Marbles, Softball, which was played with a sponge ball. Also, it seems as though I can vaguely remember something called "Kick-the-Picket".

Russell's memories are vague--he was a very quite boy--he never gave the teachers any trouble. You would hardly believe he was related to the rest of the Adams bunch.

Wallace's memories are the usual--getting into as much mischievous as possible. One time he had to march around the room with his teacher because he had been naughty.

Some of Olah Belle's memories were of the times she would walk home with Martha Leeper and Lorene Clyman and they would stop at Lorene's house and eat hot homemade bread with lots of butter. She and Bett Woods had to sit on the front seat several times.

Teachers we had were: Chauncey & Addie Briggle, Lema Withers, Glenn Magoffin, Ruth Jones, Mary O'Brian an Mae Hope.

Our memories are all of the good things that happened. We forgot about wading through the snow, driving the horse and buggy through the cold, biting wind, hovering around the pot-bellied stove. We can look back now and say it was some of the best and happiest times of our life....

Now, in the year 1989--most of us---Darieus, Louise, Wallace and Olah Belle in or around Carthage. Russell lives in the big town of Dudenville."

Courtesy of Natalie Lafon Wilson

Cost of building the Sharon School house 1898   Courtesy of Natalie Lefan Wilson

Sharon School, 1908 - Tacher, May Stiles   Courtesy of Natalie LaFon Wilson

Sharon School - Gone But Not Forgotten
Pauline Alexander Adams 1989

"Plat of Lincoln Township (1893) shows three branches of the Alexander/Confer family within school District No. 4 (Sharon). Alexander, Confer and Mills families owned property and in time sent children to Sharon. Five generations of Alexanders lived on the property acquired by Milton R. following his discharge from the Civil War (approximately 121 years).

A few old pictures of Sharon 'school days' are among mementoes of the family. Changes in modes of dress are noticeable but none show the remodeling of the school building which took place in the early 1920s. Windows were removed from the north wall of the building. Blackboards were hung on this north wall, seating rearranged so students faced north with light coming in from the south and west. No artificial light was available so the room was rather dark on cloudy days. Walter Colley was Jasper County School Superintendent and he was well liked by teachers and pupils.

Spelling Bees and ciphering matches were highlights of the week with some teachers and on special occasions, pupils, put on programs for parents. Sharon had a small but well selected library. Students who enjoyed reading read many of the books over and over. Flying Dutchman, Ante-Over, One-eyed Cat, Hide & Seek, were some of the games played outside. One teacher wanted to teach all her older girls to crochet and embroider. That was fine for a few but some of them were tomboys who wished to be outside at recess playing games. Basic subjects were taught at Sharon (the 3 R's). One term the 5th and 7th grades were taught, the following year the 6th and 8th grades were taught. Since all grades were in one open room, a lower grade student who was alert and quick to learn could hear recitations of older students and sometimes benefit greatly by this advanced classroom work. It was necessary for teachers to be very innovative to keep pupils interested. Some students would not complete the eight or nine month term because they were needed to help with farm work at home. Heating of the building was a problem so school would close during a severely cold winter.

Clay Alexander attended Sharon 1887-1895; his son Rex attended 1917-1925; daughter Pauline attended 1918-1925; daughter Agatha attended 1922-1930.

Sharon and it's many dedicated teachers helped a large number of young people to get a start in life. Such memories are GOOD."

As I remember Sharon
Oscar Clyman

"Perhaps my family's roots and connections with Sharon School go back a little farther than most people's do. I hope my recollections will be of interest to others.

My maternal grandfather, Dr. S. L. Hazen, moved to Jasper County in 1869 from Lake Champlain, New york. He was the first medical doctor in Lincoln Township. He purchased 1,300 acres of land at $2.00 per acre and built a brick house a mile north of the future location of Sharon School. His son, S. A. Hazen, donated the land which was to be the site of the school.

My grandparents were James C. Evans and Emily Hazen Evans. James C. Evans moved to Jasper Country in 1867. He married Emily Hazen, a daughter of Dr. S. L. Hazen, in 1874 in the old Sharon School. It is my understanding that the building was used as a school during the week days and a United Brethern Church on Sundays. They lived on the Jasper, Lawrence County line where we reside now. He was on the school board for many years and was school clerk when the second Sharon School was built in 1898 at a cost of $600.

My mother taught school at Sharon during the last year the old school existed - in 1897.

My father and his parents lived on the corner, just south of Sharon School for some time in approximately 1900. The house, I'm told, was used as a post-office at one time. It was said that there was a steel mail box on that corner which was kept locked and the Golden City and Bowers Mill mail carriers exchanged letters there.

My father was a director for several years and was a member at his death in 1946. I then took his place on the board and served as a member and clerk until the school closed.

My first teacher was Lema Withers. I have an older sister, Audrey, and a younger sister, Lorene, who also attended Sharon. We had recitation desks at the front and sit on two long recitation seats. We would stand for spelling and when a student misspelled a word it would pass to the student to the left. Often on Friday afternoons during the last period we would engage in spelling, geography and mathematics matches.

Most students walked to school but a few either rode horseback or drove a horse and buggy. There was a footbridge over the stream a half mile south of the school.

The teacher also acted as janitor. However, she would have some of the boys bring in coal for the coal stove we used to heat the building. It had a sort of jacket around it to conserve heat. We hung our coats and hats on the east wall and our dinner buckets on the north and south walls next to the coats. A dinner bucket was anything from a brown bag to a syrup bucket with only a few "store-bought" buckets. The boys usually ate out of doors and would eat in the garage if it was a bit cold.

We had many games we played: softball, Anti-over, Dare-base, and many others. We also play Fox and Geese in the snow."

Pleasant Memories
Alva Ellis

"I was born on May 13, 1905 to Frank and Arta Ellis, who lived one-half mile north of Sharon School. The school was located in Northwest Jasper County, approximately twenty miles from Carthage. I attended Sharon School for eight years. An older brother, Ralph, and a younger sister, Viola, also attended Sharon School.

Some things I remember about my grade school days are carrying water from my grandfather's (Issac Coplens) well which was one-fourth mile north of the school. This was a duty for two larger boys who carried the bucket twice each day as there was no well at the school at that time. The school was heated by coal from a large pot-bellied stove in the center of the room. The coal was hauled from a mine near Sylvania, north of Golden City, by horse and wagon in the early autumn. In very cold weather the pupils would sit on benches around the stove to keep warm. The older boys, fifteen to eighteen years of age, trapped furs for spending money. Rabbits were the usual prize, but if they were unfortunate enough to catch a skunk in the traps the odor was not one to be desired in the schoolroom.

The teacher drove a horse and buggy to school. A stable was built to the side of the coal house to provide

Sharon School 1909   Courtesy of Natalie Lafon Wilson

shelter for the horse.

The only playground equipment was a string ball brought by a pupil. A large stick or a flat board served as a bat. Some of the games we played were Flying Dutchman, Blackman, and Ante-over.

The mail man from Bowers Mill left mail at a corner house south of the school. He would eat his lunch and feed his team there each day.

Wed look forward to the Sharon School reunions as an opportunity to visit with friends of former years. I was honored at the reunion in June by being the oldest pupil present who had attended Sharon. I am now 84 years of age and enjoying a busy life.

Sharon School Memories
Unknown author

"Grandad and Grandmother Evans along with her brother Fred Hazen and Ava Cunningham were all married March 15, 1874 at the "Old Sharon School", which also served as a United Brothern Church at that time.

Grandad and Grandmother had four children. Dora, the oldest, Harry, Howard and Clyde. They all graduated at Sharon and Dora also taught there.

My father Howard married Florence Oliver in April 1913. They had 13 children, three sets of twins. Two of the twins died at birth. Edna was the oldest, then Wayne, Gladys & Glenn (twins), Irma (her twin Irene died at birth), Leon (died at age 17), Eugene, Thelma, Robert (his twin Billy died at birth), Ruth Ann and Wilma. Edna, Wayne, Gladys, Glenn, Irma and Leon all attended Sharon School. Edna and Wayne were the only two that graduated at Sharon. Thelma did teach at Sharon later on.

I don't remember or have a date when the new Sharon School was built, but I have heard stories of how hard Granddad worked and campaigned for the new school. There was a lot of hard feelings over the new school. Some of the landowners didn't want to be taxed any more, especially to help educate Granddad's kids, but he was very persistent and got it passed. I guess the hard feelings soon wore off.

I can remember some of the things that happened. The folks didn't want to start Edna to school by herself so they kept her out until the spring. She was almost 7 and I was 5. The first day dad walked with us 1/2 miles west of the house across the field to a gap in the hedge. He told us to go over there where some crows were setting in the field, then go on up to that gap in the hedge, then turn left and go on down to the school. We got over there okay and started out. In the road Edna was in front and back she came. There came a man up the road. So we ran back and hid behind the hedge until the man got by. It was Alvin Farmer going to school. So we went on to school and everybody looked at us like we were from another planet. Esther Hull was the teacher. She put me in a double seat with two other kids. When recess came I had a "nature call" and didn't know where to go. So I went around behind the school house. I remember I was almost through when around the corner came two girls, Pauline Alexander and Melba Harned. They let out a scream and went back. In a little bit, one of the Phipps boys, that lived on the Arthur Boyd place, came around and showed me where to go.

We walked to school the next year. We would try to get to the corner 1/2 mile south before the Delp kids came along. They drove a Shetland pony hitched to a 2-wheeled cart. They would give us a ride. Jack, Mamie, Helen, Edna and I in that little cart and that pony would trot all the way to school with a little encouragement from Jack.

I was probably about 8 years old. I would have to help dad chore, eat breakfast, go hitch up the mare to the buggy and get ready for school. On cold mornings I would have to spit on the bits to take the frost out of them or they would peel the hide off the mare's tongue. I would have to grease the buggy axles once a week. If I tried two weeks, the wheels would squeak. We would all get our dinner buckets and pile in the buggy. The dirt roads were usually terrible, ruts and frozen ground. We would try to be at the Sharon Branch by the time the five minute till 9:00 bell rang. If we were there by that time, we would usually get to school by 9:00. Some teachers went to giving us 10 minutes grace.

Dad and Alexander built us a horse shed to tie our horses in at school. there were several people who drove horses to school. The Adams kids drove "Old Neg". Alexanders drove a pretty bay mare "Old Bess". The Cearnel kids road a bay mare "Old Bab". Glen Magoffin sometimes rode a Shetland pony "Old Prince". He lived 2 1/2 miles south of Golden City, which made about 6 1/2 mile ride. He would ride it in 30 minutes. Sometimes the pony would really be lathering, but it didn't seem to hurt him.

Macie Childres rode a sorrel pacing horse and Ruth Shaffer drove a bay mare when she taught. There were others who rode horses sometimes. When the roads were bad, they didn't have much choice. Oh yes, our horse was the slowest runner of the bunch, but lived to be about 35 years old.

The schoolhouse used to face the west. Then they remodeled it and had the seats face north. I think Lemme Withers taught last when the school faced west.

I remember the teacher would send two of the big boys up to Arthur Lafons during school after a bucket of water. I thought it would sure be nice to be big and get to go, but no such luck. They drilled a well in 1924 and stopped the bucket brigade.

We all learned to entertain ourselves. If somebody would get hold of a rubber ball, we could always find a 1" x 1" x 4" board for a bat and we would sure have fun. We used to play Blackman, Bear, Darebase. When the snow was on we played "Fox and Goose". We always welcomed noon and recesses. Most of the kids had rabbit traps set to get a little spending money. I remember coming home from school I had four rabbits traps. I had a rabbit in each trap. I took them to Dudenville and got 25 cents a piece for them and $1.00 a day was the going wage then. Sometimes I would walk to school and check my traps. I remember catching a civet cat and I got stunk up. I went to school and got sent home. I thought that was a pretty good deal, had the rest of the day to do as I pleased. I tried to catch another civet cat, but no luck.

I remember another interesting thing I should remark about. Agatha Alexander would write a diary every day and would let some of us read it. It was always very interesting and I always looked forward to reading it. Wonder if she still has them?

I remember the boys always went around on the west side of the school to eat our lunch. As soon as the buckets were open, they all started trading lunches. I remember trading True Porter a boiled goose egg for a piece of raisin pie. Mother had some extra goose eggs, so I wanted her to boil one for me to take to school. I don't know which one came out ahead, but True was still eating on the goose egg after the raisin pie was gone. I still say True's mother, Nancy, made the best raisin pie I ever ate. After the Cearnel's moved out of the district, the trading stopped.

The country schools were a necessity in their day and people sure hated to give them up. Some put up quite a fight, but due to our transportation and the decline in rural population, etc., they outlived their time. I don't know where they could find anybody now who could do the janitor work, teach all eight grades and cook a hot meal for the kids. I don't ever hear of anybody wanting to go back to the one room school."

Agatha Lambeth Alexander
Sharon

"I don't remember too much about my first years of school, other than the fun my best school friend, Anise Farmer, and I used to have. We shared secrets and spent as many nights sleeping over at each others homes as our moms would allow. We also liked to spend the night with our 1st grade teacher, Ruth Shaeffer. Her mom was such a good cook and filled our dinner buckets next day with store-bought cookies and huge slices of Angel Food cake. That was something rare in a dinner bucket, when eggs had to be sold instead of using 13 of them for a cake!

I either walked the mile and a quarter through the field to school or rode "Old Bess", our fat and faithful horse.

On cold evenings, when school let Wayne Evans and I used to race to the corner on Old Bess and his black horse, Old Kate.

I remember that we girls used to trade food at lunch time. Anise and I usually brought something special to swap with each other. Her Mom canned such good peeled cucumbers. I think she must have kept a jar of them open just for me. I would trade a sandwich or most anything in my bucket for one of those pickles. Miss Mae Vanbebber was our 8th grade teacher and she prepared delicious soups and stews on the big coal heater in the schoolroom. (You will notice I'm always talking about 'food'. Something I have never outgrown.)

Another fun-thing I remember about Miss Mae's terms, was her school programs. All thought my 8 grades, teachers had good programs for parents and friends, but Miss Mae's were extra special. She loved music. She would crank up the old Victrola and we would march up and down and all around the room to the tune of "Stars & Strips Forever." Miss Mae also helped us get a school paper started. It was called "Spotlight". We had various editors for articles, such as Sports, Editorial, Cartoons & Jokes, Class work and other important items. This was copied as part of our schoolwork and given to all of the district members who wanted one.

Our school Christmas programs were always very special. We practiced for days & days on our 'pieces', songs & dialogues. When the program was over, Santa would arrive to distribute gifts. We had always drawn names before hand so everyone would get a gift. We never had much money to buy gifts, but I always thought I got to give my teachers a bottle of perfume for Christmas. That perfume always came from Kress' & probably cost about a dime. I'll bet the teachers had to hold their breath when they unwrapped the package, but of course I thought it was a grand gift.

One year Louise Adams and I sat together in a double seat and we always prided ourselves on keeping the neatest desk in school. Our school library was full of good books. I read "Tom Sawyer", "Girl of the Limberlost" and "Black Beauty" so often I just about had them memorized.

I remember that Rex made me 2 wooden rabbit traps which I set and baited with a piece of apple ever morning that I walked to school. Of course when I was lucky enough to trap a rabbit, the poor thing had to remain trapped until I got home from school that evening to tell Rex about it so he could take it out of the trap for me. After all, that rabbit skin was worth a whole nickel up at Maple Grove store and I could buy a pkg. of Juicy Fruit gum or a bottle of grape pop for a nickel!!

One evening I walked home with Edith Stiles. They had some big white ganders at their housed and one of them chased me around the house 3 times before Edith got that doggoned gander chased away from me. Another time, I was spending the night with Edith. We were sitting at a north window, coloring, when it began to storm and a bolt of lightning caused Edith to fall off her chair and affected her eyesight for several minutes. That was a scare.

I can't remember too many sad things that happened at school. We always hated to see pupils move out of our district. The saddest thing I can remember is the day Miss Ruth Jones let all of us walk to the Alfred Pennell home, about a mile south of the schoolhouse. A small child of the Pennells had passed away. The baby girl was lying in a casket in their living room. We all gathered near it and sang "Jesus Loves Me". Then walked back to school.

   I remember how badly I wanted a new dress for 8th grade graduation. That was even before we had feed sack material for dresses, etc. Material at the store cost 20 or 15 cents a yd. and even a dime was hard come-by. So Mom told me I could sell all of the eggs I found outside of the henhouse. Where the hens made nests in the barns, strawstacks, etc.) I could use the egg money to buy a new dress. I spent a lot of evenings after school & a lot of weekends chasing the hens out of the henhouse, hoping they would be forced to lay their eggs anywhere but the henhouse! I'm sure Mom knew what was going on, but she knew how badly I wanted the new dress and she never said a word about what I was doing to those poor old hens. By graduation week, I had enough egg money and with a few dimes slipped to me from Dad, to go to Bormasters Dry Goods store in Carthage and get a brand new ready-made dress. It was a beautiful blue flowery print. I'll never forget it.

   Our 8th grade class, with Miss Maes' help, had great fun writing our last will & testament and a prophecy of what we thought our classmates would be doing in 25 years. We put our documents in a fruit jar (just Like Johnny Carson) and then put the jar in the schoolhouse attic. Our intentions were to all meet there again in 25 yrs. Twenty five years seemed like a long time to us then. The plans didn't work out, we didn't have that reunion, the schoolhouse was sold & torn down without the jar ever being found. Never the less, we are at our reunions now. (60 years later).

   The old pump that was out in the northeast corner of the yard really got a workout. We would gather around it like camels in a desert. Not just because we were thirsty, but water fights were frequents. Just before time for school to resume after lunch or recess, everybody made a mad dash for that last drink of water. Soon after that, hands began to fly up into the air; 1 finger for 'toilet time' 2 for a drink and 5 for 'a question, teacher'.

   Our school would sometimes go to Bois D'arc School for baseball games. We weren't Big League players but we sure had fun. 3 or 4 of us girls doubled as players & cheerleaders. Our favorite cheer was:

> **Booma Alacka, Boom Alacka**
> Bow, bow, Bow!
> **Chicka Alacka, Chicka Alacka**
> Chow, chow, chow!
> **Booma Lacka, Chicka Lacka**
> Who are we?
> **Sharon School! Don't you see?**
> S-H-A-R-O-N !!!

   Other games we played were Needles Eye, Dressel Ply, (I never did know what dressel ply meant) but we played the game nearly every day. Also, the old games of Blackman, Dare Base, Ante-over, Ball, Hop Scotch & Tag. In the winter time it was the Wild Geese game that was played in the snow & Flying Dutchman.

   One more experience to share & then I will shut up!

   One recess, Pauline Richmond and I went down to the northwest corner of the schoolyard to the girls' business office. We found a 2 foot black snake stretched out on the 2-holer seat. Believe me, that business conference adjourned in a hurry!! Teacher & a couple of those brave Sharon boys disposed of the intruder.

Now! That's all!! Aren't you glad??"

Thomas Milbern Wright
Sharon

"I am Thomas Milburn Wright. My parents were Thomas Leroy "Roy" Wright and Fannie Mabel Boyd Wright. I was born on Feb. 4, 1923 near Dudenville, Missouri.

I started to school at Spring Hill in September 1928, and left in the fall of 1932, my dad was able to buy out Manley Jenkins who was farming Arthur Boyd's north farm. I quit school at Spring Hill immediately and went to help with sowing of wheat along with my father. I drove mules and worked the ground. When the wheat was sowed, we moved the remainder of the family.

The day we moved, we made several trips with the mules and wagons. The last trip was late in the evening and we stopped at Maple Grove Store. Mr. Floyd Moore gave my dad a can of pork and beans for us to eat. He told us Mr. Roosevelt was elected president. It was November 4, 1932.

Soon afterward I started attending school at Sharon. The teacher was Mrs. Mae Hope. This was a smaller school than Spring Hill and had fewer books available. I had many chores to do at home before and after school.

In the fall of 1933, I had a new teacher, Miss Mary O'Brien. Times were very hard. We had very little food and clothing. My father was an expert at making rabbit traps. We hunted and trapped rabbits. The store in Dudenville and Maple Grove bought them. They paid from between three and ten cents each. Usually we traded them for groceries. I hunted with Loyd and Leroy Pennel. They were excellent shots and had very good rabbit dogs.

We took whatever was available in the line of food to school for lunch - at times a rabbit leg and biscuit or molasses cake.

In the fall of 1934, wed had the same teacher, Miss Mary O'Brien. She took a group of us to put on a program for another school one Friday night. When we got back, we stayed all night at Miss Mary's house. After breakfast the next morning, her father , Mr. Pat O'Brian, gave us some fresh roasted peanuts. To this day, I still like peanuts and remember Mr. Pat O'Brian.

In the spring of 1935, Miss Mary took us to Avilla to take the test for our graduation. With the help of Miss Sylvia Mason, I managed to pass the examination, and graduated with the class of 1935. I was twelve years of age.

In the fall of 1935, I enrolled in the Golden City High School. Somehow I managed to stay in school and achieved enough credits to graduate in the spring of 1939. This was the end of my formal education."

Sharon School about 1914   Harry Curry, teacher   Courtesy Natalie Lafon Wilson

The Love of Teaching School
Mary Angie O'Brien
Sharon

"I was asked to write a history of my teaching career, and as I get pencil and paper, my mind travels back to my first school, a one-room school, and the first day of teaching. I was so happy and frightened too.

I had graduated from Golden City High School in the spring of 1933 and was hired to teach at Sharon School for the 1933-34 term. Mrs. Mae Hope had taught at Sharon for several years and I knew following a teacher like Mrs. Mae wasn't going to be easy.

I cherish all the memorials of Sharon School. The children who didn't have an opportunity to attend a one-room school with only one teacher have missed part of their education.

The older children helped the younger ones; in other wards, they were also teachers. It helped them remember their own school work.

Class periods weren't very long, not more than fifteen minutes each. One year I taught fifth and seventh grades, sixth and eighth the next. From the fifth grade you would go to the seventh grade. Then the next year back to the sixth. The students didn't seem to mind the jumping back and forth.

I taught all subjects, did the janitor work, built fires, carried coal, took out ashes, and in later years prepared lunches with food provided by the government. Sometimes the mothers would help me prepare the food.

My total salary was fifty dollars a month--four hundred dollars a year. I was so glad when I got my first paycheck. I ran about a quarter of a mile home, and was all out of breath when I got to the house. My father asked me what was wrong. I said, "Look, I have fifty dollars!" I appreciated the money and the experience from that first month of school.

That year at Sharon, we had 32 students. We entered a contest and won first prize for the best number on the program. Our prize was the picture of THE LONE SCOUT.

When Christmas came we made decoration of paper rings and hung them across the room. It was beautiful.

That first year we were practicing for Activity Day at Greenfield, so I told the children we wouldn't have hot lunches that week. The next morning a mother came to school and asked why. I told her we needed the time to practice. She was very upset. She said, "Oh, I'll have to bake bread every day." She volunteered to cook our lunches that week and they were delicious.

We won several prizes at Activity Day, and I was very pleased for we were in competition with other schools that had more experienced teachers.

At recess we played Anti-over, Blackman, Upset the Fruit Basket, I Spy. Hide the Thimble, Go In and Out the Window, Three Deep, and Whip Cracker.

The last day of school we had a program and dinner, Those parents were good cooks. In the afternoon the parents presented my with a Friendship Quilt which is beautiful. I love every stitch of it!

The next year when I taught Sharon we had 29 students. The rural schools I taught were Sharon, Monitor, and Ackley. Then at the request of the superintendent and board of directors, I moved to the Golden City Public Schools where I remained for twenty-four years.

Several years teaching as Sharon a student came to visit me. I went to the door and she walked in the house, put her arms around me and said, "I just wanted to see if you still had that little mustache." She informed me that we were going to see Sharon School. I told her I couldn't go I have to finish dressing chickens. She replied, "Well, they're dead and will be here when we get back."

I thank the Good Lord for his many blessing and the good health he has given me and thank the many parents, teachers, board members, and friend who helped make my teaching a success.

I taught school forty-five years and never missed a day for personal illness."

Irma Nelle (Evans) Erickson
Sharon

"I became a student at Sharon School in 1925. That was eighty-five years ago for that reason my memory of Sharon School is rather vague. I was five-years-old but would be six in November. I had four older brothers and sisters attending Sharon. My first teacher was Mr. Glenn Magoffin. I recall standing beside his desk and reading to him. I had to learn to read before I started to school and was pleased when he had me read to the rest of the first grade. He taught there only one year.

The second grade teacher was rather elderly and was very kind and motherly. The teacher that we had the next year lacked patience. I remember her getting angry and screaming at the students. It seemed I sensed tension the whole nine months. Being from a large family, we children decided her problem was the result of being an only child and she was spoiled.

Ruth Jones was our next teacher. My most vivid memory of that year was when a family near by had a baby that didn't live. The teacher had us walk to the home, stand around the coffin and sing "Jesus Loves Me". The next and last teacher at Sharon was Mae Vanbidder. My family moved in February to New Hope district. Miss Mae was an excellent teacher. She would have some of the classes compete for prizes for the highest grade. I treasured a copy of a small New "Testament that I was awarded and have kept.

We lived about two miles from school if we traveled on the road. Sometimes we would walk across our field and a neighbor's field to the road that led to the school building, that route was only about one mile. Other mornings our older brother Wayne would harness our house Kate and we would enjoy riding in the buggy. Later, Gladys and I would ride Kate and Glenn and Wayne would ride Bird. Edna was in high school by then. There was a shed for the horses. If the weather was really bad our father would drive us to school in our Model "A" Ford sedan if necessary.

We all enjoyed playing games during recess and noon. The Christmas programs were something to remember. I was to hug Russell Adams in a play we were to present. I flatly refused. I liked Russell but I wasn't about to hug him in front of parents and others who would come for the program. I didn't get any encouragement from Russell as he was as timid as I was.

My sister Gladys was a year ahead of me in school. She told me of an incident that happened to her the first day of school when she was in first grade. There was a large waste bucket at the side of the room. If you had waste paper you wanted to get off your desk you were allowed to leave your desk and take it to the waste basket. Gladys and Jewel Cerneal were bored as the teacher gave them nothing to do. To entertain themselves they started taking turns tearing off a little piece of paper, wadding it up and taking it to the waste basket. Instead of the teacher asking them to stop the activity after a few trips, she took them to the front of the room, took down their bloomers and spanked each of the bare behinds. Eventually Gladys became an excellent teacher of first and second grades for thirty-two years. I am confident she didn't spank any bare behinds. She said she always made sure her beginners had something to do to keep them busy. Attending a rural school for eight years was an adventure. We did our studying at school while another class was on the recitation bench. Home work was not in our vocabulary. We had to learn to change our study habits when we progressed in higher education."

Oaths of School Directors.

I do solemnly swear or affirm, that I will support the Constitution of the United States, and the Constitution of the State of Missouri, and that I will faithfully and impartially discharge the duties of School Director, in and for _Dist No. 26_ County of _Jasper_, Missouri, according to law and the best of my ability.

Clay Alexander, Director.

Sworn to and subscribed before me, this _sixth_ day of _April_, 1915.

James Farmer

I do solemnly swear or affirm, that I will support the Constitution of the United States, and the Constitution of the State of Missouri, and that I will faithfully and impartially discharge the duties of School Director, in and for _Dist No 26_ County of _Jasper_, Missouri, according to law and the best of my abilities.

Warren A. Still, Director.

Sworn to and subscribed before me, this _4_ day of _October_, 1921.

Clay Alexander

I do solemnly swear or affirm, that I will support the Constitution of the United States, and the Constitution of the State of Missouri, and that I will faithfully and impartially discharge the duties of School Director, in and for _Dist #26_ County of _Jasper_, Missouri, according to law and the best of my abilities.

A. Lofow, Director.

Sworn to and subscribed before me, this _1_ day of _April_, 1919.

Clay Alexander

I do solemnly swear or affirm, that I will support the Constitution of the United States, and the Constitution

Sheridan School

LOCATION: SECTION: 32   TOWNSHIP: 30   RANGE: 30   DISTRICT: 22

Located 3 miles SW of Jasper. organized in 1877 and annexed by the Jasper School District in 1960.

Assessed value $137,100; Teacher: Gladys Rusk-Carthage; Grade of certificate...2; Officers: Everett Bruffett-Jasper, Clerk; Oscar Fasken-Jasper, President; B. F. Miller-Jasper; Enrolled...21; No. of pupils in Class A...5, B...4, C...5, D...7; No present...19; Term...8 months; Condition of grounds...Clean; Water...Well; Condition of out-buildings...Fair; Blackboard...Good; Maps...0; Globes...1; Dictionary...1; Library: No. of vol...115; Value...$50; Suitability of books...Good; Free text books...No; Condition of school records...Good; Heating...Stove; Community meetings...Farm Club

Jasper County Superintendent's School Report 1924-25
Courtesy of the Jasper County Record Center

!887 Rules Governing Sheridan School

Article 1: That the pupils render due obedience to their teacher.

Article 2: That the students are strictly forbidden using profane or vulgar language in or around the schoolhouse.

Article 3: That the teacher is strictly required to keep order in the school. Should any pupil or pupils not comply with this article they must be punished, or, if a proper age, to be reported to the school directors.

Article 4: That the teacher shall have the oversight of the pupils during recess in regard to improper conduct and that they return to their restrictive homes as soon as they are dismissed from school.

Article 5: The teacher shall have the care of the schoolhouse and furniture.

Courtesy of Kathy Sidenstricker - www.jaspercountyschools.org

Sheridan School 1921

Sheridan School 1945-46

L-R Back Row: Wayne Smith, Wilber Smith (twins), Dorothy Grisham, Gene Bruffett, Mary Harvey, Faye Flesher, teacher, Paul Bruffett, Melvin Simmons
L-R Front Row: Joan Grisham, ____, Richard Taylor, ____, ____.

Shiloh School

LOCATION: SECTION: 8   TOWNSHIP: 29   RANGE: 31   DISTRICT: 48

Teacher: Jennie Conrad; Salary...$35 monthly; Term: 8 months; Enrolled: Male...14, Female...18, Total...32; No. present to-day...13; Board: Frank Weeks-Carthage, Clerk; John N. Weeks-Carthage, President; Clark Ale & Chids Mills

Jasper County Superintendent's School Report 1893
Courtesy of the Jasper County Record Center

Assessed value $196,100; Teacher: Emma Cooper-Carthage; Salary $75 monthly; Officers: Ernest Potter-Carthage, Clerk; C. A. Bowman-Carthage, President; O. F. Frost-Carthage, Member; Enrolled...14; No. present...13; Term...8 months; Condition of house...Clean; Condition of grounds...Clean; Water...Well; Sanitation...Good; Decoration...Good; Condition of out-buildings...Fair; Blackboard...Slate; Maps...Case; Globes...Broken; Dictionary...1; Library: No. of vol...300; Value...$75; Suitability of books...Good; Free text books...No; Condition of school records...Good; Heating...Stove

Jasper County Superintendent's School Report 1924-25
Courtesy of the Jasper County Record Center

"In 1961, the original Pleasant Valley, Mineral, Garden Dell and Shiloh school districts consolidated to form the new Pleasant Valley R-6 School District. Students were transported to the Pleasant Valley school building located in Brooklyn Heights."
Kathy Sidenstricker - www.jaspercountyschools.org

Joyce (Bowman) Carter
Shiloh and Prairie View

"I went to school at Shiloh from 2nd through 8th grade (1938 to 1943-44). In the front of the school was a room separated from the classroom where we hung our coats on hooks & benches where we put our lunch boxes and on which we sat to take off galoshes.

The main room had a big coal burning stove at the back. The teacher was responsible for starting and keeping it going and she was also the janitor. If a student sat near the stove on cold days, they were warm and up in front the students were chilly. There were either three or four large windows on both sides of the school. In the back of the building was shed for the coal. There was a large yard where we could play baseball & other things, also "Annie Over' the school house. We had teeter totters but no swings. The school yard was given half and half by the Bowman family and the Ale family who had settled here in the spring of 1873 and got school started. My great grandparents, My grandfather (Clarence Bowman) went to school here. We lived about a block through a pasture from the school and my Mother boarded the teachers so they live with us five days a week. I really didn't like this. Some of the kids thought we were "pets" so the teachers went our of their ways to prove that wasn't the case.

The old school is practically gone now. Then we had outdoor toilets built by the WPA, which were much nicer than the old ones. One day the County Superintendent, Mrs. Bertha Reed came and she complimented our teacher on how quiet her school room was when she came for a surprise visit. Mrs. Reed was my 1st & 2nd grade teacher at a large country school Prairie View, before she became Superintendent.

My two sons, Steve & Doug remember some things about their days there. The county furnished 1/2 pints of milk, chocolate or white, for each child for 1 cents each. One year they started charging 2 cents, I though doubling the price was a lot. Seems ridiculous now.

My husband, Gene, was on the school board & when they hired a new teacher, (Mrs. Gordon Lee), they warned her about one of the boys that caused trouble. She just said, "I won't have any trouble." And she didn't. The first time he acted up she boxed his ears & sent him home. When he came back he was a model pupil that liked his teacher. Imagine teachers doing that now! I remember the rest of us thought that we sure didn't want to get slapped like that & of course, no one did."

Above: Shiloh class of 1952-53
Below: Shiloh school 1954-55

Silver Creek School

LOCATION: SECTION: 22 TOWNSHIP: 30 RANGE: 33 DISTRICT: 12

"Located three miles north of Medoc; John Luster, M. K. Jones and Wm. Row, directors; J. C. Grason, teacher; Term of six months began October 21st; District enumeration 31; Enrollment 14; Present 13; Building and furniture second-class. Seating capacity 18. This is Mr. Grason's fourth term in Jasper County and he is teaching a good school. On the day of the recent election a prairie fire broke out in the neighborhood which destroyed a large amount of fencing and would have burned the school house but for the hard work of Mr. Grason and the entire force of the school."

Jasper County School Report by S. A. Underwood, 1878
Joel Thomas Livingston - A History of Jasper County, Missouri and Its People, Vol. 1, 1912, Page 103

Teacher: J. A. Swank; Salary...$40 monthly; Term...9 months; Enrolled: Male...17, Female...17, Total...34; No. present to-day...28; Board: J. B. Harpole-Opolis, Clerk; Wm. Graves-Medoc, President; John Martin-Opolis; Condition of blackboard...Excellent; Condition of building...Fine; Condition of floor...First class; Condition of furniture...Good; Condition of apparatus...None; Condition of grounds, out-houses, etc...Good

Jasper County Superintendent's School Report 1893
Courtesy of the Jasper County Record Center

Assessed value $135,917; Teacher: Atta Dick-Asbury; Grade of certificate...2; Officers: Jennie Bell Flaker-Opolis, Clerk; Orla J. Moore-Opolis, President; W. A. Herr-Medoc & A. A. Barrett-Opolis, Members; Enrollment...30; No. present...29; Term...8 months; Condition of house...Good; Condition of grounds...Clean; Water...Well; Condition of out-buildings...Needs repair; Blackboard...Good; Maps...0; Globes...1; Dictionary...1; Library: No. of vol...200; Value $75; Suitability of books...Good; Free text books...Yes; Condition of school records...Good; Ventilation...Good; Heating...Laurel

Jasper County Superintendent's School Report 1924-25
Courtesy of the Jasper County Record Center

Silver Creek 1921

Silver Creek 1912
On wonders what was going on in the left back row and left front row.

Silver Creek 1943-44
Front Row L-R: Bobby Garretson, John McCool, Jack Washburn, Orville Miller, ____, Nidiffer, ____ Vaughn

Middle Row: ____ Vaughn, Beverly Monroe

Back Row: Myrtle Vaughn, Riley Vaughn, Carl Nidiffer, Norman Monroe, Bill Marcus, Mildred Garretson, ____, Nidiffer, Eula Grace Monroe, Edith Pugh-Teacher

Snowflake School
LOCATION: SECTION: 15   TOWNSHIP: 30   RANGE: 29   DISTRICT: 1

Teacher: W. E. Johns; Salary...$30 monthly; Term...5 months; Enrolled: Male...15, Female...14, Total...29; No. present to-day...8; Board: Wm. Etter-Golden City, Clerk; Geo. A. Malltbie-Golden City, President; H. Gringrich & W. S. Evans
Jasper County Superintendent's School Report 1894 - Courtesy of the Jasper County Record Center

Assessed value $102,100; Teacher: Beulah Maddox-Golden City; Salary $70 monthly; Officers: Forest L. Maddox-Golden City, Clerk; C. W. Parker-Golden City, President; Chas. Magoffin-Golden City, Members; Enrolled...7; No. of pupils in Class A...1, B...1, C...3, D...2; No. present...7; Term...8 months; Condition of house...Clean; Condition of grounds...Mowed; Water...Carried; Condition of out-buildings...Both need repairs; Blackboard...Slate; Maps...0; Globes...0; Dictionary...Old; Library: No. of vol...150; Value...$50; Suitability of books...Good; Free text books...No; Condition of school records...Good; Heating...Modern
Jasper County Superintendent's School Report 1924-25 - Courtesy of the Jasper County Record Center

Spring Hill School
LOCATION: SECTION 6   TOWNSHIP: 29   RANGE: 29   DISTRICT: 27

Following is the term report of this school: "Length of term, 5 months; number of days actually taught, 98; enrollment, 62; total days' attendance, 3868; average number of pupils present each day, 39 23-49; average number of days' attendance by each pupil, 692 12-31.

Prizes were awarded to Mary Keller of "C" class, and to Laura Forsithe of "D" class. A large number of patrons witnessed the closing exercises, which consisted the declamations, selected reading spelling.
L Greene, teacher."
The Carthage Banner March 12, 1885

Springhill School

Assessed value $185,777; Teacher Mrs. Addie Priggle-Bower Mills; Grade of certificate...1; Officers: Claude Erwin-Golden City, Clerk; Geo. Wilson-Golden City, President; James Ziler-Reeds, Member; Enrollment...30; No. present...30; Term...8 months; Condition of house...Clean; Condition of grounds... Clean; Water...Well; Condition of out-buildings...Good; Blackboard...Slate; Maps...Case; Globes...1; Dictionary...1; Free text books...No; Heating...Modern
Jasper County Superintendent's School Report 1924-25 - Courtesy of the Jasper County Record Center

Spring Hill 1952-53 - Bernice Brown, Teacher

Spring Hill - Sylvia Baker, Teacher

Sumerset School

LOCATION: SECTION: __   TOWNSHIP: 29   RANGE: 30   DISTRICT: 1 (Early district)

Sumerset School   Courtesy of Kathy Sidenstricker

"There was no question about the type of behavior expected, even demanded of pupils of Somerset School west-northwest of Avilla during the 1880.

The code of conduct adopted by the Board of Education and carefully explained to each teacher is contained in a battered record book rescued from approaching disintegration by Dote Hall, Reeds, Route 1. The code is clear.

"Rules for the government of the district school in District 1, Township 29, Range 30."

First, all vulgar and profane language (is) forbidden in the schoolroom and on the playground.

Second, running, jumping, scuffling, throwing apples, books or anything else in the schoolroom to the detriment of the school property is strictly forbidden, also walking on top of desks and any school property damaged or destroyed in violation of this rule shall be made good by the parties, their parents or guardians.

Third, it shall be unlawful for any pupil attending school to use saucy or improper language to any teacher in said school.

Fourth, all reasonable rules made by the teacher for the government of the school will be sustained by the board.

Fifth, a persistent violation of any or all of these rules shall be considered a sufficient cause for suspension or expulsion from school.

Sixth, these rules (are) to take effect when a copy of the same is placed in the hands of the teachers.

It is apparent vandalism and use of abusive language were attempted by someone but no freedom for possible repetition was granted. The business of the school plainly was education and it was intended that business should be conducted smoothly and efficiently.

Somerset district was organized for the 1878 spring term.

In 1883, the district was divided to allow for formation of another school district, identity of which is not readily available, with part of Sumerset's assets assigned to the new district.

By order of the board W. F. Lamkin on March 29, 1883, formally appraised the school "house and property" and fixed its value for purposes of the division of $600. Somerset's classes continued at the same site.

The period of usefulness of the Somerset School apparently ended with the spring term in 1887. "The school board of District No. 1, Township 29, Range 30. will sell on Sept. 20, 1889, between the hours of 1 and 3 o'clock p.m. the Summersett (sic) schoolhouse. All parties desiring such a building will be expected to be present
at that time. Terms--to be paid within 30 to 60 days, which time will be agreed upon day of sale.

Apparently the structure sold to Spring River Church of the Brethren and converted to use as a house of worship.

An undated "expense report" included in the record is illuminating:

"Two brooms, 50 cents; butts for door, 15 cents; nails for fence, 15 cents;; door lock, 45 cents; nails for privy; 25 cents; door for privy, $1.50; lumber for privy, $1.20; daily register, $1; chalf, 20 cents; scrubbing house, $1.50; labor on lot fence, $1; wire for lot fence, $31; wire for lot fence, $3.25; work on privy, $1; building flue, $1.50; brick and fencing, 50 cents."

Enrollment totals recorded ranged from a low of 37 for the spring term of 1885 to a high of 71 for the winter term of 1880.

A typical tax levy was 22 cents per $100 assessed valuation in 1885.

Sumerset has passed into history but it made an indelible mark upon Jasper County society which has not and will not disappear."

A Brief For History by Marvin L. VanGilder, Press Historian
The Carthage Evening Press, Nov. 25, 1978
Courtesy of the Jasper County Record Center

Stone School

LOCATION: SECTION: 23 TOWNSHIP: 29 RANGE: 33 DISTRICT: 66

Assessed value $124,721; Teacher: Juanita Hammons-Oronogo; Grade of certificate...TT; Officers: Rosa Ritter-Oronogo, Clerk; A. Ritter-Oronogo, President; Mrs. L. E. Vaughn-Oronogo & H. Weaver-Oronogo, Members; Enrollment...12; No. present...12; Term...8 months; Condition of house...Good; Condition of grounds...Mowed; Water...Carried; Decoration...Good; Condition of out-buildings...Good; Blackboard...Good; Maps...Case; Globes...1; Dictionary...6 Serall; Library: No. of vol...127; Suitability of books...Good; Free text books...No; Condition of school records...Good; Heating...Stove

Jasper County Superintendent's School Report 1924-25
Courtesy of the Jasper County Record Center

Stone pupils at play. There appears to be a mine in the back-ground.

Courtesy of Kathy Sidenstricker

Dorothy Ogdon, teacher

The Old Stone School House,

Editor PRESS:—The following poem in reference to the historic Stone School House, north of town, was part of a letter written by a girl of seventeen, (with no thought of publication) to a school girl friend.

As it possesses true literary merit, and is interesting as showing the talent, latent, in our country schools, we offer it for publication:

Ah! Still it stands by the roadside there,
To the passerby it is far from fair,
For its walls of stone are gray and cold,
And its roof is blackened and covered with mud.

No cedar or pine around it stand
Above its roof, waves no old oak grand,
Nor are there trees with nuts so brown,
But a simple hedge encloses the ground.

Inside this house so old and worn,
The paper from the walls is torn.
And the seats seem just to have ended a strife,
With a a rough school boy and his pocket knife.

The desks are scratched, and cut, and scarred,
And their former beauty sadly marred;
Along the aisles where the children walk,
Are crushed small cinders and bits of chalk.

The rains through the broken window beat,'s
The battered doors on their hinges creak,
The stove is cracked and red with rust,
And the tuneless organ is covered with dust.

But despise it not, oh passerby!
Nor look on it with contemptuous eye,
We love that house with looks forlorn,
For within its walls our hopes were born.

Hopes, for many, to be realized never;
Born only for fate's cruel sword to sever,
But they were lovely and sweet in their youthful bloom.
Ere the cold hand of death laid them low in the tomb.

There our thoughts were buoyant and fresh and young,
And our hearts, with cords of ambition were strung.
We have passed from its shelter one by one,
To the great field of work which lay beyond.

Dale Craig & Donald LePanne

Richard Craig

Photos courtesy of
Kathy Sidenstricker
www.jaspercounty schools. org.

Floyd Craig

Harley Pitcher

John Ellison

Stony Point School
a/k/a Diamond
LOCATION: SECTION: 7 TOWNSHIP: 27 RANGE: 31 DISTRICT: 117

Teacher: John Fleck; Salary...$35 monthly; Term...6 months; Enrolled: Male...27, Female...17, Total...44; No. present to-day...30; Board: Chas. Randall-Fidelity, Clerk; Wm. McReynolds-Scotland, President; Jacob Grubb-Fidality; Condition of blackboard...Not very good; Condition of building...Need repairing; Condition of furniture...Fair; Condition of apparatus...Medium; Condition of grounds, out-houses, etc... Needs repairing

Jasper County Superintendent's School Report 1893
Courtesy of the Jasper County Record Center

Assessed value $ 99,730; Teacher: Josie Collings-Diamond; Grade of certificate...3; Officers: G. J. Collings-Diamond, Clerk; J. J. Duke-Carthage, President; Ed Frerer-Carthage, Member; Enrollment...48; No. present...46; Term...8 months; Condition of house...Fair; Condition of grounds...Clean; Water...Well; Condition of out-buildings...Fair; Blackboard...Fair; Maps...Case; Globes...0; Library: No. of vol...100; Value $75; Free text books...Yes; Condition of school records...Poor; Heating...Stove

Jasper County Superintendent's School Report 1924-25
Courtesy of the Jasper County Record Center

Stony Point School 1910s   Courtesy of Kathy Sidenstricker & Michelle Hansford

Stony Point 1952 - Rosetta Richardson, Teacher

Stony Point 1954-55

Summit School

LOCATION: SECTION: 23   TOWNSHIP: 30   RANGE: 30   DISTRICT: 4

Summit closed in 1960 sending students to Jasper. Pupils enrolled in 1872 was 62, in 1894 the count was 38, in 1924-25 it was 10.

"Summit school house: H. C. Parrich, teacher, wages $35; five months term; good house, large and comfortable, seated with pine desks; sixty-two pupils. This is sub-district No. 2, township 30, range 30. A very good class of pupils and pretty well drilled; school a success, all seem interested in the support of a good school and as far as I could see labor to that end. I think tardiness a bad feature of this school; also non attendance but on the whole the school is doing very well."

Assessed value $148,128; Teacher: Lottie Rogers-Jasper; Salary...$65 monthly; Grade of certificate...3; Officers: Chas. F. Thomas-Jasper, Clerk; G. A. Scheel-Jasper, President; P. B. Wright-Jasper & Floyd Thomas, Members; Enrolled...10; No. of pupils in Class A...3, B...1, C...1, D...5; No. present...10; Term...8 months; Condition of house...Clean; Condition of grounds... Clean; Water...Well; Sanitation...Good; Condition of out-buildings...Fair, boys' need repairs; Blackboard; Slate; Maps...Old case; Globes...Broken, Dictionary...2 old; Library: No. of vol...100; Value $50; Suitability of books...Some good; Free text books...No; Condition of school records...Poor; Heating...Stove; Community meetings...No

Jasper County Superintendent's School Report 1924-25
Courtesy of the Jasper County Record Center

Ella Sunderland 1941-42

Ella Marie(Sunderland) Leaming
Summit

"I began Summit School, a one room country school, the fall of 1941. Being an only child and was five years old that past January, my parents, Bud and Marcella, had not planned on me entering school till the following term. The teacher, Mildred Mae Harvey, called Mother and said Jimmie Frerer was beginning and she'd like two in the class. It would make our grades come even, not skip 5th and 7th, then 6th and 8th like we used to do. So. I did begin September, 1941. Later into the

Scrap Metal Drive

year, Gilbert Garrett moved into our neighborhood; that made ten children total in grades 1 thru 8. Lydia Jane Earl, Donna Schnell, Norma Thomas, Bell Johnston, Roger Schnell, Patsy Schnell, Wayne Johnson, Jimmie Frerer and myself. We all took sack lunches, pumped our water from a well and had outdoor toilets. Our one room school was heated with a coal stove. Country school life was fun.

We lived two full miles from school. My parents took me to school but I could walk home some times going south with Jimmie Frerer. He would chase me with wet turtles or his big German police dog. We were always in competition the whole eight years. Other times I'd walk east with the Schell Kids and we'd cut through their pasture and pick persimmons. We would get a drink from their springhouse. Either way, I had a mile to myself and could imagine many things.

The last day of school was always a big day in April, as we began in Sept. and only had eight months of school. All the parents came for a well-filled basket dinner and we had awards, a program and then all played softball.

The next year, 1942-43, we had the same teacher but only nine students this school year. We had a scrap metal drive. This became a huge scrap pile for World War II. That year we had a great Halloween party and program. Also, we all went on our first train ride. We were taken to Jasper Depot, boarded a MO. Pacific passenger train and road to Carthage. We were then taken to the Carthage fire station and we sat on the fire truck for pictures. Big. Day!

That summer Mildred Harvey married Eldon Rees and so the fall of 1943, Maurice Leaming was our new teacher and we had eight students. She later would be my aunt as I married her nephew in 1953.

During 1944-45, Helen Mae Wolfe Carlson, a doctor's wife, became our teacher for the next four years. I believe twelve children in one year were the most taught by Mrs. Carlson.

By 1948-49, my 8th grade year, Doris Jean Wardlow had her first and only teaching year. We had thirteen students.

That spring, we went to another country school, Magoffin, where Margott Manley was teacher. We had softball games and a picnic.

During 1944, the Henry boys, James and Robert, moved into our neighborhood, Robert was in our class, so now there were three boys and me. We would continue our education through 8th grade here at Summit, then on to Jasper High School, where all four of us graduated in 1953 and would all remain good friends.

The pie suppers were great once a year for fund raisers. Home made pies were auctioned off and raffle tickets sold on larger items such as blankets, etc. The school girls would make and decorate boxes, maybe shoe boxes, and fill them with sandwiches and goodies. These would be bought by the highest bidder and then the winner would eat with the girl. Our pie suppers were very successful, sometimes bringing in over $100. This money would purchase something needed for our school and some for fun games, new globes, books or new bats and balls,etc. We had a blackboard across one end and a library on one side. We had a cloak room where we hung our coats and a small kitchen. There were about five rows of wooden desks, maybe six desks to a row and they sat us in every other seat for less conversation.

We always opened the day with the Pledge of Allegiance to the Flag, sang the National Anthem and had memory Bible verses. We had two recesses, 15 minutes each, one mid-morning and the other mid-afternoon. We always played outdoors except in rain. Some games were Annie-over, Mother Mai I, Dodge Ball and Tag. There was no running water but we did have electricity. Every one was pretty healthy and turned out to be well-adjusted adults. After our one hour lunch and lay time at noon, the teacher always read us a story from books-to settle us down before studies began. The school day was done at 4:00 p.m.

I have very fond memories of my eight years of grade school at Summit. I am happy to see someone restored it and made a home there.

All this surely stays with us all, a life time of memories. A rural school was worth it all.

Bidding was high and lively for "Gravel Gertie's" cake at the Summitt School pie supper which took in $236. Rex Vonier was handling the bidding for "Gravel Gertie's" followers. Barbara Mackey was second. A total of $53. was paid for the post popular girl. "Never saw so much money in my life at a country school pie supper," was a remark many made.

Ride on Fire Truck

All Summit photos donated by:
Ella Marie Sunderland

Miss Mildred Harvey 1941-42

Miss Doris Jean Wardlow

Summit Teachers

Sunflower School

LOCATION: SECTION: 26 TOWNSHIP: 29 RANGE: 30 DISTRICT: 58

Assessed value $115,650; Teacher: Edith Lux; Salary...$75 monthly; Grade of certificate...1, Officers: W. T. ____,-Reeds, Clerk; H. O. Dinamin-Reeds, President; W. F. Ziler-Reeds, Member; Enrollment...17; No. of pupils in Class A...5, B...__, C...__, D...__, No. present...17; Term...8 months; Condition of house...Clean; Condition of grounds...Clean; Water...Well; Sanitation...Good; Condition of out-buildings...Poor, need repairs; Blackboard...Slate; Maps...2; Globes...0; Dictionary...1; Library: No. of vol...218; Value...$100, Suitability of books...Good; Care...Sectional case; Use...Good; Free text books...No; Condition of school records...Good; Heating...Stove

Jasper County Superintendent's School Report 1924-25
Courtesy of the Jasper County Record Center

Melba Hansen McCune
Sunflower and Center Point

I attended Sunflower School when I was in third grade in 1952-53 after some other rural schools had consolidated. I had attended Center Point School during my first and second grade. Sunflower School was located 6½ miles east of Carthage, Mo on old historic highway 66 which is now 96. The experience was similar to my first two years. My teacher was Ernest Evans. I was a little apprehensive at first because he was a man teacher and my first and second grade teacher had been a woman, Lucille Spenser. However, he became on of my favorite teachers. I also had him at Avilla School in the fifth and sixth grades.

Sunflower was a one-room school with two doors facing south. It had windows on the east and west sides of the building and no windows on the north side which would help to keep the building warmer in the winter. We had a coal stove in the back that Mr. Evans had to fill up every morning before school started. There was a small garage out east of the school. It was just big enough to store the coal and room for one car. There were two outhouses in the back on each side of the school house.

The student's desks were in single rows connected together and our books and supplies were under the desk top. In front of the room was the teacher's desk with a globe on it. A blackboard was on the front wall. Maps of the World and the United States were attached to the top of the blackboard. At various times different students would get to take the erasers outside and beat the chalk dust out of them. I always enjoyed doing this. Pictures of Washington and Lincoln were on the wall. There was a small bench beside the teacher' desk where students would sit during their lessons with the teacher. We had approximately 15 students all together. The teacher had to teach all eight grades. We would start the day by standing and saying the pledge of allegiance to the flag which was in the front of the room.

We had no water in the schoolhouse so we had to go outside to the well where there was a pump. One person would have to pump it while another got a drink with a cup or by cupping your hands than you would trade places and pump it for the other person. The best thing about it in the summer was that the water was good and cold. In the winter it was cold too; so you might want to use a cup instead of your hands. The teacher or the older boys would fill up a bucket full of water and take it inside for us to drink during the day. The bucket of water set in the back of the room with a dipper and we had cups for us to fill up and get a drink.

At the beginning of the school year there was another student in the third grade with me. We were able to learn things together and that made it fun. At recess we would go outside and compare our arithmetic problems and study spelling words together. Her family moved in the middle of the year and I missed her a great deal. The older students looked after me and helped me. It was like belonging to a large family. The teacher took a personal interest in each student; which made all of us feel special.

I can remember going up and sitting on the bench beside the teacher's desk and reading aloud to the teacher. We studied geography, history, science, health, arithmetic, etc. The teacher would put some of the classes together when he taught certain subjects and even if he didn't, some of us would listen and learn from the lesson he was teaching the others.

At lunch time when it was warm, we would go outside behind the schoolhouse and sit in the shade on the grass and eat lunch. Mr. Evans would sit with us and we would visit with one another. It was like having a picnic everyday when it was pretty outside. At recess we had swings and teeter totters to play on. We played various games such as Dare Base, Anti-over, Red Rover, Blackman, and softball. When we had to play inside, we would play board games, jacks, up set the fruit basket, etc. We always had lots of fun. After lunch and recess was over we would go inside and sit down and relax while Mr. Evans read to us for 15 or 20 minutes. Usually the books he would read to us were either the Hardy Boys or Nancy Drew mysteries. This helped to instill in us the love of reading.

One time when I was ill, Mr. Evans put some of the older boys and girls in charge and drove me home. He wasn't gone long and he knew he could depend on the students to take care of things. They were very good and dependable students.

Sunflower 1952-53

Swindle School

LOCATION: SECTION: 21   TOWNSHIP: 28   RANGE: 29   DISTRICT: 4 (Early District #)

"La Russell school was originally known as "Swindle" school. The La Russell school was originally organized as the Swindle School District abut 1870. It was located southwest of La Russell on the old Jacob Graff farm at the crossroads of Highway F and Second Road. It was used as a church and a school. Some years later a nice frame house was built on the Lewis Meador farm about 200 yards west to the present Meador home, but it was still called Swindle school."

"The old Swindle school house was sold at auction to N. M. Forsythe for $450. The grounds were sold to L. D. Meador for $50."
THE CARTHAGE PRESS, JULY 12, 1905
COURTESY OF CHARLES CHRISMAN

If one was to draw conclusions of what was happening surrounding the photo on the following page. There are several characters in this story. First there is the teacher, a Mr. W. M. Dennison. He is the one holding the flowers. Don't be mislead by those flowers, there is also a switch lying at his feet. Next there is a small boy at the right of the picture that has his eye on him. I think he knows something is going on or he could be the lookout.

Finally, there are the two young girls in the window. (See photo on right and following page.)

Now if my memory serves me correctly, when we knew we were to have our school picture taken, we wore our best clothes and were always told by the teacher to be on our best behavior. Parents would see the resulting picture and misbehaved children was a reflection on the teacher's disciplinary ability.

So what do you think was happening in this photo. My guess was the two girls were misbehaving and Mr. Dennison told them they could not be in the photo and sent them into the school.

Not to be outdone by a minor setback and knowing Mr. Dennison could not see them, they decided to get revenge. As you can see, one has her fingers in each side of her mouth and making a face and the other is holding her hand over her mouth.

My guess they thought they were pretty cute and had gotten away with the little prank, that is until the photo came out.

Now I don't know how harsh Mr. Dennison was but it is a fair assumption that the switch was used at school and like punishment was experienced at home.

Now I base my assumptions not on personal experience in such matters, but I do have brothers and know how those things played out............ On the other hand, I could be totally wrong and it was the big joke in the school that year and the girls were celebrities. I will let the reader be the judge.

Temperance School

LOCATION: SECTION: 17   TOWNSHIP: 29   RANGE: 30   DISTRICT: 84

Teacher: Lydia Smith; Salary...$30 monthly; Term...6 months; Enrolled: Male...10, Female...8, Total 18; No. present to-day...13; Board: J. N. Howard-Reeds, Clerk; Fred Poncot-Reeds, President; Edgar Newman & Geo. Gibson; Condition of blackboard...Very poor; Condition of building...Fair; Condition of floor... Medium; Condition of furniture...Needs repair; Condition of apparatus...None; Condition of grounds, out-houses, etc...Good

Jasper County Superintendent's School Report 1893
Courtesy of the Jasper County Record Center

Assessed value $170,173; Teacher: Clandine Shelton-Reeds; Salary $70 monthly; Grade of certificate... Repents; Officers: Ethel Brock-Reeds, Clerk; Jay H. Butcher-Reeds, President; Amos Poncot-Reeds & Roy Brock-Reeds, Members; Enrolled...30; No. of pupils in Class A...2, B...8, C...6, D...13; No. present...26; Term...8 months; Condition of house...Dirty; Condition of grounds...Clean; Water...Carried; Condition of out-buildings...Good; Blackboard...Slate; Maps...Old case; Globes...1; Dictionary...1; Library: No. of vol...100; Value $50; Suitability of books...Good; Free text books...Yes; Heating...Stove

Jasper County Superintendent's School Report 1924-25
Courtesy of the Jasper County Record Center

"The acre of land on which Temperance stands was deeded to the district by Gustave Poncot who traded that acre for a piece of land on which the original school of red brick was burned. In 1888, there were 48 attending this school. From records available, the present Temperance school building was planned and built in 1896. The cost, $500, was raised from a bond issue. The first teacher, William Dennison, was given a contract for six months at $35 per month by District 3, Township 28, Range 29.

Thirty-six pupils attended school the first year. School opened Oct. 19, 1896.

Temperance was one of the first 4-H clubs organized in Jasper County in 1931. It had been a year around club ever since with 246 boys and girls enrolled during years 1947 to 1958. The enrollment in 1958 was 29.

For several years there had been rumors that the Temperance School would be consolidated with one of the other districts. Leaders of the 4-H, Mrs. R. F. McQuilken and Vera Mae McQuilken (now Mrs. Otis Lytle) made plans to buy the building when it came up for sale.

Temperance school building was the headquarters for the 4-H club and the Extension club and other in the community felt it necessary to save the building for that purpose. The auction was held on May 4, 1957 with Jack McCormick as the designated bidder. More than one bidder wanted the building driving the price higher than expected but the community won the bid. However, the auction was followed by a lawsuit. The owner of the land surrounding the acre of property claimed the property since it would no longer be used for school purposes. After nearly a year's litigation, a ruling was made in favor of the school district, On March 4, 1958, the district deeded the property to the Temperance Community Center trustees and their successors".

The Carthage Evening Press March 14, 1958
Courtesy of the Jasper County Record

Tower of Light School

LOCATION: SECTION: 20   TOWNSHIP: 29   RANGE: 32   DISTRICT: 65

Situated 1 1/2 miles SW of Purcell.

Teacher: Lida Alwetz; Salary...$30 monthly; Term...7 months; Enrolled: Male...22, Female...24, Total...46; No. present to-day...27; Board: Mrs. C. E. Berrian-Oronogo, Clerk; Jas. Sylvey-Oronogo, President; Jacob Shelton & Geo. Buck
Jasper County Superintendent's School Report 1893
Courtesy of the Jasper County Record Center

Assessed value $138,024; Teacher: Edith Neiman-Webb City; Salary $75 monthly; Officers: C. C. Potts-Oronogo, Clerk; Elmer Byler-Oronogo, President; Jess Gillard-Oronogo, & Jas. Mays, Members; Enrolled...22; No. present...22; Term...8 months; Condition of house...Clean; Condition of grounds...Clean; Water...Well; Condition of out-buildings...Good; Blackboard...Good; Maps...Old case; Globes...1; Dictionary...1; Library: No. of vol...200; Value...$100; Care...Good case; Use...Good; Free text books...Good; "Condition of school records...Good; Ventilation...Good; Heating...Hart
Jasper County Superintendent's School Report 1924-25   Courtesy of the Jasper County Record Center

First established in middle 1800s. Purchased and rebuilt into a church in 1952 It was then moved to the present church site.

Tower of Light school was damaged in the 2003 tornado. It was torn down in 2005.

No. Renewal   May 15   1946

Teacher's Certificate
Public Schools of Missouri

FIRST   GRADE

It is Hereby Certified, that Jesse M. Henneka has furnished satisfactory evidence of good moral character, and has, upon examination by the State Superintendent of Public Schools, attained Grades as indicated in the following subjects: Orthography 90, Reading 95, Language Lessons 92, Writing 88, English Grammar 90, Geography 91, Arithmetic 92, U. S. History 90, Civil Government 85, Physiology 90, Agriculture 89, Pedagogy 89, Algebra 80, Literature 80, Adv. History 92, Physical Geography 91, and has obtained the following professional grades based on teaching experience: Teaching Ability 90, Management 95, Average 90, and has furnished satisfactory evidence of having completed 4 years of high school work.

Therefore, Authority is hereby given him, to teach in the Public Schools of any County in the State of Missouri, for the term of three years from this date, unless this certificate be revoked.

John F. Wilson
County Superintendent.

Average required 90. Minimum Grade 60. Sec. 10625, R. S., 1939.

MIDLAND PRINTING CO. JEFFERSON CITY, MO.   X26921

Twin Groves School
a/k/a Burton
LOCATION: SECTION: 28   TOWNSHIP: 29   RANGE: 33   DISTRICT: 67

Twin Groves was consolided to Waco R-4 November 1, 1949

Twin Groves   Courtesy of Sue Fredrickson

Shirley Sue Costley

Twin Groves As Remembered
Sue Fredrickson

The Twin Groves (one room school) located on highway 96 midway between highways 43 and 171 closed it's doors for the last time as a school at the end of the 1942-43 school term. The teacher that term was Miss Phoebe Creel. She boarded with Ella and Ed Stuckey who lived in the first house east of the school on the same side of the road..just a quarter of a mile down.

With beautiful penmanship Miss Creel wrote these words in the autograph book of second grader Shirley Sue Costley on February 5, 1943; "In the Book of Life--God's album, may your name be penned with care."

The teacher for the previous school term of 1941-42 was Mrs. Grace Gosch who lived in Webb City. I recall that our school presented a Christmas program to the parents and that Mrs. Gosch gave me a small baby doll that I named Grace. During the summer she had me spend a day with her at her home. I went with her to the beauty shop.

Outside the school building there was a well with a pump over it. Water was pumped into a bucket and taken into the entry hall where it was placed on shelf for use. There was a wash pan nearby for hand washing. There were two outhouses in back of the building...one for the boys and one for the girls.

At recess and after lunch I remember playing softball, Annie-Over, Red Rover-Come Over, Flying Dutchman, Two-deep, and Drop the Handkerchief. In inclement weather I remember playing I spy, checkers and jacks in the building.

The school had a door in the center front and an entry hall all the way across the front end of the building that held a water bucket from which students could get a drink throughout the day. There were hooks where coats could be hung and a shelf on which to lay lunches and books. There was a cabinet which held books and miscellaneous supplies. There were two doors going into the classroom. Near the front and to the side there was a big pot-bellied stove. Beyond it was a raised area or stage. At the far end of the building there was a chalkboard all the way across the wall. At one side of the stage there was an outside door. Both sides of the building had numerous windows. There were benches along the sides of the building and in the center there were student desks with the teacher's desk being in front of theirs. The stage had a curtain that could be rolled up and down. It had a pretty scenic picture on it. There were also maps that could be rolled up or down.

The alphabet was just above the chalkboard. At one side away from the stove, there was a piano and glass covered book shelves called the library.

The teacher worked with individual students or small groups. Sometimes older or more competent students worked with the younger and less competent students. It was a good learning environment. You were encouraged by others and felt safe and comfortable in the company of siblings and neighbors.

In the fall of 1943 there were only seven students in District 67 so our district Board of Education met with the Carl Junction Board and we were then bused to school in town. I experienced a culture shock when I was placed in a class of over thirty third graders. I felt alienated in a sea of unknowns.

Twin Groves — Courtesy of Shirley Sue (Costley) Fredrickson
Front Row L-R: Shirley Sue Costley, ____, Rosamary Jewsbury, Eleanor Kimmel, Ray Reis, Paul Reis, John Jewsbury
Back Row: ____ Grace Gosch, teacher, Harry Swager, William (Bill) Costley

In about 1949 or 1950 when schools all over the state of Missouri were being reorganized, the Twin Groves building was purchased by funds raised by the community through donations and pie suppers to use it as a meeting place for the Twin Groves 4-H club, the Peg-a-way Extension Club and other community events like wedding showers, square dances, etc. Sometime in the 1980's it ceased being used for this purpose. The property with the building reverted back to the owner of the adjoining property from whence it came and has since been sold.

I do not know when Twin Groves came into existence but I can confirm that it was there in 1906-07 when my mother, Leota Johnson Costley, wa six years old and in the first grade there. Her teacher was Elsie H. Heaton. Two other teachers that I have heard her mention were Harry Rhule and Victor McDowell.

My brother, Bill Costley, remembers that there is a hiding place in the door jam of the west door where a fire extinguisher was kept.

Three of my five sibling and I attended Twin Groves School. They were Ralph Costley, Paula Rose Costley Dill (deceased), and William (Bill) Costley. Our family moved to the community in the spring of 1938.

Underwood School
a/k/a Atlas
LOCATION: SECTION: 35   TOWNSHIP: 28   RANGE: 31   DISTRICT: 100

"A new school building is to be erected in the Underwood district, eight miles southwest of Carthage and two miles east of Porto Rico. It is to cost $1200 and will be begin next week. It will be a one room structure with two cloak closets, porch, belfry, etc., with modern appliances for heating, ventilation, etc. It will probably be the best one-room school building in the county when done. The former building in this district was burned down last April and school had to be dismissed before the term was out, because of the fire. Insurance to the amount of $600 was secured on account of the loss and now with the equipment of the new building the district will be in much better shape for educational advantages than ever before."

The Carthage Evening Press, Friday, June 1, 1906
Courtesy of the Jasper County Record Center

Assessed value $607,894; Teachers Inez Setser-Carterville & Pearl Murphy; Grade of certificate...1 & 3; Officers: ___ Marchbanks-Carthage, Clerk; L. F. Wilson-Carthage, President; J. H. Barhern-Carthage & Jack Mayfield-Carterville, Members; Enrollment...33 + 30; No. of pupils in Class A...18, B...15, C...__, D...__; No. present...30 + 29; Condition of house...A; Condition of grounds...Clean; Water...Well; Sanitation...Good; Decoration...Good; Condition of out-buildings...Good; Blackboard...Hyloplate; Maps...Set; Charts...1; Globes...1; Dictionary...1; Free text books...Yes; Condition of school records...Good; School approved...No; Heating...2 Smith

Jasper County Superintendent's School Report 1924-25
Courtesy of the Jasper County Record Center

Underwood School   Courtesy of Kathy Sidenstricker & Dona Cupp

Underwood School   Courtesy of Kathy Sidenstricker & Tom Rogers

Underwood School 1959-1960

Union School

LOCATION: SECTION: 3   TOWNSHIP: 27/28   RANGE: 30   DISTRICT: 105

Teacher: J. D. Prigmore; Salary...$30; Term...6 months; Enrolled: Male...12, Female...7, Total...19; No. present to-day...8; Board: W. N. Stroup-Reeds, Clerk; Danl. Prigmore-Reeds, President; Taylor Hood-Reeds
Jasper County Superintendent's School Report 1894
Courtesy of the Jasper County Record Center

Assessed value $86,895; Teacher: Emma Fullerton-Sarcoxie; Salary...$70 monthly; Grade of certificatge...3; Officers: Ernest Haggard-Reeds, Clerk; E. E. Hood-Sarcoxie, President; Reese Mears-Reeds, Member; Enrollment...14; No. of pupils in Class A...4, B...3, C...4, D...3; No. present...13; Term...8 months; Condition of house...Poor; Condition of grounds...Dry; Water...Carried; Condition of out-buildings...Boys' poor - need repairs; Blackboard...Good; Maps...0; Globes...1; Dictionary...Old; Library: No. of vol...200; Value...$50; Suitability of books...Fair; Care...Case; Free text books...Yes; Condition of school records...Poor; Ventilation...Too much; Heating...Wood stove
Jasper County Superintendent's School Report 1924-25
Courtesy of the Jasper County Record Center

Union 1895 circa   Courtesy of Kathy Sidenstricker & Rebecca Woodworth

"For the month commencing Nov. the 2nd, ending Nov. the 27th, 1885. No. of pupils enrolled during the month: Male 19, female, 17, total 36. No. of days attendance of all pupils, 564. Average no. of pupils attending each day, 28. Average no. of days attendance by each pupil, 15 1/2. No. of days taught, 20. The following are the names of those entitled to the 'roll of honor'; Edith Curtis, Don Davis, Sallie Dodson, Meda Hood, Mattie Mitchell, Mollie Wood, Henry Davis, Lee Dodson, James Michael, Dick Prigmore, Iodie Prigmore. Parents are invited to visit our school. Dora Haggard, Teacher"
Carthage Banner Dec. 10, 1885

Rural School Days in Jasper County
Mary Jane Hicks - Teacher
Union, Pleasant Valley, Green Grove

Rural schools were a way of life for those of us living in the forties in Jasper County.

My first school experience was at Pleasant Valley, a beautiful big school building with three rooms. First and second grade was taught by Miss Kathryn Yankee and then Miss Hazel Brock. Third, fourth and fifth grades were grades were taught by Mrs. Lura Robinson and then sixth, seventh and eighth grades were taught by Mr. Marshall.

I think there were around 75 to 80 students in that school. My brother, Bill, sister Louise, and I all enjoyed going to Pleasant Valley School. There was a wonderful playground, and I remember playing at recess down under some lovely big trees.

Another memory I have of that school was when I was in the first grade, my mother came to visit, and brought my sister Shirley, not yet in school. Shirley, the bright little girl that she was, counted to one hundred and I couldn't do that. I was quite jealous when the teacher gave her a little ball as a prize for her counting ability.

One incident I remember happening in that school was when my brother, Bill, refused to recite his multiplication tables for Mrs. Robinson. He promised he would say them the next day, but she did not buy that. He stayed in from recess, and the next day he happily recited his tables.

Next, my family purchased a farm on Airport Road east of Carthage and we were enrolled in Green Grove School. World War II was raging and teachers were scarce. I am not sure how qualified or enthusiastic some of the teachers were that taught us during those war years. The teachers who worked there were Miss Berry, Mrs. Edith Coffield, Mrs. Van Horn, and Mr. Harold Schmidly.

I remember lots of confusion at that school with few books to read for enjoyment. One year, I won a prize for perfect attendance. The prize was the book, <u>Campfire Girls.</u> My sisters and I took turns reading that book all summer.

Playground was always fun and I think we spent more time playing than we did studying in the classroom. One of our teachers liked to walk across the street during noon break and visit with the lady who lived there. Looking back, one wonders what was happening there while we were all running wild on the playground. I remember there were times the students just jumped out the windows instead of using the doors.

The county Superintendent of Schools, Bertha Reed, came to visit the schools in Jasper County each year. On that day we were cautioned to be especially good, and I believe we did behave well while she was visiting.

At one time, there were approximately 40 students attending that school. In order for the teacher to have recitation time for all the students, one of the teachers had my sister, Louise and I moved to the next higher grade. Louise and I loved school so that move did not cause any academic problems.

We moved next into the Prairie View School District. I was in the eighth grade and was surprised and happy to find my second grade teacher, Miss Brock teaching the upper grades at that school. Mrs. Ruth Heisten was the lower grades teacher.

Total enrollment in that school was around 40, but there were two teachers in two rooms so that was a nice peaceful learning atmosphere. The teachers were strict and we all learned what was being taught. We had more books to read for enjoyment also.

Again, my fondest memories are of all the fun on the playground. We played games like Red Rover, Dare Base, and softball. Mrs. Heiston was a fast runner and enjoyed playing with us at recess. We all wanted her on our team.

I graduated from the eighth grade with a little ceremony.

Another move found my family living in Sarcoxie where we all enrolled in the Sarcoxie Public Schools. My brother finished high school in Carthage, but Louise, Shirley and I all graduated from the Sarcoxie High School.

We girls were all thrilled to be able to find books in their library that we devoured with great enthusiasm.

Sixteen and a graduate of High School found me wondering how I was going to earn enough money for college expenses. My Aunt Geneva in Tulsa, Oklahoma invited me to live with her for the summer. I found a job working as a secretary for the President and Vice President of Brown Duncan, a big department store in downtown Tulsa.

I rode the bus to and from work and saw the black people forced to sit in the back. It was my first experience being with black people, and I never thought anything about the fact that they couldn't sit where they pleased.

Summer quickly passed and I headed for home on the Greyhound Bus. I was able to save $100 from my pay checks and with that amount; I was able to enroll at Southwest Missouri State in Springfield, Missouri. The tuition was $26.50 for each quarter, and books were less that $10 each. That left me with a little spending money.

After I enrolled in college, I immediately found a job in the Placement Office which was housed in the same office as Dean Willard Graff and President Roy Ellis. My boss was Hazel Ponder, Placement Director. She took me under her wing and helped me with decision making. She tried to encourage me to stay in school after I finished my freshman year in college.

Most of my work was typing recommendations from professors for graduating seniors. We made several copies of each recommendation, and that was done with carbon paper. Oh, the terror of a typing error.

My job allowed me to pay my room rent which was $4.00 a week.

There was a small kitchen in the basement where we prepared our meals with food we had brought from home. We had two beds in our room where we slept two to each bed. There was a bathroom on the 2nd floor where we lived, and it was shared by about twelve girls. We all got along very well with this arrangement.

The only phone in the house was on the first floor. Lots of running and yelling when the phone rang.

The home was owned by Mrs. De Frieze who made wedding cakes as a business. We were always getting nibbles of cake and icing in her delicious smelling kitchen.

Her son, David, lived there. I thought he seemed really old, but he was only in his early twenties. We girls all thought he was very cute, but he never paid any attention to any of us.

I was asked to Homecoming that year by someone from one of my classes. I purchased a beautiful blue strapless, black lace trimmed, long dress to wear to the dance. I still have fond memories of that beautiful dress.

One of my roommates, Judy, dropped out of school that fall and I, wore the blue dress to be her maid of honor in her wedding. I took the lace off the dress and wore a blue net shawl to cover my shoulders. She married Bill Hasselbring, her high school sweetheart. They have been happily married since, but she does regret not finishing college.

At the end of my freshman year of college, I was eager to have some money for a few extras. I left school and began trying to find a rural school where I could teach and go back to school in the summers to finish my degree.

Lucky for me, Vance Meares, Board President of Union School District took a chance on me and gave me a job at that school. The community was small with about six families attending the school. My salary was $165 a month for 8 months.

I did the janitor work for an additional $10 a month. My work consisted of sweeping, dusting and building fires in a big black stove in the back of the room. We would all huddle around that stove until it warmed the building enough for us to move into the desks which were screwed onto 1x4 boards that kept them in straight lines. The teacher's desk was on a little raised platform.

Some of the families seemed to have enough money to dress their children well and send them to school with healthy lunches. Others were having a very hard time finding enough money for the basic necessities of life.

My memories of one of my students in that first year are clear. I was 17 years old with a 16 year old student in my class. He was a big boy and fairly compliant but far too old to be attending elementary school. I discussed this student with my former high school superintendent, Charles Sloan. He was able to enroll Deloit in Sarcoxie High School and after a short time, my 17 year old student joined the United States Navy. I believe that was a good move for all involved.

There were 14 students in the school when it opened in September, 1950. That was the beginning of my education as a teacher. Some of my students were very bright and especially quick with arithmetic facts. I soon brushed up on my facts in order to stay ahead of them. The students were eager to learn and loved being in school. There were very few books and paper was scarce also.

We were able to make copies of test, maps, arithmetic facts, and sheets to color. I am not sure what the device was called, but it was made of two pieces of wood filled with a jelly-type substance. You wrote what you wanted copied on a piece of paper with a special pencil, wet the jelly with a little sponge, laid your copy on the jelly for a minute or so and then took it off and you had made your copies. I think the little box was called a hectograph, but the dictionary does not tell me that.

John F. Wilson, County Superintendent of Schools, made an annual visit to see how school was working. I did encourage the children to be on their best behavior, and I did my best to impress him with my teaching abilities. I was always happy when that visit ended.

Another visitor each year was an inspector of our well to be sure the water was pure. We always passed which also made all of us happy.

After a long week of school we would celebrate Friday, by having spelling, arithmetic and geography matches either at our school or another county school nearby.

During my second year of teaching, I developed appendicitis while at school. I had had two other serious attacks without going to the doctor. This time I knew that I should see a doctor quickly.

I sent the children home and drove to Dr. Byrd's office in Carthage. Being young and dumb, I sat in his office waiting my turn. When I got in to see him, he took one look at me, and said, "We are going to the hospital." We arrived at McCune Brooks Hospital where I was soon in surgery. Luckily, my appendix did not rupture, but it was a close call.

My recovery was slow because the doctor was not sure exactly what was wrong. He made a very long incision which was very slow to heal. Restrictions were place on my activities. I believe a parent taught for me during that recovery period.

Another year, we had a sleet storm on Valentine's Day. I had baked cookies and brought soda pop for our Valentine Party. We had our party early and I dismissed the children to walk home in the sleet while I tried to drive home in about 12 inches of sleet ot move the car. I walked abut three miles up to Highway 166 to catch a ride home with my father.

I continued teaching at Union School for three years. During this time, I kept going back to Southwest Missouri State working toward my degree in teaching. At that time the school had mid-term sessions where you were able to enroll late and make up what you had missed. Credit hours were assigned according to your grades. If you made an E, you would earn three credit hours. You were allowed to take six hours at that session making it possible to earn six hours. Summer sessions allowed you to earn up to fifteen hours depending upon your grades, and there was an August session allowing students to earn six more hours. I finally earned my Bachelor of Science Degree in Education 1957.

At the end of my third year of teaching at Union School in 1953, Floyd Cochran, the principal of Avilla, a reorganized district offered me a job teaching in his school. I was thrilled and eagerly accepted. I was assigned to teach third and fourth grades in one room with about thirty-five students in the two grades.

This school was like night and day compared to Union School where I had been teaching. The students were bright, well dressed and very competitive. Their families earned good incomes and were very supportive of what we were doing at school. By this time, I had learned quite a lot about children and teaching. I never thought I knew all I should know, but the children were happy and progressed well during my two year at Avilla.

The school had a cafeteria that served delicious hot meals. On stormy days, the children were able to play in that space. There was a janitor and a principal to provide support. I loved working with the other staff members.

After two years teaching at Avilla, the enrollment declined, and the staff had to be cut. I was the last teacher hired so my contract was not renewed for the next year.

I learned of a vacancy at a school in Carl Junction, Missouri. There was a teacher for each grade and the School Board chose to hire me even though I had not completed my degree from Southwest Missouri State. I was assigned the fifth grade and there were fifty plus in that one grade, but I never thought of not taking the position. It was at this school that my years of association with county schools ended.

Summit 1910   Pearl Johnson, teacher

Rural School Souvenirs

Wealth may seek us, but Wisdom must be sought

Though lost to sight to memory dear
Thou ever wilt remain
One only hope my heart can cheer
The hope to meet again

Summit 1911   Stella Thomas, teacher

Union Valley School

LOCATION: SECTION: 20   TOWNSHIP: 30   RANGE: 30   DISTRICT: 6

Teacher: Carrie Magers; Salary...$34.33 1/3 per month; Term...7 months; Enrolled: Male...16, Female...8, Total...24; No present to-day...14; Board: J. S. Laforce-Jasper, Clerk; Geo. Gray-Jasper, President; Jas. Leary-Jasper

Jasper County Superintendent's School Report 1893
Courtesy of the Jasper County Record Center

Assessed value $96,400; Teacher: Jennie Conrad-Jasper; Grade of certificate...1; Officers: B. B. Earl-Jasper, Clerk; J. M. Carter-Jasper, President; George Probert-Jasper, Member; Enrollment...18; No. present...17; Term...8 months; Condition of house...Good; Condition of grounds...Grassy; Water...Carried; Condition of out-buildings...Good; Blackboard...Good; Maps...Old case; Globes...0; Dictionary...1; Library: No. of vol...100; Value $0; Free text books...No; Condition of school records...Good; Heating...Stove; Community Meetings...4 library

Jasper County Superintendent's School Report 1924-25
Courtesy of the Jasper County Record Center

Union Valley 1922-23

Front Row: Talma McClintock, Pauline Winder, Verna Mae Billington, Della Isenmann, Ella Mae McClintock, Fred Isenmann, Jr., John Probert

2nd Row: Winston Carter, Harvey Earl, Paul Probert, Chauncey Earl, Lester Probert, Wieford Southern

3rd Row: Howard Probert, Ellis Fasken, Wilma Faskin, Chester Faskin Margaret Probert

"Coon Creek, Union Valley School, two miles east of Midway (later Jasper City), sub-district No. 1, Township30, Range 30, John Weed, teacher, wages $40. Here I found a good school, good desks, good blackboard, plenty of chalk and directors not afraid to have it used. Appearance of pupils good, clean, sprightly and intelligent; recitations good. Weed is a good teacher. His pupils love him and the district appreciates his labors. The patrons of this school deserve credit for their mutual effort to sustain a good school."

Joel Thomas Livingston - Jasper County Missouri and Its People, Vol. 1, 1912 Page 101
Courtesy of the Jasper County Record Center

"Union Valley District--...W. H. Rhoads, George F. Bowers and Isaac Hendricks, directors; A. R. Haughawout, teacher. Term of four months began Oct. 28th. District enumeration 72, enrollment over fifteen years of age, total 46, present 43. Building and furniture second-class. Seating capacity 44, The policy of the directors has been to pay the best wages and employ the best teachers, and they have thereby given the district a school that in point of advancement and thoroughness, ranks with the first district schools of the county. Mr. Haughawout is teaching his fifth term, and is doing good work, especially with arithmetic. Any teacher not in possession of good methods in primary work would do well to witness the exercises of this school."

Joel Thomas Livingston - Jasper County Missouri and Its People, Vol. 1, 1912 Page 106
Courtesy of the Jasper County Record Center

"In April of 1903 a proposition to issue $800 bonds was voted on and carried by a vote of 8 to 3 for a new school house. Plans were to build it during the summer. In July of that same year, the school board advertised for bids for the erection of the new school building. Later in Oct. of that same year, a notice was printed in the newspaper indicating the "old school house" will go to the highest bidder for cash at 2 o'clock p.m. Saturday, October 10, 1903."

The Jasper News
Courtesy of Kathy Sidenstricker - www.jaspercountyschools.org

Union Valley opened its doors in the late 1860 and closed its doors in 1960.

Left to Right: Thelma Fasken, Paul McClintock, Winena Probert, Donald Probert, Phyllis Probert, Barbara Earl, Miss Erwin, teacher

Unity School

LOCATION: SECTION: 22   TOWNSHIP: 30   RANGE: 29   DISTRICT: 25

Assessed value $132,693; Teacher: Alice Salout-Golden City; Salary...$75 monthly; Grade of certificate...TT; Officers: Chas. McGuire-Golden City, G. N. Maxwsell-Golden City; Discipline...A; Enrollment...12; No. present...11; Term...8 months; Condition of house...Good; Water...Well; Sanitation...Good; Condition of out-buildings...Good; Blackboard...Good; Maps...Case; Globes...0; Dictionary...1; Suitability of books...Good; Free text books... Yes; Condition of school records... Good; Ventilation...Good; Heating... Smith

Jasper County Superintendent's School Report 1924-25
Courtesy of the Jasper County Record Center

Unity — Courtesy of Kathy Sidensticker

"The final act in the life of a rural school -- a most typical one -- was enacted Saturday, Aug. 10, when an auctioneer's chant became the funeral dirge of the old Unity school in the extreme northeast corner of Jasper county. The school furnishings already had been removed and, at the final auction, the building itself was sold, title to the land reverting to the pre-school owner.

The Unity building and grounds are situated one mile south of the Barton county line and 1 1/4 miles west of the Dade county line, a mile west of the village of Dudenville.

The Unity district was organized May 1, 1872, in a public meeting, where O. Little presided and James R. Williams served as secretary. Named to the initial board of education were Little, Williams and T. J. Cunningham.

According to The Golden City Herald of Thursday, Aug. 1963. "the selection of the name Unity probably came about in the way:

"The war between the states had ended only seven years previous and feelings had been evenly divided in Jasper county. The prairie was now beginning to fill with settlers, some being Federal soldiers of the late war, who had acquired acreages cheaply by reason of army services.

"Unity naturally was the thought uppermost in the minds of many and it seemed only proper that such a name should be given to this new school district."For many years the original frame building, which stood several yards north of the structure just sold, served as a community center as Dudenville, then known also as Chambersburg, and each Sunday housed the community Sunday school.

The first classes were conducted only four months of each year, the change to a 7-month term coming in 1875, with seven or eight months of instruction being the general rule for many years thereafter.

When the 1873 term opened Sept. 30 for a period which would conclude at Christmas time, the school records listed total enrollment of 29, 19 boys and 10 girls, who attended the then new building erected at

Courtesy of Kathy Sidenstricker

a cost of $558.44 and were taught by a teacher who received the comparatively large income of $28 per month.

The first building was destroyed in 1900 by fire, one of the major calamities in the history of Unity-Dudenville community. The present structure was erected shortly thereafter and had served constantly since that time.....

Mrs. Ida Parker Bawbell, writing for The Golden City Herald, remembered:

"All community activities were centered at the school. The regular school program, spelling bees, ciphering matches, Christmas programs.

"The there were the debates, Literary societies and other adult activities. The bi-monthly Literary was a gala affair and the whole community participated in it. Also writing schools, singing schools were held at night during the week.

"Itinerant traveling shows and demonstrations were held at the schoolhouse."

Mrs. Bawbell enrolled at Unity in 1875.

The operation of the district as a separate administrative unit came to an end June 6, 1960, when the patrons voted to annex to the Golden City district in Barton county. However, classes were continued for a time.

When school opens the fall, however, all pupils of old Unity district will be transported to Golden City, traveling by school bus to more modern facilities and a more diversified faculty."

Marvin VanGilder, Press Staff Member
The Carthage Evening Press Aug. 20, 1963
Courtesy of the Jasper County Record Center

Memories Attending Jasper Co. Rural School
Joan Kentner Tierney
Unity

My story will be mostly short since I did not attend Unity School until the last two years. Passing through 7th and 8th grades and graduating on to Golden City High School. My father, Lyman W. Kentner purchased the Richard Patterson Farm in 1944 and our family of 7 and soon to be 8 children moved to Jasper county. The teacher was Grace Smith and I believe she had been at this location several years. Many students in the area walked 1-2 miles each day. A few had transportation by car and 1 young boy, Jackie Cearnel always rode his horse. The horse was sheltered in the coal and storage shed. He waited patiently until the return trip home in the afternoon. My 8th grade was completed with one other student Bert Kaderly.

Valley Dell School
LOCATION: SECTION: 20   TOWNSHIP: 30   RANGE: 32   DISTRICT: 16

"Valley Dell school was built in the 1890's and closed in the 1950's. The building was purchased by Calvin Ridgeway to be used as a hay barn."
Courtesy of Kathy Sidenstricker - www.jaspercountyschool.org

Assessed value $105,948; Teacher: Erma Kilmer-Medoc; Grade of certificate...2; Officers: Ina A. Scott-Medoc, Clerk; R. C. Ridgway-Medoc, President; M. M. Doubledec-Medoc, Member; Enrollment...20; No. of pupils in Class A...7, B...2, C...6, D...5; No. present...19; Condition of house...Old; Condition of grounds...Weedy; Water...Carried; Condition of out-buildings...Boy's poor; Blackboard...Slate; Maps...Old case; Globes...0; Dictionary...Old; Library: No. of vol...50; Value...$25; Suitability of books...New ones ordered; Care...Case; Free text books...No; Condition of school records...Good; Heating...Stove

Jasper County Superintendent's School Report 1924-25
Courtesy of the Jasper County Record Center

Valley Dell 1953   Teacher, Clyde Condon
Pupils attending Valley Dell during the 1952-53 term: Wanda Ridgway, Dennis Hight, Judy Vette, Leslie Sisseck, Ronnie Smith, Darrel Sisseck, Jack Vette, Sandra Smith, Lois Doubledee, Johnny Doubledee, Ronald Condon, Jeannetta Ferguson, Barbara O'Neal, Don Hight, Joe Sisseck, Pat Tiberghien

Valley Dell 1956-57

Victory School

LOCATION: SECTION: 4 TOWNSHIP: 27/28 RANGE: 31 DISTRICT: 115

"I believe that Victory and Victor are the same schools. The 1920 picture labeled Victor has many children of the Siler family listed. In 1920, they lived in Jasper County, Jackson township, East 7th Street. The 1895 plat book for Jasper County lists this area as the Victory school district."
Courtesy of Kathy Sidenstricker - www.jaspercountyschools.org

"The Victor school, five miles south of Carthage, was entered Friday or Saturday night by prowlers. So far as was determined yesterday nothing of value was taken. Entry was taken by tearing a wire netting off a window. The prowler or prowlers went out through the door. Burnt matches were found strewn over the floor when the burglary was discovered Sunday. Miss Helen Dyer is teacher at the school."
The Carthage Evening Press, Jan. 29, 1929, Page 2
Courtesy of Kathy Sidenstricker - www.jaspercountyschools.org

Teacher: Clara B. Lundy; Salary...$30 monthly; Term...6 months; Enrolled: Male...15, Female...14, Total,,,29; No. present to-day...20; Board: N. Hutton-Carthage, Clerk; John Haithcook-Carthage, President; A. Barlow-Carthage; Condition of blackboard...Poor; Condition of furniture...Fair; Condition of apparatus...None; Condition of grounds, out-buildings, etc...Poor
Jasper County Superintendent's School Report 1893
Courtesy of the Jasper County Record Center

Assessed value $65,883; Teacher: Maude Scott-Carthage; Salary $65 monthly; Grade of certificate...3; Officers: C. P. Burkholder-Carthage, Clerk; A. M. Fike-Carthage, President; W. D. Stokes-Carthage, Member; Enrollment...30; Term...8 months; Condition of house...Clean; Condition of grounds...Clean; Water...Carried; Condition of out-buildings...Good; Blackboard...Needs resurfacing; Map...Old case; Globes...Small; Library: No. of vol...100; Value $100; Free text books...No; Heating...Wood stove
Jasper County Superintendent's School Report 1924-25
Courtesy of the Jasper County Record Center

Victory School 1914

Viewbank School
a/k/a Dog Trot
LOCATION: SECTION: 2   TOWNSHIP: 29   RANGE: 33   DISTRICT: 36

"Located 1 1/2 miles northeast of Galesburg. The first school house was erected in 1848 and located at the corner of Pine Road and County Rd. 238. School was taught the following winter (1849).

The building was moved around the corner on Highway 43 about one mile southwest of the old location in section 1 to section 2 with the second location near North Fork River sometime after 1911. This may have been when school changed its name."
Submitted by Goldie Smith Kirk
Courtesy of the Jasper County Record Center

Viewbank School 1911

Teacher: Joseph Sailor; Salary...$30 monthly; Term...5 months; Enrolled: Male,,,11, Female...11, Total...22; No. present to-day...11; Board: Wm. Dick-Medoc, Clerk; Wm. Smith-Breeze, President; Leonard Bowers-Breeze
Jasper County Superintendent's School Report 189
Courtesy of the Jasper County Record Center

Assessed value $116,378; Teacher: Helen Roberts-Oronogo; Salary $85 monthly; Grade of certificate...1; Officers: J. E. Smith-Oronogo, Clerk; C. N. Montgomery-Alba, President; F. C. Smith-Alba & R. M. Storms-Alba, Members; No. of pupils in Class A...6, B...7, C...9, D...4; No. present...21; Term...8 months; Condition of house...Good; Condition of grounds...Clean; Water...Carried; Condition of out-buildings... Remodeled; Blackboard...Painted; Globes...1; Library: No. of vol...100; Value...$50; Suitability...Good; Care...Case; Free text books...Yes; Condition of school records...Good; Heating...Stove; REMARKS...Set of playground apparatus
Jasper County Superintendent's School Report 1924-25
Courtesy of the Jasper County Record Center

Goldie (Smith) Kirk - Viewbank

"My Dad was on the school board. We lived on the house where I was born on Base Line. When I was about five we moved to grandpa's house because my grandmother had passed away. Dad had come home and said

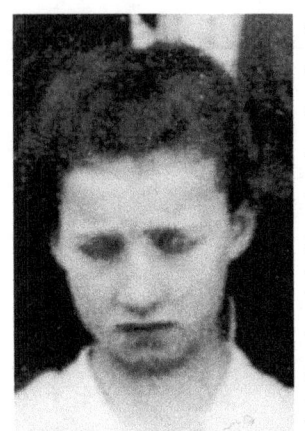

Goldie Smith 1921

we needed to go up and take care of him. Well, I think we started to school after we moved but my brother was going to Viewbank. Originally, the building was not where it is now. That was Dog Trot. We lived here and right up here on the corner was where it was. I remember my Dad coming home, he was on the board, and said to mother that they were going to have to move it because there was a new ruling that no child should have to walk more than a mile and a half to school. That's the part I remember that definitely he said. Now, I was awful little then but that impressed me and my brother went and at the time he was going to have to walk three miles to school but there was a path across some fields and he would cut across the he did not have so far to go. They went ahead and moved the school because there were other children and they would not have so far to walk.

At that time it was called Dog Trot. I have this fixed in my mind and I don't know if it is true but I think the dogs followed the kids to school and that is why they called it Dog Trot.

I don't know whether I started to school after it was moved or before. I have not memory of it being where it used to be.

My maiden name was Smith. My dad's name was Tom Smith. My grandfather was James Preston. There was nine in the family and they all settled around here.

I started to school when I was five years old in 1918. My mother started me a year ahead of what they do now.

I went to school there until I graduated from the 8th grade. Out of the five kinds in my class, I was the valedictorian. I always had women teachers.

Our main subjects were spelling, arithmetic and spelling and once a week we had history of the United States. There was some writing lessons but not very much instructions.

At recess we would go out and play

Viewbank 1919
Front Row: Roy Hobbs, Avis Smith, Hazel ____, Imogene Shepherd, ____ ____,
Back Row: Dora Williams, Gladys Williams, Hazel Shepherd, Francis Ferguson-Teacher, Herbert Williams

dodge ball or something like that. We took turns but probably played more at noon hour after we had lunch. I probably had a sandwich or left over pie or something. I don't remember any fruit. In those days, we didn't have too much fruit except what was canned. We always took our lunch and when it was real cold, sometimes we would lay it on top of the stove and toast it a little bit.

We had spelling matches. They would give you a word and you stood up as long as you could spell the word. Somehow we had contests about arithmetic spelling. I always liked arithmetic spelling and that was the only thing I could spell was those words.

We had a graduation at the end of the year and I had to memorized a little speech I went on to four years of high school and wanted to go to business college but I got married and my husband didn't want me to."

White Hall School
LOCATION: SECTION: 11   TOWNSHIP: 29   RANGE: 33   DISTRICT: 44

Teacher: Eliza Lanson; Salary...$32 monthly; Term...7 months; Enrolled: Male...22, Female...9, Total...31; No. present to-day...15; Board: B. F. Weaver-Oronogo, Clerk; E. Billingslea-Oronogo, President; R. Heilig-Oronogo

Jasper County Superintendent's School Report 1893
Courtesy of the Jasper County Record Center

White Hall 1923

Assessed value $107,572; Teacher: Lucille Petefish-Oronogo; Salary...$82 1/2 Monthly; Grade of certificate...1; Officers: D. C. Kutz-Oronogo, Clerk; Jess Weaver-Oronogo, President; A. G. Kimmel-Oronogo, Member; Enrolled...26; No. of pupils in Class A...7, B...6, C...6, D...7; No. present...26; Term...8 months; Condition of house...Clean; Condition of grounds...Clean; Water...Well; Condition of out-buildings...Fair; Blackboard...Fair; Globes...1; Dictionary...1; Library: No. of vol...150; Value...$75; Suitability of books...Good; Care...Case; Free text books...Yes; Condition of school records...Good; Heating...Hart

Jasper County Superintendent's School Report 1924-25
Courtesy of the Jasper County Record Center

White Hall 2003

"White Hall School's 50th year was in 1923"

"The one-room, rural White Hall School, located on the northwest corner of what is now Maple Road and County Road 240 in northwestern Jasper County, open in 1873.....The first school house in this district was a log affair, standing about a quarter of a mile south of the present building, on the opposite side of the road. It was used for five years or more and was known as the "Back Door School," because the only entrance was at the end of the building which was painted white, the latter looked so fine in the then new country, that it was called the White Hall school house and the district took its name from that....

The first White Hall building was its occupancy by a summer school in 1873, taught by F. A. Hubbard....
The present enrollment of the school is 30, and it has been seldom more than this for many years past. So the population of school age in the district has grown permanently less than it was for the years when the district was first settled up following the Civil War.

The Carthage Evening Press
Friday, April 20, 1923

White Hall School, 1941-42 - 1st row: Earl Honey, Jamie Marner, Billie Joe Weaver, Rose Marie Jantz.
2nd row: Jimmy Butler, Joe Butler, Janet Berkey, Lois Honey, Charles Honey, Lois Bennett, Marilyn Marner. Teacher, Glenna [Decker] Munson.

White Hall School, 1942-43 - front row: Rose Marie Jantz, Wanda Louise Jantz, Earl Honey, Jamie Marner, Charles Jarman, Billie Joe Marner.
2nd row: Marilyn Marner, Charles Honey, Lois Honey, Janet Berkey, Twila Jarman [teacher], Joe Butler, Jimmy Butler, Lois Bennett.

Unkown School

Chapter 10

Stories From Rural Schools in other Counties

Life of a Rural School Teacher in Missouri and Kansas
Virginia Clark

"Rural schools in the Midwest and elsewhere were usually one-room frame buildings, often with only one entrance; although an occasional did have a two-room school building. The buildings were often rectangular with a row of windows along each side. Sometimes there was a partition across the back with a cloakroom behind the classrooms. Other school had an ell on one corner that served as a cloakroom, a counter for hand washing facilities, and perhaps a storage cabinet. Coat hooks lined the walls at a height that the students could reach to hang their coats and caps. Galoshes, overshoes and other protective footwear were stashed below.

In an earlier day, these school buildings were often multipurpose, being used for community meeting, the Grange and other gatherings.

Most were heated by a coal stove with a metal jacket encircling it, although my first school had a furnace in the basement.

It was part of the teacher's responsibility to arrive early enough to get the fire going so the building would be warm when the children arrived. If one happened to be lucky, and skillful, the fire would have been banked before leaving the building after school. If not, the fire had to be started from scratch. The teacher was also responsible for janitorial duties. Sometimes a student would clean the building daily for a small fee. It was the teacher's choice.

In the early days of rural education there was, of course, no electricity. Kerosene lamps were sometimes used; and, later, gasoline lamps hung from the ceiling gave sufficient light that evening meetings could be held. After rural electric service (REA) became available schools sometimes had electric lighting.

Water was available only from a well with a hand-operated pump. The handle sometimes became very cold, or even ice-coated. There was also no sewage system. Two outhouses (toilets) were built; one for use by the girls and one for the boys. They were surrounded by a tall fence and neither sex was expected ever to enter the building of the opposite sex. It was an absolute NO-NO.

There was frequently a stage across the front that was six to eight inches above the rest of the room, and frequently there would be wires strung to support a curtain as well as others to create partitions for the stage to be used by actors when their roles did not require their presence on stage.

The school yard was an acre or more and space for a ball diamond; usually there would be a basketball court with goals at each end, and the well to provide water for general use. There was also a flag pole. Some school yards had pipe fencing on which the children loved doing somersaults or hanging with their knees hooked over the pipe. Before automobiles came into general use, some schools had a shelter for the teacher's horse or an occasional student's horse.

Often times the teacher boarded in local homes through the week, sometimes boarding around at different homes in the district. Other times the teacher arranged to board for a fee at the same home for the entire school year and would go home for the weekends. One year, my sister and I taught at schools some distance apart, so we shared transportation. On Sunday evenings, she had the use of the car after returning me to my district home. Then, I would walk the mile to school. The next week I would keep the car after taking her to her district home.

The furnishings in the school building were utilitarian with little surplus furniture. In the early days, the students shared double width desks, two to a desk. I did not see those particular desks when I went to grade school myself, but there were still a few of them in the school where I taught. However, the enrollment figures never required their being used by two students. Every desktop had its own inkwell.

Other furniture consisted of a teacher's desk (some had a covered compartment such as a box with a slanted hinged top and two flat sections on either side), a teacher's chair, a recitation bench, a storage cabinet, a piano, and bench or stool for it. Sometimes there was a table, and usually there was a blackboard all across the front of the room. Sometimes there would be smaller sections of blackboard beside the windows near the front of the building on ether side.

The term was eight months in most rural schools by the time I started teaching, but I think it may have been a shorter period at an earlier time in history. The age of the students normally ranged from five years to fourteen or fifteen; however, there were areas and times when the older students, especially the boys, were kept at home to help with farm work, especially crop harvest. So, sometimes boys of seventeen or over attended during the winter months to catch up with education they had missed when they were younger.

In a one-room school, the teacher played many roles: instructor, disciplinarian, planner, scheduler, song leader, pianist if possible, health nurse, art teacher, playground supervisor, coach, administrator, public relation advocate, and so forth. I agree that teachers today also play many of these roles and answer too many of the same demands and expectations, but it was still a unique position. There were many rewards, although monetary ones were not outstanding. Many dedicated teachers did then and still do derive great personal reward from the profession. I do not know how a teacher acquired teaching credentials in the early years of education in the Midwestern states. I suspect being willing to try was probably all it took.

Sometime in the early twentieth century it became necessary to pass an examination in both Missouri and Kansas. However, there were a few high schools in Kansas that offered normal training (teacher training) classes. Completion of that course qualified a high school graduate to receive a two-year certificate to teach grades one through eight. Continuing eligibility to teach require being able to pass the teacher's examination or some college credit.

The number of students attending a one-room school ranged from a few as three or four up to forth. I started with ten students one year. On March 1, the traditional time for a farm lease to expire, six children from three families moved away for that reason, and no new families with children moved into the district. For that reason, we finished the year with four students. There were only four students for the next term. The school closed the following year and the few children were transported to the nearby town school.

During the last two years I taught, I had a total of thirty-six pupils, in all eight grades, and I had the assistance of an aide. I never felt I had done justice to the job, but we all tried our best.

There are pros and cons regarding rural one-teacher school: proximity to home as opposed to bus transportation, community control as opposed to federal control, limited exposure to other adults and resources, limited financial resources, and greater opportunities in larger districts. The list could go on and on, but the fact remains that these one-teacher schools did provide educational opportunity that could not always have been supplied by parents at home, and it was not often feasible to send children to boarding school.

It was an era that served its purpose all over the rural areas of the Midwest and other sections of our country. These schools came closer to providing universal literacy for the United States as compared with areas of the world where girls in particular were denied education opportunity."

Nelda Rathman Dennison

I"n 1919, I started school at the age of six years. The walk was a mile and one-half. I spoke only German; the teacher spoke on English. The teacher, a local girl, also walked a mile and one-half. We had a later teacher, a marred man with a mustache, who had a horse and buggy. Icicles formed on his mustache when it was very cold. We had a coal-burning furnace to heat the room.

About ten children sat on the bench for lessons. We each carried our own drinking glass. It snowed while we were in school; old family members would piggy-back the children to school. Above the blackboard of the classroom were the letters of the alphabet, and they were written as capital letters. The lower case letters were also displayed. We had an American flag in our school that was made by the teacher and students. It stood in front of the room and was made from construction paper and folded in such a way as to look like a proper United States flag.

Every Friday we had a spelling bee. Classes lasted for six months of the year. Some students were older and stayed in school longer because they couldn't learn as quickly; however, no one had to say past the age of 16. Discipline was delivered by hand or by sitting with the face in the corner.

The County Superintendent of Schools visited every county school every year to inspect the building, outhouses, library books, heating facilities and water wells. It was always a treat for the school children for much time was spent preparing and cleaning for the visit.

There were many games for us to enjoy at recess: Ante-Over, Fox & Geese (when it snowed), Baseball, Hide & Seek, Hop Scotch and Whip Lash were our favorites."

Ed Browning
Chihuahua, Higginsville

When I was six years old, I started the first grade in a public school with about 25 other kids my age in a town of about 3000 to 5000 inhabitants. Just prior to my seventh birthday, my family moved about 80 miles to the rural community where my parents had been raised. Following a two-week illness, I began my stint in the local rural school-the same one my mother attended. What a culture shock! There were less than 25 kids in the whole school; that's first through eight grade. I took right up with the older boys. Not that I was popular or anything like that. It's just that there were so few of us, they needed help playing Red Rover with the girls.

The kids attending school there thought I was pretty smart. I could count to 100 before any of the others my age. Of course, there was only one girl and one other boy my age, so that may not have been a very significant point. All the boys hounded Mrs. Erdman, our teacher, to advance me to second grade because I was so smart, but she wouldn't hear of it. Mrs. Erdman taught all eight grades, you know. She'd teach us first graders and give us an assignment then while we studied, she'd teach the next level. By the way, she taught my mother too, which is dangerous for the offspring. That seemed to be the story of my life. I had so many teachers that had taught my mother 20 years earlier, I've lost count, and every one of them remembered her.

My family lived about three quarters of a mile from the school, which at the time seemed about ten miles. I grew up hearing my dad reminisce about having to ride a horse ten miles to school and my paternal grandmother and her sister doing the same thing. I guess walking as little as I did wasn't like riding a horse through the snow and cold all winter.

I remember my maternal grandfather picking his two youngest daughters and me up from school one day. It was raining cat and dogs and a few cows. The roads back then were dirt road—not gravel—dirt! Except when it rained. Then they were mud. The ruts in the road—there were two sets by that time—were about 10" to 12" deep. My grandfather was driving a '36 five-window Ford sedan (I wish I had inherited it) from the best I remember. He was fighting the steering wheel tooth and toenail to keep it in one of the sets of ruts. That's when he laid one of life's rules on me. "Find a rut and stay in it."

The next fall I started second grade in town. Boy, there sure was a lot more competition there. While there were a lot more opportunities and friends in the bigger school, that four or five months in the one room country school are memorable.

Richard Wardlow
Diamond

"I went for eight years to a one-room country school called "Diamond" located about 7 miles NW of Jasper. It would be interesting to know how and when the establishment of such schools was mandated and, particularly, how the location of each school was chosen.

There seems to have been a random pattern of locations. Roughly, one school was surrounded in all four directions by two or three square miles of land, but...with many variations and no set pattern.

For instance, only two miles west of Diamond was the "Shapley" school. Three miles west of it was "Nashville". Three miles north was "Duval", Three miles south was "Rosebank". Some three miles east of Diamond was "Blue", three miles south and another mile east of Diamond was "Lynnland". However, to the north of Diamond there was not another such school (to the best of my memory) until "Iantha" --which was distant some 12 miles or more.

In general the physical layout was the same for most one-room schools: One square acre (208.7' X 208.7') located the corner on a 1 square mile section. An outhouse or privy was located at each of the two rear most corners of the tract: the girl's toilet and the boy's toilet. The school building was usually located about 20 feet from the road front, and a few yards to the side of the schoolhouse was the coal and woodshed for storing the fuel of the school stove. The balance of the land was for playground, and sometimes auto parking.

The schoolhouse itself was a clapboard rectangle about 20 feet wide and 40 feet long, 3 or 4 sash windows on each side, a door (and only one door) in the center front, and a blank wall at the opposite end. All buildings had white exteriors and wooden shingled roofs.

Near the one door there was usually a well with a pump handle type pump and a flag pole.

Immediately to the right, on entering the doorway, and against the wall stood a wooden bench, about 1 1/2 feet high. Students put their lunch pails on this bench. They put their overshoes and galoshes under the bench. They hung their caps and coats on wall-hooks just above the lunch pails.

The lunch pail was one of the few items denoting social distinction among an otherwise totally (we were all poor) homogenous group. The lowest level of social achievement was the 1-gallon syrup bucket (label removed) ;lunch pail. Above that was the square tin box with detachable lid, double folding carrying bails, brightly painted in red or blue cute designs. But the real Cadillac of lunch pails was the black, oblong box with a "covered-wagon" style hinged lid, which accommodated a thermos bottle!! Among the males, this kind of lunch box was the *sine qua non* of social achievement...especially if the thermos contained hot coffee, and not girly-sissy cocoa or milk.

Later, when the burden of carrying the lunch pail all the way home at day's end became too taxing -- it was considered very smart to bring one's lunch in a brown paper bag that could be disposed comfortably.

The library stood in the corner at the end of the lunch pail bench. The library consisted of a green metal upright cabinet, abut five feet high and containing a few shelves of nondescript and inappropriate books...and a few worthwhile ones. Titles: "Smoky, a Cow Pony" written and illustrated by Will James was my favorite. Jean Stratton Porter's "Girl of the Limberlost", Harold Bell Wright's various Ozark stories, and a few Zane Grey novels. There was no encyclopedia. There was no large "unabridged" dictionary. There must have been a dictionary of some sort, but I don't recall any.

The central floor area had a center and two side aisles running between rows of desks toward the "teacher's desk". The primary, the 2nd, 3rd an 4th grade desks were small, single seat jobs. The upper classmen had double or two-seater desks, but there was never enough students so as to require double occupancy. Behind the teacher's desk, against the rear wall was the blackboard above which hung a copy of Gilbert Stuart's "Portrait of George Washington" and a copy of Millet's "The Angelus". I went thru all eight years puzzled by the two mounds of foamy white fluff raising round George Washington's chest, no teacher ever explained it. I think it took a college education to learn that the portrait was just incomplete. Also, for some months I was under the impression that it was a picture of our neighbor 'The' (Theodore) Mitchell. I was admittedly not the sharpest knife in Diamond's draw of intellectuals.

Each school had 3 "directors elected by the residents of the school district. The directors hired the teacher for a one-year term and did little else, as far as school duties were concerned. They fixed the teacher's salary. The County Superintendent of Schools (in Barton County: the excellent Elgin Dermott) really "ran" the schools and supervised the teaching curriculum. I don't know who delivered the monthly paycheck to the teachers. Did the 3 directors maintain a school bank account? Did the County Sup't write the checks? Even though I, myself, finished out a year of such school teaching, I haven't the faintest memory of how I received my pay. (P.S. I do remember that my pay was $60 per month, and I was rehired at $75)

Many of the teachers were girls just out of high school (they'd had a few summer weeks of "teacher training") who wanted to accumulate a few dollars for her 'hope chest' or dowry, and those usually taught only until they snagged a husband. However, there were a number of career teachers who bore excellent reputations. Among them: the Rosebaugh sisters: Lillian (Lee) and Marie, Glenna Gresham, Elbert Overfman, Nora Lawless Cones, Jennie Wright Vincent, etc.

To start school one was supposed to be, or become, six years of age by the end of the calendar year. My birthday is Jan., 5th, so I didn't legally qualify to begin school in 1928, but since it was a matter of only a few days, I started school at age 5. There were probably about 18 students (grades 1 thru 8) but to me it seemed a multitude. My brother Hubert was in the eighth grade. He and his classmates seemed like giants. The teacher was a beginner and rather sour. I don't recall that she even taught me a single thing. At home I'd learned my ABC's and could identify the sound that each letter represented, and I knew to count to 100. Lucky for us, after only 3 weeks or so our teacher found that she was somewhat pregnant, so she made a quick marriage, resigned and moved away. Maybe she had good reason to be so sour and disagreeable. The silver lining to the sour dark departed cloud, was that the directors replaced her by hiring, out of retirement, Mrs. Nora Cones from the Rock Mount neighborhood. Mrs. Cones had taught 5 of my older brothers at the Blue School. And now, her hiring, during Hubert's final year and my first year of school, made our family record complete. Mrs. Cones taught Reading by phonetics: learn to sound the letters, put the sounds together and you have the word - even though you'd never heard or known the word before. She taught beginner arithmetic by having us put together various objects for addition, take some away for subtraction, put objects into groups for multiplication and division, proceeding into counting by twos', threes' etc. Thence into reciting the multiplication tables through the "twelves".

My first year classmates were Dorothy Spoon, Owen Law, Elzie Black, and Marjorie Crabtree. Since several of the families were farm renters, and not owners, ever year there were changes on March 1st. This was the tenancy change date for Duval Mortgage Company, the major landlord via a number of farm foreclosures. Maybe moving to the new tenancy on March 1st gave time to get the year's crops planted.

In any event, this meant annual changes in the school enrollment. As a result, we had new and different classmates each year. However, Dorothy Spoon and I remained the never-changing 'regulars'. Dorothy and I began school the same day and continued together through Jasper High School graduation, 12 years later in 1940. We were then, and remain, good friends. During my Army service I was in D.C. for a short while and got to visit Dorothy there. We've visited since at a couple of Jasper High reunions. Naturally, seeing my oldest friend is the high point of those reunions.

I would have liked for Mrs. Cone to remain our teacher, but she had "filled in" just for that year. For our second year the directors hired Miss Clara McCune. She was also a 'natural-born ' teacher and somewhat strict. To our disappointment and, I think, also to hers, she was not rehired for the following year. The McCunes were fine local family of the Lynnland community. Shortly thereafter Miss Clara married Mr. Earl Patterson. They lived in Carthage and still contributed to the Lynnland neighborhood by bringing singers and musicians (some Black or African-Americans) up from Carthage to perform for a really appreciative audience.

Instead of rehiring Miss Clara, the directors hired a gorgeous brunette beauty, fresh out of high school. She was movie-star pretty and totally charming. I think her educational capacities may have been limited. Sometimes, as a treat, the teacher would read, for the final ten minutes of the 'noon recess' from a novel. One novel was about a gang of boys, one named "Stephen". Our lovely teacher pronounced this as 'Step' 'Hen'. She was never corrected and we didn't know the difference. Also, near the end of October, I asked her about the origin and meaning of "Halloween" (though, I'm sure I didn't use those words). She thought a while and said it was called 'Holloween' because it came at that time of year when so many things were 'hollow' such as trees,

pumpkins, and such like!!!!
It never occurred to anybody to 'look it up'.

Some decades later I hound that 'hallows' is an Old English term for 'holy', 'saintly'; e'en is for 'eve' or 'evening;--thus Halloween is the Evening before All Saints Day (Nov. 1).

However, our brunette charmer was rehired and she was my 3rd and 4th grade teacher. During her 2nd year she married. Her charm and beauty brought us all such pleasure.

1928 was the first year that Missouri schools had "free text books". I recall that most of our texts were from Ginn & Co. in Chicago. I remember reading Arithmetic, Horn-Ashaugh Spellers, Health & Sanitation texts. I don't remember any history or civic texts.

Our Readers (Field Readers, Pathway to Reading, etc., (we had sometimes as many as four different text per grade) were truly marvels. Our primer was definitely NOT the Dick & Jane, See Spot Run variety. We began with Mother Goose, from there to Eugene Field. By 3rd & 4th grade, and definitely by grade 6th, we were exposed to masterpieces of children's literature.

The 3rd grade Reader had some Oscar Wilde fairy tales: The Selfish Giant, also H. C. Anderson's Little Match Girl, Little Lame prince; Eugene Field (the 'Missouri Post) Little Boy Blue.

I was captivated by excerpts: Mr. Toad's Wild Ride and Maggie and the Gypsies. Years later I discovered Kenneth Graham's "Wind and the Willows' and George Eliot's 'The Mill on the Floss'. Then I got to read the entire work, whose source-unacknowledged excerpt I'd loved back when I was maybe ten or eleven years of age.

I have often wondered, "Who were those wonderful people who chose the selections for public school texts"? It had to have been done during the 1910's. They must have been brave souls to put into innocent hands such works and authors: Oscar Wilde, Tennyson-'Crossing the Bar'; Browning-'How They Brought the News from Ghent to Aix; Defoe's-'Robinson Crusoe', etc. Not that the content was scandalous, but MATURE.

How did one teacher manage to handle so many grades and so many students all in a 9 a.m. to 4 p.m. day of only 5 1/2 hours teaching time? She did it. While instructing the lower grades during the morning, the upper grades were studying. Afternoons, after finishing with one class, the brighter of that class were assigned to 'monitor' those in the lower four grades. This monitoring consisted of hearing reading assignments, helping with new words, correcting spellings and pronunciations, drilling addition and subtraction fluency with the use of "Flash Cards" - a set of approx. 5" X 8" cardboards with the numbers to be added, subtracted, multiplied, etc. appearing in large black letters on the front, and repeated in small letters in a upper corner of the letters on the front, and repeated in small letters in an upper corner of the back side for the teacher or monitor to know the numbers being shown on the front.

For the students the school day began at 9 a.m. For the teacher it began much earlier. In winter, she had to start the fire in the stove to get the large room warmed by 9. This meant carrying away ashes, bringing in kindling and coal and building a fire. Sometimes some coals would be glowing from the previous day -- only if she'd properly 'banked' the fire then by covering it with dead ashes. Sometimes older students would help with sweeping the floor, pumping and carrying in a pail of drinking water, (younger ones could dust the chalk erasers). But, would you believe this? Some parents objected to this practice of student help on the grounds that the teacher was **being paid** to do this work!!!

First bell rand at 5 minutes to 9. Last bell rand at 9, at which time all were to be at their desks and ready to LEARN. The handball resided on the teacher's desk alongside the pencil sharpener. More elegant schools, such as Rocky Mount had a big bell in a belfry on the roof. But Diamond and other schools did not aspire to such grandeur. First recess was a 15-minute bread beginning at 10:30. Hardly time for any extended outdoor game, but greatly anticipated nonetheless. Noon recess (now: lunch hour) was from noon to 1 p.m. Afternoon recess was a 15-minute break at 2:30. Resumption of classes was signalled by the 5-min. first bell and the last bell. This 1 1/2 hour total recess time seriously reduced reaching and learning time down to only 5 1/2 hours per day.

The noon recess began with Hand Washing Drill. The teacher made liquid soap by shaving a bar of Lifebuoy into a quart of water. One older student manned the pump handle at the well, another poured on a bit of soap, the line of students went through, once under the pump for water, then the soap then under the pump again for rinsing. Paper towels had probably not yet been invented. I don't know about the girls, but the boys dried their hands by wiping them on their overalls or pant legs. I guess this program kept head coals to the minimum, but it seems that someone always had the sniffles.

Our main games took place during the noon period. We had one bat, one soft ball, and one catcher's mitt, but seldom enough students to field any sort of opposing teams. One Eyed Cat: two bases, 4 players, a hedge-limb club for the second batter. Sometimes a mean boy would slip in a 'hedge apple' (an Osage Orange) as a substitute softball. The milk of the hedge apple is sticky, glue-like, rubbery substance. It was generally pitched to the boy with the real baseball bat. When the hedge-apple was stuck, its nasty white gook splattered all over the batter and his clothes...ugh!!! This was considered quite a sophisticated antic.

Generally, our games were Andy-over, Prisoner's Base, Red Rover and Goose. I've forgotten the point of all of those games. Basically, they were combinations of running, tagging, confinement and rescue. Some of these games came from, and are described in, Edward Eggleston's Hoosier Schoolboy and Hoosier Schoolmaster.

The games were such that all pupils, from first grade on to eighth could play. Andy-over: half the pupils on one side of the schoolhouse, the other half on the other side, throw a ball over the top of the building to the opposite side, at some signal or other each 'side' ran to the other and, I think, you tried to tag as many kids as you could by touching them with the ball.

Fox and Goose was play only after a snowfall. A circle or wheel with a hub and four 'spokes' was trampled out in the snow. The Fox tried to catch the Geese by tagging them and bringing them to the center Hub, other Geese tried to free them, etc. (refer again to Eggleston).

During one 6th grade game of A Prisoner's Base, I caught Otto Waldbuesse and imprisoned him in the Coal Shed (which was the official 'prison'). Otto was so angry at being tagged that he picked a lump of coal, threw it and smacked me in the forehead, knocking me out for a few seconds. That night I had a big knot on my forehead and a mildly high fever. The fever continued for a couple of days and I was out of school. Apparently, Otto's 'violent' act grew in the telling, for that evening Anna Obgerfels came to our house with Otto in tow, to make him apologize. (The Obgerfels, along with the Rehmns, were one of the leading families of the German settlers, and unofficially saw to it that no German family every gave cause for offense. Mr. Obgerfel (Andy) was the lay minister of the 'German Church'...

We were all setting around the stove in our dining-living room. On the pretext of an interest in something in mom's kitchen, Anna and Mom absented themselves, leaving me and Otto alone. He took my hand (probably under dire threats from Anna) and murmured that he was sorry for what he'd done. I told him everything was OK. As it turned out, Otto had done the Diamond School a big favor because my fever was not from being beaned with a coal lump, but was coming down with chicken pox. By the following morning I was totally covered with the pimples and sparkles of chicken pox. So Otto did not get the pox, even though we'd been close together during my contagious fever period.

Otto and I remained affectionate friends across the years. I last saw him a my Dad's funeral in 1957. Otto looked so youthful and vigorous that I accused him of having discovered the Fountain of Youth. Then, shortly thereafter, I learned he had died suddenly, apparently heart failure while out in a field. So, go figure!

Miss Jennie Wright (later Vincent) was my 5th & 6th grade teacher. Before Diamond, she'd taught at Nashville. Apparently, while there she had exercise corporal punishment (i.e. given a few kids a 'licken'). So she came to us with the reputation of a strict harridan. Some parents, including my own mother, had serious misgivings and fears for their children's safety. Their worries were needless. There was never a kinder and more competent instructor than Miss Jenny. Arithmetic had always been my weakest subject. Somehow she took all the mystery and difficulty out of long division, fractions, decimals, and made math enjoyable. She boarded with Marvin and Clarice Buzzard at their home only a few steps from the schoolhouse. There was never an unheated school on cold winter mornings, she made cloth window screens so we had open windows and fresh air in the classroom.

With the help of some concerned parents, such as Beatrice Spoon, Ethel Angles Wardlow, she organized an unofficial P. T. A. This was a monthly evening social at the school, pupils did small skits and playlets, performed as a Rhythm Band, and recited. The grown-ups visited and applauded. The mothers brought food for the supper (now, we'd call it Covered Dish). I remember that at the very first evening, Miss Jenny brought food which was her fresh baked gingerbread covered with fresh whipped cream. Shed whipped gallons of fresh cream in an

enormous circular 'dish-pan' while the pupils' performances were in progress. It must have cost her most of her meager monthly 'teacher's pay'.

Miss Mary Carnes (Heckmann) was my 7th & 8th grade teacher. She was a pretty blond with blue eyes. At that time we had another classmate - the pretty Pauline Zaerr, Willy Waldbuesser (a year ahead of me and Ot's older brother) had a crush on Pauline. He expressed his admiration by carving a art of her name on the upper unloading-chute door of the Coal Shed. He only got as far as her first name, and had misspelled that as Pualine.

Then someone ratted on Willy to Miss Mary. The resulting furor was apparently limited to the student body. But we were all extremely upset by this heinous deed. Our malaise must have lasted all week long. Meanwhile, Pauline reacted with her little Mona Lisa smile, as was her gentle wont.

Needless to say, under Miss Mary's tutelage we, Dorothy, Pauline and I, were well prepared for the Finals - which we took at the Duval School along with pupils from several surrounding districts. We all 'passed' and got our diplomas at a grand Last Day of School picnic. There, Lillian Shapely Golliday gave me an autographed volume of Winston Churchill's (the novelist, not the statesman) Richard Carvel, as Lillian put it, congratulation on my First Step. I left that book at my farm home-I wonder whatever happened to it.

First Airplane To Come To Carthage
Alma Kasper Trent

""When I was in the second grade I started attending Mark Twain School in Carthage, I lived out west of Carthage and had to ride the street car back and forth to school. I had to pay 5 cents to ride into town and 5 cents to ride back home in the afternoon.

It was about 1918 or 1919 as I remember, and it was recess time. All the kids were playing when we saw the airplane flying slowly around. Some of the older kids started to follow the plane so the rest of us followed, too.

You must remember that at that time most of the property going down Centennial Street was open fields, so we cut across the fields and kept following the airplane until it finally landed at the corner of Fairview and Baker, about where H. E. Williams is now. A big crowd had gathered and we all stood around for quite a while looking at the plane.

The plane had two wings, one on top of the other and only one man flew the plane. It was so fascinating because we had never seen anything like that before, at least not in person.

When we got back to school, of course, we were in trouble. In my class, we all had to form a line, go up to the teacher's desk, apologize and kiss the teacher's hand.

Index

Achey, Alvin 206
Adams, Darieus III, 255, 256
Adams, Louise 255
Adams, Mollie 115
Adams, Olah Belle 255, 256
Adams, Pauline 255, 257
Adams, Russell 255, 267
Adams, Wallace 255, 256
Adams. B. F. 35
Ale, Clark 274
Alexander, Agatha 258, 261, 262
Alexander, Clay 258, 261
Alexander, J. C. 260
Alexander, Pauline 255, 257,
Alexander, Rex 258
Allen, Ben 153
Allen, Erma 144
Allen, J. W. 251
Allison, William 199
Almegard, I. J. 63
Alombaugh, Manda 246
Alombaugh, Sam 246
Alumbaugh, Sherry 164
Alumbaugh. Mary 246
Alwetz, Lida 293
Amity 55, 59
Amos, Helen, 81
Amos, Mary 111
Amour, Cary 249
Anderson, Mrs. 83
Armstrong, R. C. 235
Arnett, Twyla 150
Arnold, Phillip 35
Arthur 55, 61, 63
Arthur, Lilburn Q. 59
Ashley, Clifford 205
Ashley, Lavina 205
Askins, Mr. 204
Atherton, Amos 106
Atkinson, John 115
Atlas 55, 297
Aubrey, Carolyn 214
Ault, Edna 105
Ault, Issac 105
Bacon, John R. 124
Bacon, Sarah Ann 124
Bailey, Bert 63
Bailey, Martha 63
Bailey, Rex 68
Bailey, Verna 63
Baily, Anna 63
Baily, Finis 63
Baily, Juanita 63
Baker, Billie 228
Baker, Charlotte 201
Baker, Don 97
Baker, Edith Gladys 97
Baker, Ester Nell 97
Baker, Farris 206
Baker, G. W. 193
Baker, George 206
Baker, Greory 71
Baker, Harold 228
Baker, Helen 197
Baker, Martha 97

Baker, Mrs. Laura 153
Baker, Sylvia 61, 254, 276
Baldwin, Bobby 130
Baldwin, Gladys 130
Baldwin, Mrs. Belle 1150
Ball, Barbara 97
Ball, Charles 99
Ballard, Esther 83
Banner 55, 63
Bardoe, Cara 137
Barhern, J. H. 297
Barkley, C. O. 239
Barkley, Gerald 97, 240
Barley, Pauline 218, 220
Barlow, A. 311
Barnes, Lois J. 79
Barrett, A. A. 211, 273
Barson, J. W. 227
Bartosh, John III
Bartosh, John, 235
Bass, Clyde 243
Bass, Lee 243
Bass, Wanda 243
Bastin, Bobby 130
Bastin, Chas. 129
Bastin, Earl 213
Bastin, Russell 213
Batton, J. W. 219
Bauer, John 235
Baugh, Butter 153
Baugh, Clarence 185
Bawbell, Ida 308
Bayless, Christine 102
Bayless, Jimmy 102
Bayless, Mike 102
Beavan, Violet 202
Beaver, Ferman Clyde, 192
Beaver, Marvin, Dean 192
Beckett, Ruth 186
Begley, Chas. 141
Beldon, Trixie 200
Bell, George L. 199
Bell, Jennnie 69, 128, 211
Bell, Walter 97
Belle Center 56
Bender, Helen 72
Bender, Kathryn 72
Bennett, Lola 316
Bennett, Rose Ann 97
Bensing, B. F. 185
Bentley, John 103
Berean 55, 65, 68
Berkey, Jane 319
Berkey, Janet 319
Berkley, Bob 104
Berkley, Janet 316
Berrian, Mrs. C. E. 293
Berry, Bernice 162
Berry, J. G. 239
Berry, Kathryn 122
Berry, Neta 162
Betts, Kenda 124
Biffee, Mamie, 115
Billingslea, E, 215
Billingsley, C. A. 145

Billington, Verna Mae 305
Binney, Geo. 183
Binney, Libby 59
Bird, Emma 65
Bird, Jas. 209
Bird, O. L. 65
Bird, Willa 189
Bishop, Lenno 70
Bissell, Charles 163
Bistline, Wayne 219
Black Jack 56, 253
Black, Barbara 202
Black, Billie 164
Black, Pattty 164
Black, Ramona 164
Black, Sherye 164
Blackberry 55, 67
Blake School 55, 69
Bleam, O. D. 115
Blevins, Martha 86
Block, Anna 63, 64
Block, Betty Jo 63, 64
Block, Billie Jean 63, 64
Block, Elmer 64
Block, James 64
Block, Leroy 65, 64
Block, Samuel Charles 64
Blood 55
Bloomindale 55, 71, 121
Bock, Barbara 184
Bois 'D Arc 55, 73
Boling, Connie 218
Booton 150
Bower, G. W. 199
Bowers, Alice 60
Bowers, George F. 306
Bowers, Leonard 313
Bowlen, Miss Susan 20
Bowman, Barbara 192
Bowman, C. A. 271
Bowman, Helen Bender 72
Bowman, Morris Gene 130
Bowman, P. C. 129
Boyd, H. M. 11,12
Bradford, Clarence 249
Bradford, Clayton 249
Bradford, Ray 254
Bradley, H. W. 133
Bradley, H. W. 140
Bragdon, Geo. H. 245
Branson, Matie 227
Brick 55, 75
Bricker, Billy 64
Bricker, Nadine 64
Bridges, Evan 204
Bridgewater, G. A. 151
Briggle, Addie 256
Briggle, C. H. 115
Briggle, Mrs. C. 115
Briggle, Chanuncy 254, 256
Briggle, Mrs. C. 122
Briggle, Mrss. C. 117
Briggle, Vivian 74
Bright, Samuel 13
Britten, Wiley 22, 52

Broadaway, Imogene 63, 64
Brock, Ethel 291
Brock, Hazel 237, 300
Brock, Roy 294
Brooks, Kennedy 49
Brooks, Opal 193
Brown, Bernice 276
Brown, Crayton 162
Brown, Hattie 162
Brown, Homer 162
Brown, Judge Marion 159
Brown, Marlin 64
Brown, Phyllis 64
Brown, Thaine 63, 64
Brown, W. S. 159
Brown, Walter P. 159
Browning, Ed 320
Bruffett, Everett 269
Bruffett, Gene 270
Bruffett, Paul 270
Bruffett, Sharon 197
Brummett, Mrs. James 13
Brush College 62,
Bryan, John 115
Bryant, Fannie 146
Buchanan, G. W. 191
Buck, Geo. 293
Buck, Thomas 103
Buerge, Orville 97
Bull, Kathy Sue 124
Bull, Lora 124
Bull, Marjorie III, 87, 130, 139
Bull, Vance 124
Burbridge, W. N. 243
Burch, Fred 83
Burgi, Eva 207
Burgi, J. T, 73
Burgi, Lloyd 74
Burgie, Frank 190
Burkholder, C. P. 311
Burnett, Alfred 193
Burns, F. R. 181
Burton 55, 81
Busby, Eva 247
Buston, Mrs. Frank 189
Butcher, Garnet 204
Butcher, Jay H. 291
Butcher, Martha 204
Butcher, Rose 204
Butcher, Walter 204
Butler, Jimmy 316
Butler, Joe 316
Buxton, Betty 97
Buxton, David 97
Buxton, Doris 97
Byler, Elmer 293
Byon, Beatrice 208
Callary, Phil 159
Callison, A. B. 115, 183, 199
Campbell, Charlyn 761
Campbell, Warren 253
Cannon, Maud 75
Capps, Joyce 218
Capps, Nancy 218
Capps, Richard 218

Index

Carlson, Helen Mae Wolfe 284
Carmical, Martha 243
Carneal, Gladys 267
Carnes, Mary (Heckmann) 327
Carpenter, Effie 246
Carpenter, S. D. 31
Carr, Harry 107
Carr, Jim 71
Carr, John R. 245
Carr, Jonnie J. 71
Carr, Margaret 129
Carr, W. W. 36
Carson, Belle 153
Carson, Helen Mae Wolfe 287
Carter, Boyd 130
Carter, C. W, 245
Carter, Florence 127
Carter, G. L. 96
Carter, J. G. L. 89
Carter, J. M. 305
Carter, Joyce Bowman 271
Carter, Lorena Frost 244
Carter, Ruth 119, 137
Carter, Winston 116, 305
Cartwright, J. C. 183
Carvel, Richard 328
Carytown School 55, 85
Case, Velma 153
Caster, Elvis 70
Cather, Joseph 209
Cave Spring 55, 85, 89
Cave Spring 91, 92, 93, 94
Cave Springs 55, 95
Cearnel, Jackie 308
Cedar Bluff 55, 97, 102
Centennial 55, 101
Center 55, 107
Center Point 55, 107, 109, 287
Central City 55, 111
Cernel, Jewel 267
Chaddle, M. E, 29
Chandler, Everett 72
Chandler, Freda 70
Chandler, Homer 70
Chandler, Jerry 70
Chandler, May 70
Chandler, Myra 70
Chandler, Ruby 70
Chapman School 155
Chapman, Clarence 207
Chapman, Clarence Seta 207, 208
Chapman, Cloyd 207, 208
Chapman, D. A. 207
Chapman, Zeta 207
Charity 22
Charter Oak 55, 115
Chenault, John R. 13,
Childres, Macie 261
Chitwood 56
Chrisman, Charles 76
Chrisman, Etlon 70
Chrisman, Goldia 70
Chrisman, Jessie 70
Clark, M. G. 188
Clouser, Helen 119,

Clyman, Lorene 256
Clyman, Oscar 258
Coates, Don 139
Coates, Gary 139
Coates, William 140
Coats, Charley 204
Coats, Jackie 71
Coats, Jo Ann 71
Coats, Marie 204
Coats, Mildred 204
Cobine, Mildred 64
Cochran, Beverly 70
Cochran, Floyd 306
Cochran, May 142
Coffield, Edith 303
Cole, Brenda 103
Cole, Connie 103
Cole, Ricky 103
Colley, W. B. 41, 49, 257
Collings, G. J. 284
Collings, Josie 284
Compton, Bobby 129, 130
Conder, A. B. 183
Conder, J. S. 183
Condon, Clyde 312
Condon, Ronald 312
Cones, Nora 325
Conrad, Jennie 271
Conray, Ed 183
Conroy, Kathleen 248
Cook, Judy 184
Cooley, Samuel B. 13
Coon Foot 55, 117
Cooper, A. 239
Cooper, Arthur 42
Cooper, Emma 271
Coren, Vina Van 2246
Corwine, Gabie 139
Costley, Bill 296
Costley, Leota Johnson 296
Costley, Paula Rose 296
Costley, Ralph 296
Costley, Shirley Sue 295
Cottingham, C. 129
Couard, Jennie 240
Cowan, Carol 142
Cowan, Marcia 142
Cowen, Diana 142
Cox Diggings 56
Crabtree, Marjorie 325, 326
Crabtree, Marjorie 326
Craig, Dale 280
Craig, Floyd 280
Craig, Richard 280
Cramer, Charlie 162
Cramer, Emma 162
Cramer, Lizzie 162
Cramer, Zelpha 162
Cravens, Jeremiah 9, 12
Crawford, John C. 115
Crawford, Walter 73
Creel, Phoebe 295
Cribbs, Barbara 192
Cribbs, Mary Ann 192
Culley, Gary 70

Culley, Lenero 70
Culpepper, Josie 106
Cunningham, T. J. 309
Cupp, Bertie 139
Cupp, Maud 146
Cupp, Myrta 137
Cupp, Ora 146
Curry, Brent 142
Curry, Peggy 142
Curtis, Edith 299
Curtis, Mary 127
Daggy, Leona 204
Daggy, Leonard 204
Daisy, Alice 213
Daniels, Lawrence 126
Darrel, N. 127
Daugherty, Tresa 213
Dauray, Alta Jo 139
Davey, Myrtle F. 235
Davidson, Betty Joyce 64
Davidson, Dorothy 64
Davidson, Doyle 64
Davidson, Jas. I. 63
Davis, Don 299
Davis, Hardy 229
Davis, Harry 211
Davis, Henry 299
Davis, Jos. 211
Davis, Lowell 127
Davis, Mable 70
Davis, Nell 219
Davis, Rosemary 144
Deck, John 140
Deer Creek 55, 119
Denison, E. D. 38
Denison, James 243
Denison, Ruth 243
Dennison, Jess 140
Dennison, John W. 140
Dennison, Margie 186
Dennison, Nelda Rathman 319
Dennison, W. M. 140, 289, 291
Denton, Marybeth 122
Dewey 55, 121, 122
Diamond School 55, 326, 327
Dick, Atta 273
Dick, John 231
Dick, Wm. 313
Dickson, Martha 77
Dilworth, Jackie 139
Dinamin, H. O. 287
Ditto, Carrie 245
Dixie 55, 125
Dixon 56
Dixon, Connie 164
Dixon, Danny 164
Dobbins, Phyllis 144
Dodson, Anna 135
Dodson, Edith 118
Dodson, Jack 118
Dodson, Lee 299
Dodson, Mary Lon 118
Dodson, R. L. 219
Dodson, Sallie 299
Dog Trot 55, 313, 314

Doke, Delpha 111
Doubledee, Johnny 309
Doubledee, Lois 309
Doubledee, M. M. 309
Downer, Ella 162
Drake, Charles 23
Dry Valley School 155
Duke, J. J. 284
Dumar, Mrs. Lee 148
Dumm, Johnnie 142
Duncan, Hirman 9
Duncan, Lee 69
Duncan, S. F. 69
Duncan, William 3, 85
Dunn, Chalmer 205
Dunn, Iven 70
Duty, Andrew 245
Duty, Olive 245
Duval 56, 253
Dyer, Helen 122
Earl, B. B. 305
Earl, Barbara 306
Earl, Bonnie Tiller 194
Earl, Chauncey 305
Earl, Harvey 305
Earl, Kenneth 210
Earl, Lydia Jane 284
Earl, Marvin 206
Earl, Robert 210
Earnst, Effie 213
East Hollow School 55
Edwards, Alma 133
Edwards, Buster 190
Edwards, Iva 162
Edwards, J. B. 221
Edwards, Mona 141
Edwards, Stella 162
Edwards, Vera 218
Edwards,Governor 11, 12
Eilway, J. P. 151
Elliason, Oma Howell 245
Ellingsworth, Caroll 63
Ellingsworth, Leroy 63
Ellingsworth, Marie 63
Ellingsworth, Norman 63
Ellis, Alva 259
Ellis, Ralph 259
Ellis, Viola 259
Ellison, J. F. 159
Ellison, John 279
Elmira 55, 127
Ely, Maggie 246
Emery, Lula 121
Empire 55, 110, 129, 142
Enis, H. W. 151
Enos, Thomas 151
Enterprise 55, 131
Erickson, Irma Nell Evans 266
Erie 55, 133
Erwin, 306
Erwin, Claude 275
Esther Ballard
Etter, Gertrude 127
Etter, Wm. 275
Evans, Dora 264

Index

Evans, Ernest 287
Evans, Gladys 271
Evans, Glen 264
Evans, Harry 264
Evans, Howard 264
Evans, James C. 258
Evans, Pearl 141
Evans, W. P. 44
Evans, W. S. 275
Evans, Wayne 266
Everet, David 211
Everhand, Bobby 184
Everhand, Nina Beth 184
Excelsior 55, 135
Fadler, Geo. 246
Famer's Union 56
Fannin, Betty 74
Fannin, Eldon 74
Faradar, Tom 111
Farmer, Alvin 260
Farmer, Anise 262
Faskin, Chester 305
Faskin, Ellis 305
Faskin, Oscar 269
Faskin, Thelma 306
Fassen, W. G. 115
Felkins, Martha 80
Fenner, Mrs. Roy 221
Ferguson, Frances 317
Ferguson, Jeanetta 309
Ferguson, Opal 141
Ferguson, Thos. 235
Ferguson, Tom 228
Ferree, Charles 146
Fidelity School 55, 137
Fieker, 94, 95, 96
Fieker, Selma 51, 89,
Fieker, Selma 91, 93, 94
Fike, A. M. 311
Filarski, Anges 63
Filarski, Mary 63
Fingerle, George 211
Finic Baily, 68
Finley, Helen 135
Finn, Perry 159
Fishburn, Peter 153
Flaker, Jennie Bell 273
Fleck, John 284
Flenniken, Carl 122
Flesher, Barbara 97
Flesher, Faye 270
Flesher, Frances 199
Flesher, Hattie 235
Flesher, Patricia 97
Fleshes, Ida 227
Flowers, Aretha 121
Flowers, Fern 122
Flowers, T. A. 121
Foght, Harold W. 45
Foley, Geo. 249
Folger, Fannie 146
Folger, Frank 146
Folger, Jennie 146
Folger, Mary 146
Folger, Olive 146

Ford, Myrtle 179
Forest 55, 139
Forest Mills 55, 96, 101, 141
Forsithe, Laura 278
Fosclick, F. S. 211
Fosdick, Mona 227
Fosdick, Tommy 227
Foster, Eugene 210
Fox, Larry 155
Fox, Nora 209
Fox, Tillman 207
Fox, Verna 145
Franklin, Belle 153
Franklin, Hattie 153
Franks, J. H. 33
Franks, Mamie 65
Frazae, Viva 118
Frazar, Vivian 118
Frederickson, C. 231
Fredrickson, John 231
Fredrickson, Sue 69, 105, 131, 295
Frerer, Ed 284
Frerer, Jimmie 283, 284
Frost, Aaron 165
Frost, Carolyn 46, 180, 173
Frost, Charlotte 173
Frost, Clarence 165
Frost, Cy 165
Frost, Dorothy 46, 179
Frost, Nell 13
Frost, O. F. 271
Frost, Orville 167
Frost, T. J. 173
Frost, Walter 174
Fullerton, Emma 299
Fullerton, John M. 3
Fullerton, Ronnie 94
Fullmer, G. E. 231
Funk, Lolly 70
Gaddis, J. A. 83
Galesburg 55, 143
Gandy, J. W. 153
Garber, Aline 243
Garden Dell 55, 145
Garner, Jerry 35
Garret, Kay 248
Garret, Ricky 248
Garret, Ruth 248
Garret, Stanley 248
Garretson, Bobby 274
Garretson, Mildred 274
Garrett, Gilbert 284
Garrison, Joe 70
Garrison, Rabbit 70
Gass, Howard 42
Gause, Emma 146
Gem 55, 147
Georgia City 62, 153
Gibson, Geo. 291
Gilbreath, Weslen 214
Gillard, Jess 293
Gillman, Lester 203
Giterly, Mr. 115
Glasscock, Ethal 75
Goff, Danial 121

Golliday, Lillian Shapely 328
Good, Jerry 164
Good, Jimmy 164
Good, Ricky 102, 164
Goodnight, Carl 135
Goodson, Linda 164
Goodson, Tommy 164
Graber, Billy 249
Graber, Ella 249
Grace, Tommy 139
Grason, J. C. 273
Graves, Wm. 273
Gray, Geo. 305
Gray, Ira 106
Gray, Sue 151
Gray, Wm. 205
Grayson, Nora 67
Greathouse, Frankie 139
Greathouse, Roy 139
Greeley, Horace 22
Green Grove 55, 101, 153,
Green, Arba 146
Greene, L. 275
Greenlee, Mary 210
Greninger, Joe 135
Grenninger, Helen 133
Gresham, Fred 247
Gresham, Glenna 173, 174
Gresham, Jerry 248
Grieb, Mary 64
Grieb, R. E. 146
Griffih, Lila 240
Grimes, Glenda 192
Gringrich, H. 275
Grisham, Dorothy 270
Grisham, Joan 270
Grubb, Joacob 284
Grubb, Victoria 137
Guinn, Codine 74
Guinn, John C. 151
Guinn, R. T. 30
Guinn, Rodney 70
Gully, Shirley 144
Gunlock, Carlene 144
Gunlock, Carol 144
Gunlock, Ronnie 144
Gurley, Mabel 63, 64
Hadley, Lois 60
Haggard, Dora 299
Haggard, Ernest 299
Haggard, J. W. 63 70
Haggler, Neva 204
Haithcock, John 311
Hale, Pearl 225
Hale, R. W. 225
Hall, Dote 280
Hall, John Phillips 97
Hall, Juarita 97
Hall, Noah 146
Hall, Standley 97
Halloman, John B. 9
Hamilton, Carolyn III
Hamley, S. G, 111
Hammons, Juanita 279
Hancock, D. L. 143
Hane, Nellie 249

Hanna, Chrystina III
Hannah, Marie 189
Harbison, John 124
Harbison, Mary 217
Hardaway, Luther 42, 191
Hardscrabble 55
Harmon, Jacob 105
Harned, Alexander 260
Harned, Melba 260
Harned, Pauline 260
Harper, Mitia 70
Harpole, J. B. 273
Harris, Charles 253
Harrison, Gerald 219
Harry, Hiram 115
Harry, Nathaniel, 115
Harvery, Mildred 289
Harvey, Mary 270
Harvey, Mildred 283, 286, 287
Hathaway, Luther 49
Hatten, Cora 153
Hatten, Ina 153
Haughawout, A. R. 306
Havens, Geo. 181
Hawkins, Robert 204
Hawkins, T. J. 107
Hazen 55
Hazen, Dr. S. L. 258
Hazen, S. A. 258
Heaps, Jaunita 248
Heaps, Larry 248
Heaton, Elsie, H. 296
Heckert, Marjorie 237
Hedworth, B. 235
Hegar, James 97
Hegar, Paul 97
Heger, Leo 97
Heger, Luke 97
Heger, Rose Ann 97
Heisten, Rugh Gipson 107
Heisten, Ruth 70, 300
Heiston, George 153
Heman, Kenneth 70
Hemphill, Lizzie 115
Henderson, Eugene (Ted) 189
Henderson, Jene 189
Hendricks, Aline 164
Hendricks, Isaac 306
Hendricks, John 152
Hendricks, Larry 164
Hendricks, Sue 164
Henry 55, 153
Henry, A. D. 101, 102
Henry, Bev. 155
Henry, Brice 189
Henry, Eugene 189
Henry, Gary 102
Henry, Gaylon 240
Henry, Guy E. 131
Henry, J. E. 155
Henry, James 284
Henry, Johnny 189
Henry, Pete 194
Henry, Robert 284
Henry, Roscoe 141

Index

Henry, Ruth 240
Hensley, Danny 103
Hensley, Mike 103
Herr, W. A. 273
Herrell, James 161
Herring, Isaac 209
Hickler, H. 107
Hickman, Judge J. M. 159
Hickman, Mead 146
Hickman, Robinette Langley 15
Hicks, Linda Marie 214
Hicks, Mary Jane 300
Hicks, Rebecca 213
High Hill 55, 157
High Point 55, 159
Hight, Dennis 309
Hight, Don 309
Hill, Allen 184
Hill, Cecil 243
Hill, Dorothy 243
Hill, Grace Livingston 200
Hill, Jeanie III, 170
Hill, Lemoine Cabin 248
Hill, Marvin 123
Hill, Velma 248
Hine, Geo. 246
Hine, Idea 246
Hine, Mary 246
Hirshey, Henry 243
Hnter, W. T. 142
Hntley, George 209
Hobbs, Gloria 192
Hobbs, Judy 192
Hobbs, Roy 317
Hobbs. Kay 317
Hodges, W. G. 185
Hoenshell, Nelle 196
Hoght, Harold W. 53
Holderman, Ed 129
Holderman, Saml. 209
Holland, Debbie 142
Holland, Karen 14
Hollman, John B. 16
Holmes, Altehta 208
Holmes, Harriet 107
Holmes, Mrs. Allen 254
Holmes, Robert 212
Holmes, T. D. 129
Holroyd, Flora E.
Honey Charles 316
Honey, Earl 316
Honey, Jim III
Honey, Lois 316
Hood, Bertha 254
Hood, Deloris 71
Hood, E. E. 299
Hood, Jerry 70
Hood, K. C. 103
Hood, Larry 70
Hood, Meda 299
Hood, Mollie 149
Hood, Roberta 120
Hood, T. B. 157
Hood, Taylor 299
Hoofnagle, A. 213

Hoofnagle, Gary Dean 214
Hoofnagle, Larry 192
Hoofnagle, Nancy 214
Hoofnagle, Russell Lee 214
Hoover, Steve 153
Hope, Mae 256, 264
Hopkins, Andrew 137
Hopkins, S. A. 57
Horrell, Bill 64
Horrell, Olive 64
Horrell, Paul 64
Horton, Helene 204
Horton, Pete 204
Houk, L. E. 243
Houseman, John 227
Hout, Gus 205
Howard, Barbara 135
Howard, Catherine 144
Howard, Charlotte 135
Howard, Edna 265
Howard, Ethel 144
Howard, Gladys 265
Howard, Glenn 265
Howard, Irma 265
Howard, J. N. 291
Howard, Leon 265
Howard, Wayne 265
Howell, Brenda 142
Howell, Louis 240
Howell, Odell 240
Hubbard School 55, 243
Hubbard, Carolyn 210
Hubbard, Elaine 210
Hubbard, F. A. 318
Hubbard, Henry 97
Huddleston, Lavern 74
Hull, Betty 74
Hull, Esther 260
Hull, Loren 70
Humbard, 55
Humickhorn, J. F. 161
Hummel, Alpheres 215
Hunter, Helen K. Fullerton 89
Hunter, Pricilla 30
Hunter, W, T, 135
Huntley Bill 204
Huntley, Ellen,204
Huntley, Genevieve 204
Huntley, George 204
Hutton, N. 311
Hyde, Virginia 107
Independence 55, 161
Isemann, Anna 72
Isemann, George 72
Isemann, Verna 72
Isenmann, Della 205
Isenmann, Doris 210
Isenmann, Dorothy 210
Isenmann, Fred 305
Isenmann, Paul 210
Jaccard, Flora 81
Jackson 55
Jackson, Maggie 2207
Jacob. J. W. 29
Jacobs, George M. 115

Jantz, Rose Marle 316
Jantz, Wanda Louise 316
Jarman, Charles 316
Jarman, Twila 316
Jasper 62,
Jenkins, Bud 118
Jenkins, Ruth Ann 118
Jenkyn, Thomas 177
Jennings, Edmund 1
Jewell, Lena 115
Jewsbury, John 299
Jewsbury, Rosemary 299
Johannes, Carolyn 170
Johns, W. E. 275
Johnson, Isaac N. 165
Johnson, J. W. 147
Johnson, S. W. 147
Johnson, T. W. 140
Johnson, Wayne 284
Johnston, Bell 284
Johnston, C. S. 71
Johnston, Fred M. 71
Johnston, Jonnie 184
Johson, J. W. 152
Joice, Mary 247
Jones School 55
Jones, Carten E. 124
Jones, Claude B. 124
Jones, F. E. 219
Jones, Golda 205
Jones, H. J. 229
Jones, J. K. 253
Jones, Junior 63
Jones, Lois 205
Jones, M. K. 273
Jones, Melvin 205
Jones, Oliver 213
Jones, Owen 205
Jones, Peggy 124
Jones, Ruth 256, 263
Jones, Sylvia 153
Jones, Thelma 205
Jones, Velda 72
Jones, W. H. 251
Joslin, Wayne 204
Junge, Dolores 79
Kaderly, Bert 309
Katzfey, Mary 64
Kauffman, T. 247
Kaylor, Sue 139
Keeling, A. J. 153
Keeper, Reba III
Keeppes, Carl 183
Keller, Mary 278
Kennedy, Carroll 63, 64
Kennedy, Inice 66
Kennedy, Loveta 215
Kennedy, Shirley III, 63
Kennell, J. T. 163
Kentner, Pearl 119
Kilmer, Erma 309
Kilpatirck, Leonard 74
Kilpatrick, Carl 74
Kilpatrick, Paul 74
Kimberlin, Helen 64

Kimmel, A. G. 315
Kimmel, Eleanor 299
King School 55, 165
King, Delpha Stone 95
King, Mounte 205
King, Myrtle 157
Kinney, F. 249
Kinney, G. E. 147
Kirk, Goldie (Smith) 313
Kirksey, Miss Elton 159
Kiser, Everett 243
Kiser, Florence 243
Kiser, Freddie 243
Kiser, Lorra 243
Kling, Frankie 190
Knell, Delores 130
Knell, Frank 130
Knell, Fred 130
Knight, Annie 175
Knight, L. Gale 124
Knight, Loren 174
Knight, Ruby 165, 170, 186, 187, 188
Knights School 55, 101
Knights Station 109
Kollenborn, Gayreet 213
Kollenborn, Lavina 213
Kollenborn, Romaine 213
Kutz, D. C. 315
La Grange 55, 177
La Russell 101
Ladd, S. S. 105
Lafons, Arthur 261
LaForce, J. S. 305
LaForce, Martha 177
LaForce, Samuel B. 177
Lakeside School 55, 179
Lamb, Nora 162
Lambeth, Ella 135
Lambeth, Gene 142
Lambeth, James 64
Lambeth, Raymond 159
Lamkin, W. F. 280
Landers, Dorothy 192
Landers, Ina 251
Landers, Marjorie 214
Landes, Albert 144
Landes, Arthur 144
Landes, Carl 144
Landes, George 144
Lane, Daisy 209
Lanson, Eliza 215
LaPanne 280
Largent, Carolyn 192
Lasiter, Dennis 142
Lasiter, Eugene 142
Lasiter, Maety 142
Law, Donald 228
Law, Dorothy 228
Law, Owen 325
Lawerance, Linda Lou 71
Lawrence, Ann 164
Lawrence, Jack 72
Lawrence, Jane 164
Leaming, Charles 197
Leaming, Ella Marie 283

Index

Leaming, Maurice 240, 284
Leary, Jas 305
Lee, Allen 142
Lee, Beverly 70
Lee, Gary 70
Lee, Kenneth 70
Lee, Mrs. Gordon 243, 275
Lee, Ralph 72
Lee, Steven 142
Lee, Thomas Edward 201
Leeper, Martha 256
Leggett, Laurence 118
Leggett, Mary 144
Leggett, Wm. 105
Leidy, F. B. 159
LeMasters, Bessie 72
LeMasters, Hester 72
LeMasters, Lee 79
Lett, Lola 75, 78, 79, 80, 81, 82
Lewis, Billy 139
Lewis, Robyn 139
Liberal 55, 181
Liberty 55, 183
Lincoln School 35
Lincoln, Abraham 116
Little, Barbara III
Little, O. 309
Livingston, Joel T. III, 9, 13, 16,
Livingston, Tom 29
Lofan, A. 255
Lombard, Darrell 70
Lombard, Gene 70
Lone Elm 30
Lone Star 55, 185
Long, Amelia 63
Long, Charlene 70
Long, Judy Ann 135
Long, Masine 70
Long, Russell, 142
Lorenz, Bruce 189
Lorenz, Evelyn 189
Lortz, Marguerite 158, 216
Loudenslayer, Earl 221
Lovecamp, Mary Ann 153
Loveland, Erpil 135
Loveland, Jerry 135
Loveland, Steve 135
Loveless, Jonathan 159
Lowell 56
Lown, Marguerite 157
Lowry, G. R. 183
Lucas, Donnie 144
Lucas, Freeman 115
Luman, John R. 118
Lumbattis, J. A. 231
Lunderman, Mary 162
Lunderman, Nick 162
Lundy, Clara B. 139, 213
Lundy, Joseph 137
Luster, John 273
Lux, Edith 63, 287
Lyngar, Dr. 211
Lynnland 55, 189
Lytle, Mrs. Otis 294
Mackey, Harold 118

MacNeil, Denny 164
Maddos, Forest L. 275
Maddox, Beulah 275
Madsen, Edwin 192
Magers, Carrie 305
Magnet 55, 141
Magoffin 55, 225
Magoffin, Chas. 275
Magoffin, Glen 225, 256, 261, 266
Magoffin, Retta 129
Maize, Elmo 209
Maky, Harold 120
Malltbie, Geo. A. 275
Manley, Margaret 97, 226, 284
Manley, Richard 226
Mansfield, John J. 124
Maple Grove 55, 253
March, David D. PHD 10, 28
Marcus, Bill 274
Marion 55, 191
Marlin, Carolyn 214
Marlin, Jerry Ray 214
Marner, Billie Joe 316
Marner, Jamie 316
Marner, Marilyn 316
Marrett, Chas. 245
Marshall, G. S. 161
Martin, Evelyn 107
Martin, John 273
Mason, Sylvia 73, 264
Massey, Frank 87, 88
Massley, H. C. 73
Masters, Vernon 144
Mathews, Regan 63
Mathews, Valgene 63
Matthews, D. 121
Matthews, Dan 85
Matthews, Vernon 85
Maxell, E. L. 221
Maxwell, Bob 77
Maxwell, G. N. 307
Maxwell, Ruth 77
Maxwell, Virginia 77
Maxwell, William 9
Mayfield, Jack 297
Mayflower 55, 193,
Mays, Jas. 293
Mazur, Joanne 164
Mc Daniel, E. 108
McBain, Dyer 107
McBride, W. R. 243
McCall, Thos. 193
McClanahan, Charleen 118
McClanahan, Kathaleen 118
McClintock, Ella Mae 305
McClintock, Gene 210
McClintock, Paul 306
McClintock, Talma 305
McConnell, Betty 97
McCool, John 274
McCormack, L. L. 249
McCormick, Geo. 225
McCormick, Jack 291
McCormick, Pauline 129
McCune, Clara 325

McCune, Joan Johnson 231, 232
McCune, Melba Hansen 108, 287
McCune, Orie 189
McDaniel, Elizabeth 108, 129, 130
McDaniels, Chas. 129
McDowell, C. B. 129
McDowell, Vicor 296
McFaddon, Harry 155
McGee, Tommy Melton 71
McGowern, John 163
McGuire, Chas. 307
McIntyre, Geraldine 226
McKelvey, Frank 219
McKelvey, Tom 254
McLane, W. R. 38
McMahan, Geneva 107
McMullen, Mrs. Jessie 143
McMullen, Bess 143
McNary, Dan 71
McNew, Rex 157
McQuilken, R. F. 291
McQuilken, Vera Mae 291
McRae, J. D. 153
McReynolds, Ruth 79
McReynolds, Wm. 284
McVey, Kenneth 130
McWilliams, Moses 117
McWilliams, Rebecca Ann 214
Meador, John 140
Means, Weldon 228
Meares, Vance 302
Mears, Reese 299
Medoc 55, 199
Meligun, Buelah 63
Melin, F. E. 155
Melton, David R. 59
Melugin, Frank 245
Melvgin, Janet 192
Melvgin, Jimmy 192
Merker, J. P. 231
Mers, Charleston 108
Mers, Zelda 108
Meyer, Brenda Fay 135
Meyer, Linda Kay 135
Michael, James 299
Michael, Mae 243
Miller, B. F. 269
Miller, Beverly 144
Miller, David 144
Miller, Florence 37
Miller, Herbert 144
Miller, Larry 144
Miller, Mrs. 156
Miller, Orville 274
Miller, Robert 144
Millet 55
Mills, Ale 271
Mills, Chids 271
Mineral 55, 201
Mink, Frank 239
Mink, Louis F. 239
Mink, Maurine 122
Minkler, Gary 144
Mitchell, C. R. 143
Mitchell, Ginger 142

Mitchell, M. A. 209
Mitchell, Mattie 299
Mitchell, Peggy 144
Mitchell, Theodore 48
Mitchell, Wydonna 192
Miterly, Mr 122
Monitor 55, 148, 203
Monroe, Beverly 274
Monroe, Eula Grace 274
Monroe, Norman 274
Montgomery, C. N. 316
Moore, Chris 192
Moore, Henry 59
Moore, Orla J. 273
Moore, Peggy 192
More, Eddyth 229
Morning Star 55, 205
Moser, Herbert 122
Moss, Carl 243
Moss, Cren 243
Moss, Crystal 243
Moss, Doris 243
Moss, Gene 243
Moss, Harris 243
Moss, June 243
Moss, Myrta 213
Moss, Terry 135
Motley, J. D. 199
Motley, N. C. 243
Munson, Glenna 316
Murphy, Pearl 297
Murray, A. D. 81
Murto, Arria 177
Murto, Sam 177
Myers, Earl 240
Myers, Elma 240
Myers, Jacob 151
Myers, Paul 240
Nagle, Elina Rugh 161
Nally, Alvin 218
Nally, Gary 218
Nally, Sharon 218
Napper, Renward 103
Neely, Mrs. William 208
Neil, Jerry 164
Neiman, Edith 293
Nelson, Gary Lee 201
Nelson, Patricia 202
New Hope 55, 207
Newberry, Margaret 30
Newman, Edgar 291
Newton, Vilah 137
Nichols, Billy 202
Niditter, Carl 274
Nixon, Vertile 204
Normal School 42, 45, 50
North Fork 55, 209
North Star 55, 209
North, F. A. 1
Nowell, W. H. 245
O'Banion, Florence 64
O'Banion, Margaret 64
Obgerfels, Anna 327
O'Brian, Mary 256, 264, 265
Ogle, Edna 135

Index

Ogle, Lilian 135
Ohler, Geneva 211
Oldhan, Alva 219
Oliver, J. B. 251
Olson, N. 181
O'Neal, Barbara 309
Opolis 55, 211
Osborn, A. M. 215
Osborn, Anna Lee 64
Osborn, Bob 64
Osborn, Colleen 64
Osborn, J. W. 63
Osborn, L. B. 57
Osborn, Leon 64
Owens, Alberta 72
Owens, Arde 146
Owens, Bertie 146
Owens, Cletis 70
Owens, Ed. 247
Owens, Evertt 70
Owings, Jasper 247
Ozburn, T. C. 249
Pace, Gloria Jean 214
Page, Darlene 202
Page, Dianne 202
Palmer, Andy 162
Palmer, Clarence 162
Palmer, Paul 91
Palmer, Racine 85
Palmer, V. F. 161
Palmer, Volly 162
Palmer, Wilma Jean 119
Parker Laws 31
Parker, C. W. 275
Parker, Donna 199
Parker, Thoma A. 23
Parlor, Anna E. 63
Parrich, H. C. 283
Parsley 156
Patterson, Charles 192
Patterson, Darrel 189
Patterson, Janice Sue 192
Patterson, Margaret Anne 192
Patterson, Mrs. 126
Patterson, Naomi 247
Patterson, Patsy 189
Patterson, Samuel 246
Paugh, E. F. 241
Payne, Marcia 184
Payne, Max 184
Payne, Peggy 184
Payton, Billy Vasco 201
Peace Church 37, 55, 131
Pearl Hill 55, 213
Peck, John Mason 10
Pennel, Leroy 264
Pennell, Alfred 263
Pennell, Loyd 264
Pennington, Duane 142
Pennington, Floyd 116
Pennington, Valorie 142
Perkins, Charley 259
Perry 55
Perservance 55, 215
Pershing, Gen. John J. 34

Petefish, Lucille 315
Petefish, Mattie 227
Petefish, Rosalie 71
Peter Hill 55
Peters, Raymond 192
Peterson, Alice 165
Phiefer, Vivian 74
Phillips, Jas. 246
Pickering 69
Pickering, 225
Piercy, Pleasant 178
Piercy, Ralph M. 178
Pine 55, 217
Pine, Maggie 153
Pippen, Clel 70
Pitcher, Harley 280
Pitts, James 165
Pleasant Grove 55, 219
Pleasant Hill 55, 221
Pleasant Valley 55, 201, 223
Pleasant View 55, 98, 99, 100, 225
Poncot, Amos 291
Poncot, Fred 291
Poncot, Gustave 291
Porter, True 266
Possum Creek 55
Potter, Earnest 271
Potter, Janice Ann 214
Potter, Lany 153
Potter, Mrs. Frank 145
Potter, Nellie 217
Potts, C. C. 293
Potts, Euphemia 227
Potts, Johnnie 227
Potts, L. A. 226
Poundston, A. W. 105
Powell, Dick 124
Powell, Ralph 124
Powell, Shirley 124
Powers, Augusta 240
Powers, Fred 244
Prairie Dale 55, 227
Prairie Flower 55, 229, 230
Prairie Hill 55, 231, 232
Prairie Star 55, 111, 235
Prairie View 55, 237
Pratt, Blanche 163
Presley, Opal 239
Preston 38 104
Preston School 55, 239
Priggle, Mrs. Addie 275
Prigmore, Danl. 299
Prigmore, Dick 299
Prigmore, J. D. 299
Prigmore, Jodie 299
Probert, Arlene 226
Probert, Donald 306
Probert, Doris 226
Probert, Ethal 205
Probert, Howard 305
Probert, J. A. 225
Probert, J. L. 205
Probert, Jerry 226
Probert, John 305
Probert, Lester 305

Probert, Margaret 305
Probert, Paul 305
Probert, Phyllis Bull 121
Probert, Winena 306
Pugh, Edith 111, 274
Purviance, Charlene 148
Purviance, Isabel 64
Quaker School 56
Rader, Robert L. 114
Radium 55, 101, 241
Ralston, Claude 153
Randall, Chas. 284
Randall, Emma 115
Redwood 55, 243, 243
Reed, Bertha 114, 124, 245, 272, 300
Reed, E. P. 205
Reeds 142, 245, 246
Rees, Eldon 284
Reinheimer, Chas. 81
Replogle, Mrs. S.M. 83
Replogle, S. M. 83
Rhoads, W. H. 306
Rhule, Harry 296
Rice 55
Rice, Blance 124
Rice, Charles, A. 124
Rice, Jeanette 124
Rice, Jos. E. 247
Richardson, J. M. 17
Richardson, Rosetta 282
Richie, Beulah 63
Richmond, Pauline 268
Rickman, M. C. 229
Ridway, R. C. 309
Ridway, Wanda 309
Riffee, Lena 115
Riffie, U. A. 107
Riggs, Orlea 70
Rinner, Jacob 140
Rising Sun 55, 121, 122, 247
Ritter, Rosa 279
Rittter, A. 272
Robb, Gary 65, 66
Roberts, Evaline 23
Roberts, Helen 313
Robertson, W. R. 185
Robinson, John 202
Robinson, Lura 300
Robinson, Ray 202
Robinson, Wayne 173
Rogers, Lottie 283
Rois, Ray 299
Rols, Paul 299
Roosevelt, Theodore 52
Roper, Lester 197
Roper, Madge 133
Roper, Marcella Sweet 197
Roper, T. A. 135
Rose, Silas 65
Rosebank 55, 121, 122, 249
Rosebaugh, J. C. 251
Ross, Allen Lee 214
Ross, Gaylen 139
Ross, L. R. 249
Ross, Linda 139

Ross, Robert 146
Round Prairie 55, 96, 250
Row, William 273
Royer, T. A. 219
Rudy, Charlie 249
Rudy, Minnie 235
Rush, Agnes 173
Rush, Anamae 173
Rush, Eva 213
Rush, Hiram 123
Rush, Ivon 71
Rush, Lloyd 185
Rush, Neal 71
Rusk 55, 253
Rusk, Elmer 253
Rusk, Gladys 269
Rusk, J. O. 229
Rusk, Wes 90
Russell, Julia 75
Russell, Lena 203
Sailer, Anna 151
Sailor, Joseph 313
Sailor, William J. 199
Salisbury, Maurice 157
Salout, Alice 307
Sample, Charles 205
Sanders, Floyd 123
Sanders, Lena 70
Sanders, Silas 116
Sandy, Evelyn 83
Sandy, John 76
Sandy, Pete 76, 83
Sandy, Peter 78
Sandy, Richard 75, 77
Sanley, Ada 148
Scantlin, Alice E. 146, 153
Scantlin, Bill 204
Scantling, W. W. 231
Schaeffer, Marva Lee 63, 64
Schantz, Ward 26
Scheel, G. A. 283
Schell, Peter 225
Schmidly, Mrs. Harold 303
Schnell, Donna 284
Schnell, Patsy 284
Schnell, Roger 284
Schooler, H. R. 205
Scotland 55
Scott, Barney 178
Scott, Ina A. 309
Scott, Maude 311
Scott, Orie 240
Scott, Roy 240.
Scroggs, B. F. 251
Scroggs, H. N. 251
Seela, Ed 59
Seela, J. N. U. 117
Seela, Valera 141
Sellers, Doris Jean 97
Seneker, Loren 162
Serrel, John 71
Setser, Inez 297
Sevens, Tommas 207
Shackelford, Ruth 241
Shaffer, Ruth 261, 262

Index

Shank, W. W, 20
Shantz, Ward 22
Sharon 55, 255, 269
Sheets, Paul 208
Sheldon, John 208
Shelton, Clandine 291
Shelton, Jacob 291
Shelton, Ray 70
Shelton, Tom 70
Shelton, Winnie 70
Shepherd, Hazel 317
Shepherd, Imogene 317
Shepherd, R. W. 208
Sheridan 55, 269
Sherrel, H.G. 205
Sherrell, Boyd 205
Sherrell, Mary Louise 205
Sherrill, E. C. 153
Sherrit, Jim 71
Shields, Darrell 228
Shields, Darrell 233
Shields, Mary Jean 228
Shields, Nancy Ann 228
Shiloh 55. 201, 271
Shipman, P. J. 133
Shippen, Flora 227
Shively, Lois 76
Shivley, George 137
Shivley, Rachel 137
Shoemaker, Floyd C. 10, 11
Shore, Freda Mae 65
Shubert, Clifford 248
Shull, Dorothy 172
Shuper, B. A. 145
Sidenstricker 125, 133, 143, 159, 177
Sidenstricker, Kathy III, 179, 201, 247
Sigel 109
Silver Creek 55, 111, 113
Simmons, Billy 243
Simmons, David 192
Simmons, Edward 243
Simmons, Freda 243
Simmons, Mary Ellen 192
Simmons, Melvin 270
Simmons, Wm. 121
Sisseck, Darrel 309
Sisseck, Joe 309
Sisseck, Leslie 309
Sloan, Charles 309
Sloan, Loyd K. 124
Smih, Mattie 160
Smith, Annie 153
Smith, Avis 317
Smith, Ben 71
Smith, C. J. 117
Smith, Cora 246
Smith, Elvis 227
Smith, F. C. 313
Smith, Grace 308
Smith, J. E. 117
Smith, Lela 117
Smith, Marietta 144
Smith, Mary 144
Smith, Mattie 153
Smith, Ronnie 309

Smith, S. M. 163
Smith, Sandra 309
Smith, Sue 144
Smith, Thos. 137
Smith, Uriah 125
Smith, W. E. 159
Smith, Wayne 270
Smith, Wilber 270
Smith, Wm. 313
Smithfield 56
Smoker, Carolyn 144
Smoker, Rosalie 144
Sneed, Ruth 142
Snider, Stephen 214
Snowflake 55, 275
Snyder, Glen 63
Snyder, Rex 63
Snyder, Virginia
Snyder,Vesta 63
Southard, Della 135
Southard, Frances 79
Southard, G. W. 157
Southard, G. W. 157
Southern, J. R. 141
Southern, Wieford 305
Spaid, J. W. 209
Spence, Jim 64
Spence, Wayne 64
Spencer, C. L. 245
Spencer, Etta 237
Spencer, Lucille 107, 109, 110
Spoon, Bertrice 327
Spoon, Dorothy 325
Spor, Linda Sue 135
Spout Springs 55
Spring Hill 55, 275
Sprouse, Elmer 246
Sprouse, Lee 246
Stamp, Barbara 164
Standley, J. T. 251
Stanley, Ada 141
Staples, S. B. 251
Stauffacher, Marjorie 201
Stauffacher, Shirley 201, 202
Stebbins, Fred W. 251
Stemmons, A. C. 63
Stemmons, Clay 254
Stemmons, W. F. 225
Stevens, Bonnie 201
Stevens, Carol 202
Stevens, John Elwood 201
Stevens, Oscar 246
Stevens, Thomas 201, 202
Stevenson, J. M. 35
Stevenson, Judge 90
Stevent, John 245
Stewart, Linda Kay 214
Stickney, Robert 28
Stiles, Edith 262
Stiles, May 227
Stiles, Warren A. 255
Still, Betty Fullerton 90
Still, Bonibel 74
Still, Harvey 74
Still, Jr. 74

Still, Margaret 74
Still, Mermyl 74
Still, Richard 74
Stneed, Ruth 149
Stocker, Jo III
Stokes, W. D. 311
Stone 55, 279
Stoner, Albert 213
Stoner, Cora 213
Stoner, Emma 213
Stoner, Sarah 213
Stony Point 55, 281
Storbeck, Karen 226
Storbeck, Marilyn 226
Storms, R. M. 313
Stoup 55
Stour, Billy Ray 201
Stover, Isabelle 105
Stricker, F. L. 71
Stroup, W. N. 299
Stuart, Gilbert 48
Stuckmyer, Frank 145
Stump, Berniece 210
Stump, Floyd 210
Stump, Harlen 210
Stump, Ilene 210
Stump, Virginia 210
Sumerset 55, 277
Summit 55, 283
Sunderland, Clara 122
Sunderland, Dick 119
Sunderland, Ella Marie 288
Sunflower 55, 287
Sunnyside 55
Surface, Chuck 230
Swager, Harry 299
Swain, Grace 141
Swank, J. A. 273
Swin, Nellie Carter 61
Swindle School 55, 289
Swingle, Mabel 141
Swingle, Mrs. Jeff 163
Sylvey, Jas. 293
Taggart, A. E. 211
Tatum, Lillie Thorn 143
Tatum, Ron 61
Taylor, Floyd 243
Taylor, Myrtle 162
Taylor, Nelly M. 162
Taylor, Richard 270
Teague, Earl 64, 207
Teague, Robert 64
Teas, Samual 12
Temperance 55, 291
Thacker, Mahala 185
Thacker, Mrs. Mahala 228
Thetge, Mary 190
Thetge, Susan 190
Thomas, Chas. F. 286
Thomas, Evert 110, 149
Thomas, Floyd 283
Thomas, Mildred 131
Thomas, Norma 283, 284
Thomas, R. C. 235
Thomas, Ruth 175

Thompson, Betty Jane 204
Thompson, Margaret 74
Thompson, Ralph 74
Thorn, David 116
Thorn, Judy 70
Thorn, Linda 70
Thorn, Noah 116
Thorn, Robert 116
Tiberghien, Pat 309
Tidball, J. C. 115
Tierney, Joan Kentner 308
Tiller, Donna Sue 71
Tiller, Emerald "Pete" 194
Tiller, Faye Bruffett 194
Tiller, Jerry Dean 71
Tilley, Larry 248
Tilley, Richard 248
Tilton, Steven 142
Timble, Janelle 71
Toomy, Tobe 181
Tower of Light 55, 293
Tremble, Walter 155
Trent, Alma Kasper 325
Trimble, Joy 226
Trimble, Loy Hale 226
Troyer, Judith 144
Truan, Harry 101
Tubbs, Carolyn 204
Tubbs, Leoa 205
Tubbs, O'Neill 205
Turkey Creek 38
Turner, Anniece 133
Turner, Benjamin 13
Turner, Evelyn 133
Turner, Helen 133
Twin Grove 55, 295
Uaryan, B. H. 105
Underwood School 55, 297
Underwood, J. W. 209
Underwood, Laura Beth 133
Underwood, Otis 133
Underwood, S. A. 30, 33
Underwood, W. 127
Union 55, 148, 299
Union Valley 55, 305
Unity 55, 307
Utter, Ruth 213
Valley Dell 55, 309
Van Gilder, Marvin III, 145, 153, 163
Van Gilder M. 178, 254, 278, 308
Vanbebber, Mae 267
VanCoran, Vina 246
VanCuren, Harry 246
VanDyke, Leroy 70
Vanway, Debie 103
Vanway, Mike 103
Varney, Walter 181
Vaughn, Mrs. L. E. 279
Vaughn, Myrtle 274
Vaughn, Riley 274
Vaught, Jackie 184
Veills, Ralph 207
Vette, Jack 309
Vette, Judy 309
Viala, Frances 212

Index

Victor School 62, 312
Victory 55, 311
Viele, Frances 208
Viewbank 55, 313
Waco 56
Wade, Geo. 209
Waerf, L. A. 249
Wagner, Geo. 209
Waight, J. A. 243
Waldbuesse, Otto 327
Waldbuesser, Willy 327
Walker, Cleo 243
Walker, G. B. 159
Wallace, Miss 115
Waller, John 209
Warden, Alice 213
Warden, Daisy 213
Warden, Herman 213
Warden, J. R. 135
Warden, Linnie 213
Wardlow, Doris Carter III, 83, 89, 239, 241
Wardlow, Doris Jean 284, 286
Wardlow, Ethel 190
Wardlow, Richard 47, 48, 320
Wardow, Ethel 253
Warnick, Mrs. Gladys 231
Warwick, Gladys 236, 238
Washburn, Jack 274
Watchorn, Judy 71
Watchorn, Nancy Kay 71
Watson, B. R. 219
Weatherman, William 192
Weaver, H. 279
Weaver, Jess 315
Webb City 54
Weber, T. F. 247
Webster, U. B. 29
Wecker, Laura Rose 64
Wecker, Phyllis 64
Wecker, Sonny 64
Weed, John 306
Weeks, Anna 146
Weeks, Frank 271
Weeks, George 146
Weeks, John N. 271
Weeks, Owen 146
Weir, J. J. 117
Welde, Billy 64
Welde, Patty 64
Weldon, Steve III
Wendleston, Susan 142
Wescott, Kathryn 190
Wescott, Marvin 190
Wescott, Richard 190
Wescott, Velma 190
Wheat, Kenneth 208
Wheat, Myrlin 208
Wheat, Myrtle 208
Wheat, Nadine 153
Wheat, W. B. 207
Wheeler, E. S. 227
Wherton, W. M. 38
Whisner 62, 141
Whisner, Jay 77
Whisner, Richard 77

Whisner, S. D. 140
Whisner, Vernie 140
Whitaker, Ada 246
Whitaker, Laura 246
Whitaker, Lela 246
White 56
White Hall 55, 315
White Oak 55, 253
White, Rex 208
White, Ross 208
Whitehead, Mr. 122
Whiters, Lema 258
Whitlock, S. G. 163
Whitmore 244
Wicker, Bobby 103
Wicker, Janet 103
Wicker, Karen 103
Wickstrom, John 141, 142
Wickstrom, Teresa 142
Wickstrom, Wm. 163
Wiese, Clarence 64
Wiggins, Henry 64
Wilhite, Ovilla 70
Wilks, J. E. 213
Williams, Alice 202
Williams, Donnie 202
Williams, Dora 317
Williams, George 213
Williams, Glenda 202
Williams, Herbert 317
Williams, James R. 310
Williams, Marvin 139
Williams, Maxine Mink 245
Williams, R. 235
Williams, Rachel 59
Williams, Sarah 59
Williams, Virginia 116
Williams, W. H. 155
Williams, Wayne 60
Willoughby, A. 163
Willoughby, J. C. 25
Willoughby, Wm. G. 243
Wiloughly, Robyn 142
Wilson, Carol 210
Wilson, Elsie 210
Wilson, Geo. 275
Wilson, J. A. 106
Wilson, Joan McCune 237
Wilson, John F. 302
Wilson, June 210
Wilson, L. F. 297
Wilson, LeRoy 77
Wilson, Natalie Lafon 256
Wilson, Swely 210
Wilson, Wm. 127
Wimsett, Inez 202
Winder, H. S. 147
Winder, Pauline 305
Wingfield, Travis 239
Winsett, Inez 207
Wise, D. 81
Wiseman, Lena 183
Withers, Lema 256
Wittenmans, E. B. 241
Wolf, John 115

Womack, Dorothy 130
Wood, Doris 97
Wood, Erma 97
Wood, I. J. 215
Wood, Mollie 299
Woods, Bert 260
Woods, M. J. 83
Woods, Matilda 139
Woodson, Governor Silas 29
Woolen Mills Spring 20
Woolomes, J. M. 151
Worst, S. N. 239
Wright, Jennie 71, 121
Wright, Margaret 201
Wright, Mrs. R. 145
Wright, P. B. 283
Wright, R. C. 145
Wright, Thomas Milbern 264
Wyat, Carolyn L. 191
Wyatt, Frances 80,
Wyatt, Jas. 243
Yankee, Kathryn 300
Yaryon, Jas. 231
Yoes, Austin 130
Yoes, Ellen III, 107
Yoes, Pauline 130
Yoes, Thedaway 205
York, Bonnie 189
York, Dean 189
Young, Jean 65
Young, Jim 213
Young, Mrs. Guinn 151
Young, Nettie 137
Youngblood, Annabell 213
Youngblood, Clay 213
Youngblood, Freddie 213
Zaerr, Celia 189
Zaerr, Jess Jr. 189
Zaerr, John 72
Zaerr, Pauline 327
Zergler, J. 231
Ziegler, J. 236
Ziler, Aletha 213
Ziler, James 275
Ziler, Ollie 213
Ziler, Orville 213
Ziler, W. F. 287
Zinite 56
Zinn, Bob 204

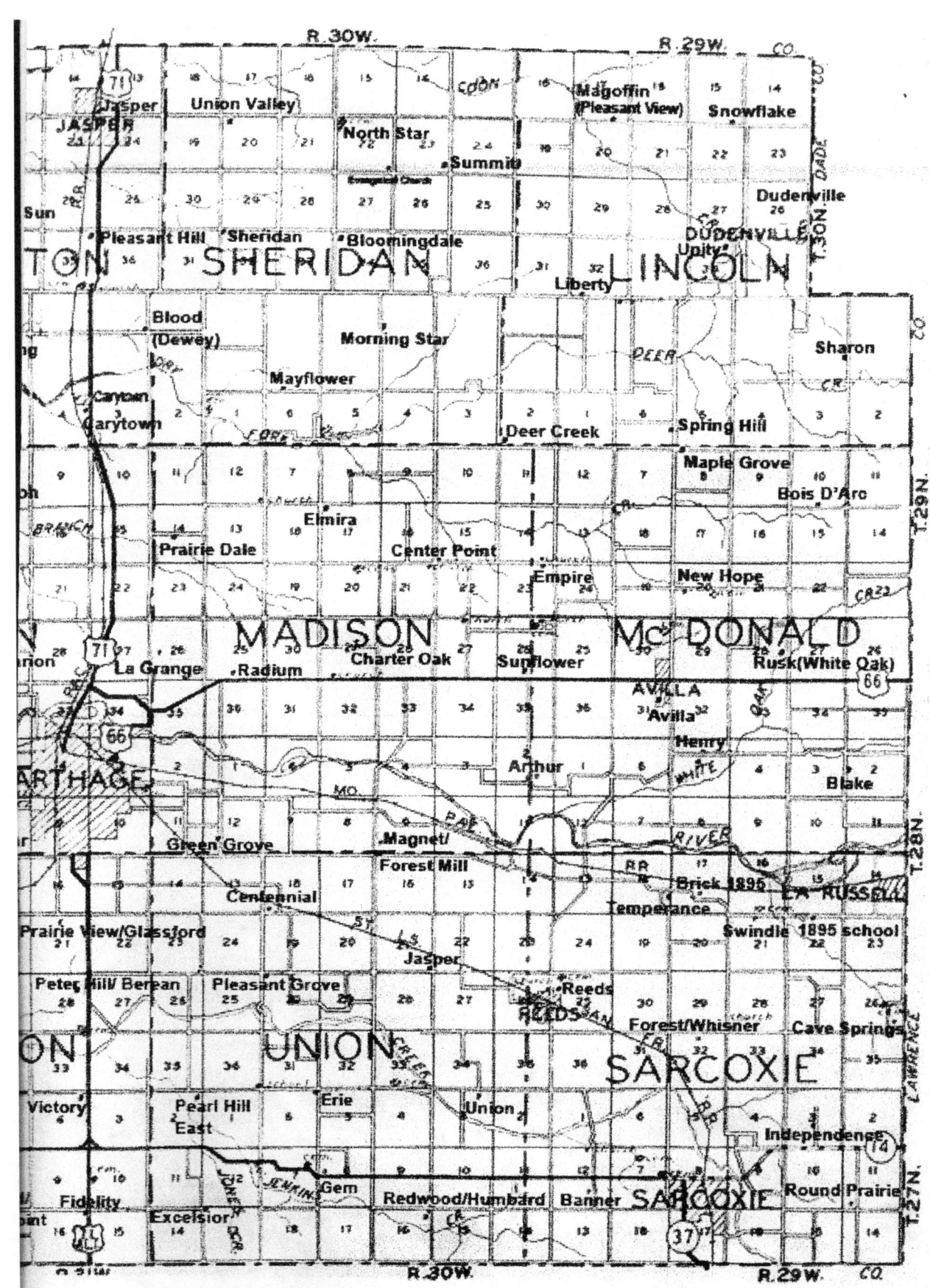

Jasper County School Map - East